FOR THOSE WHO FELL

A LEGION OF THE DAMNED NOVEL

WILLIAM C. DIETZ

FOR THOSE WHO FELL

A LEGION OF THE DAMNED NOVEL

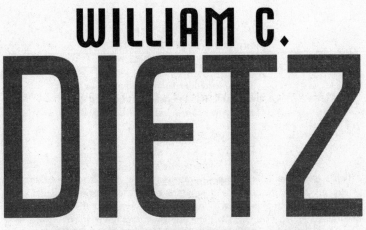

TITAN BOOKS

For Those Who Fell
Print edition ISBN: 9781783290468
E-book edition ISBN: 9781783290475

Published by Titan Books
A division of Titan Publishing Group Ltd
144 Southwark Street, London SE1 0UP

First edition: July 2015
2 4 6 8 10 9 7 5 3 1

A CIP catalogue record for this title is available from the British Library.

Printed and bound by CPI Group (UK) Ltd, Croydon, CR0 4YY.

DID YOU ENJOY THIS BOOK?
We love to hear from our readers. Please email us at:
readerfeedback@titanemail.com or write to us at Reader Feedback at the
above address.

To receive advance information, news, competitions, and exclusive offers
online, please sign up for the Titan newsletter on our website.

www.titanbooks.com

This one is for Richard Curtis, in appreciation for his friendship, sage advice, and considerable patience.

1

War is commonly supposed to be a matter for Generals and Admirals, in the camp, or at sea. It would be as reasonable to say that a duel is a matter for pistols and swords. Generals with their armies and Admirals with their fleets are mere weapons by the hand of the statesman.

SIR JOHN FORTESCUE

LECTURE

Standard year 1911

Planet Algeron, the Confederacy of Sentient Beings

The planet blocked the sun, so that Algeron was momentarily backlit as the shuttle started its descent, and plunged into the darkness below. The hull shook like a thing possessed as powerful winds battered the vessel, and snow sleeted through the wing lights. Though already strapped into his seat, President Marcott Nankool grabbed on to the chair's armrests. "My God, General," the politician exclaimed to the man seated beside him, "is it always like this?"

Legion General William "Bill" Booly III had close-cropped salt-and-pepper hair, steady gray eyes, and a long, lean frame. He shook his head and grinned. "No, sometimes it's worse."

A sudden gust of wind hit the port side, the pilot made the necessary correction, and Nankool battled to keep his lunch down as the ship lost fifty feet's worth of altitude. Algeron wasn't his first, second, or even third choice as the Confederacy's interim capital. Unfortunately for him, and the thousands of government officials about to take up residence on the planet's surface, it was the *only* place available.

Ever since the ex-battleship that served the sprawling Confederacy as a capital had been destroyed by the Ramanthians, he and his staff had searched for a more developed world on which the reconstituted government could convene, but to no avail. While generally supportive of the war effort, none of the member states were interested in playing host to the Senate, only to have the world in question automatically soar to the top of the enemy's hit list. With the exception of the Hudathans, who lived on a planet so inhospitable that they would eventually be forced to evacuate it, not a single race had been willing to offer the government sanctuary. Not the Clone Hegemony, the Dwellers, the Arballazanies, or a half dozen others. All of which explained why Algeron had been chosen.

"There," Booly said, as he pointed toward the viewport to the politician's right. "Can you see the lights? That's Fort Camerone."

The shuttle banked, snow swirled, and Nankool saw the ghostly glow of what looked like a small city but was actually a fortress. An anachronism really, but the same could be said of the Legion, which had originally been created to serve the colonial needs of a long-defunct nation-state yet continued to live on.

Eventually, when the people of Earth ventured out from their native planet and made homes among the stars, the Legion had gone with them, growing as it took on new responsibilities, until it became the means by which a succession of human governments had been able to impose their will on a network of far-flung colonies. A function similar to the one for which the organization had originally been invented.

Then, in the aftermath of the Hudathan wars, the Legion had repeatedly been used to defend the Confederacy of Sentient Beings, and the peace that the new organization had imposed. But no one wants soldiers hanging around, not during peacetime, which was why a long-dead emperor had ceded Algeron to the Legion and why successor governments allowed the arrangement to continue. That, plus the fact that no one else seemed to want the place. No one except the indigenous Naa, that is, who had a long-running love-hate relationship with the Legion, and were increasingly restive of late.

Fort Camerone had been named after a battle that took place in 1863. A battle in which Captain Jean Danjou and a company of sixty-two legionnaires took on thousands of Mexican regulars and continued to fight until only three of them were left. A battle lost, yet strangely won, and celebrated once each year.

The politician's thoughts were interrupted as the wedge-shaped shuttle passed over the three-cornered fort and settled toward one of the brightly lit landing platforms beyond. There were pads within the walls as well, but those were reserved for the cybernetic fly-forms that remained on standby around the clock. Not to deal with the Ramanthians, although an attack from that quarter was possible, but to respond to the Naa should one of the more radical clans decide to flex its muscles. Booly felt a solid thump as the shuttle touched down, then hit the release on his harness as the pilot spoke over the intercom. "It's twenty below, windy, and snowing. Welcome to Algeron."

Longshot Suremake watched the white, green, and red lights circle the fort and grinned in the darkness. The Naa was about fifteen hundred yards away from the landing platforms, a theoretically impossible shot during ideal conditions, never mind at night in the midst of a storm. But Suremake was no ordinary marksman, the carefully maintained rifle was no ordinary weapon, and the hand-loaded .50 caliber cartridge that was seated in the chamber was no ordinary round.

The shuttle fired its repellors, fried the snow that the internally heated platform hadn't managed to melt yet, and settled into a cloud of steam. But that blew away, just as the Naa knew it would, revealing a rectangle of bright light. A tiny stick figure passed through the shuttle's open hatch and was immediately followed by a second. Together the two targets made their way down a short flight of fold-down stairs and entered the light pooled below. That was where another individual stepped forward, and the threesome paused to speak with each other.

Suremake allowed the crosshairs of his powerful telescopic

sight to drift across the potential targets and considered each in turn. Then, the sniper let out a long steady breath, exerted a steady pressure on the trigger, and felt it give. There was a muffled *bang!* followed by a kick in the shoulder, and what felt like an eternity as the metallic messenger sped through the intervening snow and darkness.

Commandant Colonel Kitty Kirby smiled and stepped forward to take Nankool's hand. She wore her hair high and tight and had a rapier-thin body that looked larger than it actually was thanks to a heavy olive drab parka. The light hit the president from above and threw his shadow onto the duracrete beneath his feet. The officer noticed that the politician was lightly dressed and made a note to keep her greeting short. She'd seen his face on countless holo vids but never actually met him before. The legionnaire was surprised by how short Nankool was, but liked the way that his eyes met hers and the strength of his grip.

"Colonel Kirby! It's a pleasure to meet you. General Booly speaks very highly of you."

Kirby was about to respond, about to say something self-effacing, when she heard a loud metallic *clang*. The report was so muffled by the combined effects of distance and snow that the civilian failed to recognize the sound for what it was. Nankool looked back toward the shuttle. "What the hell was *that?*"

"That was a gunshot," Booly replied lightly, "fired from a hill to the east. Try to think of it as a one-gun salute."

"My God!" the president replied in alarm. "Shouldn't we take cover?"

"There wouldn't be much point," Kirby replied. "The warrior who fired the shot is long gone by now."

"Really?" Nankool inquired uncertainly. "Well, I certainly hope you're right. At least he missed."

"Oh, he didn't miss," Booly replied as the two of them followed Kirby down off the platform. "That was just his way of saying hello. Had he wanted to kill one of us, he certainly could have."

"How do you know that?" the politician demanded. "It seems hard to believe."

"Because I was born here," Booly replied matter-of-factly, "and my grandmother was Naa."

Nankool had been told that, but forgotten it, and tried to think of something pertinent to say. Nothing came, however, so he said, "Oh," and stepped onto a thick layer of well-packed snow. The president had arrived—which meant that the Confederacy had arrived as well. Suddenly, and without any of the fanfare usually attendant on such occasions, a new capital had been born. If the planet felt honored, there was certainly no sign of it, as the wind howled, and snow attacked the fortress walls.

Planet Starfall, the Confederacy Of Sentient Beings

The sun shone from a clear blue sky, the air was clean and crisp, and the streets were packed with small furry bodies as thousands of Thrakies made their way to work. Whatever architectural traditions the Thraks possessed before they boarded their giant arks to flee from the robotic Sheen had been lost during hundreds of years in space.

Now, having settled on the planet they chose to call Starfall, the aliens were starting from scratch. And, thanks to the hierarchical nature of Thraki culture, everything Christine Vanderveen saw as she left her apartment building smacked of centralized planning. That included the intentionally narrow streets, the complete absence of vehicular traffic, and the regimented buildings that were reminiscent of the gigantic arks on which the Thrakies had lived for so long before taking up residence within the Confederacy.

Though impressive, Vanderveen knew that the city was a far cry from the multicolored glass metropolis that occupied the same spot back before the Hudathans laid waste to it. That was when the race who called themselves the N'awatha committed mass suicide in an attempt to protect their carefully concealed grubs, only to have the brutal off-world troopers break into the birthing chambers and slaughter all that they found there.

But that was ancient history now that the Sheen had been defeated, and the Confederacy had grudgingly ceded the planet to the Thraki people in hopes that they would settle down and become good citizens.

Well, they have settled in, Vanderveen thought to herself as she allowed the river of pedestrians to carry her around a corner, *but good citizens? That remains to be seen.*

The blocky five-story building had been constructed according to the complex set of specs that governed construction of all the Confederacy's multitudinous embassies, consulates, and legations. That meant it could survive anything short of a direct hit from a bunker buster but looked very strange crouched among the metal-and-glass-clad structures that surrounded it.

A pair of smartly uniformed legionnaires stood in front of the building and snapped to attention as Vanderveen approached. The soldiers reminded the diplomat of Lieutenant Antonio Santana, the long, bloody siege on LaNor, and the few precious weeks that followed. A time during which they had grown closer even as they struggled to figure out where their relationship was headed. The problem was that both of them were at the beginning of what promised to be demanding careers, and it was difficult to figure out how they would ever spend much time together, unless one of them quit. Something neither was willing to do.

As the diplomat nodded to the legionnaires and mounted the front steps, she wondered where Santana was and hoped that he was safe. A stupid thought, really, given the reality of war, but sincere nevertheless.

Security had been tightened at all of the Confederacy's embassies by then, and even though the legionnaires in the lobby knew Vanderveen by sight, it still required the better part of five minutes to wade through all the various scans and retrieve her briefcase on the other side of the checkpoint. The process was annoying but necessary, since it was the only thing that kept races like the Ramanthians from murdering one of the embassy's staff, putting an agent into a virtually identical electromechanical body, and marching it into the building.

A lift tube carried the diplomat up to the fourth floor. The lifts, restrooms, and all of the utilities were clustered at the building's center, which left the outside walls free for cubes and offices. A gleaming hallway led Vanderveen to her pride and joy—an office that not only included the five additional square feet of space to which her new rank of FSO-4 entitled her, but a western exposure as well.

Unfortunately other things went with her new responsibilities, not the least of which was the care and feeding of newly appointed Ambassador Kay Wilmot, who, if not the most obnoxious person in the foreign service, had to be among the top five. That impression was reinforced when the diplomat's desk comp sensed her presence and granted itself permission to speak. "You have three messages... The first was left at 6:11 by Ambassador Wilmot... The second was left at 7:03 by Ambassador Wilmot... And the third was..."

"I get the general idea," Vanderveen responded, as she draped her coat over one of the guest chairs and glanced at her wrist term. It was 7:46, and the official workday began at 8:00, which meant she was early.

Vanderveen hadn't reported to Wilmot for very long, but it didn't take a genius to figure out that the early-morning messages had been left for the sole purpose of establishing the fact that the Ambassador had already been at work for hours when the FSO-4 arrived. Never mind the fact that nothing ever seemed to be accomplished during that period of time, or that Wilmot took two-hour lunches, and generally disappeared halfway through the afternoon.

The whole thing was part of a thus-far-successful charade that had enabled Wilmot to scale the diplomatic ladder in record time, score what promised to be a rather cushy post, and avoid being transferred to Algeron, which, if the buzz was correct, had been chosen as the next capital. A bleak wasteland by most accounts—although Santana talked about how beautiful it was.

But the game had to be played, which was why Vanderveen took a moment to send the briefing paper to Wilmot, grabbed her hand comp, and stepped out into the hall. The rest of the staff had started to arrive by then. Most were human, but the FSO exchanged greetings with a spindly exoskeleton-clad Dweller, a colorful Prithian, and a stolid looking Turr as well.

The last of the crowd, an FSO-5 named Mitsi Ang, stepped off the lift just as Vanderveen entered. She had short black hair, almond-shaped eyes, and a wicked grin. She had worked for

Wilmot during a previous posting and had a pretty good idea what Vanderveen had to cope with. "Going upstairs are we?"

Vanderveen made a face. One had to be careful, especially since Wilmot had some well-placed sycophants, but the diplomat had already come to trust Ang. "I'm supposed to brief her on the local situation. Never mind the fact that I arrived on the same ship she did, there are at least twenty staff people who know the Thraks better than I do, and that most of the information she asked for is contained in the backgrounder that you handed her on day one."

Ang laughed. It was early yet, but Vanderveen looked like she might be one of the good ones, and Ang had decided to help her. "Welcome to the life of an FSO-4! Just give her the summary— she has the attention span of a gork monkey."

Vanderveen waved as the doors hissed closed. Three minutes later the diplomat approached the durasteel-lined wooden barricade that served Wilmot's secretary as a desk but could also function as a defensive barrier should that become necessary.

The secretary, an officious young man named Has Benz, prided himself on his pumped-up physique. He monitored Vanderveen's face to see if she would react to it, was disappointed when she didn't, and used a well-manicured finger to stab a button. "FSO Vanderveen is here to see you, Ambassador, shall I send her in?"

Wilmot glanced at the handcrafted clock that President Nankool had sent in recognition of her work on a diplomatic reception, registered the fact that Vanderveen was right on time, and frowned in disappointment. She had already come to the conclusion that the FSO-4 was the only flaw in an otherwise perfect assignment.

There were a number of things the diplomat didn't like about Vanderveen, starting with her blond hair and slim good looks, qualities that were almost certain to make the ambassador seem less attractive by comparison. Just one of the reasons why Wilmot had a male secretary. Then, as if Vanderveen's physical attributes weren't bad enough, there was the fact that the FSO was the recipient of the Citizen's Medal for Distinguished Service, a rather rare honor and one which the ambassador envied.

Of course even the most promising career can be destroyed by a superior who is determined to bring it down, but to do so would incur the wrath of Charles Winther Vanderveen, Christine's father, and an advisor to the president. All of which meant that it was best to tolerate the little bitch, look for an opportunity to transfer her to some hellhole, and bring in a more amenable staffer.

Wilmot grabbed a fistful of hard copy, fanned it out in front of her, and touched the appropriate button. "Send her in."

One of two metal-core doors opened, and Vanderveen entered. Wilmot summoned her best, "I'm terribly busy but still pleased to see you" smiles, and said, "Good morning." Vanderveen answered in kind and took one of two guest chairs. It faced the ambassador's rather imposing desk and the huge window beyond. A low-flying air car zipped past, slowed as it approached a building to the south, and entered via a sixth-floor parking bay.

Vanderveen noticed that all the objects on the surface of the ambassador's desk had been chosen with care. There was the clock that Nankool had given her, a chunk of rock crystal from Earth, and a photo of her standing next to Earth's governor.

As for the woman herself, Wilmot appeared to be in her late thirties, was attractive rather than beautiful, and slightly overweight. Not much, only ten pounds or so, but just enough to exaggerate the roundness of her face and the fullness of her breasts. Physical attributes that the ambassador took advantage of at times yet sought to hide at others, as if her chest was something of an embarrassment. Wilmot cleared her throat. "So, is the briefing ready?"

Vanderveen nodded. "I sent a copy. If you would be so kind as to pull it up, we can review it."

"Good," Wilmot said as she turned in the direction of her desk comp, "I'm looking forward to…"

But Vanderveen never got to hear what the ambassador was looking forward to because that was the moment when the Prithian appeared outside the window, hit the hardened glass at full speed, and caused it to shatter. His body made a loud *thump* as it hit the floor. Wilmot screamed, and attempted to escape, only to have her chair fall over sideways.

Vanderveen felt a sudden stab of fear, but, thanks to the rebellion on LaNor, had become somewhat inured to sudden violence. There was no mistaking Sok Tok's yellow beak, white head feathers, and blue shoulder plumage. The translator issued a croaking sound as Vanderveen went to the Prithian's aid. Though not a diplomat, Sok Tok was a member of the embassy's staff, and Vanderveen liked him. One of the alien's wings fluttered weakly, and the other was clearly broken. There was blood, a lot of blood, and Vanderveen called to Wilmot, who was up on her feet by then. "Call Dr. Fortu! Tell her to hurry! Sok Tok is bleeding to death."

"No," Tok warbled, as the fingers of his right wrapped themselves around her left ankle. "It's too late…" The Prithian coughed and a half cup's worth of blood spilled out onto the hardwood floor. That was when Vanderveen noticed the dagger that protruded from the alien's back. He'd been stabbed, yet managed to fly to the embassy.

"Save your strength," Vanderveen said, "the doctor will be here in a moment, and…"

"There is nothing she can do," Tok croaked. "Now listen carefully, whatever you do, don't trust the Thrakies. They claim to be neutral, but…"

The Prithian's words were interrupted by another racking cough followed by a second rush of blood. But it just kept coming this time, flooding the area around his head, and drowning his words. Dr. Fortu burst into the office right about then and rushed to his side, but it was too late. Tok was gone, taking whatever he had hoped to warn his employers about with him, his fingers still locked around Vanderveen's ankle. Fortu pried them off, but a circle of blood remained and proved difficult to remove.

Planet Algeron, the Confederacy of Sentient Beings

Corporal Nowake Longsleep stood on a rocky ledge not far from the village in which he had been born and looked toward the east. He'd been part of the Legion for seven years by then and fought on three planets, none of which were as beautiful as his native Algeron, a world that completed a full rotation every two hours and forty-two minutes. The phenomenon created a world-spanning mountain range called the Towers of Algeron. Longsleep knew that the highest peaks, some of which topped eighty thousand feet, would dwarf Earth's Mount Everest, and the knowledge made him proud.

All of which was intellectually interesting but didn't begin to describe the sheer beauty of the quickly rising sun, the soft pink light that glazed the snowcapped peaks to the south, or the feeling that rose to fill his chest. He'd been away too long—and it felt good to be home.

A light breeze ruffled the short gray fur on Longsleep's unprotected back and brought him the fresh clean scent of his sister's perfume. The legionnaire turned as a rock clattered, and she climbed to join him. "I thought I'd find you here," Lighttouch Healsong said, reaching up to take his hand. "Nodoubt Truespeak wants to see you."

Longsleep was on leave, Truespeak was the village chief and would be eager for news. The soldier nodded. "Of course… I'll follow you back."

Lighttouch had big eyes, full lips, and was dressed in an everyday outfit of blouse, jerkin, and black pantaloons. The fur that remained visible was gray, interrupted by streaks of black, just like her mother's. She was pretty, very pretty, and would take a mate soon. Not the old way, by an arranged marriage, but someone of *her* choosing.

The legionnaire followed his sibling back along the cliff-hugging trail, down a series of hand-cut steps, and onto the granite ledge where more than three dozen earthen domes steamed under the quickly rising sun. At least a third of the homes were abandoned now, slowly melting away as the wind, rain, and snow conspired to wear them down. Eventually, after three or four years, they would be little more than mounds on which wild grasses would grow.

Longsleep knew that most, if not all, of the empty dwellings resulted from families leaving the village when one or more of their males joined the Legion. Odds were that they lived in the squalor adjacent to Fort Cameron. A vast labyrinth of mud huts that the humans referred to as Naa Town. Life was hard there, but very few of them ever came back, suggesting that conditions were even worse in Sunsee.

The soldier sidestepped a mound of steaming dooth droppings, kept to the relatively clean stepping-stones that the villagers employed to keep themselves up out of the muck, and said good-bye to his sister as she set off on an errand.

As befitted the owner's status, Truespeak's house was one of the largest and sat at the center of the village. Longsleep sat on a bench outside, removed his Legion-issue boots, and tapped a brass cylinder with a hammer made of bone. Many hours of painstaking craftsmanship had gone into cutting designs into the metal, but the howitzer casing still looked like what it was and bore Legion markings. There was a resonant *bong*, followed by a basso voice, and the word "Come!"

It was warm inside thanks to the nearly odorless dried dooth dung fire and the blankets that served to seal the narrow door. Longsleep slid between them, made his way down a short flight of stairs, and found himself on the main level.

The interior was carpeted with colorful hand-loomed rugs, each overlapping the next so they covered the earthen floor. An open fire pit and a funnel-shaped chimney dominated the center of the home. One section of the circular space that surrounded it was reserved for cooking, while others had been set aside for sitting or sleeping. "Welcome," Truespeak said from his place by the fire. "Sit and tell me of other worlds." The invitation was that of one warrior to another. A tacit recognition of Longsleep's status as a legionnaire and a far cry from the almost dismissive attitude that Truespeak had shown toward the youngster before he left.

The chieftain was big, and his shaggy orange fur made him look even bigger. He didn't rise, which would have been normal, but waved the legionnaire over. "Excuse me for not getting up to greet you, but I took a fall and broke my leg."

Now, as the soldier sat down on the semicircular bench-style seat, he realized that a homemade wooden brace had been applied to the chieftain's stiffly extended leg. It was a reminder of the crude medicine that most villages still relied upon. "I'm sorry, sir. Is there anything I can do?"

"Tell me what you've been up to for the last seven years," Truespeak suggested gruffly. "It will take my mind off my leg, and give me a better picture of what's going on out there. We get more news than we did when you were a cub, but it still tends to be spotty."

Longsleep chose to pick up the story at the point where he left the village, and spoke for the next two hours. Truespeak listened carefully, occasionally interrupted with a question, but generally remained silent while the legionnaire told his tale. But that changed when Longsleep spoke of the *Friendship*, the bomb that had been assembled deep inside the hull, and the subsequent evacuation. The soldier had been there, among the legionnaires assigned to protect the president, and that seemed to pique the chieftain's interest. "You must tell me about him," Truespeak said urgently, "every detail, no matter how small it may be."

So Longsleep did, describing how Nankool handled the chaos that followed the destruction of the ship, what he had heard about initial skirmishes with the buglike Ramanthians, and the president's efforts to find a new capital. And it was then that the chieftain seized the younger warrior by the arm and stared into his eyes. "You speak truly? Nankool is *here*? With General Booly?"

Longsleep nodded. "Yes, I speak truly. Why? Is that important?"

"It could be," Truespeak said, releasing his grip to stare into the fire. "The humans have used Algeron for a long time. Thousands of Naa have died in their battles. And for what? A few supply drops during the winter? Doctors who visit twice a year? The metal we salvage from their garbage pits?

"Now they plan to convene their government *here*, rather than on a planet like Earth, and their new enemy will follow them. Just as the Hudathans did in my father's time. They owe us more, *much* more, and debts must be paid."

The words were said with such passion, such conviction, that Longsleep was taken aback. The humans were far from perfect, as was the Legion, but there were other evils, some of which were pretty nasty. "Much of what you say is true, sir, but not entirely fair. It's worth pointing out that the Council of Chiefs is represented on Earth."

"Yes," Truespeak agreed bitterly, "and what good has it done us? General Booly's grandfather served as our first representative, and things improved for a time. But the humans always look to their needs before ours. The Naa people deserve more, they deserve a seat on the Senate itself and a say in what the Confederacy does. Not as subjects of Earth—but as an independent people. Now, as the government meets on Algeron, we must demand that which is rightfully ours. There will never be a better time."

It was an audacious idea, one that was almost certain to run into a great deal of resistance, especially since the very beings who would have to approve it represented the space-faring races. Not only were they unlikely to want their power diluted, but if a Naa senator was admitted to the Senate, other heretofore marginalized races would demand representation, too, thereby raising all sorts of complicated questions having to do with definitions of sentience, the meaning of the word "civilization," and levels of racial maturity.

Still, Truespeak was correct, or so it seemed to Longsleep, and the legionnaire felt a sudden surge of anger. "I see your point, sir. Is there anything I can do to help?"

Truespeak smiled grimly as he made use of both hands to shift his injured leg. "Why yes, son, as a matter of fact there is."

Ramanthian Planet, Hive

The security around Hive had always been tight, but now, in a time of all-out war, it could only be described as intense. An entire fleet had been assigned to protect the Ramanthian home world, and in recognition of his role in what the Queen liked to refer to as the "Sheen affair," Admiral Enko Norr had been placed in command of it.

Though not an especially brilliant individual, he was extremely diligent, a virtue where military officers are concerned. And because of his diligence Norr had gone to great lengths to protect the *entire* solar system, realizing that even though the other four planets were largely uninhabited, it was extremely important not to let the enemy gain a foothold on any of them.

That was why a destroyer escort issued a challenge to Ambassador Alway Orno's ship only seconds after it dropped hyper and appeared in-system. Codes were exchanged, checked, and double-checked. Then, and only then, was the sleek courier ship allowed to proceed toward the precious mottled brown sphere beyond.

A senator until the destruction of the *Friendship*, the politician had become an overnight hero on Hive and cemented his position among the ranks of the Queen's most trusted advisors. Now, having assumed the mantle of Ambassador at Large, he was returning from a visit to the Clone Hegemony.

But no one, not even the great Orno, was allowed to bypass the orbital security system that kept the home world free of contamination. The word had come to mean not only off-world microorganisms, but all manner of cyborgs and cleverly designed robots as well. An exhausting task, since every race that had the capacity to do so, spent billions of credits each year trying to penetrate Ramanthian security. The efforts would only increase now that hostilities were under way.

The first stop was one of the twenty-four heavily armed space stations that orbited Hive, where Orno had to disembark and pass through a detox center. Then, having been cleansed of artificial contaminants, the diplomat was scanned and sampled to ensure that he was who he claimed to be, before being released into the station proper.

But, rather than waiting for a regular shuttle as he had in the past, Orno was escorted to one of the vessels reserved for top government officials. The ship broke contact with the space station, bumped its way through the atmosphere, and entered a high-priority flight path. Orno, who never tired of looking at his home planet, peered through a viewport. Thanks to the common vision that had been passed from one queen to the next, Hive looked much the way it had during preindustrial times, only better.

In marked contrast to the sprawling cities that covered Earth like a scabrous disease, Hive was the very picture of refinement. Once undisciplined rivers flowed within carefully shaped banks, rows of fruit trees marched army-like across low green hills, and crops flourished within well-irrigated circles. All of which was made possible by the fact that consistent with both their instincts and the dictates of reason, the insectoid species lived underground. That strategy maximized the use of arable land, made the industrial base almost impervious to attack, and protected the citizenry.

Provident though the race had been, however, the gods of evolution had still seen fit to challenge Ramanthian ingenuity. Rather than rely on the three eggs produced by each three-person family unit for its survival, the race had been gifted with a secondary means of reproduction, one that threatened as well as served them. Every three hundred years or so the current queen would produce *billions* of eggs, a number so large that previous hatchings had triggered significant advances, one of which opened the way to interstellar travel and enabled the Ramanthian people to journey among the stars.

Of course there was a dark side as well, because more often than not, the sudden increase in population resulted in famine and civil war. Now, with an estimated 5 billion new souls on the way, the race was struggling to cope.

However, thanks to the advent of spaceflight, it was now possible to ship most of the excess population off-planet. That was why the Queen and senior members of her government had worked so hard to secure additional planets, the spaceships required to move billions of eggs, and the infrastructure required to support the newborn nymphs. Not just for days, weeks, or months, but for *years*.

It was an enormous challenge, and one for which a great deal had been sacrificed, even including one of Orno's mates. But such service was an honor, and trying though it might be, the Ramanthian was determined to do his best.

The shuttle swooped in for a vertical landing, jerked as a platform lowered the vessel into the ground, and soon vanished from sight. A few minutes later Orno disembarked in the underground city called The Place Where The Queen Dwells, entered a government vehicle, and was whisked away.

The cell-powered car carried him along busy arterials, through vast chambers, and under a heavily reinforced arch. The diplomat knew that a blastproof door was hidden above the structure and stood ready to fall if the planet were attacked.

The Queen, not to mention billions of eggs stored in the climate-controlled vaults below, lived within walls so strong that not even a subsurface torpedo could destroy them.

The car was forced to stop for two different identity checks before being allowed to proceed through the royal gardens, along a gently curving ramp, and up to the royal residence itself. The carvings that hung above the entryway told the story of the first egg, the first hatching, and a glorious future. They were said to be more than three thousand Hive-years old.

The car came to a stop, an attendant opened the rear door, and a squad of heavily armed warriors came to attention as Orno backed his way out of the vehicle. Then, unsure of the reception he might receive, the diplomat entered the building.

A series of ramps led up to a broad, scrupulously clean platform that surrounded the hive mother. Her body, which had once been of average size, had grown steadily over the last year until it was so huge that it required the support of a specially designed cradle. Though swathed in colorful silk and tended by dozens of retainers, Orno knew that the Queen felt like a prisoner. Something that made her cranky, unpredictable, and therefore dangerous.

The diplomat's sense of smell was centered on the two short antennae that sprouted from his upper forehead. The rich pungent odor of recently laid eggs triggered the release of certain chemicals into his bloodstream causing the functionary to feel protective, receptive, and subservient, reactions that 98 percent of the race felt in the presence of their Queen. That made it difficult for subjects to lie to her, but it also limited the amount of objective advice the monarch received, something she had a tendency to forget at times.

Though trapped within her factory-like body, and confined to the eggery, the Queen missed very little of what went on around her. She watched, via one of the monitors arrayed in front of her, Orno shuffle up onto the platform. He paused to speak with one of her functionaries, and that was sufficient to summon her wrath. "Well, Ambassador Orno... Did you come here to speak with me? Or to exchange gossip with my staff?" The Queen's voice was electronically amplified and boomed throughout the enormous bombproof chamber.

Orno, who had paused to find out what sort of mood the monarch was in, had his answer. Not wanting to annoy her further, the diplomat hurried toward the other end of the Queen's enormous body, and turned to face her. He bent a knee. "I come to see *you*, Majesty. May I inquire as to your health?"

"The egg factory is running at full tilt, if that's what you mean," the royal answered irritably. "Now, what news do you bring me?"

Like all his kind, Orno had two short antennae, compound eyes, and a parrotlike beak. A pair of seldom-used wings were folded along his back but hidden by the loose-fitting scarlet robe that hung nearly to the floor. He bowed by way of apology, then looked up again. The single aspect of the Queen's physiology that hadn't grown any larger was her head. It looked tiny by comparison with the rest of her grossly distended body, but he harbored no doubts regarding the strength of the mind that lurked within. As always the diplomat chose his words with care. One aspect of his mission had met with success. It seemed best to begin with that. "I'm pleased to announce that negotiations with the Drac Axis were successful. They have agreed to join their forces with ours."

The Queen rotated her head slightly. "Excellent. I'm glad to hear it. What about the question of command?"

The Dracs had been understandably reluctant to place their forces under Ramanthian command, but had finally agreed, conditional on representation at theater-level command conferences. Ramanthian officers would hate the requirement but be forced to accept if they wanted to add some five hundred heavily armed warships to the force already at their disposal. "We retain command," Orno replied, "but they have the right to monitor the decision-making process. They fear some of our officers might spend Drac lives too freely otherwise."

The Queen offered the Ramanthian equivalent of a grimace. "Unfortunate but understandable. Well done. I know the Hudathans stand against us—but what of the Clone Hegemony?"

That was the question that Orno had been dreading. He steeled himself against what might be an extremely negative response. "In spite of the fact that they have worked closely with us in the past, the Clones have grown closer to what they refer to as 'the free breeders' over the last year or so and are presently unwilling to ally themselves with us."

The Queen's eyes seemed to narrow. "What does that mean? Will they support the Confederacy?"

"I don't know for sure," Orno replied, "but if I were forced to guess, I'd say 'yes.'"

"That's regrettable," the Queen said, as if thinking out loud. "It's my understanding that their military is quite strong. What of the Thrakies?"

"The Thraks claim to be neutral," Orno replied, "but they tend to be rather pragmatic where political relationships are concerned, and could prove useful. Not as formal allies, mind you, but as go-betweens, through whom we can interact with others. Of more immediate importance is the need for technical assistance where the newly acquired Sheen ships are concerned. They need to be retrofitted in order for the navy to make full use of them. The Thrakies have the necessary know-how."

"Yes," the Queen replied, "the War Norr mentioned the matter to me. I assured the admiral that you and your staff would do everything in your power to resolve the matter."

There had been no firestorm of criticism, and insofar as Orno could tell, there wasn't going to be. He allowed himself to relax slightly. "Yes, Highness, please rest assured that we will."

"Good," the Queen replied. "Give my best to the Egg Orno... and may the gods guard your travels."

Orno, knowing a dismissal when he heard one, bent a knee and withdrew. Meanwhile, during the relatively brief conversation, 1,754 eggs had been added to the repository below. The race continued to grow.

Planet Algeron, the Confederacy of Sentient Beings

In spite of the fact that the cyborg was dressed in civilian attire, the officer of the day (ODD), knew who Sergi Chien-Chu was, and shouted "Atten-hut!" as the man that many called the Father of the Confederacy stepped out onto one of Fort Camerone's snow-encrusted ramparts. His appearance was that of a twenty-five-year-old male with blond hair and a woodenly handsome face. The reality was something else. While his brain continued to function, the rest of his biological body had been dead for many years.

It was daytime, for the next seventy-two minutes at least, and the former president of the Confederacy, founder of Chien-Chu Enterprises, and Reserve Navy admiral wanted to take a brief look around prior to plunging into what promised to be a long series of meetings. He nodded to the parka-clad ODD. When he spoke no vapor appeared. "As you were, Captain... Do you mind if I take a little stroll?"

The captain wanted to say, "Yes," she did mind, but Chien-Chu's naval rank was equivalent to that of a two-comet general, and there was only one answer she could properly give. "No, sir. Watch out for the ice—it's kind of slippery."

Chien-Chu could see the concern in her eyes and knew it didn't have anything to do with the ice. He smiled. "Don't worry—I'll keep moving. Besides, I have a backup body back in my room."

The captain laughed at the joke, but she knew that if the cyborg took a high-velocity slug through his brain box, it would put him down just as effectively as a bio bod such as herself. The moment the admiral was out of earshot the ODD triggered her belt radio and spoke into the boom-style mike that curved out in front of her lips. "Blue Six to Blue Five. Launch two fly-forms and tell them to pull a check on the surrounding hills. Over."

There was a double click by way of response followed by a steadily rising scream as four engines wound up, and two of the skeletal fly-forms jumped into the air. Outside of the heavily armored brain boxes that housed the pilots, the aircraft were unmanned. That meant every bit of their considerable payload could be devoted to ordnance. Each ship mounted a laser cannon in its blunt nose, a .50 caliber machine gun on each stubby wing, and enough rockets and bombs to put the hurt on an entire battalion of dooth-mounted indigs.

Not that there was any likelihood of that. It was the ODD's hope that the fly-forms would cause any snipers who might be hanging around to dig in deep—if only for the period of time that the admiral was out wandering around.

Chien-Chu, who was oblivious to the efforts on his behalf, continued along the top of the thick outer wall. His sensors took in the white maze that was Naa Town, the lacy fingers of smoke that drifted up to merge with the lead gray sky, and the hills that lay beyond. But his thoughts were focused on the past rather than the present.

A different war had been under way during his last trip to Algeron, a war in which the Ramanthians had been allies and the Hudathans had been enemies. A desperate battle had been fought on and around the planet, and, if it hadn't been for the efforts of the Say'lynt, as well as thousands of legionnaires and the Naa who fought alongside them, the Confederacy would have been destroyed. Yet, even as *that* war was won, another had been brewing. It never seemed to end.

An internal alarm went off, a message flashed in one corner of his electronic "vision," and Chien-Chu turned to retrace his steps. The meeting was about to begin.

The top portion of the fort, the part that could be seen above ground, represented only 20 percent of the total structure. The rest, including vast storage rooms, living quarters, mess halls, classrooms, maintenance bays, and a first-class hospital, were all underground.

Work was already under way to construct an extension of the fort to house the Senate, but that effort was far from complete, and the steadily growing contingent of government personnel was being crammed into every conceivable corner of the existing structure. Officers were being forced out of their quarters to make room for Senators, one section of the mess hall had been roped off for civilian use, and staff people were living in what had been barracks.

It made for a chaotic environment, and as Booly made his way through a crowded passageway, he found himself rubbing shoulders with sharp-looking legionnaires, skeletal spider forms, and harried civilians, many of whom appeared to be disoriented, confused, or lost.

Booly handed out directions, returned dozens of salutes,

and finally made his way into the base theater. It boasted five hundred seats, a steeply slanting floor, and a raised stage. Above the platform, in letters six feet tall, were the words, "Legio patria nostra," The Legion Is Our Country. A reminder that the sentients who made up the Legion were loyal to each other first—and whatever political structure they might serve second. Yet, in spite of that, the increasingly diverse organization had come to be the one force that people everywhere could count on.

Booly's shoes made a clacking sound as he walked down the right aisle toward the stage. The theater wasn't especially fancy, but it was large enough to seat the Senate and associated staff, which would have to do. Some of the politicians had arrived, but most remained in transit, which meant that the first full session wouldn't begin for three standard days yet. In the meantime President Nankool hoped to make some progress where overall strategy was concerned and had convened a meeting of what he referred to as his "brain trust," a high-powered group that included Booly, senior military officers, and a number of key civilian advisors like Sergi Chien-Chu, Charles Vanderveen, and Margaret Rutherford Xanith.

Given the relatively small number of participants, the decision had been made to meet up on the stage. Booly climbed a short flight of stairs and saw that a number of smaller tables had been combined to make a larger one—which had been covered with a light-duty duralon field tarp. The random blotches of brown-and-tan camouflage added a somewhat martial air to the proceedings, as did the olive drab chairs.

Chien-Chu was already present and turned as Booly crossed the stage. The two men were related, thanks to the fact that Booly had married the industrialist's niece, and they had been friends for quite a while by then. But it still felt strange to shake hands with a man who was more than a hundred years old, looked like he was twenty-five, and seemed to be ageless. Both men grinned as they came together. "Sergi! It's good to see you!"

"And you," Chien-Chu replied, "although I wish the circumstances were different."

They would have said more, but President Nankool arrived then, along with Charles Winther Vanderveen, his senior political advisor, Margaret Rutherford Xanith, the head of the Confederacy's Department of Intelligence (CONINT), and a phalanx of support staff.

Booly's team consisted of Colonel Kitty Kirby, his chief of staff, Colonel Tom Leeger, and the recently appointed head of Inter-Arm Operations, Major Drik Seeba-Ka, a dour Hudathan who had distinguished himself during the recent hostilities on LaNor and been cajoled into accepting a staff position.

There were others, too, including a six-officer naval contingent and all manner of specialists, analysts, and liaison people. There was a certain amount of milling around as each participant looked for a place card with his or her name on it, took a seat, and settled in for what promised to be a long session.

President Nankool opened the meeting by thanking those who had organized it, joking about the tablecloth, and giving everyone an opportunity to introduce themselves. Then, after activating his hand comp, he read the agenda. "We'll start with a review of the political situation, followed by the military summary and the strategy discussion. I think you'll all agree that it's absolutely critical for this group to achieve consensus on a general approach *before* we make presentations to the Senate requesting funding. All right, let's get on with it."

Charles Winter Vanderveen was a tall, patrician-looking man, with carefully combed gray hair, and piercing blue eyes. He stood, took a moment to remind his audience that all the information at his disposal was at least six standard days old, and began his presentation. The essence of the situation was that, while the Dracs hadn't allied themselves with the Ramanthians, not formally at any rate, Confederacy intelligence analysts assumed that they would.

Vanderveen went on to indicate that both sides were hard at work trying to woo the Clone Hegemony, and, while it was not yet clear which side the Clones would come down on, the answer would soon be apparent. If Senator Ishimoto-Six arrived on Algeron during the next few days, it could be assumed that the Hegemony had decided either to fight on behalf of the Confederacy or assume a neutral posture. Either of these would be acceptable, although it was Vanderveen's hope that the Clones would add their military clout to the anti-Ramanthian alliance.

"Fortunately," Vanderveen continued, "the Thraks refused to ally themselves with the Ramanthians, as some of us feared they might, and declared their neutrality instead. All of their warships have been pulled back to their home system to protect Starfall. If you want more granularity, check your hand comp. My report is titled 'Political Summary,' and bears today's date."

A murmur of approval and relief ran around the table. The Thrakies possessed a large armada of ships and were skillful fighters where space combat was concerned. Their ground forces were something of a joke—but that wasn't at issue. "That's good news indeed," Nankool said. "Thank you. Colonel Leeger?"

Leeger had white sidewalls, a stiff crew cut, and ears that protruded like the handles on a jug. His uniform looked like it had been sprayed on, and there were four rows of ribbons over his left shirt pocket. Dark brown eyes stared out from under craggy brows. There was no preamble—just a straight-on attack. "Having hijacked thousands of ships, many of us expected the bugs to go on a rampage, attacking anything having strategic value. That hasn't been the case. Rather than lash out, the Ramanthians have assumed what amounts to a defensive posture, and we think we understand why.

"Based on what *we* know about the Sheen ships, which is a great deal since we still have the balance of the fleet, every single one of them is robotic. An approach that has certain advantages, but lacks flexibility, and runs counter to Ramanthian culture. That means the bugs have to retrofit all three thousand vessels before they can put them to use. No small task, and something that will be especially difficult without assistance from the Thrakies, who invented the technologies involved. That buys time, valuable time, which we can use to move against the Ramanthians. I guess that's all, sir. More when we have it. My full report can be found on your comps under 'Military Summary' with today's date."

Nankool thanked the officer and declared a bio break. Twenty minutes later, when the meeting reconvened, Chien-Chu noticed that Xanith, often referred to as Madam X, had disappeared. He wondered why.

Once the strategy discussion got under way, a number of things became apparent, the first of which was that in spite of the fact that all of the armed forces reported to Booly, the navy was firmly in the lead. That was sensible because if the swabbies could find a way to defeat the Ramanthian fleets, there wouldn't be a need for ground combat.

What made less sense, to Chien-Chu's mind at least, was the fact that Admiral Yato wanted to precipitate a series of large-scale space battles in hopes of cutting the enemy down to size before the Sheen ships could be brought on-line. The strategy wouldn't work if the Ramanthians were smart enough to avoid it, which the industrialist believed they were.

The discussion, which had come to center on how the Confederacy might draw the Ramanthians out into the open, had been under way for more than an hour when Nankool decided to intervene. "I've been watching my old friend Sergi Chien-Chu for some time now, and he's starting to fidget. That usually means that he has something to say."

Most of the group chuckled, but the diminutive Admiral Yato didn't, and the industrialist knew why. The regular officer considered Chien-Chu's naval rank to be more honorary than real—and was nervous lest the ex-politician suck energy away from the strategy that he favored. Knowing that, Chien-Chu sought to disarm the naval chief while still getting his concerns across. "Thank you, Mr. President. As everyone here knows I'm a much better businessman than I am an admiral—which means that I tend to look at things from a slightly different perspective. And, while I see the necessity to draw the enemy out prior to the point when they can bring the Sheen vessels into play, I wonder if there isn't something we should work on first."

The combination of self-effacing humor and the nod toward Yato's point of view acted to mollify the admiral if not satisfy him. The senior officer forced a smile.

"While the Ramanthians certainly qualify as an aggressive, expansionist race," Chien-Chu continued, "those qualities are not responsible for this war.

"The bugs went to war because they were about to experience a population explosion so large that it threatens the well-being of the rest of their race, they knew we would perceive the situation as a threat, and sought to preempt an attack by us."

The industrialist paused to eye the faces around him. "I know you're aware of all that—but I would like you to consider the implications. Because of the unique nature of their situation, the bugs are focused on moving billions of eggs from Hive to their colony planets. Not only that, but they will have to move billions of tons' worth of supplies in order to support not only the nymphs but the adults charged with raising them.

"So, if you want to hit them where it hurts, use commerce raiders to go after their supply lines. Force the bastards to put more and more armed escorts on each convoy, drain assets away from their battle fleets, *then* attack head-on."

A long moment of silence followed Chien-Chu's remarks, and to his credit, Yato spoke first. "I don't know what the rest of you think, but for an individual who refers to himself as a businessman, I'd say Sergi is a pretty good admiral."

There was laughter, followed by a flurry of positive comments, and Booly knew that the first part of the puzzle had fallen into place. Though relatively easy to describe, the strategy would be damned hard to execute, and an incredible amount of work lay ahead.

It was time for lunch, and Nankool was about to announce a break, when Xanith rushed into the theater, ran up the stairs, and bent to whisper in his ear. The president listened, said something in return, and raised a hand. "I know we're overdue for lunch and that General Booly's cooks are the finest on Algeron, but Margaret would like a few moments of your time first. Margaret?"

Xanith took a moment to establish a link between her comp and the holo tank, accepted a laser pointer from one of her staff, and tapped a hand mike to make sure that it was on. Those who knew Xanith well, and that included most of the people on the stage, recognized the quick, almost birdlike movements as being typical of the intelligence chief when she was excited about something. Xanith had a head of carefully styled salt-and-pepper hair, a curiously unlined face, and a look of almost perpetual disapproval. She tapped some keys, and a star map blossomed within the holo tank. All of them knew it by heart and had no difficulty understanding what was going on when Xanith zoomed in on a remote area that lay right at the point where the human and Ramanthian empires touched each other. "*This*," the intelligence chief said, "is the planet Savas."

The symbol for Savas expanded into an actual shot of the planet taken from space, which dissolved into a montage of desolate plains, searing desert, and thick jungle. "Savas is a Class III planet," Xanith continued, "although I'm sorry to say that the restrictions normally imposed on such worlds have been largely ignored.

"It's an Earth-like, Hive-like planet, which is why both races would like to settle it. When the war started Savas was classified as a joint protectorate under the control of both humans *and* Ramanthians. Those of you who want more detail regarding this world will find that a background document has been downloaded to your comps. The focus of my report is the Ramanthian fortress called Hagala Nor, which as you can see on this map is located toward the northern part of the planet's single world-spanning continent. It is, or was, a volcano, which the bugs converted into a military base.

"Now, as we look at an aerial reconnaissance vid shot sixty-two standard days ago, please take note of the equipment located along the rim of the crater."

The audience followed the red dot as it touched some blocky structures and a rectangular piece of metal mesh. "This is an antenna," Xanith said, "and not just *any* antenna, but a brand-new configuration our experts have never seen before.

"The purpose of this antenna is to pick up electronic messages sent from distant star systems and to send messages in return. The Ramanthians refer to the prototype as a 'hypercom,' and the truly amazing thing is that it actually works!"

There was a moment of silence, followed by an explosion of conversation, as everyone attempted to speak at once. Booly stood up. "Quiet! Let's handle this one person at a time. Mr. President?"

Nankool was nonplussed. "What are you saying, Margaret? That after decades of trying to come up with a means of faster-than-ship communications the bugs beat us to it? And they cobbled together some sort of super-radio that allows them to communicate from one end of the galaxy to the other?"

"That's exactly what I'm saying," the intelligence chief responded. "Remember that the equipment on Savas is experimental in nature and that the Ramanthian military hasn't had a chance to assimilate the new technology yet. It won't take them long to do so, however, and, once the bugs distribute workable units to their fleets, they'll be able to fight a lot more effectively. *So* effectively that they will win the war."

There was another explosion of conversation, but Admiral Yato had a voice all out of proportion to his relatively small body and managed to cut through the chatter. "No offense, Margaret, but how reliable is your information?"

"*Very* reliable," Xanith replied. "I can't go into detail for security reasons, but suffice it to say that a Ramanthian air car crashed in the desert, two of their scientists were killed, and one of my operatives had the good fortune to reach the wreckage before the bugs did. Among the items recovered from the crash site was a comp loaded with technical data. Not design information, but detailed notes and initial test results."

"But what if that material is fake?" one of the staffers wanted to know. "We could waste a whole lot of energy chasing a technology that doesn't exist."

"But what if they're *real?*" Leeger countered. "A device like that would change everything. If they have it, and we don't, the war is over."

Nankool looked at Xanith. "Margaret? What do you think?"

The intelligence chief took a deep breath. "I trust the operative on Savas, and, while I can't guarantee that the information isn't part of some elaborate scam, that seems highly unlikely. The scenario put forward asks us to believe that the Ramanthians knew exactly where my operative was, were willing to kill two valuable scientists to make the crash look real, all in an attempt to burn some of our bandwidth. I don't buy it."

"So," Nankool said, "what would you recommend?"

"Assemble a naval strike force, take control of Savas, and seize the research facility intact," Xanith said levelly. "It's too late to put a lid on the technology—but we need to have it."

Nankool nodded and turned to Yato. "How come I know you won't agree?"

The naval officer made a face. "We're stretched tight, sir. Lord knows my people would love to get their hands on some sort of hypercom, but we don't have any reserves. A battle group of that size is out of the question."

"All right," Nankool replied patiently, "what *can* you do?"

One of Yato's aides whispered something in the admiral's ear, and the naval chief nodded. "We could scrape up a couple of troop transports, give them a destroyer escort to keep them company, drop the group in-system. That's about it unless you want us to detach a strike force from one of the fleets."

Nankool winced. He knew that all of the fleets were understrength and overcommitted. The president swiveled toward Booly. "How 'bout it, General? Could you spare some troops?"

Booly nodded soberly. "Sir, yes, sir. A battalion should do it. Assuming the navy can put our people on the ground near the objective, they'll take Hagala Nor, *and* the hypercom. They're going to need a ride home though—a battalion isn't strong enough to hold an entire planet."

"The same transports that take the troops in can take them out," Yato replied confidently. "Barring the unexpected, of course."

The reply was glib, a little too glib for Booly's taste, especially given what the unexpected could do to even the best-laid battle plan. "Yes," the legionnaire said gently. "And that's the problem, isn't it? Nothing ever goes quite the way we expect it to. Let's hope that this operation is the exception."

2

An officer's first duty is to the well-being of his troops.
—GRAND MARSHAL NIMU WORLA-KA (RET.)
INSTRUCTOR, HUDATHAN WAR COLLEGE
Standard year 1956

Planet Adobe, the Confederacy of Sentient Beings

According to the orientation materials that First Lieutenant Antonio Santana had reviewed on the trip to Adobe, 10 percent of the planet's surface was covered with water. But the cavalry officer hadn't seen any patches of blue on his way down through the atmosphere, and, now that the shuttle was on the ground, the legionnaire figured the brief had been written by some REMF (rear echelon motherfucker) who had reviewed some survey data but never set foot on the place. Heat flooded the shuttle's interior as the ramp hit the ground and sent a puff of bone-dry dust up into the air. "Welcome to Adobe," the pilot said over the intercom, "and don't forget your sunscreen."

Some of the other passengers seemed especially eager to rush out into the noonday sun, so Santana let them go before picking up his T-1 bags and starting down the ramp.

Meanwhile, toward the rear of the crowd that had assembled outside, Mora Haaby peered over the kepi-clad heads gathered in front of her. The ten-foot-tall Trooper II had a vaguely humanoid appearance, although there was nothing human about the air-cooled .50 caliber machine gun built into her right arm, or the fast-recovery laser cannon that was an integral part of her left. Even minus the missile launchers that could be mounted on her shoulders, Haaby was still one of the most effective killing machines ever devised. She could run at speeds up to fifty miles per hour, operate in a vacuum, and walk across the bottom of a lake. Assuming that Adobe had one.

The atmosphere-scarred shuttle shimmered as heat rose off its angular hull, and a khaki-clad officer made his way down the ramp and paused to look around. Haaby superimposed the picture she had been given to that of the man in front of her and came up with a match. The T-2 said, "Excuse me," stepped through the hole the bio bods made for her, and took six giant strides forward.

Santana felt a shadow fall across him, heard the whir of servos, and turned toward the sound. Now that she was closer Haaby could see that in addition to the collar badge that denoted membership in the 1st Foreign Cavalry Regiment (1st REC), and a row of campaign ribbons, the newly arrived officer also wore bars that stood for an MFV (Medal For Valor) and a DSC (Distinguished Service Cross). All of which could signify that he was one hell of an officer or a glory boy who would be happy to trade her life for another decoration. Only time would tell.

"Lieutenant Santana? My name is Haaby, Corporal Haaby. Welcome to Adobe. Captain Gaphy sent me to pick you up."

Santana nodded. "Glad to meet you, Corporal. Especially since I don't have the vaguest notion of where I am."

Haaby decided that she liked the officer's open, unassuming manner and used her graspers to pick up the bags. "Here, let me take those, sir. I can give you some of the scoop on the way back. The base was built after the first Hudathan war. It's laid out in concentric circles. The center, the area where the larger ships land, is designated A-1. This is A-5. The maintenance shops are located along B-1, and so forth, all the way out to F-3, which is where the regiment set up shop. Just watch for the signs."

Santana said, "Thanks," circled behind the cyborg, and made

use of the steps built into the back of her thick legs to climb up level with the top of her head. Once in position he strapped himself into the recess provided for that purpose, removed his kepi long enough to don the headset stored in a recess next to the small control panel, and automatically requested a com check.

"I have you loud and clear," Haaby replied. "Hang on."

Santana hadn't ridden a T-2 since the rebellion on LaNor—and the long dangerous trip through the Claw-held countryside. But he was a cavalry officer, and the old skills came flooding back. The key was to relax, allow the harness to accept his weight, and use his knees as shock absorbers. The rhythmic motion, plus the odor of hot metal, were like old friends.

Thanks to the fact that Haaby was taking care of the navigation, Santana was free to examine his surroundings. The military base wasn't just large, it was *huge*, and bustling with activity. Thanks to the fact that Adobe was just a few thousand lights away from Ramanthian-held space, the planet was the perfect jumping-off place for raids into the so-called contested zone. As the cyborg made her way down one of the ruler-straight streets that radiated out from A-1, the legionnaire spotted elements of the 1st Foreign Regiment, the 3rd Foreign Infantry Regiment, the 13th Foreign Half-Brigade, a contingent of militia from Earth, a battalion of Hudathan regulars, a detachment of colorful Prithians, and an engineering outfit made up of personnel from half a dozen different species.

All the troops appeared to be in the process of building things, moving things, or tearing things down. Dust rose in clouds as all manner of tracked, wheeled, and articulated vehicles crawled, rolled, or walked along the reddish-colored streets. A company of marines jogged past. They wore sweat-stained caps, T-shirts, and shorts. Each carried a camel-pack filled with a solution that would keep them hydrated.

But if the sights were something to behold, the sounds were no less varied, and came together to create a discordant symphony. Power wrenches shrieked, NCO's shouted, servos whined, radios crackled, music blared, chains rattled, and all manner of other noises battled each other for dominance. It was horrible, yet strangely wonderful, as all of them came together to create a sense of energy.

Haaby made comments from time to time, even pausing to point out the officer's club, the open-air showers, and the area where Santana's new platoon was quartered before taking the officer to battalion HQ. Like most of the more important structures Santana had seen thus far, the shelter was shaped like a half cylinder laid on its side, was olive drab in color, and covered with a thick patina of reddish dust.

The cavalry officer removed the headset, hit the harness release, and jumped to the ground. His Class B uniform was creased in all the wrong places, covered with dust, and stained with sweat. Not the way one wanted to look when reporting for duty but there wasn't much the officer could do about it. Santana thanked Haaby for the ride, picked up his bags, and went inside. The outer door opened into a lock that could be used as a decontamination chamber but also served to keep the worst of the dust out of the interior. The inner door opened into a large room that was so cool it felt like the Arctic region on Earth. The forward section of the long narrow space was taken up with two dozen folding field desks, all occupied, with an aisle down the middle. Farther back Santana could see the com section, with equipment racked to both sides of the throughway, tended by three bio bods and a spider form.

The space along the back wall was split between a conference room with a zip-seal see-through plastic wall, and an office, which was dark and presumably empty. The overall feeling was one of quiet professionalism. An excellent sign.

A sergeant rose from one of the desks and came out to greet the officer as he lowered his bags to the floor. She had short rusty red hair, fair skin, and a scattering of freckles across the bridge of her nose. "Lieutenant Santana? I'm Sergeant Conte. Welcome to Adobe. Both the CO and the XO are away at the moment, but I can check you in, and the colonel left a package for you."

Santana gave silent thanks for the momentary reprieve, removed his kepi, and followed the NCO to her desk. "A copy of your P-l arrived a couple of weeks ago," Conte said, "but I need your card to make sure everything is up to date." Santana took a seat, fished the wallet-sized nearly indestructible data card out of his right shirt pocket, and handed it over.

Conte pushed the card into a slot on her comp, watched as the officer's personnel file and medical history were downloaded to the battalion's field comp, and gave the plastic rectangle back to its owner. With that taken care of she asked Santana to press his thumb into a small device that sampled his DNA, so the bat comp could compare it with the profile that had arrived earlier, and verify his identity. They matched.

"That's it, sir," Conte announced. "The XO assigned you to Bravo Company, 2nd Platoon, under Captain Gaphy. A supply bot will draw your gear for you and leave it in your shelter. In the meantime Colonel Kobbi asked me to give you *this*."

Conte took something off the floor and handed it over. Santana opened the roll to find that it consisted of a set of overalls with a note inside. The message read, "Alpha Company, 1st Platoon. Kobbi."

Santana looked up to see Conte grin. "Colonel Kobbi is a jacker. He spent two years as a tech and likes to keep his hand in."

Like all legionnaires Santana knew that "jacker" was slang for an officer who had come up through the ranks rather than graduate from the academy as he had. There weren't that many of them, and most never rose beyond the rank of captain, which suggested that Kobbi was an unusual man indeed.

Conte's comment had been by way of a kindness, since she could have just as well kept her mouth shut, and Santana smiled. "Thank you, Sergeant. I'll keep that in mind. Can I leave my bags here?"

"I'll have them sent to your squat," Conte replied, "and here's a map."

Santana accepted a piece of paper that showed the battalion HQ, a number of landmarks, and a dotted line that led to a spot marked "Alpha Company, 1st Platoon."

It was still another kindness, and the officer nodded appreciatively. "I owe you a cold one, Sergeant... They do have beer here, don't they?"

Conte managed to look shocked. "This is the Legion, sir. Of course we have beer!"

"I'm gratified to hear it," Santana replied. "Buy your friends a round tonight and bill it to me."

They couldn't drink together, the gulf between officer and

NCO didn't allow for that, but by buying a round for Conte and her friends Santana could not only express his appreciation of the sergeant's help, he could indirectly score some points with some other noncoms as well. An investment that would be almost certain to pay off during the days, weeks, and months ahead.

Santana left the office, paused to don the overalls that Kobbi had left for him, and stepped out into what felt like a blast furnace. A large shadow passed over him as a heavily burdened fly-form whined overhead. It had a fifty-ton quad clutched under its belly and carried it off to the west.

The cavalry officer glanced at the map Conte had prepared, set off down a heavily trafficked street, and was about halfway to his destination when he saw a neatly printed sign that read, "Bravo Company, 2nd Battalion, 1st REC," and knew that the camo netting and the dusty tent that crouched beneath it were the property of his new company commander. It was tempting to stop in, but it seemed as though Kobbi was expecting him, which meant that it was best to continue on his way.

Santana had passed the company HQ by, and had just drawn level with a field hospital, when a huge Hudathan stepped out of the shade produced by a land crawler. Like most members of his race he was about seven feet tall, weighed something like three hundred pounds, and had a humanoid head. His white kepi hid the half-inch dorsal fin that ran front to back along the top of the legionnaire's skull, but not his funnel-shaped ears, and froglike mouth. His skin was white at the moment but would turn black if exposed to cold temperatures. In spite of the heat the Hudathan boasted a uniform so crisp that it looked as if it had just been removed from a hanger. The big legionnaire wore the chevrons and rocker that denoted a gunnery sergeant. He pointed a sausage-sized finger at Santana, and said, *"You!* Hold it right there."

That was when the cavalry officer realized that he had left his blue kepi back at battalion HQ—and that the overalls served to conceal the bars on his collar. He could have set the matter straight by revealing his identity, but there was something about the sergeant that bothered him. The feeling was reinforced when a human and a Naa drifted out of the shadows to stand behind the NCO. He paused. "Yes, gunny?"

Gunnery Sergeant Hreemo Kuga-Ka was a natural-born predator, a vicious fighter, and a sadist. That was why he had been discharged from the Hudathan army, and, having nowhere else to go, had joined the Legion. Then, relying on his skill as a warrior, native guile, and crude political skills, Kuga-Ka had risen to the rank of company sergeant—a lofty position from which he ruled with an iron hand. Now, having spotted what he assumed was a private, who had not only forgotten to put on his cover, but was dressed in sloppy overalls, the NCO was looking forward to exercising his power. The human was tall, but the Hudathan was taller, and that gave him the advantage. Kuga-Ka tried to place the soldier as he moved closer but drew a blank. "What outfit are you with?"

"Bravo Company, 2nd Battalion, 1st REC," Santana answered truthfully. "And you?"

The bland, clearly fearless reply served to infuriate the Hudathan, who clenched both of his ham-sized fists. His toadies grinned and waited for the show to begin. "I'll tell you who I am, slimeball," Kuga-Ka growled, "I'm your company sergeant, your new best friend, and your worst nightmare. I'm the one who's going to take you out of the box in the morning, run your ass all day, and put it back at night! Does that answer your fucking question?"

"Yeah," Santana replied calmly, "it does. I look forward to hearing more about your motivational techniques in the future, but I'm kind of busy at the moment. If you see Captain Gaphy, please inform him that First Lieutenant Santana is dirtside, and on his way to meet with Colonel Kobbi."

The blow fell with such speed that it took Kuga-Ka a moment to absorb what had taken place. The Hudathan experienced a moment of genuine fear, since officers, especially strong ones, were a threat to his invisible empire. Still, lieutenants were a dime a dozen, and could usually be dealt with. The Hudathan came to attention. "Sorry, sir. The sergeant couldn't see your rank, sir. It might be a good idea to wear a kepi, sir. What with the sun and all."

Santana nodded gravely. "I'll keep that in mind, Sergeant. Dismissed."

Kuga-Ka wanted to say something more, wanted to find a way to gain the upper hand, but the dismissal made that impossible. The Hudathan offered his best salute, received one in return, and did a smart about-face. His toadies knew they were in for a rough afternoon but followed anyway.

Santana made a mental note to pull the gunny's P-1, took another look at the map, and continued on his way.

Once, back when he was eighteen years old, before he had been executed for murder, snatched from the brink of death, and dropped into cybernetic boot camp, Lance Corporal Bud Wilker had been six feet tall, and weighed 173 pounds. Now, only four years later, his *new* body stood twenty-five feet tall, weighed fifty tons, and could carry two squads of legionnaires into battle. Assuming it was fully operational that is—which it currently wasn't. The "up" actuator on his right foreleg had sheared in two, transforming him into what his fellow quads jokingly referred to as "a tripod." Efforts were under way to correct the problem however—with none other than Colonel Kobbi in the role of lead tech.

The battalion commander would have been bald if he hadn't chosen to shave his head, possessed a face like a bulldog, and sported a full day's stubble. He was five-eight, had a barrel-like chest, and slightly bowed legs. He wore filthy overalls, and the only thing that served to distinguish him from the rest of the maintenance crew was the eagle pinned to one of his epaulettes and the fact that he swore a lot more than they did. Most tech types would have been embarrassed, not to mention resentful, had their battalion CO found it necessary to involve him- or herself in a routine maintenance procedure. But Kobbi's people knew that the old man was there because he genuinely loved to get his hands dirty, liked to hang out with "real soldiers," and was passionately interested in every aspect of his command.

That wasn't to say that the cavalry officer was unaware of the credibility that such activities earned him, the example it set for junior officers, or manner in which it shaped the battalion's personality. Because although he was a jacker, Kobbi was extremely intelligent and happy to exploit any advantage that came his way.

That was why a small crowd watched with interest as Kobbi directed a sergeant to, "put the frigging support stand under the frigging support plate, so we can work on the frigging actuator."

Wilker could have stood on three legs while the repair was made, and would have had the battalion been out in the field, but the regs called on them to, "Implement Class Three safety procedures, while in areas not categorized as hostile imminent zones as defined in section twelve, part two, of standing LEGCOM orders."

Metal squealed as a group of soldiers pushed the stand in under Wilker's armored belly. "Colonel Kobbi? First Lieutenant Antonio Santana, reporting as ordered, sir."

Kobbi turned toward the voice and saw that an officer with dark hair and even features was standing at rigid attention. "You can skip the parade ground crap, son. We're working on a quad—not kissing some general's ass."

Santana allowed himself to relax. Kobbi was different, that was for sure, and there was something about the colonel that he liked. "Sir, yes, sir."

"So," Kobbi said, looking the newcomer up and down. "I understand that a bug named Hakk Batth ordered you to fire on some unarmed Thrakies during the Sheen conflict, you told him to shove it up his ass, and the brass brought you up on charges. Then, after face-fucking each other for a while, they broke you to second louie while the bug took a walk. How did you feel about that?"

The unexpected question, combined with the unusual setting, hit Santana like a bucket of cold water—especially with so many other people around. That was when Santana realized that the nearest legionnaire was fifteen feet away, that Kobbi's voice was pitched low enough that only he could hear it, and that the assault was by way of a test. The battalion commander wanted to see whether his newest officer would stand and stutter, try to deflect the question, or tackle the subject head-on. The cavalry officer looked Kobbi in the eye. "It really pissed me off, sir. It still does."

Kobbi laughed and punched the younger officer in the shoulder. It hurt, but Santana did his best to pretend that it didn't. "Good! So, think about that the next time you order some poor sonofabitch to go die for you. Officers, even good officers, make mistakes. Besides, even though that passel of idiots broke you, somebody else promoted you back to first lieutenant again. The Legion isn't perfect, but it's been my experience that things level out over the long run, assuming that you live long enough to enjoy it. See that quad?" Wilker was so huge that he blotted out most of the sky. It would have been impossible not to see him. Santana nodded. "Sir, yes, sir."

"We're getting ready to replace his right front 'up' actuator. The only problem is that the shafts for the forward frigging 'up' actuators are two inches longer than the shafts for the rear frigging 'up' actuators, and while we don't have any forward frigging actuator shafts, we have plenty of rear frigging actuator shafts. All because some supply bozo screwed up. Do you follow me?"

"Sir, yes, sir."

"Good. So, if you were in charge here, what would you do?"

In spite of the fact that such matters were normally handled by the battalion maintenance officer and the techs who worked for him or her, Santana took pride in knowing everything he could about the cyborgs under his command and answered without hesitation. "I would mount a second actuator bracket two inches down from the first, thereby allowing us to use a rear actuator shaft up front. In fact, based on the supply situation that you describe, I would have additional brackets welded to *all* of my quads, thereby facilitating maintenance under combat conditions."

Kobbi pretended to look amazed. "Well, I'll be damned! A ring knocker who not only knows a thing or two about maintenance but understands the relationship between maintenance and combat. Sergeant Bolas! Meet Lieutenant Santana. The loot offered to weld that bracket for you, and even though I know you love welding brackets, I thought you might enjoy seeing an officer perform some useful work for once."

The comment was loud enough so everyone could hear it, and the crowd laughed. It was another test, and a rather public one, although Kobbi had seen the advance copy of Santana's P-1 and had seen the welding endorsement that was listed under the subhead "Technical Skills."

It took the better part of twenty minutes for Santana to carry out a weld that any competent tech would have completed in half the time, and the result was somewhat crude, but it didn't matter. The metal had just started to cool when the word started to spread: "The new loot knows his shit—so don't try to push anything past him."

Kobbi had sources, lots of them, and by the time night fell, and he retreated to the privacy of his tent, the buzz regarding Santana had already circled back to him. The officer poured three fingers of amber liquid into a dirty glass and paused to remember the crusty NCO who had believed in him before he had come to believe in himself. A really obnoxious old bastard who had bullied him into submitting an application for officer training school, then made use of twenty years' worth of contacts to make sure that it went through. Kobbi raised his drink. "To Top Santana, the best first sergeant the Legion ever had, and my first real friend. He's a fine young man, Top—and you have every reason to be proud."

A sudden breeze came up, stirred the tent flap, and sent a breath of cool air into the tent. Kobbi downed the whiskey, killed the light, and went to bed.

The sun was up, and the streets were damp from the early-morning spray-down, but would soon be forced to surrender their moisture to the sun. Regimental headquarters occupied four interconnected inflatable buildings, which made sense, since it took a lot of people to support three battalions of cavalry. Like most organizations of its type it was top-heavy. All manner of captains, majors, and colonels prowled the busy, air-conditioned halls. Each had responsibility for some aspect of the regiment's administrative, logistical, technical, medical, intelligence, and air support functions. And while all of them were supposedly on the same side, they typically spent part of each day competing with each other for more budget, clout, or recognition.

But regimental headquarters wasn't a democracy, and at the end of the day there was only one officer who really mattered, and that was General Lani Ibo, sometimes referred to as the Iron

Lady. Ibo had a tight cap of close-cropped gray hair, black skin, and high cheekbones. Her uniform was as spotless as her record and the metal table that served in lieu of a desk. She wasn't one for knickknacks and never had been. The surface in front of her supported nothing other than a hand comp, coffee cup, and two sheets of badly mutilated hard copy. Not because she couldn't read the orders off the screen, but because she liked to sleep with her problems, and computers make poor bedfellows.

But the strategy was successful, the general awoke with the decision made, and was in the process of reviewing it one last time. Ibo scanned the printout again. LEGCOM was located on Algeron, which meant that the NOVA-class orders had been approved by Bill Booly himself, and maybe the president as well. The directive called on her to dispatch a battalion of heavy cavalry to a planet called Savas, "…where the commanding officer will carry out his or her orders by whatever means possible."

Orders which *she*, as the battalion's commanding officer, wasn't privy to. That was unusual, but not without precedent, given the need for security.

But the next part of the cover letter, the part intended to guide her decision, was entirely unique. "Because of the particulars of this mission LEGCOM recommends that the officer tasked with this mission be extremely experienced, utterly reliable, and suited for independent command."

And then, as if Booly had seen fit to add a postscript himself, it said, "If the entire war hung on one battle—who would you choose to fight it?"

That was the line that captured Ibo's attention, caused her to delay a final decision until morning, and served to pique her curiosity. *Ah well*, the general thought, *I'll find out what was so goddamned important eventually.*

Ibo touched a button. A staff sergeant responded immediately. "Ma'am?"

"Get hold of Colonel Kobbi… Tell him I'd like to see him at 0930."

"Ma'am, yes, ma'am."

"And, sergeant…"

"Ma'am?"

"Find Captain what's-his-name, you know, the naval liaison officer. Tell him to join the colonel and me at 1000 hours."

"Ma'am, yes, ma'am."

Ibo touched the button for the second time and took a moment to lean back in her chair. The decision felt good.

Had she been selecting an individual to serve as an aide, a diplomatic attache, or a liaison officer, Kobbi would have ranked at the bottom of her list. But when it came to the most important battle of the war? The general felt confident that she had the right man.

As the sun inched higher in the sky, and cool morning air began to warm, B Company stood at parade rest. The company consisted of a headquarters platoon, a scout platoon, and two quad platoons.

Santana, who had been assigned to the 2nd, or scout platoon, had been introduced to the various beings under his command the afternoon before, but the process of getting to know them had barely begun. What were their strengths? Where could they improve? And what could he do to help? It was too early to know.

The platoon's mission was to serve as eyes and ears for both the company and the battalion. Consistent with that mission Santana had two squads of fast moving Trooper IIs. There were three cyborgs and three observers on each squad. That made a total of eleven sentients not counting himself. A lot less people than an infantry platoon would include, but more lethal, given the amount of firepower that six T-2s could put out.

Now, as he and the other bio bods stood at parade rest in front of their assigned T-2s, the platoon leader spotted movement out of the corner of his eye. Captain Dil Gaphy appeared a few seconds later, with Gunnery Sergeant Hreemo Kuga-Ka walking a respectful three paces behind, like the tail on a dog.

The two of them marched out to the point where the company's scarlet guidon hung limply from its metal pole and executed a perfectly synchronised left face. That was formal, *very* formal for a training day, and Santana wondered why. Was the emphasis on ceremony a reflection of Kobbi's personality?

Or did it say something about Gaphy's? Having met the colonel the previous day, and seen him in his grease-stained overalls, the platoon leader would have put his money on option two.

Lieutenant Lis Awanda served as both a platoon leader and the company's executive officer (XO). She shouted, "Company… Atten-hut!" and waited a beat before the follow-up. "B Company is ready for roll call and inspection, *sir!*"

The cyborgs were already at what amounted to attention, but the bio bods snapped to, and roll call began. The NCOs handled most of it, which meant that Santana had an additional opportunity to examine his new CO. Gaphy was around six feet tall and rail-thin. What flesh he had clung to his bones as if most of his substance had been sucked out of him. The company commander's face was little more than skin stretched over a skull, his eyes were nearly lost in deep-set sockets, and his ears looked as if they had been pinned to his head. Gaphy's uniform was immaculate, but the shirt he wore appeared to be a full size too large, while his trousers fit to perfection.

As the roll call came to an end, and the morning inspection began, Haaby felt a growing sense of anxiety. She was designated as Santana's mount, stood directly behind the lieutenant, and could see over the platoon leader's head.

Kuga-Ka was pissed about something, she could tell from subtle clues learned over the last few months, and that was a bad sign. Because whenever the gunny was unhappy, he had a tendency to take it out on the troops, and cyborgs in particular.

Things had been especially difficult during the weeks since Lieutenant Quito had transferred out. As senior NCO, Kuga-Ka had been assigned to lead the 2nd platoon until a new officer arrived. Except that rather than lead the 2nd, he bullied it, riding the T-2s like they were horses, forcing them to carry him around when they were supposed to be off duty, and making liberal use of a bootlegged neural input device. Drill instructors were allowed to use "zappers" during basic training, and military police carried them as a matter of course, but no one else was supposed to have or use one of the controllers. But Kuga-Ka not only had one, he loved to use it, and Haaby had been zapped two times. Once when she refused to wrestle another T-2 out behind the NCO club—and once when the Hudathan forgot to strap himself in and fell off her back.

Now, as Gaphy and Kuga-Ka finished inspecting the 1st platoon, Haaby was worried but wasn't sure why. She and her comrades had a *real* platoon leader now, and if appearances meant anything, a good one. But the feeling wouldn't go away, and the T-2 felt herself tense up as Gaphy stopped in front of Santana, and the Hudathan moved in to examine her readouts.

As with all Trooper IIs, inspection plates were located on various parts of Haaby's mechanical anatomy. In order to thumb the higher ones open most humans had to stand on a footstool, but thanks to his additional height, Kuga-Ka had no need for such assistance.

The Hudathan called each reading out as he checked them. "Power, 98 percent. Coolant, 94 percent. Ammo, zero. Life support, 100 percent. Communications, uh-oh, what have we here? I'm sorry, Lieutenant Santana, but at 56 percent readiness, Corporal Haaby's com status falls well below minimums. Not a very good showing is it, sir?"

Haaby checked her own internal readouts, experienced a feeling of horror when she realized that the accusation was true, and wondered how such a thing could have occurred. In fact, one of the maintenance techs had checked her systems earlier that morning, and... Then it came to her. The tech had been bribed or forced to disable part of her com system. Not the short-range stuff, since she'd been using that, but something else. But why?

Santana heard the patronizing, almost condescending tone in the Hudathan's voice, and knew that whatever had occurred was payback for the incident the day before. Kuga-Ka knew the new lieutenant would want to make a good impression on Gaphy and was determined to embarrass him. Just as *he* had been embarrassed in front of his toadies. The cavalry officer looked up into the Hudathan's mocking eyes. "Yes, Sergeant. I would have to agree. Come see me about 1400 hours. I'd like to discuss what we can do to make sure that nothing like this *ever* happens again."

It was an order—which meant Kuga-Ka had no choice but to

obey. Not only that, but the way the response was worded, and the slight emphasis on *"ever"* had a slightly ominous quality. "Sir, yes, sir."

"If you two have completed your little chat, it would be nice if we could move this process along," Gaphy said irritably. "I realize that you have been dirtside for less than a full rotation, Lieutenant Santana, and am willing to grant you some momentary slack, but not after today. Corporal Haaby is *your* responsibility, and I expect more of my officers, especially those with your experience."

It was a proper dressing-down, made all the more humiliating by the fact that it had been delivered in front of the 2nd platoon, not to mention the rest of the company. Santana felt the blood rush to his face as he stared at a point one foot above Gaphy's head. "Sir! Yes, sir!"

Kuga-Ka smiled thinly—and the inspection continued. The sun inched higher, the temperature continued to climb, and the Legion baked in the sun.

A cold lunch had been brought into General Ibo's office fifteen minutes earlier. It sat mostly untouched as the increasingly heated discussion continued. The meeting with Kobbi had gone well, but taken a turn for the worse when Naval Captain Horace Yantz arrived, and immediately launched into a list of all the things that the navy couldn't possibly provide, starting with armed escorts, and extending to the request for a Leviathan-class transport.

"So," Yantz said, flicking an imaginary piece of lint off an immaculate sleeve, "the *Mothri Sun* and the *Spirit of Natu* are the best that I can do. Both of them are smaller than the type of transport you requested, but there's a war on, and we must work with what we have. Especially where these off-the-cuff special ops missions are concerned. There's only so much we can do you know."

Ibo watched the naval officer stroke his well-manicured mustache with the back of a finger and wondered if he had ever been shot at. It seemed unlikely.

Kobbi, his face bright red with barely contained anger, leaned forward in his seat. His voice was so low, so hoarse, that it resembled a growl. "What can you tell me about those frigging ships? My battalion includes cyborgs as well as bio bods... Do both ships have the necessary life-support systems?"

Yantz frowned, used a silver stylus to tap a series of comp keys, and peered at the data that morphed onto the screen. "It looks like the *Natu* has racks for 150 brain boxes—but the *Sun* doesn't have any. It shouldn't matter, though... we'll put all of your borgs on the *Natu*."

"The hell you will," Kobbi said thickly. "Think about it... If the ship carrying the brain boxes is destroyed—the war forms on the other vessel will be frigging useless! The boxes have to be split in two so that each cyborg is on the same vessel with his or her body. Need I remind you that this mission has a NOVA-class priority?"

"Sorry, old boy," Yantz replied smugly. "Mission priority doesn't matter... It just isn't on. You can take what we have or walk to Savas. The choice is up to you."

Kobbi started to come up out of his chair but hesitated when Ibo placed a hand on his arm. "As you were, Colonel."

"Captain, I can't say that I think much of your attitude, something I intend to make clear to Admiral Sato. In the meantime make whatever arrangements are necessary to board Colonel Kobbi's battalion in three days' time.

"Oh, and one more thing, you will either find some sort of believable escort for the transports, or I will remove this comet from my collar and personally kick your chair-bound ass. Do I make myself clear?"

Yantz was an expert at bureaucratic warfare, but didn't relish the prospect of an actual fight with the tough-looking general, even though he outweighed her by a good thirty pounds. The naval officer rose from the table and reached for his hat. "That won't be necessary, General. I'll see what I can do."

The legionnaires waited for Yantz to leave, looked at each other, and grinned. "I would pay good money to see you kick his ass," Kobbi said.

"It would be hard to miss," Ibo growled, "but I won't get the chance. He'll come up with some sort of escort. But what about the brain boxes? You could leave them in their war forms."

"Yeah," Kobbi agreed, "I could. But it's a three-week trip. Each borg would be buried in a hold—and locked up with his or her own personal devils. Half of them are convicted murderers—so who knows what would happen if they were isolated for a prolonged period of time? I'll put most of them in the racks and take my chances. We can put a few in spider forms and put them aboard the second ship. It sucks—but it's the best I can do."

"Yes," Ibo agreed soberly. "Well, odds are that both ships will make it through, and everything will be fine."

Kobbi nodded, and even managed a smile; but there was an empty place in his gut, and the battalion commander wished he could find something that would fill it.

The boxy eight-by-eight paused just long enough for Sergeant "Dice" Dietrich and Private Suresee Fareye to hop off the tailgate before it lunged forward and growled into a higher gear. Dietrich waved his thanks to the truck's rearview mirror, took a scrap of paper out of his pocket, and was about to examine it when Fareye spoke. "It's over there, Sarge, next to the water tank."

Dietrich put the piece of paper away. "All right then—let's see if the loot is home."

Though unarmed, the legionnaires advanced the way they would have on LaNor. Together, yet separated by enough space that a single burst of machine-gun fire wouldn't kill both of them, eyes scanning the area for danger. Not because they expected trouble on Adobe, but because they expected trouble everywhere, and were ready for it.

Platoon leaders rated a four-person shelter or squat all to themselves, and like everything else in the area, Santana's was covered with dust. The legionnaires were about ten feet away from the front of the dome-shaped tent when a Hudathan emerged. He scowled at them. "Who the hell are you?"

"I'm Sergeant Dietrich—and this is Private Fareye. We're with the 2nd platoon, Alpha Company, 1st REC. And you are?"

"I'm the one who's about to call your company sergeant and tell her that you're out roaming around where you shouldn't be," the gunnery sergeant replied. "Or should I call your platoon leader instead?"

Dietrich had been in the Legion a long time, had dealt with every kind of NCO there was, and the expression on his leathery face didn't change one iota. "Call anyone you like, gunny. We have passes. Is the lieutenant in?"

Kuga-Ka made no reply other than to grunt, barge between them, and stomp away.

The legionnaires looked at each other and shook their heads in mutual amazement as they approached the tent.

"Lieutenant Santana?" Dietrich called. "Are you in there?" But there was no response. A quick peek confirmed that the squat was empty.

"So what was that about?" Fareye wondered out loud. Dietrich shrugged. "Beats the hell out of me. Well, let's grab some shade and take a load off. The loot will probably turn up soon."

Santana returned twenty minutes later, spotted the twosome emerging from a patch of shade, and returned their salutes. "Well, I'll be damned... Aren't you two supposed to be back on LaNor?" Dietrich had a tendency to be rather ruthless at times, and Fareye wasn't above a bit of larceny, but he felt a real sense of affection for both of them. In a tight situation, when the chips were down, no officer could ask for better soldiers.

"No, sir," Dietrich replied, stepping forward to shake the platoon leader's hand. "You left, the captain took some staff job on Algeron, and the new CO arrived. There wasn't anything wrong with her except for the fact that she's infantry, and we're cavalry. If you take my meaning, sir."

Santana grinned, read between the lines, and figured the new officer was green as grass, something of a tight-ass, or a combination of both. "Well, we're lucky to have you whatever the reason. Which outfit were you assigned to?"

"Alpha Company, sir. Second platoon," Dietrich answered. "It's a good group but we wondered if the lieutenant's platoon is up to full strength?"

"It is," Santana answered, "but I'll check with the company sergeant. Maybe we have some slots in one of the other platoons."

Dietrich nodded. Once he and Fareye were on the company's

muster sheet they'd find a way to join Santana's platoon. "Thank you, sir. Your company sergeant… Is he Hudathan by any chance?"

"Why yes," Santana replied, "he is. How did you know?"

"A Hudathan gunnery sergeant was leaving your tent just as we arrived," Fareye responded. "It said 'Kuga-Ka' on his name tag."

"Thanks," Santana said, his eyes narrowing. "I'm scheduled to meet with him later this afternoon. I'll check on those slots when I do."

"Thank you, sir," Dietrich replied. "Well, we'd better get going, but we'll see you around."

"That's affirmative," Santana said. "Camerone!"

"Camerone!" the legionnaires answered, as they snapped to attention and saluted.

Santana responded in kind, watched them depart, and wondered what Kuga-Ka had been doing inside his tent. Searching it probably—looking for some sort of leverage.

"So," Fareye said once he and his companion were out of earshot. "Did you see the loot's face when you told him about the Hudathan?"

"Yeah," Dietrich replied, "I sure as hell did."

"So, what do you think?"

"I think the loot has a big ugly three-hundred-pound problem."

"So, what should we do?"

"We'll do what we always do," the NCO answered calmly, "we'll cover the loot's six."

The grapevine was usually faster than official channels of communication, though often less accurate, which was why battalion maintenance officer Captain Beverly "Bev" Calvo already knew the battalion was going to be deployed *before* she took the call from Colonel Kobbi. The destination was wrong, though, not that it mattered, since she'd never been to Worber's World *or* Savas.

All Calvo cared about was the fact that there were only three standard days in which to prepare, the brass was going to split the brain boxes and war forms between two different ships, and the battalion would have to operate independently for an extended period of time.

That was why both she and the battalion supply officer, Captain Rono-Ra, had mustered their forces at the center of the 1st REC's cavernous maintenance center. It was chow time, which meant that members of the other battalions weren't likely to be around, and that was just as well. The prefab structure dated back to the inception of the now defunct Trooper III program and was forever imbued with the odors of hot metal, lubricants, and ozone.

The Maintenance Officer (MO) was only five feet five inches tall—which was why she stood on the second step of a three-step maintenance ladder. Rono-Ra needed no such assistance.

Calvo wore her usual combination of a blue kepi, stained overalls, and scuffed combat boots. She had a pretty face, but rarely gave the matter much thought or sought to emphasize the fact. What Calvo was known for was the specially equipped artificial right arm which she had been fitted with after losing the flesh-and-blood version to Thraki shrapnel. The MO had modified the artificial limb so that it could accept a full array of tools, including a cutting torch, impact hammer, and power wrench. Her fingers whirred as she motioned the audience forward. "Close it up, people… We don't have much time.

"Those of you assigned to snatch teams have been given lists of must-have high-priority parts. You were chosen for this assignment because of your contacts, your discretion, and your complete lack of scruples. Please don't disappoint us."

Those assigned to the snatch teams knew the cap was telling them to steal the items on the list from the other battalions. They also knew that their peers would expect such a move and defend against it. But they laughed nonetheless and were in high spirits as they streamed out of the building through a quad-sized door.

"All right," Calvo continued, "it's up to the rest of you to prep the war forms, load the transit containers with supplies, and put the boxes aboard the ships. Check your hand comps for lists of what goes where and the load sequence.

"Finally, hear this, and hear it good... Lieutenant Rono-Ra and I want every quad, RAV (Robotic All-terrain Vehicle), and tac box filled with food, ammo, and spare parts before they are loaded into the transit containers. Then, before the cargo modules are sealed, we want *more* stuff crammed into all the nooks and crannies. If you do it, and do it right, Lieutenant Rono-Ra calculates that we can increase the amount of supplies we take with us by a full 10 percent."

"That's right," the Hudathan put in. "And when the troops board, feed them first, fill their pockets with loose rounds, and tuck a roll of toilet paper under each arm. Does everyone read me?"

There was a loud, "Sir! Yes, sir!" followed by more laughter.

"*Good*," Calvo concluded soberly, "because where we're going there aren't any pre-positioned supplies, shopping malls, or packages from home. Consult your NCOs if you have questions. We'll be working sixteen hours on and eight hours off until the ships lift. That will be all."

The crowd scattered as Calvo stepped down, thought about the task ahead, and looked at Rono-Ra. "So what do you think? Can we pull everything together?"

The supply officer produced the Hudathan equivalent of a smile. "Oh, we'll pull it together all right... But General Ibo would be well advised to keep one hand on her skivvies. There won't be much left around here when we're done."

The Hudathan arrived on time, filled the entrance to the squat with his considerable bulk, and announced his presence. "Gunnery Sergeant Kuga-Ka, reporting as ordered, sir!"

Santana was seated behind his folding field desk. Its surface was bare except for a zapper identical to the one that the NCO had used on Haaby and quite possibly others as well. The officer eyed the silhouette, wondered if the meeting was a mistake, and said, "Enter."

Kuga-Ka took three Hudathan-sized paces forward, came to attention, and held it. Normally Santana would have said, "At ease," and invited the NCO to sit down, but the present circumstances were anything but normal. His status as an officer gave him an important advantage—and he had every intention of using it.

The Hudathan spotted the zapper, knew it was there for a reason, and felt something cold trickle into his veins. How much did the officer know? And more importantly, did he have any proof?

"No, it isn't yours," Santana said, taking the remote off the table. "But it's similar. I wanted to see how hard they were to come by and learned that half a dozen of them were stolen from the military police a few months back. Did you or one of your toadies steal them?"

"Sir! No, sir!"

"That's good, very good," Santana replied, "not that I'm inclined to believe it. Here's what I've learned so far... Ever since you arrived on Adobe you have used your authority to abuse, degrade, and torture the very beings you are sworn to protect. And, because you are so violent, people have been understandably reluctant to file charges against you.

"Now, based on what I'm telling you, a normal person would stop such activities so that he or she wouldn't get caught. But you believe you're smarter than your officers are—and take pleasure in carrying out your little games right under their noses. That, plus the fact that you are addicted to the pleasure you derive from abusing others, means that you'll continue even as some aspect of your tiny little brain tells you that it's dangerous to do so. And it is dangerous, because I'm going to catch you at it, and bring you up on charges.

"Or, and I suspect you're thinking about this one right now, you can attempt to kill me. I say 'attempt,' because a whole lot of people have tried to kill me in the past, and I'm still around. How 'bout it, gunny? Would you like to take a shot at me?"

Kuga-Ka wanted to kill Santana, was determined to kill Santana, not to mention Haaby. The freak had been warned, the freak had spilled her guts, and the freak was going to suffer. But not here, not now, and not while Santana held all the cards. The squat could be bugged, and there was no guarantee that he would be able to find such a device in the aftermath of the murder. Not only that, but other people were aware of the meeting and could testify to it. He kept his eyes focused on a point over the officer's head. "Sir! No, sir!"

"That's what I thought you'd say," Santana said easily. "Now, one last thing, is the company full up? Or do we have some open slots?"

"We have three open slots, sir."

"Good. I have excellent candidates for two of them. I will provide their names to Captain Gaphy—and you will endorse them. Gaphy owns the company, but I run one-third of it, and I can find ways to make your life a living hell. Do we understand each other?"

"Sir! Yes, sir!"

"Excellent. Now, get out of here before the very sight of you causes me to throw up."

The Hudathan executed a perfect about-face, marched out of the tent, and soon disappeared from sight.

Santana let out a long slow breath, removed the pistol from his lap, and placed it on the desk. It had taken the better part of two hours to coax the truth out of Haaby—and only after a promise that he wouldn't take the matter upstairs. Not only was the cyborg afraid of Kuga-Ka, but she had the Hudathan's toadies to consider, along with one of the Legion's most venerable laws. Members of the enlisted ranks solved their own problems, never took interpersonal issues up the chain of command, and were sanctioned if they did.

Was it right? No. Was it real? Yes. That was why Santana had decided to bait the Hudathan and lure the noncom out into the open, where official action could be taken. Would Kuga-Ka move against his enemies before the battalion lifted off? The cavalry officer believed that he would because once the techs jerked Haaby's brain box the zapper wouldn't work, and the noncom's leverage would be lost. Not only that, but the T-2's brain box would be racked along with all the others, and kept under lock and key until just prior to landing.

All of which meant that, in addition to preparing his platoon for deployment and trying to snatch a few hours of sleep every now and then, Santana had to protect both the cyborg and himself. No small task with a potentially homicidal Hudathan on the loose.

The officer rose, slipped the pistol into the shoulder holster that most members of the 1st REC preferred, and left the squat. There was a whole lot of work to do—and less than three standard days in which to get it done.

The sun had gone down, the air had started to cool, and it was as if the entire planet had heaved a sigh of relief as the evening breezes started to stir. There were no Ramanthians in-system, not yet anyway, which meant the streetlights were on. They created pools of green luminescence linked by areas of darkness. Gunnery Sergeant Kuga-Ka paused in one such refuge and froze. There was noise, plenty of it, including the sound of a fly-form passing overhead, the growl of a truck engine, and the distant blare of Earth music. None of which held any interest for the NCO. He was listening for more subtle sounds. The scrape of a boot on gravel, the clink of metal, or the distinctive *click* that a safety made as it was released. But there were no suspicious sounds, which meant Kuga-Ka was free to focus his attention on the four-person squat and the dim glow within. The officer was present—but was he alone?

The Hudathan could move with considerable speed given the size of his body. He dashed through the intervening pool of light, entered the shadow that bordered the tent, and crept up to a window. It was open to let the cool evening air flood in. A single glance was sufficient to establish that the human was all by himself.

Thus reassured, Kuga-Ka withdrew the specially engineered tube from the cargo pocket on the side of his pant leg and approached the door. The duralon whispered as he slipped inside. The officer sat in semidarkness, shoulders slumped, eyes focused on the desk in front of him. He heard the slither of fabric and looked up. Something big blocked the streetlight beyond. "Kuga-Ka? Is that you?"

"Yes, sir," the Hudathan replied gently. "It's me."

"Did you bring it?"

The cylinder felt cool in Kuga-Ka's hand. "Yes, I brought it."

"Then give it to me."

"You have three already, sir. Another could kill you."

"Don't be absurd," the officer replied loftily. "I know how much I can handle. Besides, the battalion is about to lift, and I won't be able to get any more. Now stop wasting my time and hand it over. Or, would you like a transfer to another company? One where your rather exotic notions of entertainment wouldn't be tolerated?"

It was a potent threat and one that would rob the Hudathan of that which he valued most. Kuga-Ka sighed, and the tube changed hands. "I hope you're right, sir."

Gaphy welcomed the coolness of the metal, the moment of anticipation as he unscrewed the lid, and the gentle hissing sound as air pressures were equalized.

Then, unable to wait a moment longer, Gaphy used his left hand to unbutton his shirt, tapped the cylinder with his right index finger, and whispered to the creature within. "Time to come out, my sweet... That's right... You'll like what you find."

There was a wet popping sound as the six-inch-long joy-leech sensed the presence of food, propelled itself out of the canister, and landed on Gaphy's skin.

Kuga-Ka heard the human whimper as the alien life form pushed a needle-sharp penetrator through the surface of his skin. That noise was followed by a long, drawn-out groan of pleasure as the wormlike creature injected powerful endorphins into the company commander's bloodstream, and a wave of ecstasy carried him away. Gaphy's eyes rolled back in his head, and he passed out.

The Hudathan waited for a moment, rebuttoned the officer's shirt, and extinguished the single light. Loading would continue far into the night, but Kuga-Ka would cover for the officer and wake him just before dawn.

The NCO exited the tent, paused to let his eyes adjust to the dark, and slipped into the night. Suresee Fareye followed.

3

*The popular conception of a court-martial is half a dozen bloodthirsty
old Colonel Blimps, who take it for granted that anyone brought before
them is guilty... In reality courts-martial are... so anxious to avoid a
miscarriage of justice that they are, at times, ready to allow
the accused any loophole of escape...*

SIR WILLIAM SLIM
UNOFFICIAL HISTORY
Standard year 1959

Planet Adobe, the Confederacy of Sentient Beings

In spite of the fact that there were three additional people in the
room, General Ibo's office was almost entirely silent as she sat
and stared out through the single window. Maintenance bots
had washed the entire headquarters building down during the
night, but a thin layer of dust had already accumulated on the
plastic and distorted the view. It was kind of like trying to look
into the future, where one could make out the general outline of
what would probably take place, while the all-important details
remained vague and undefined. Not that the dust mattered,
since the *real* purpose of sitting with her back to the room was
to signal the full extent of her displeasure, and provide his
subordinates with time in which to stew.

Finally, after what seemed like an eternity to those who stood
waiting, Ibo swiveled her chair back toward them. Colonel

Kobbi, along with Captains Calvo and Rono-Ra, kept their eyes focused on a point over the general's head. They stood at rigid attention. "Well, Colonel," Ibo began ominously, "let's begin with *you*. You command the 2nd Battalion. That's what it says on the TO (Table of Organization) although some people wonder who's in charge. Especially your peers, who point to the pirates in your maintenance and supply sections as being responsible for the recent crime wave.

"That brings us to *you*, Captain Calvo, and *you*, Captain Rono-Ra, who, if the rumors can be believed, organized what your subordinates refer to as 'snatch teams' to prey on the other battalions."

Kobbi cleared his throat, but Ibo shook her head. "When I want to hear from you, Colonel, I'll pull your chain. Now, where was I? Oh, yes, the snatch teams. Now, while I realize that scrounging for parts and supplies is a time-honored tradition within the Legion, what you two unleashed is well beyond the boundaries of anything that could be called normal. I'm talking about forged requisitions, looted warehouses, and midnight burglaries. This sort of activity will not be tolerated. I realize that the 2nd may receive a mission with little to no possibility of resupply, but the rest of the regiment could receive similar orders any day now, and they will need spares as well." Ibo transferred her gaze from Calvo to Rono-Ra. "Do I make myself clear?"

The officers answered in unison. "Ma'am! Yes, ma'am!"

"Good. Now, one more theft, and I will bring all three of you up on charges. Dismissed."

Rono-Ra did a smart about-face and marched out of the office, closely followed by Calvo and Kobbi. Once outside the threesome paused. "Sorry, sir," Calvo said, her face reflecting the misery she felt.

"For what?" Kobbi answered cheerfully.

"For getting you in trouble, sir," Rono-Ra responded. "The general was pissed."

"No she wasn't," Kobbi countered confidently. "She knows what we're up against. It wasn't so long ago that she led a battalion herself."

Calvo looked doubtful. "Yes, sir. But..."

"'But' nothing," Kobbi insisted. "Answer me this... Did she order you to return the supplies and parts?"

Calvo's eyebrows rose. "No, I guess she didn't, but I assumed..."

"Good officers never assume," Kobbi replied tartly. "Now, don't you two have some work to do?"

"Sir! Yes, sir."

"That's what I thought... We lift tonight, so this is not the time to let up. One thing however... If these so-called snatch teams exist, and I'm not saying that they do, someone should order them to stop. That was the *real* message that you heard from General Ibo. Dismissed."

Kobbi, who rarely took advantage of the T-2 at his disposal, walked away. He was whistling. Ibo watched through her dirty window, wished that she could trade places with the jacker, and went back to work. It seemed that a staff officer on Algeron thought it would be a good idea if the 1st REC started a choir—and challenged other regiments to do likewise. She was about to realign his priorities.

The scene in and around the spaceport's center was one of barely controlled chaos. A tall minaret-like control tower marked the epicenter of the action. Air cars and fly-forms crisscrossed the sky, repellors screamed as a bright orange traffic control monitor led a destroyer escort to its assigned pad, a never-ending stream of announcements poured out of omnipresent loudspeakers, a crane swung a heavily shielded drive into position over a deep-space tug, and robots hurried to service an admiral's gig as the 2nd Battalion's war forms filed into the long, narrow decontamination stations.

Santana watched Haaby follow another T-2 into one of the chambers, where she soon disappeared into a welter of chemical sprays, pressurized rinse water, and billowing steam. The idea was to kill as many of Adobe's microscopic life forms as possible so none of them would be transferred to Savas, where they could potentially play hell with the local ecosystems. Later, after the war forms had been loaded into their transit containers, each cargo module would be irradiated just to make sure.

As Santana paralleled the decontamination chamber and waited for Haaby to emerge from the far end, he saw Kuga-Ka in the distance. The Hudathan offered a completely unnecessary salute that Santana was then obliged to return. The NCO was mocking him, and had been ever since their meeting, as if to say, "See? I *am* in control of what I do."

And Santana was starting to believe it. Though not part of his platoon, both Dietrich and Fareye had successfully transferred into Gaphy's company and somehow managed to pick up on the threat that Kuga-Ka posed. But, outside of the single seemingly surreptitious visit that the Hudathan had made to Gaphy's squat, their efforts to catch the gunnery sergeant doing something wrong had been futile. Now, contrary to Santana's earlier predictions, it seemed as if the Hudathan was determined to ignore the bait and leave both the cyborg and her protector alone.

The officer yawned, watched Haaby emerge from a cloud of steam and enter the next station, where she would be blown dry. Other cyborgs were present, not to mention more than a dozen bio bods, which made any attack on the T-2 highly unlikely. The perfect time to go in search of some much-needed food.

The cooks had established stands here and there throughout the loading area so hardworking legionnaires could grab snacks on the fly. Santana commandeered a sandwich, poured himself a cold drink, and looked for a place to sit down. The officer spotted a likely-looking cooler, sat on it, and took his first sip of the refreshing liquid as he keyed his platoon's frequency. "Red Six to Red Five... Over."

There was a burst of static followed by sound of Haaby's synthesized voice. "This is Red Five. Over."

"Have you completed the decontamination sequence yet? Over."

"We're entering the shipping container now," the cyborg said, as a tech motioned for her to enter the durasteel transit box. Though grateful for the fact that the loot was keeping an eye on her, she hoped Santana would come up with a less direct way to check on her safety, since it was unusual for a platoon commander to track the activities of a single legionnaire, and her squad mates would soon take notice.

The cargo module's interior had been fitted with special clamps that would hold the bipedal war forms in place during transit. Each box was designed to hold six T-2s, which meant that Santana's entire platoon would make the trip in a single container.

A second tech directed Haaby into slot five, and just as the cyborg started to turn, she recognized the bio bod. "Wait a minute," she said out loud. "What's the gunny doing in here? He's supposed to be…"

Someone threw a switch, a pair of hydraulically operated arms reached out to grab the T-2 and wrap her in an unbreakable hug. Fear caused Haaby to drop all pretences and make a direct appeal to her platoon leader. "Sir! I can't move! They…"

The sandwich fell as Santana came to his feet. "Haaby? What's happening? Over."

But Haaby could no longer reply. Kuga-Ka was up on her back by then. He flipped the protective cover up out of the way, grabbed the red, T-shaped handle, and gave it one full turn to the right. That was sufficient to disconnect her brain from the war form and all of its capabilities. Then, by pulling on the same handle, the Hudathan removed the cyborg's bio support module from the back of her massive head. Sedatives flooded Haaby's brain, and the outside world snapped to black.

Santana swore and started to run. The loading area wasn't far, no more than a few hundred feet away, and the officer arrived in front of the transit box just as a tech placed the last of six brain boxes on a specially designed cart. "Corporal Haaby," the platoon leader demanded. "Where is she?"

The tech was a tired-looking woman with a serpent tattooed onto her scalp. She eyed the boxes. "Right there, sir. Left side, bottom row."

Santana followed the pointing finger, saw the green indicator light, and heaved a sigh of relief. The cyborg was okay.

That was when Fareye appeared at his elbow. "I was monitoring your freq, sir. Gunnery Sergeant Kuga-Ka just left. He had what looked like an ammo box tucked under his arm."

Santana felt a lead weight hit the bottom of his stomach. "An ammo box? Are you sure? Is there any chance it could have been a brain box instead?"

The Naa glanced at the cart. The possibility that the NCO might abscond with one of the brain boxes hadn't occurred to him. "Yes, sir. They're about the same size."

Santana grabbed the tech's arm. "Haaby's brain box... Who pulled it?"

The tech looked confused. "I'm not sure, sir. I was outside."

"Damn! Which way did Kuga-Ka go? We've got to catch the bastard."

"That way, sir," Fareye said, and pointed back toward some long, low maintenance buildings.

Santana nodded. "See if you can catch up... Stay in touch by radio, but remember Kuga-Ka can hear what you say, and he's a helluva lot bigger than you are."

Even as Fareye took off, the officer turned to the tech and eyed her name tag. "Specialist Fahd... Secure this cart and everything on it. Nobody is to touch it without my permission. Understand?"

Fahd looked startled. "I guess so, sir, except that I'm supposed to..."

"Forget what you're supposed to do. I gave you an order. Follow it."

The tech said, "Sir! Yes, sir!" but Santana was already running by that time. He was in good shape, but it was hellishly hot, and it wasn't long before his breath came in short gasps. The cavalry officer wanted to call for help, but feared the Hudathan would hear him and hide Haaby's brain box somewhere. The built-in life-support system would sustain the cyborg for a few hours but no more than that. Assuming the object Fareye had seen was a brain box. But what if Haaby's brain was sitting on the cart? And Kuga-Ka was carrying a box full of spares? Maybe the whole thing was a setup! A deliberate attempt to discredit the noncom's pursuers and escape punishment. But the alternative, which was to do nothing, was unacceptable.

Those concerns were still churning through the officer's mind when Fareye's voice came in via his earpiece. The Naa was intentionally cryptic and chose to omit his call sign so that only someone who was familiar with his voice would know who had sent it. "Target sighted. Look for the radio mast. Over."

Santana looked ahead, spotted the fifty-foot-tall antenna that towered over the maintenance sheds, and knew the Hudathan was somewhere in that vicinity. He ran even harder.

Then a second voice was heard. This one belonged to Sergeant Dietrich. It was cold as ice. "I have him, sir. Maintenance Shed Six."

Santana gave silent thanks. "Good... Does he have a brain box with him?"

There was a pause. "He has something with him. It's wrapped in fabric."

"Okay, hold the bastard. Fareye—call the MPs. Tell them we have a thief in Maintenance Shed Six."

A would-be murderer was more like it, but the exact charge didn't matter, so long as they got some help soon. The officer slowed to a jog, rounded a structure labeled "Maintenance Shed Five," and heard Fareye's voice in his ear. "The MPs are on the way, sir."

A small crowd had gathered just outside Maintenance Shed Six. It consisted of human techs, a couple of Prithians, and three utility bots. As Santana pushed his way through he could hear Kuga-Ka shouting. "What's wrong with you people? Can't you see that this man is crazy? Take his weapon!"

But Dietrich was armed with a CA-10 carbine that was capable of firing eight hundred rounds per minute. It was shaped like a wedge with a peg-style grip mounted behind the muzzle, a combination pistol grip and trigger assembly to the rear of that, and a thirty-round magazine that protruded from the receiver. With the exception of the robots, the rest of those present had qualified with the weapon and were familiar with its capabilities. So, given the fact that none of them were armed, it made sense to wait and let someone else straighten the situation out.

The maintenance shed's service door was open, and just as Santana arrived in front of it, a wheeled vehicle screeched to a stop. Captain Gaphy swung a pair of highly polished boots out onto the tarmac. In spite of months spent on Adobe, his skin still looked like white parchment. He pointed a long thin finger at Santana. "Lieutenant! What's going on here? Why is that man pointing a weapon at Gunnery Sergeant Kuga-Ka?"

There was another screech as a scout car full of MPs arrived.

Santana sighed. If he was wrong, if the object clutched under Kuga-Ka's massive arm was anything other than Haaby's brain box, his career was over. "I have reason to believe that the Gunnery Sergeant removed Corporal Haaby's brain box from her war form and brought her to this location to kill her."

Gaphy looked incredulous. "Are you out of your mind? Why would Kuga-Ka do something like that? I can only imagine that you have taken leave of your senses.

"Sergeant! Place that weapon on the ground! That's an order."

Dietrich glanced at Santana, saw the officer nod, and put the CA-10 on the oil-stained duracrete floor.

"All right," Gaphy said as he strode toward Kuga-Ka, "let's settle this nonsense right now…"

Kuga-Ka stood at attention and made no attempt to resist as the cavalry officer removed the package from his grasp, turned toward the crowd, and removed the wrapping.

Santana held his breath as the duralon fell away, saw Gaphy frown, and heard someone gasp. "It's a brain box!"

Kuga-Ka made no attempt to run. There was no place to go. The Hudathan knew that his best chance, his *only* chance, was to pretend innocence and hope for some sort of break. "Sir! The gunnery sergeant thought it was an ammo box, sir."

Gaphy knew it was a lie, but didn't want Kuga-Ka to reveal his addiction, which meant he had to be careful. "Really? Well, if so, the gunnery sergeant needs to have his eyes examined. It says 'Corporal Mora Haaby' right here on the box. Still, I suppose some sort of mix-up is possible."

"I don't think so, sir," Santana put in, as he felt a tremendous sense of relief flood his body. "Someone gave a fake brain box to the life-support techs. That makes some sort of mix-up very unlikely."

Gaphy swore silently. The Hudathan had been stupid, extremely stupid, but it was critical to maintain some sort of front lest the idiot spill his guts regarding the joy-leeches. "Yes, well that's what investigations are for, aren't they? It will all come out in due time.

"Corporal!" Gaphy said, motioning to one of the MPs. "Take the gunnery sergeant into custody. I want full reports on everything you saw here. That goes for you, too, Lieutenant…

I'll be interested to hear how you came to be so knowledgeable about this situation, why you decided to keep such knowledge to yourself, and when you planned to let your superiors in on it."

"I look forward to that as well," Colonel Kobbi said grimly, having arrived in time to hear the last few paragraphs. "All right, let's break it up. I don't know what the hell is going on here, but those transports will lift off in four hours and twenty-three frigging minutes. We don't have time for distractions, so get your asses back to work."

Santana watched the MPs take control of Kuga-Ka, saw the noncom turn to look into his eyes, and felt the full impact of the Hudathan's hatred. That was when he realized it wasn't over, and wouldn't be, not so long as both of them were alive.

Aboard the *Mothri Sun*
In spite of the fact that the freighter was relatively small as transports go, the number two cargo hold looked huge as Calvo stepped down onto a catwalk, and peered into the dimly lit durasteel cavern below. The liftoff had gone without a hitch from the maintenance officer's perspective, since all the war forms, munitions, and spares had been loaded aboard the *Mothri Sun* on time and stored in a manner that would allow her technicians to access them during the trip. Something they needed to do since the days prior to departure had been spent rounding up spares rather than performing precombat maintenance checks.

Lights appeared in the murk below as the MO's crew of twenty-four maintenance techs entered the hold. Though normally embedded in the four companies that went together to comprise the battalion, the "gear heads" as they were sometimes known, had been stripped out of their units and put aboard the *Sun*. Sixteen members of her crew were bio bods and eight were borgs. They "wore" specially equipped six-legged spider forms.

Owing to a shortage of space on the *Spirit of Natu*, a lieutenant and two squads of infantry had boarded the *Mothri Sun* as well. Though normally charged with providing security for battalion HQ, the ground pounders had been put to work humping tools and diagnostic equipment.

Metal clanged on metal as the first transit container was breached and the technicians entered. Each war form in that particular module would be checked, serviced, and rechecked. Once that was accomplished the durasteel box would be resealed and the four-person team would move on. Meanwhile, other teams, each working under the supervision of a non-com, were following the same process. It represented a great deal of work, but that didn't trouble Calvo, who relished such activity.

A power wrench chattered as a spider form made use of one of a tool arm to remove the bolts on an inspection plate. Calvo grinned, made her way to the far side of the hold, and descended a ladder. There, down in the gloom, was the world that she loved best.

Aboard the *Spirit of Natu*

The *Spirit of Natu* was and always had been a military vessel, which meant that as Santana made his way down the ship's main passageways there was nothing to see beyond overhead cable trays, regularly spaced lights, bare bulkheads, directional signs, side corridors, and the gray nonslip matting that covered the decks. The cavalry officer was furious, and at least some of that must have been apparent, because those coming from the opposite direction were careful to stay out of his way.

Once Santana arrived in the section of the ship where Alpha Company personnel were quartered, he followed a narrow passageway inward and stopped in front of an open hatch. The compartment was tiny, but private, a fact for which Captain Gaphy was grateful. The officer heard a couple of dull thumps and looked up to find Santana framed by the hatchway. He had been expecting the visit but saw no reason to signal the fact. "Yes? What is it?"

The platoon leader stood at attention, but rather than staring at a point over Gaphy's head, he looked the officer in the eye. "Lieutenant Antonio Santana, requesting permission to speak with the captain, sir."

"Enter."

Santana took two steps forward. Gaphy was seated on the

opposite side of a fold-down worktable. He sat very straight so as to maintain at least three inches of space between his body and the metal bulkhead. An important precaution lest the officer lean backward, apply pressure to the leech that had taken up residence in the cleft between his shoulder blades, and suffer the painful consequences. "Yes?" the company commander demanded. "What do you want?"

Santana felt his hands start to tremble and balled his fingers into fists. "I was told that Gunnery Sergeant Kuga-Ka was released from the ship's brig. Is that true, sir?"

"Yes," Gaphy replied calmly, "but only after consultations with Colonel Kobbi. The gunnery sergeant has an impeccable record, there's still a possibility that there was some sort of unfortunate mix-up where Haaby's brain box is concerned, and the ship is in hyperspace. All of those factors were taken into account while making the decision to release Kuga-Ka. Does that answer your question?"

The whole thing had a rehearsed quality and made no sense to Santana, but there was only one reply that he could give. "Sir! Yes, sir."

"Good. I read your statement, and while I find the accusations you made against Kuga-Ka hard to believe, I know you were sincere in lodging them. There will be a court of inquiry, similar to the one mentioned in your P-l, which will provide you with an opportunity to testify. In the meantime I suggest that you focus on your responsibilities as a platoon leader—and leave matters of military justice to your superiors. Dismissed."

The mention of his own court of inquiry, combined with the curt dismissal, had their intended effect. Santana clenched his jaw, delivered his best salute, and turned on his heel. It wasn't right, not by a long shot, but Kuga-Ka was on the loose.

Though nicer than most, the cabin was still no larger than the average walk-in closet, and extremely spartan. Colonel Kobbi closed the door to his cabin, felt his heart beat just a little bit faster, and stood in front of the wall safe. The battalion commander felt both a sense of anticipation and dread as he prepared to read the orders locked within. The metal felt cool as he pressed his palm against the print-sensitive plate, there was a distinct *click* as the lock was released, and a whiff of stale air as the nearly indestructible door swung open. The O-4 package wasn't much to look at, just a gray duraplast case, with "Command Eyes Only" embossed on its cover. But inside, nestled within a circular recess, was a data disk that detailed the battalion's mission.

Kobbi checked his watch and noted the time so he could include it in the ops diary that he updated each day. Then the officer removed the case from the safe, took a seat behind his fold-down desk, and slipped a thumbnail under the removable sticker. It came off easily. With that out of the way the jacker applied his thumb to the print-sensitive oval, and the cover popped open. The battalion commander knew that had he, or someone else, attempted to open the case with a tool, the resulting explosion would have destroyed both the disk *and* the person trying to access it.

The disk was shiny and about two inches across. Kobbi dropped the device into a slot on his hand comp and was rewarded with a nearly instantaneous response. Because the question had been drawn from his private life, the answer couldn't be found in his P-l file. "Who is your favorite author?"

Kobbi cleared his throat. "Sun Tzu."

The computer checked the disk for a matching voice-print, found it, and checked the answer. It was correct. Text flooded the screen. There was a preface, followed by the orders themselves and background information on Savas.

Kobbi read for the next five minutes, went back to the beginning, and reread the orders again. The essence of the mission was clear. The battalion would put down near a fortress called Hagala Nor, capture something called a hypercom, and haul ass.

The bugs had an armored unit in the area, plus the equivalent of half a battalion of ground troops, or so the briefing document claimed. But that information dated back to the point before the planet had been cut off, which meant that the force could have grown during the intervening time, or been withdrawn. There was no way to know.

Adding to the uncertainty was the fact that outside of some

rather sketchy data gathered by an unmanned recon drone more than a standard month earlier, the three-ship task force was going to drop out of hyperspace blind, and hope that their single escort would be sufficient to protect them from any ships that the bugs had in-system.

But Kobbi was a realist—and knew that no amount of wishing would make the situation any better than it was. The only thing he could do was to brief his officers, insist that they plan for every possible contingency, and hope for the best. The jacker went to work.

In spite of the fact that Gunnery Sergeant Hreemo Kuga-Ka was free, he didn't *feel* all that free, not with a full-fledged investigation under way. Rumors suggested that Haaby had been talking and that even more cyberfreaks were prepared to testify. That meant his freedom wasn't likely to last very long, and if the noncom wanted to lay the groundwork for an escape, he needed to do it *now*.

That was why the Hudathan made his way up-ship to officer country. Maybe, if he was lucky, Kuga-Ka could gather some intel regarding the battalion's mission, information that would help him create a realistic plan. In spite of the suspicion focused on the noncom, the combination of his size, "don't fuck with me" attitude, and the clipboard tucked under his arm conveyed the impression that he was on an official errand.

Conscious of the fact that someone on official business wouldn't skulk about, Kuga-Ka marched straight into the intel officer's tiny cubicle, only to discover that its owner was in residence. The noncom saluted. "Sorry to bother you, sir. I have something for Captain Gaphy... Have you seen him? No? Thank you."

Having struck out where the intel officer's cabin was concerned, Kuga-Ka was on his way to Kobbi's quarters when a group of officers appeared, and one of them said something about it being time to "... drain my tanks."

A quick check was sufficient to verify that they had been meeting in the wardroom. The table that dominated the center of the room was strewn with all manner of hand comps, printouts, and half-empty coffee cups.

Well aware that it would be only a matter of minutes before the officers returned, the noncom completed a quick circuit of the table and paused when he saw the words "LEGCOM, Command Eyes Only," on one of the glowing screens.

A quick scan of the first paragraph was sufficient to confirm that the file was what he had hoped for, and a few quick key strokes were sufficient to send a copy to himself. The message would show up if the computer's owner were to check—but that was a chance that the Hudathan was willing to take.

Seconds later, his eyes on the clipboard, Kuga-Ka was walking down the corridor when Major Tik Matala, the battalion's Executive Officer returned. He saw the noncom, but wasn't aware that the Hudathan had been in the wardroom, and had no reason to be concerned. There weren't any Ramanthians on the ship, and it was isolated in hyperspace, which meant that the battalion's security was intact.

Clouds could be seen high in the searingly blue sky, the hillside in front of them was covered with loose rock, and what looked like a well-packed trail beckoned. But trails are the perfect place to lay mines, so even though it meant more work for Haaby, Santana ordered the T-2 to climb up through the loose scree. Even though the harness served to hold the platoon leader in place, the motion of the T-2's body still threw the human back and forth, forcing him to hang on. There were moments when the loose rock threatened to send both of them tumbling down the slope, something that would not only be hard on Haaby, but worse for the bio bod should the cyborg roll over on top of him.

Then, after ten minutes of hard climbing, they neared the top of the rise. Santana ordered the T-2 to stop just short of the crest rather than expose herself on the skyline. Anyone watching from the opposite direction would see nothing more than a tiny irregularity on the horizon.

A single glance at the heads-up display (HUD) projected on the inside surface of the platoon leader's visor was sufficient to verify that the other members of the first squad were in position. Private Su Theek, and a T-2 named Private Hooly Lukk, were about a hundred yards off to the left, while Private Lynn Cho, and a borg named Fas Nulla were stationed an equal distance to the rear. Their job was to guard the back door in case the enemy attempted to sweep in behind the squad and cut it off.

Confident that his troops were properly positioned, Santana let his weight rest on the harness, raised his electrobinoculars, and scanned the valley ahead. Targeting information scrolled down the side of the viewfinder as he panned from left to right. With the exception of clumps of trees, all of which looked too similar to be real, the terrain was open and inviting. *Too* inviting.

The squad's mission was to scout ahead, locate the enemy, and warn the quads that were theoretically following behind. That meant Santana had to keep going, keep covering new ground, lest the huge cyborgs overtake him and bring the assault to a stop.

But there were times when a platoon or squad leader had to ignore such pressures and make sure of the terrain in front of him or her. The key was to understand which situation was which. The sky shivered, turned an unlikely shade of green, and snapped back to blue. Santana keyed his mike. "Blue Six to Blue Five. Over."

"This is Five," Theek replied. "Over."

"See anything suspicious? Over."

"No, sir. Over."

Santana took another look, and was just about to order Haaby upslope, when a cluster of boulders slid sideways. Not far, but given the fact that boulders are supposed to be inert, they weren't supposed to move at all. "Did you see that group of boulders shift left? Over."

"Sir! Yes, sir," Theek replied excitedly. "I think those other rock formations are fake, too! Ground effect vehicles is my guess—waiting in ambush. Over."

"Well, let's find out," Santana replied, and put in a call for air support. The voice arrived before the fly-form did. "Red Six to Blue Six... Did someone find something for us to shoot at? Over."

"Welcome to the party, Red Six... We have a targeting laser on what may or may not be a ground effect vehicle approximately two thousand yards forward of our position. Over."

"Roger that," the airborne cyborg answered cheerfully. "Tally ho! Over."

And with that three heavily armed fly-forms came out of the sun just as a volley of surface-to-air (SAM) missiles flashed up to meet them. A combination of chaff and electronic countermeasures (ECM) proved sufficient to neutralize the threat as one SAM detonated harmlessly and the rest took off in pursuit of phantom targets.

The fly-forms pulled up, dumped multiple sticks of bombs on the target, and accelerated away. Explosions marched along the bottom of the valley, tossed half a dozen limpet-shaped ground effect vehicles up into the air, and left a line of blackened craters in their wake. A mixture of rock, dirt, and scrap metal was still raining down from the sky when the words "Mission Complete" flashed in front of those taking part in the training scenario.

"All right," the platoon leader said, as he started to remove the leads that connected him to the virtual reality (VR) training system, "good job. The system will provide each of us with personal feedback. Study it and log some solo hours if you scored anything less than 90 percent.

"We're going to link up with the second squad during the next session, so you might want to review the company's call signs. Things start to get complicated with six T-2s plus a whole bunch of quads to keep track of. Any questions?"

There weren't any, so Santana removed the VR helmet and nodded to both Theek and Cho. Like their platoon leader, the other legionnaires were strapped onto blocky constructs that provided the same kind of kinesthetic feedback that riding a real T-2 did.

As for the cyborgs, they had taken part in the exercise from the racks where their brain boxes were temporarily housed, and were now free to use the same system for recreational purposes.

It wasn't perfect, but the system helped compensate for the fact that there hadn't been any opportunity for training on Adobe, and Santana was grateful. The platoon leader unhooked himself, followed the other two bio bods out into the hall, and decided to return to the compartment he shared with the ship's third officer. The court of inquiry was a mere thirteen hours away—and he wanted to be ready.

Aboard the *Mothri Sun*

Video blossomed as one of the bio bods inserted Kitamoto's brain box into the back of a war form's head and the T-2's systems came on-line. The onboard computer took what the cyborg could "see" via its eye cams, combined that with data provided by infrared sensors, and sent the result to the technician's brain.

Like the other cybernetic tech heads, Kitamoto had been through basic training but wasn't expected to fight. So, because the vast majority of her time was spent in spider forms, the big bulky T-2 felt exceedingly awkward as she backed the machine out of its retaining clamps, managed a poorly executed turn, and marched the body out of the transit container.

The check ride called for her to walk to the far end of the hold and back, run diagnostics on all the onboard systems, and put the T-2 away. The quads were too large for such a stroll, which meant that all the techs could do was start them up, and run a full battery of tests. Not a step listed in the manuals—but something Captain Calvo insisted on.

Kitamoto clumped her way down the corridor between the cargo modules, stopped in front of the bulkhead, and did a clumsy about-face. Meanwhile, all of the navigation, com, and targeting systems tested green. "This unit looks good," the technician reported via short-range radio. "Put it down as good to go."

Calvo said, "Good work," ran her stylus down her hand comp's touch-sensitive screen, and tapped a serial number. The officer didn't know Corporal Haaby—but assumed the trooper would be pleased.

Aboard the *Spirit Of Natu*

The ship's wardroom was the largest space available other than one of the ship's holds, and it was packed with people. There was a loud buzz of conversation as those present discussed

Gunnery Sergeant Kuga-Ka, the charges brought against him, and what they knew about the case. Heads turned, and all conversation ceased as Colonel Kobbi brought the ceremonial gavel down with a loud *bang*.

"Okay, people," the battalion commander said, "let's get this thing under way. Let the official record show that a military court of inquiry was held on this date, at this time, aboard the navy vessel *Spirit of Natu* for the purpose of reviewing charges brought against Gunnery Sergeant Hreemo Kuga-Ka, in order to determine whether there is sufficient evidence to justify court-martial proceedings, or lacking such evidence, whether the charges should be dropped.

"Because this court of inquiry is taking place during a time of war, and Gunnery Sergeant Kuga-Ka does not have benefit of qualified counsel, the findings of this court will be considered provisional and subject to review when conditions allow. Are there any questions? No? Then I will ask Major Matala to read the charges."

Santana, who was seated in the front row, looked at Kuga-Ka as the XO started to read. The noncom's face wasn't just blank, it was *professionally* blank, as it would be on parade. Owing to the almost paranoid distrust that Hudathans had for each other, never mind other beings, the noncom had been allowed to place the back of his chair against a steel bulkhead. His uniform was impeccable, his posture was upright, and he looked every inch a noncommissioned officer.

"...And," Matala continued, "having removed Corporal Haaby's brain box from her war form, it is further alleged that said noncom substituted a fake box to try to conceal the abduction.

"Having abused the corporal and other subordinates in the past, and fearful that she might talk, it is further alleged that the goal of the abduction was to murder Corporal Haaby and thereby silence her."

Matala looked up from his comp. Kobbi nodded and consulted the list in front of him. "The first witness is Corporal Haaby. She is present in the room, but since her war form is not presently available, she and other cyborgs from Alpha company will testify via electronic hookup."

Like many in the room, Santana turned to look at a life-support cart loaded with five olive drab boxes. Cables and hoses connected each brain box to the equipment on the cart, which was plugged into a jack panel mounted on the bulkhead. A tech sat next to the cart, where she could monitor a bank of readouts.

"Corporal," Kobbi said, "can you hear the proceedings?"

"Yes, sir," the cyborg said, "and I can see via the camera mounted in the back of the room."

"Excellent," Kobbi replied. "You may swear the witness in and proceed with her testimony."

Kuga-Ka was well aware of the ways in which he had abused not only Haaby, but the other cyberfreaks as well, so he saw very little reason to listen to their whining. Instead, the Hudathan took advantage of the time to consider the cards that remained in his hand and how he could best play them. The first was Captain Gaphy. He could ruin the company commander—and the skeletal slope knew it. But, rather than simply rat him out, Kuga-Ka planned to use the officer one last time.

Beyond that, the Hudathan had his toadies to call upon. Neither had been charged—and both remained at liberty. Lance Corporal Sawicki was a lazy sort, but wonderfully malleable, and a good hand with explosives. Private Knifethrow was a bit more ambitious and could be relied on to take the initiative from time to time.

Both legionnaires were far more devoted to him than the Legion and could be counted upon when the time came. Kobbi interrupted his thoughts. "Gunnery Sergeant Kuga-Ka? Would you like to question the witness?"

The Hudathan realized that the question had been asked before and that his answer had been "no." He looked defiant. "The box heads are lying, sir. They're lazy, incompetent, and stupid. This is their way of getting back at me for forcing them to perform their duties."

Kobbi raised an eyebrow, looked at Captain Gaphy, and back to the Hudathan. The more the jacker heard from Kuga-Ka the more he wondered about all the glowing evaluations that the company commander had submitted. His voice was cold as ice. "Perhaps you misunderstood, Sergeant. I asked if you wanted to question the last witness. If your statement was intended to summarize your defense, please hold it for the end of the proceedings. In the meantime, further use of derogatory language regarding your fellow legionnaires will result in disciplinary action. Is that clear?"

"Sir, yes, sir."

"All right. Major? Who's next?"

Santana took the necessary oath, delivered a detailed chronology of what had occurred, and was followed by testimony from Fareye and Dietrich.

Dietrich had just completed his statement, and was looking forward to an escape from officer-held territory, when Kobbi pounced on him. "So, Sergeant, you say that Private Fareye directed you to the maintenance shed where Gunnery Sergeant Kuga-Ka was found to be in possession of Corporal Haaby's brain box. Why were you involved in this matter to begin with?"

It felt hot in the room. Dietrich wanted to wipe the thin sheen of perspiration off his forehead but managed to resist the temptation to do so. "As I stated earlier, sir, Private Fareye and I saw the gunnery sergeant leave Lieutenant Santana's squat under suspicious circumstances. We were concerned for the lieutenant's safety."

Kobbi raised both eyebrows. "Are you and Private Fareye members of Lieutenant Santana's platoon?"

"No, sir."

"Then why the interest in his welfare?"

"We served with Lieutenant Santana on LaNor, sir."

Kuga-Ka, who had lapsed into a dull, semilethargic state by that time, took note of the question and sat a little bit straighter.

Santana felt dozens of eyes turn in his direction, swore silently, and waited for the axe to fall. "Yes," Kobbi continued thoughtfully, "that's correct. And who submitted your name for promotion from corporal to sergeant?"

Dietrich could see where the questions were headed but was powerless to intervene. "Lieutenant Santana, sir."

Kuga-Ka blinked, nodded knowingly, and grinned. Kobbi nodded in agreement. "Based on your relationship with the lieutenant, did you approach him regarding the possibility of being assigned to his platoon?"

Dietrich swallowed. "Yes, sir."

"And what did Lieutenant Santana say?"

"He said that his platoon was full up—but that he would talk to Captain Gaphy about a transfer to Alpha Company."

"And were you subsequently transferred?"

"Yes, sir."

"Which was when you came under Gunnery Sergeant Kuga-Ka's authority and started to follow him around."

Dietrich had never been so miserable. He looked down then up again. "Yes, sir."

Santana felt his spirits slide into an emotional crevasse and was wondering why Kobbi was siding with Kuga-Ka, when the questioning took another turn.

"Did Lieutenant Santana order you to follow the gunnery sergeant?"

"No, sir."

"Did he know what you were doing on his behalf?"

"No, sir."

"So, your efforts were not intended to undermine Gunnery Sergeant's career, but to protect an officer you had come to trust... Is that correct?"

Dietrich felt a sudden surge of relief. "Sir! Yes, sir!"

Kuga-Ka, his hopes crushed, lowered his eyes.

"One more thing before you go," Kobbi said ominously. "According to the statement that you gave, and subsequently signed, you were armed with a carbine when you took the gunnery sergeant into custody. I spoke with your platoon leader, and while the CA-10 had been issued some days before, none of my troops were authorized to have live ammunition at that time. How did you obtain ammo for your weapon—and where is it now?"

When Dietrich smiled, it was the Dietrich of old, the one who never lost his cool. "I didn't have any ammo, sir. I simply pretended that I did. One of the MPs took a moment to inspect my weapon and will verify that the magazine was empty."

Rage mixed with a feeling of shame filled Kuga-Ka's chest.

He of all people should have considered the possibility that the weapon was empty but had failed to do so. He stood, shouted, "You slope-headed bastard!" and charged. It took three MPs, one of whom was Hudathan, to bring the noncom under control.

The balance of the hearing went rather quickly. A panel consisting of Colonel Kobbi, Major Matala, and the transport's commanding officer found that there was sufficient reason to bind Kuga-Ka over for court-martial, and he was sent to the ship's brig.

Santana felt emotionally drained by the time he stepped out into the passageway. He was just about to return to his quarters when someone grabbed his arm. He turned to find that Colonel Kobbi was standing next to him. The jacker smiled. "So, did I scare the shit out of you?"

Santana nodded soberly. "Sir, yes, sir."

"Good. It's my opinion that most lieutenants need a laxative from time to time. Now that the material regarding Fareye and Dietrich is on the record, it won't come back to haunt you later. It's far better for us to document that stuff than wait and have a review board stacked with legal beagles do it for us."

Kobbi eyed the junior officer. "It's pretty clear that the gunny was a very bad apple—so thanks for weeding him out. A bad noncom, especially one in a position like Kuga-Ka's, can destroy an entire company. A piece of advice though… We have a chain of command—try using it sometime."

That being said Kobbi turned and left. And it was then, as the short stocky officer walked away, that Santana realized something interesting. Even though the jacker had done most of the talking during the court of inquiry, he hadn't used the word "frigging" once.

Aboard the destroyer escort, DE-10786, the *Javelin*

In many respects the atmosphere within the *Javelin*'s modest control room felt more like that of a well-managed multimedia library than the bridge of a vessel that might find itself fighting for its life within the next fifteen minutes. The command position was located at the center of the semicircular space with the first officer on one side and the navigator on the other. The rest of the bridge crew were seated one level below. All wore space armor minus the helmets racked nearby. The glow generated by their instruments gave their faces a greenish cast as the ship's pilot, weapons officer, and lead com tech exchanged information via their headsets.

Lieutenant Commander Amy Exton did her best to look professionally impassive as the ship's crew made final preparations to exit hyperspace, and reenter normal space. The good news was that 98.7 percent of all such transitions were successful. The bad news was that 1.3 percent were not.

All it took was the tiniest of navigational errors, a faulty hyperspace drive, or a random space-time discontinuity, and a ship could drop into the center of a black hole, wind up in an unknown galaxy, or never return to normal space at all. That's what the experts claimed, but the people who really knew were dead, or probably wished they were.

As a result most space travelers felt a little bit of apprehension every time their ship exited hyperspace, but that sense of tension was greatly heightened when a ship like the thirty-five-year-old *Javelin* prepared to not only drop hyper, but do so in what might be enemy-occupied space. The Savas system had been cut off for months, which meant it was quite possible that Ramanthian naval units were in the area. The thought made Exton's mouth feel dry. The *Javelin* was her first command, and even though the naval officer was proud of the aging ship, she understood the destroyer escort's considerable limitations. The old lady was slow by modern standards, her shields were subject to intermittent phase problems, and her tiny flight deck boasted only six in-system fighters.

On the other hand, Savas system amounted to an interstellar backwater. So, given all the space they had to defend, there was very little reason for the bugs to put any resources there. *But,* Exton cautioned herself, *if the area is so insignificant, why drop a battalion of legionnaires on Savas?*

Making the situation even worse was the certain knowledge that after the *Javelin* dropped in-system, two transports loaded with legionnaires would drop hyper about five minutes later.

Exton had no idea what the troops were supposed to accomplish on Savas, only that it was her job to ensure that they landed safely and hold the high ground until they were ready to depart. And not just hold it, but "hold it at any cost," which the naval officer took to mean that the brass were a good deal more concerned about whatever the Legion was up to than the fate of her ship and its crew.

But all of those thoughts were forced aside as Exton watched the final seconds melt away, tightened her grip on the seat's armrests, and waited for the telltale lurch at the pit of her stomach. Suddenly, previously dark screens came to life, the *Javelin*'s NAVCOMP reported a successful transition, and was almost immediately subsumed by the Command and Control (C&C) computer.

"Three targets have been acquired, indexed according to standard threat protocols, and tagged with firing priorities. Target one is a 96.7 percent match with a Ramanthian Slith-class destroyer. Targets two and three are an 87.3 percent match with Ramanthian Chak-class patrol vessels. All targets are accelerating to intercept. Estimated time to contact at extreme range is four minutes twenty-two seconds."

Exton swore. She had hoped, no, *prayed*, that if the Ramanthians were waiting, their ships would not only be a lot farther away, but of a type that she might be able to destroy. Now it looked like she and her crew were severely outnumbered, outclassed, and outgunned. Her voice could be heard throughout the ship. It was hard and cold. "We will engage. Launch fighters, bring the shields up, and give me full military power."

Then, in a voice that only *she* could hear, the naval officer said, *And may God be with us.*

4

*It is upon the navy, under the good Providence of God, that the wealth, safety
and strength of the kingdom do chiefly depend.*

CHARLES II
PREAMBLE TO THE ARTICLES OF WAR
Standard year 1670

Aboard the Ramanthian destroyer *Star Ravager*, off the Planet Savas

Ramanthian Naval Commander Jos Satto made use of a single-tined fork to spear one of the large, sauce-drenched grubs inching around at the bottom of his bowl, watched it wiggle for a moment, and shoved it in under his beak. Then, having flipped a large white napkin up over his head, the officer bit down. The wormlike creature was delectably ripe. There was an audible pop as the Ramanthian bit through the grub's tightly stretched skin followed by the usual spray of blood and intestinal matter. The warm liquid hit the napkin and formed a large round stain. Though ship-grown, and therefore less flavorful than its wild cousins, the taste was excellent.

Satto was still savoring the rich, mellow taste when the destroyer's battle alarm sounded, and he felt the ship start to accelerate. A less-seasoned officer might have abandoned his meal at that point, or placed a call to the bridge, but Satto did neither. To interrupt his midmeal would be unseemly, his executive officer was competent, and the Savas system amounted to an interplanetary backwater, which made it highly unlikely that an actual threat was in the offing.

Of course there was the possibility that Olthobo had located the human blockade runner—which would be good news indeed. The alien ship had dropped in-system three standard days before, given one of Satto's patrol boats the slip, and promptly disappeared. A gun smuggler most likely, intent on selling weapons to the indigenes on Savas, which ran counter to Ramanthian interests. Especially if the guns wound up in the wrong hands.

The blockade runner theory made sense, and Satto had so much faith in it that he was still eating when he heard a staccato popping noise and replied in kind. Olthobo shuffled into the compartment. The fact that he had chosen to leave his duty station rather than use the intercom indicated that whatever the situation was, the junior officer had it under control. Like all his kind, the naval officer had multifaceted eyes, a parrotlike beak, tool legs rather than arms, and a pair of narrow, seldom-used wings. He bowed his head to the exact point consistent with Satto's status and raised it again. "What appears to be a human destroyer escort dropped in-system, sir. We are moving to intercept."

The older officer was surprised but took pains to conceal it. "Time to contact?"

"Three-plus units at extreme range, sir. The patrol boats are closing in on the target as well."

Satto ingested a sip of water and brought a clean napkin up to his beak. All manner of thoughts swirled through his mind. "Extreme range" was defined as the point at which a torpedo would run out of fuel. Only a fool would fire that early—which meant he had plenty of time.

The decision to tackle the invading ship head-on was consistent with standard doctrine, which called for defending units to confront an enemy ship as quickly as possible, thereby taking advantage of the brief period during which its systems and crew were orienting themselves to a new system. The whole idea was to seize the initiative, put the newcomers on the defensive, and prevent them from reaching their objective.

All of which was fine so long as the defenders had equal or superior throw weight. But what if the destroyer escort was little more than the tip of a spear? Backed by a shaft consisting of more powerful vessels? It was a sobering thought, and Satto reacted accordingly. "Reduce speed by 50 percent—and order the patrol vessels to do likewise. Let's see what sort of gift we have before we rush to accept it."

Olthobo understood the nature of Satto's concern, knew that some of the crew might interpret the change as a sign that the commanding officer didn't trust his judgment, and felt a twinge of resentment. His head jerked forward, then back. "I understand and will comply."

Olthobo left, Satto felt the ship decelerate and rose from his table. Five of the grubs remained uneaten. Unaware that death had already passed them by, they continued to struggle.

Aboard the Confederacy destroyer escort DE-10786, the *Javelin*, off the Planet Savas

Lieutenant Commander Amy Exton watched the Ramanthian task force begin to slow and knew why. Her opposite number was worried that there might be a destroyer, cruiser, or battle group following along behind her. Had he been aware of the fact that the only vessels about to emerge from hyperspace were a pair of transports the Ramanthian would have hurried to close. "Full flank speed," Exton ordered grimly. "We need to buy the freighters some time. Order the fighters to engage the patrol vessels."

The orders were passed, and the *Javelin* leaped forward. "We're in range," the weapons officer intoned.

"Prepare to fire launchers one and two," Exton replied. "Fire."

The *Javelin* was small enough that her crew could actually feel the destroyer escort lurch as the torpedoes left their launchers and sought the enemy. But the Ramanthians had launched as well, and it was only a matter of minutes before their antimissile missiles intercepted the human torpedoes and destroyed them. They blossomed like miniature suns.

Meanwhile, the *Spirit of Natu*, and the *Mothri Sun* dropped in-system. Exton felt a sense of emptiness at the pit of her stomach as she watched the two additional symbols appear on the screens and accelerate toward Savas. All her cards were on the table now—and it looked like a losing hand.

Lieutenant Commander Stef Anders dispatched Lieutenant Shoshawna McKay and the other two daggers in her flight to deal with the patrol vessel that the *Javelin*'s C&C computer had arbitrarily tagged as "Bogey Two." *His* target, and that of his two wingmen, turned to meet them.

Though not equipped with cloaking technology that the more advanced 190s had, the CF-184 Dagger was a good fighter, and Anders felt his squadron had a slight advantage where the Ramanthian Chak-class patrol boats were concerned. Although the bug vessels were three times larger and heavily armed, they were less maneuverable.

The *real* problem, from the squadron leader's perspective at least, were the twelve fighters the Ramanthian destroyer had launched, and which were now wiping themselves onto his HUD. Half had turned toward the Confederacy transports— while the rest came to the aid of the patrol boats.

But there was no time left in which to think as Bogey Three opened fire with its laser cannons, blips of light raced past the dagger's canopy, and Anders went in for the kill. "Blue Leader to Blue Flight... There are more bogeys on the way. Let's take this bastard on the first pass. Over."

"Roger that!" Lieutenant Kai Hoguto replied enthusiastically, and followed Anders in. Like the daggers that were trying to destroy them, the Chak-class patrol boats weren't large enough to carry the equipment required to generate a defensive screen, which meant that they were forced to rely on their weapons and thick hull armor.

Knowing that, Anders readied a pair of lancer missiles and picked them off. Hoguto and the third member of the flight did likewise, which meant that the patrol boat had six incoming targets to contend with.

Bogey Three's commander ordered his weapons officer to fire

defensive missiles, blow chaff, and trigger the ECM generator. Two of the incoming weapons exploded harmlessly, and three were lured away from the actual target, but one was dead on. It struck the Ramanthian vessel in the side, blew a hole through the ship's armor, and sent a column of superheated gases into the starboard magazine. There was an explosion, followed by a second explosion, followed by a *third* explosion, which tore the vessel apart.

Hoguto yelled, "Yahoo!" pulled a high-gee turn, and ran into a burst of cannon fire from a Ramanthian fighter. The dagger exploded, Anders swore, and fought for position. Once he had it, the squadron commander triggered a pair of lancers, saw a flash of orange-red light, and flew through the resulting debris field.

Anders checked his six to make sure that it was clean, verified that it was, and Anders took a moment to check his HUD. He saw symbols for the Ramanthian destroyer, the surviving patrol boat, the destroyer escort, and two transports, but no sign of the green deltas that represented Shoshawna McKay and her flight. That was when he realized that they were dead, that 80 percent of his squadron had been eliminated, and that the bugs were winning.

Aboard the Confederacy transport *Spirit of Natu*, off the Planet Savas

Like many transports, the *Spirit of Natu* had a fairly spacious bridge, which meant that Colonel Kobbi could sit toward the rear of the control room and observe as the ship left the nowhere land of hyperspace for the Savas system. Having made the transition, the battalion commander watched with a growing sense of horror as the *Javelin* traded torpedoes with a larger vessel, four of the destroyer escort's fighters were blown to bits, and a swarm of Ramanthian interceptors attacked the transports.

Both ships mounted a dozen laser cannons each, and burped coherent light as the dart-shaped fighters crisscrossed the bulky hulls and pounded the transports with cannon fire. But the freighters had shields, *good* shields, and as they flared the incoming energy was neutralized.

But the best way to ensure their survival was to reach Savas as quickly as possible. The planet was enormous by then, a white-striated, mocha-colored marble that hung huge in the sky. If the *Javelin* could hold, maybe, just maybe, the *Natu* and the *Sun* could enter the planet's atmosphere where the Ramanthian destroyer wouldn't be able to follow. It was all Kobbi and the others could hope for, and with nothing else to do, the jacker said a silent prayer. *God, I know you're busy, but if you would take a moment to kill the frigging bugs, I would sure as hell appreciate it.*

But God was not so inclined, or that's the way it seemed, because that was the moment when Lieutenant Commander Anders's dagger took a Ramanthian missile and blew up. Tor Obbo, the last member of the dagger squadron, died ten seconds later.

Aboard the Confederacy destroyer escort DE-10786, the *Javelin*, off the Planet Savas

The two warships were relatively close by that time, too close from Lieutenant Commander Exton's perspective, but the bugs had closed the distance. The destroyer escort shuddered as another missile exploded against her shields. "They're going to overload!" the XO warned, and his prophecy quickly came true as the energy field that protected the ship flashed incandescent and went down.

Exton thought about her orders, the phrase "at any cost," and felt a deep sense of regret for her ship, for her crew, and for herself. Her voice was hoarse. "Pass the con to me, delegate the rest of the systems to the C&C, and abandon ship. That's an order."

Aboard the Ramanthian destroyer *Star Ravager*, off the Planet Savas

Rather than place a large number of critical personnel in one place the way the humans did, Ramanthian naval architects preferred to distribute them throughout the ship, a strategy intended to ensure that a single hit wouldn't kill all of the senior officers. That was why the *Ravager*'s control room was relatively small. Commander Jos Satto, the ship's pilot, and a com tech sat side by side, their compound eyes scanning the screens arrayed in front of them.

There was a flash of light as the human warship's screens went down, and Olthobo, who was monitoring the action from a station toward the ship's stern, was the first to comment. "Their screens went down, sir. We have them now!"

Satto felt a sense of jubilation and was just about to agree, when the enemy ship turned inward and started to accelerate. What looked like sparks, but were actually lifeboats, darted away. "They're going to ram!"

The pilot knew what to do. He applied full power and turned the ship to port. But the *Ravager* was big, which meant less maneuverable, and the destroyer's bow had just started to turn when the *Javelin* struck.

The destroyer escort was little more than a pile of scrap metal by then, having taken an incredible amount of damage during the minutes since her screens had failed. But her starboard in-system drive was still functioning, and Exton made use of it to propel what remained of her ship forward, and whooped into her helmet as metal touched metal.

The officer was gone after that, her space-armored body having been consumed by the white-hot gases of the resulting explosion, but not in vain. Because even as the human died, a significant chunk of the destroyer's bow was blown away, the *Ravager* lost a third of her offensive weaponry and a quarter of her crew.

The ship shuddered as secondary explosions strobed the blackness of space, fires burned for a matter of seconds before running out of oxygen, and those who had survived fought to save what remained of their ship.

Aboard the Confederacy transport *Spirit Of Natu*, off the Planet Savas

"My God," the captain of the *Natu* said, as the explosion lit up the control room's screens, "Exton rammed the bastard!" Colonel Kobbi, still watching from the aft part of the bridge, saw that the other officer was correct, and felt sick to his stomach as the destroyer escort blew up, and the Ramanthian interceptors went after her defenseless lifeboats.

"Look!" the navigator said, "they're still under way!" And it was true, because even as the transports closed with Savas, what remained of the enemy destroyer turned toward the transports. Though missing the point of her wedge-shaped bow, there was no air to contend with, which meant that so long as her airtight hatches held she could continue to fight. So, even as the two freighters continued to take fire from the Ramanthian fighters, the destroyer launched torpedoes in their direction.

The *Mothri Sun* took two hits in quick succession, lost her shields, and suffered still another blow as she entered the planet's atmosphere. Like the men and women around her, Captain Beverly Calvo wore full space armor and was strapped into an acceleration couch. The officer couldn't see anything other than the gray overhead, and wasn't connected to the ship's intercom, but it didn't take a genius to figure out that that transport had been hit. The ship shook like a thing gone mad as the planet's upper atmosphere tore at her hull, and the crew struggled to keep key systems online, as a pair of enemy fighters followed transport down.

"My mother said that it was a mistake to join the Legion," a technician named Lars Moy said via the suit-to-suit frequency. "I wonder if this is the kind of thing she had in mind."

There was laughter—followed by a barrage of insults. Calvo grinned, gave thanks for Moy, and prayed she wouldn't pee in her armor.

Aboard the Confederacy transport *Spirit Of Natu*, off the Planet Savas

Such was the captain's eagerness to escape the clutches of the Ramanthian destroyer that the freighter hit the atmosphere at a steeper angle and higher rate of speed than was either normal or safe. Colonel Kobbi's teeth rattled, plasma flared around the ship, and a host of audible alarms sounded. Someone said, "Shit! There goes the power dispersal grid..." and the freighter started to wobble as the drives fell out of phase.

"Cut the grid out of the system," the captain ordered grimly. "Switch to manual."

The ship continued to buck its way down through the planet's atmosphere, but without the computer-controlled system that fed precisely equal amounts of power to the in-system engines, there were discrepancies so subtle that a human brain couldn't even detect the differentials, much less balance them out. The pilot battled for control and gave thanks as the transport broke through the high cloud cover. Given the fact that their fuel was running low, and they were almost out of ordnance, the Ramanthian fighters had been forced to withdraw by then. That, plus the fact that the destroyer couldn't enter the atmosphere, meant that the crew could concentrate on putting the freighter down.

The captain considered his options, decided there weren't any, and made the only decision that he could. "We'll never make it to Hagala Nor. Put her down at Savas Prime instead."

Kobbi heard the order, summoned a mental map of the planet's western hemisphere, and felt a sudden sense of alarm. If the *Natu* landed near the human population center to the southeast, and the *Sun* put down near the Ramanthian-held city to the northwest, the battalion would be split in two! Not only that, but the cyborgs would be cut off from their war forms, which would make both groups vulnerable. The battalion commander opened his mouth to object, heard someone scream, and felt the huge ship roll over onto its back.

Aboard the Confederacy transport *Mothri Sun*, Planet Savas
Like all vessels her size, the *Mothri Sun* had the glide characteristics of a huge rock. That meant that it was nothing short of a miracle when the pilot managed to bring the transport's bow up and prevent the ship from corkscrewing into the desert below. The surface was tan in color, streaked with iron oxide, and interrupted by occasional rock formations. The pilot thought she saw a large cluster of domed tents at one point, but the ship was still traveling at better than 600 mph, so the surface was little more than a blur.

A series of lights morphed from green, to amber, to red as a series of audibles sounded. The ship started to shake as one of the drives cut in and out and fingers flew as the pilot fired the *Sun*'s retros, deployed the freighter's air brakes, and felt the transport slow. That was good, especially if they were going to land in one piece, but bad as well. Hagala Nor lay hundreds of miles to the northwest—and they weren't going to make it. "I'm putting her down, sir. There isn't any choice."

Captain Sahleen Amdo knew the pilot was correct. He nodded. "I concur."

With the decision made, the pilot eyed the slightly undulating terrain ahead, spotted a pair of tall rock formations, and aimed the ship for the U-shaped space between them. Slowly, because it would be easy to overcorrect, the pilot pushed the vessel down until the transport was flying fifty feet above the surface of the sand. Then, with the retros still firing, she put the transport down.

The acceleration couch served to absorb a great deal of the impact, but Calvo still felt a bone-jarring thud as the hull hit, bounced back into the air and hit again. That was followed by the shriek of tortured metal, and a cacophony of alarms as the ship's computers hurried to tell the crew and passengers what all of them already knew: The *Mothri Sun* had crashed.

Finally, after bursting through a succession of three sand dunes and plowing a two-mile-long furrow through the open desert, the ship came to a halt. The Legion had landed.

Aboard the Confederacy transport *Spirit Of Natu*, Planet Savas
All kinds of items that had been on the deck rained down upon those aboard the *Spirit of Natu* as the starboard drive quit, and the ship rolled over onto its back. Colonel Kobbi figured the ride was over and was waiting for the final body-crushing impact, when the NAVCOMP fired a series of steering jets and flipped the transport right side up. Cheers could be heard over the intercom as the captain said, "Belay that!" and the hard-pressed pilot assumed control and put the vessel into a series of wide spiraling turns. Fleecy clouds parted to let the freighter through. What looked like a thick green carpet appeared and laser fire stuttered up past the bow. "The idiots are firing at us!" the captain exclaimed. "Tell them who we are!"

A com tech ran through a number of commonly used

frequencies before landing on the one being used by the local colonists. It took the tech the better part of a minute to convince the civilians that the ship was friendly, but she finally succeeded, and the laser fire stopped.

Savas Prime sat in a valley embraced by low, softly rounded hills. A river flowed through the center of town and made a long series of lazy loops, before emptying into the southern sea some thirty miles beyond. Significant sections of the jungle had been logged, mine tailings spilled down some of the hillsides, and a network of dirt roads wandered back and forth.

The settlement itself consisted of a cluster of prefab domes, some of which were blackened as a result of Ramanthian air attacks, and hundreds of wooden dwellings. Some were quite substantial, and reminiscent of expensive homes on Earth, but the vast majority were little more than crudely built shacks.

The spaceport had never been much, but now, after repeated attacks, the control tower resembled a burned-out stump, fire-blackened skeletons of what had once been atmospheric craft lined a debris-strewn taxiway, and the sign that read, "Welcome to Savas Prime," hung askew from the front of the small terminal building.

It hadn't rained for a few days, so dust billowed up to surround the battle-scarred transport as the pilot fired his repellors and lowered the transport onto the much-abused duracrete. Colonel Kobbi waited for the solid thud as the huge landing skids touched down, triggered his suit radio, and switched to the command override. Everyone could hear him except for the cyborgs.

"This is Colonel Kobbi... The bugs know we're here. They have a warship in orbit, a patrol boat with atmospheric capabilities, and an unknown number of aerospace fighters. That means they'll come after us sooner rather than later. Check for casualties, patch 'em up, and get our gear off this ship in record time. I don't think we're going to get much help, so Alpha company will throw a security perimeter around the ship while Bravo, Charlie, and Delta Companies hump gear. Let's get started. Company commanders report to me in fifteen minutes. That is all."

* * *

Fire Base Alpha, the Great Pandu Desert, Planet Savas

It was extremely hot, and Calvo had already stripped down to her olive drab T-shirt. A single circuit of the downed ship had been sufficient to leave dark circles under her bare arms. Having just spent weeks aboard ship, the combined impact of the vast overarching sky and the seemingly endless desert was nearly overwhelming. But Calvo knew there wasn't any time for sightseeing. She had problems, lots of problems, the first of which loomed above her.

Thanks to the pilot's skill, plus the cushioning effect of the deep sand, the transport had suffered relatively little damage during the landing. Not the hull at any rate, something for which the MO was grateful, since the battalion's war forms were stored in her holds. Now, standing in the shade cast by the freighter, it was up to Calvo and Captain Amdo to figure out what to do next. "As near as I can figure we're about *here*," the naval officer said, tapping the hand comp's screen with a long, narrow finger. "About halfway between Savas Prime and Hagala Nor."

Calvo shook her head in disgust. It wasn't Amdo's fault, but if it weren't for the navy, the battalion would have been on a single ship. But that was history. The first thing they needed to do was fortify the wreckage in case the bugs decided to attack. The MO was about to say as much when Amdo's eyes narrowed, and the naval officer raised a hand. It appeared that someone was talking to Amdo via his headset. That impression was confirmed when he looked at Calvo. "The *Natu* put down at Savas Prime. Colonel Kobbi wants to speak with you."

The rest of the battalion was safe! Calvo felt a sudden surge of hope as she ran for the ship, thundered up a durasteel ramp, and passed between the containers that held the war forms. The ship's power plant was still functional. That meant the lights were on, and her techs could check each transit box for damage. Captain Rono-Ra called to her, but the MO waved as she hurried past.

Outside of the fact that the deck was tilted ten degrees to port, the ship's corridors looked quite normal as Calvo made her way into the control room, where a com tech handed her a headset. A servo whined as the MO used her artificial hand to pull the device down over her head. The ship wasn't really a ship anymore—so the officer gave a call sign consistent with Legion practice. "This is Fire Base Alpha, Captain Beverly Calvo speaking, sir. Over."

The *Natu* made a big fat target sitting as it was at the center of the settlement's spaceport. It was being stripped and Kobbi was forced to step aside as a heavily laden tech managed to squeeze past him. He heard the designator Calvo had invented and grinned. "Roger that... Please use the call sign Pandu Six from this point forward. There's no point in providing the bugs with more information than they already have. I know Amdo outranks you, and that Rono-Ra is present, but it's my opinion that you are best qualified for this particular command. Organize personnel as you see fit.

"Now, here's the plan... It's pretty simple. Fortify your position and hold it regardless of cost. We'll join you as soon as we can. At that point we will have one helluva reunion if you take my meaning. Over."

Calvo's mind raced. The message was clear. Kobbi intended to bring the brain boxes up through jungle and desert to Fire Base Alpha. At that point the cyborgs would be reunited with their war forms and the battalion would proceed on to Hagala Nor. The plan was courageous, stubborn, and almost certainly doomed to defeat. Especially since it would take the rest of the battalion weeks, if not months, to reach her position. Still, there was only one response that Calvo could give, and she gave it. "Sir, yes, sir. Over."

"Good," Kobbi replied. "The com people will establish a contact schedule so we can stay in touch. You know what to do—so do it. Nomad Six, out."

Calvo returned the headset to the com tech, got up, and made her way back down to the ship's number two hold. Both Amdo and Rono-Ra spotted the MO and hurried to join her. "So," the supply officer said, "what did the old man have to say?"

"We're supposed to hold here," Calvo replied, "until the rest of the battalion can join us."

Amdo gave a long slow whistle. "That won't be easy."

"No," the MO agreed, "it won't. There was one other thing—something I wish you had heard firsthand."

"Kobbi put you in command," Rono-Ra said, eyeing her face.

"Yeah, he did."

The Hudathan nodded. "He made a good choice. You'll have my full support."

"This is a ground operation, so I'm naming Rono-Ra as XO," Calvo said, turning to Amdo, "but I'd like you to accept the number three slot. I know it's a weird job for a naval officer, especially one of your seniority, but we need your help."

"Count me in," Amdo responded, "and my crew as well. So, what's first?"

"Defense," the MO answered grimly. "Are the ship's laser cannons functional?"

"Yes," Amdo replied, "with the exception of those that are buried under the sand."

"Excellent. Place them on standby—and keep them there. It won't be long before the bugs spot us from orbit and send some fighters. Let's prepare a warm reception."

"No problem," the naval officer assured her, "I'll get on it,"

"How about the cannons that are buried?" Rono-Ra inquired. "Could we dig them out? And if we did, could we place them three or four hundred yards out?"

Calvo brightened. "That's a great idea! Will it work?"

Amdo rubbed the stubble that covered his chin. It made a rasping noise. "We'd have to build some sort of cofferdams to keep the sand out, and it would involve a lot of hard work, but yes, it might be feasible. One question though... Assuming we succeed, how will you get power to them?"

"We'll strip conduit out of the ship," the Hudathan replied, "run it out to the gun positions, and bury it under the sand."

Amdo winced at the thought of doing further damage to his precious ship, but knew she would never lift again. He nodded. "I'll put a team on it."

"Good," Calvo put in, "and we'll help by activating eight of the battalion's war forms. Most will take up defensive positions, but we can equip a couple of them for construction work, and that will speed things along."

Rono-Ra looked as surprised as a Hudathan can. "Really? No offense, ma'am, but outside of some VR time during basic, the techs weren't trained for combat."

The supply officer towered above her, and the MO looked up at him. "First, cut the 'ma'am' crap. I may be in command, but I'm still a captain. Second, look who's talking! Maybe you've seen combat—but I haven't. We're REMFs remember? None of us are combat vets. But if we're going to hang on to this piece of real estate we're going to have to learn. So, the faster we load some war forms and get our techs some on-the-job training, the better off we'll be."

The Hudathan nodded ponderously. "What you say makes sense. How about some fly-forms? It would be nice to carry out a little reconnaissance."

"Not yet," Calvo answered. "The techs need to walk before they try to fly."

Amdo narrowed his eyes. "I might be able to help with that one... The port bay is buried—but the starboard bay is exposed. Given some prep work, and a bit of good luck, we might be able to launch the number two lifeboat. Though never intended for prolonged atmospheric use, we might be able to get two or three hops out of her."

"That would allow Lieutenant Farner and his people to scope the surrounding area," Calvo said enthusiastically. "Maybe they could place some remote sensors. I don't know much about the locals, but the briefing materials describe them as 'warlike,' so we may have to contend with them as well.

"Okay, I know there will be more issues to resolve, but let's put our people to work. It will be dark in a few hours, and I'll sleep a helluva lot better if we have some sort of defense in place by then."

Savas Prime, Planet Savas

It was dark outside, and rectangles of buttery yellow light revealed the presence of nearby homes as Colonel Jon Kobbi, Dil Gaphy, and Lieutenant Antonio Santana left the embrace of a broad porch, passed through a doorway, and clumped into a richly paneled reception area. A flood of Jithi servants rushed to offer the off-world guests hot towels, cups of fragrant tea, and the soft slippers that the locals wore inside their houses.

The Jithi were a humanoid race that had split away from the nomadic Paguum hundreds of local years before to make permanent homes in the verdant rain forests that girdled most of the planet. Over many successive generations Jithi physiology had evolved to better meet the demands of their tropical environment. They had light green skin, their hair took the form of thick dreadlocklike fronds, and they boasted tail tentacles that functioned as highly specialized hands. All wore crisp white jackets, matching trousers and black slippers.

Colonel Kobbi took a seat on one of the benches that lined the walls of the reception area and allowed one of the Jithi to remove his combat boots and fit him with a pair of slippers. Once that was accomplished, the jacker removed his sidearm from its holster, ejected the magazine, and slipped the clip into his pocket.

The rest of the officers did likewise. A servant accepted the weapons, put tags on them, and locked the guns inside a beautifully carved cabinet.

Then, as if summoned by a signal, their host appeared. He was human, of average height and rather handsome. What hair he had was black, his eyes had an Asian cast, and he had a round, open-looking face. He wore a dark blue shirt that hung down past his waist, white pantaloons, and blue slippers with red embroidery. A few quick steps carried him forward to greet Kobbi. "Colonel! What an unexpected pleasure! My name is Qwan, Cam Qwan, welcome to our home."

After each officer had been introduced the legionnaires were led through a formal sitting area into a softly lit dining room. A long, linen-covered table ran down the center of it and nearly a dozen people rose to greet the soldiers as they entered. Large mirrors threw their images back and forth, candles flickered as a breeze found its way in through louvered windows, and a round of introductions began.

Santana exchanged greetings with each of his fellow guests but quickly lost track of their names, and was left with the impression that Qwan's guests were movers and shakers within the local community. It was the sort of situation in which

Christine excelled—but made him feel uncomfortable.

The platoon leader had no idea why he had been selected to accompany Kobbi, nor did Captain Gaphy, who clearly would have preferred someone else. The fact that he was attired in camos, rather than a dress uniform, added to Santana's discomfort. But formal kit, like the other items not required for combat, were back on Adobe.

Lin Qwan, Cam Qwan's extremely attractive wife, moved to the far end of the table and stood behind her chair. She had shoulder-length hair, a slender face, and a trim figure.

Cam announced dinner, and the officers were shown to their seats. Santana found himself halfway down the table between the local representative of an off-planet mining company and an empty chair.

The guests were seated, and Cam Qwan was just about to propose a toast, when a door slid open and a beautiful young woman entered the room. She had long black hair that was tied back with a simple ribbon. Jewels sparkled at her ears, and the ankle-length red sheath dress was slit up the side, which allowed the occasional glimpse of her shapely legs. "Most of you know my daughter Qwis," Cam Qwan said, "but for those of you who don't, I suggest that you steer clear of the planet's legal status unless you want to hear a two-hour seminar on the subject."

Such was the young woman's reputation within the small community that most of those present laughed, while all of the males stood. Santana found himself enveloped by a cloud of extremely intoxicating perfume as the younger Qwan arrived at his side. Qwis had serious brown eyes, even features, and a beautiful smile. The officer held her chair, waited for the young woman to sit, and took his seat. She offered her hand. Her skin felt cool but slightly rough, a sure sign that she did more than sit around and look pretty. Her voice was soft and melodic. "Thank you, Lieutenant. Welcome to Savas. I wish the circumstances were different."

"You're welcome. This must be a very difficult time for you and your family."

A look of amusement entered her eyes. "Yes, it is. And you are?"

"Santana, ma'am, Lieutenant Antonio Santana."

It appeared as if she were going to say something further, but her father chose that moment to propose a toast. "To the Confederacy! To the Legion! To the 1st REC!"

There was hearty agreement, followed by more toasts, and the first of what proved to be a delicious seven-course meal. Santana wasn't entirely sure what occupied his plate most of the time, but was accustomed to all manner of exotic food, and happy to consume whatever was placed in front of him so long as it tasted good.

The mine manager seated to Santana's left proved to be a demanding conversationalist, which meant that there wasn't much opportunity to speak with Qwis, but there were some enjoyable moments, including one exchange when her leg made prolonged contact with his.

But such intervals were rare since the main topic of dinner conversation was the war, the Legion, and the battalion's presence on Savas. A subject of considerable interest to the colonists but one Kobbi couldn't address without revealing the nature of their mission. That made one guest more than a little testy. "So let me see if I understand," the store owner said. "You weren't sent here to protect us, but you won't tell us what the purpose of your mission is."

"*Can't* is more like it," Kobbi said matter-of-factly. "I'm sorry, but that's how it is."

"But what about *us*?" a matron demanded plaintively. "The bugs have already attacked the settlement on three different occasions. What if they land? We'll be slaughtered."

"Not if the militia has anything to say about it," another man said staunchly. "We'll fight them in the jungle."

"They *evolved* in the jungle," Cam Qwan said pointedly, "which means they would most likely win."

"Perhaps," the militia leader allowed expansively, "but the Jithi would cut them down to size... Isn't that right, Yamba?"

One of the Jithi servants, a large specimen with bright yellow eyes, lowered a tray loaded with desserts onto a folding stand. "Yes, siba (sir), that is correct. The jungle belongs to *us*."

Something about the way the Jithi put the emphasis on the word "us" caused Santana to wonder if the indig was sending the off-worlders a message, but no one else seemed to take it that way, so the platoon leader assumed he was wrong.

"I understand how you feel, and wish things were different," Kobbi assured them, "but rather than offer you help, I'm afraid that I must request it instead. Half the battalion landed in the desert—and I need your help in order to reach them."

That produced a cacophony of commentary, and finally, after repeated attempts to quell the uproar, Cam Qwan used a dinner knife to tap his water goblet. "One at a time please!"

The ensuing conversation was more confusing than useful, as all manner of views, plans, and proposals were put forward only to be knocked down by one or more of the guests. Finally, after the dishes had been cleared, Kobbi pushed his chair back and stood. "Tomorrow is going to be a long day, so the time has come for my officers and me to excuse ourselves. I would like to thank the Qwan family for their hospitality—and the rest of you for the warmth of your welcome."

Santana rose, said good-bye to the mine manager, and turned toward Qwis. Her eyes were waiting for him. "Is the Colonel a good officer?"

Santana nodded. "The best."

Qwis was silent for a moment. When she spoke her voice was serious. "Good. Savas is a hard planet. You will need his leadership."

Lin Qwan arrived at that point, took her daughter's arm, and followed their guests out into the reception area where the legionnaires retrieved their sidearms and exchanged their slippers for boots.

The air was cool outside, and the night creatures were in full cry. They trilled, grunted, and hooted as the legionnaires piled into a beat-up ground car. It rattled as a Jithi driver took them down toward the scattering of lights below. There were no streetlights to compete with—and the stars glittered like shards of broken glass.

The transport crouched on the tarmac like a gigantic toad. The area immediately below its open belly was flooded with light as legionnaires, Jithi laborers, and two dozen robots worked through the night. The goal was to not only unload the ship by morning if at all possible, but move the battalion's gear away from the spaceport, and into a safer location.

Engines growled as a succession of brutish mining trucks hauled tons of food, ammo, and equipment up through a series of switchbacks to an inactive mine. Then, once the ore haulers were unloaded, a second crew had to hump everything back into the hillside, where it was sorted, indexed, and stored. Exhausting work, but necessary, if the battalion wanted to protect the materials that enabled it to fight.

Meanwhile, at the edge of the spaceport, only three hundred feet from the transport itself, two legionnaires stood guard over an old storage shed. The roof consisted of a single sheet of corrugated metal, the walls were made of thick duracrete blocks, and the hatchlike door had been salvaged from a wreck years before.

Now, emptied of the maintenance equipment previously stored there, the shack housed Gunnery Sergeant Hreemo Kuga-Ka, the battalion's only prisoner. There was power to the structure, but the Hudathan had extinguished the single light fifteen minutes earlier, so that his eyes could adjust to the dark. The noncom's skin, which had been nearly white during the late-afternoon heat, had turned dark gray. There was a ventilation slit over the door, and if the Hudathan strained, he could hear the mutter of truck engines, the scrape of a combat boot, and the sound of desultory conversation. Having little else to do, the guards were passing the time by speculating on the battalion's mission, and what would happen next. One of them believed that the outfit would remain in Savas Prime—while the other figured a transport would arrive to pull them out.

Kuga-Ka, who had the honor of being the only enlisted person who actually knew what the battalion was supposed to accomplish on Savas, grinned as the legionnaires gave voice to their contending theories.

Not far away, in the darkness that defined the edge of the spaceport, camo-clad legionnaires slipped through the shadows. Corporal Surehand Knifethrow had black-brown fur and shifty eyes. His loyalty to Kuga-Ka was based on the privileges that the senior NCO had granted him, an appetite for loot, and a healthy dash of fear. He paused to sample the air with his supersensitive nostrils before waving his companion forward.

Private Kras Sawicki was a lazy sort, who hated the Legion's spit-and-polish ways, and was happy to let Knifethrow do his thinking for him. If the Naa wanted to break the gunny out, and the two of them were going over the hill, then he wanted to go along. He saw Knifethrow's wave, crept forward, and turned his attention outward. The Naa would take care of the guards. It was his job to provide security and make sure that no one interfered.

While under strict orders to keep the prisoner secured, neither guard had any reason to expect an external attack, especially from a fellow legionnaire. So, when Private Knifethrow emerged from the darkness and sauntered up to them, there was no reason to be alarmed. The Naa's teeth gleamed in the murk. "Hey, guys, how are they hanging?"

Lance Corporal Sootha grinned, and was just about to answer in kind, when something blurred past his chin. It was only when he felt the pain and saw the jet of inky black blood, that he realized it was his. He tried to speak, tried to shout, but couldn't summon the necessary air. That was when he felt dizzy, lost consciousness, and collapsed.

Private Fortu had enough time to say, "What the hell?" and reach toward the weapon slung over his shoulder, but that was all. The already bloodied knife flashed again, the legionnaire staggered, and went down in a welter of his own blood.

Never one to settle for half measures Knifethrow checked both bodies to ensure that they were truly dead and waved Sawicki forward. Kuga-Ka had heard the sounds of muffled combat and was ready when the door squealed open, allowing humid air to flood the shed. "Well done," he said approvingly, as the Naa stood framed in the doorway. "Drag them inside."

The legionnaires obeyed, and the NCO took the opportunity to arm himself with Lance Corporal Sootha's weapons, including a holstered zapper. "All right," the renegade said as he loosened the dead soldier's pistol belt so it would fit around his enormous waist. "Are the supplies ready?"

Knifethrow nodded. "Each of us will carry a thirty-pound pack that includes emergency rations, med kits, and reserve ammo."

"And my personal stuff?"

"It's in your pack. So that, plus the stuff Sawicki loaded into the RAV, should take care of our needs for quite some time."

Kuga-Ka nodded. A single RAV could carry up to four thousand pounds' worth of food, ammo, and other gear. Just the thing for a stroll on a primitive planet. "Good work. So, where are they?"

There was no need to ask who "they" were since both the Naa and the human knew who the Hudathan was referring to. "Santana went to dinner with Kobbi," Knifethrow answered, "and the brain boxes are stored in the terminal building. Or *were* at any rate—since they could have been moved by now."

Kuga-Ka swore. He had hoped to kill both Santana *and* Haaby before slipping out of the settlement, but that was impossible now. Still, it sounded as though Haaby was vulnerable, and something was a helluva lot better than nothing. "All right," the renegade replied, "let's pay the terminal a visit. If the freak's there, we'll kill her. As a matter of fact, we'll kill *all* of them if we have time."

There were times when Knifethrow wished that Kuga-Ka was a bit more rational, and this was one of them. Rather than waste time killing cyborgs, the Naa would have preferred to hit the trail and put as much distance between himself and the rest of the battalion as possible. But there was no reasoning with the ridge head on such matters so he didn't try. "Sure, gunny, whatever you say."

Lights glowed within the terminal building as a team of four life-support techs finalized preparations to move the brain boxes to a safer location. Special backpacks had been prepared, each having a cradle for one box, a small power source, and the systems necessary to ensure that the cyborgs received oxygenated blood substitute, nutrition, and electronic communications. The plan, which had come down from the colonel himself, was to rig the box heads for a long march.

None of the techs were armed, so when the double doors flew open, and three heavily armed legionnaires rushed in, there was nothing they could do but look surprised and raise their hands. The assault weapon looked like a toy in Kuga-Ka's hands, and he used it like a pointer. "Herd them into the office. Push a desk in front of the door. If they give you any trouble, shoot them."

Sawicki nodded cheerfully. "You heard the gunny—get in there."

One of the techs, a woman who knew the noncom, looked back over her shoulder as she entered the office. "What the hell are you doing, Sawicki? They'll find you and hang your ass."

"Maybe," the human allowed, "and maybe not. But at least I won't be here with you, polishing boots and taking shit from officers all day. Now move it."

Wood rubbed on wood as the legionnaire pushed a desk in front of the door. "Watch out front," Kuga-Ka instructed. "We don't want any surprises."

It was an important task, so Knifethrow assigned it to himself. Doors squeaked as he slipped outside.

"Now," Kuga-Ka said eagerly, as he eyed the rows of specially made-up packs. "I wonder where my little friend Haaby is hiding."

For her part the cyborg was awake, but completely unaware of what was going on around her, as she played a virtual card game with one of her peers. The sound of Kuga-Ka's voice was like a bolt out of the blue. "Hey, freak, remember *me*?"

Haaby felt a sudden, nearly paralyzing fear, ordered her war form to move, and felt an overwhelming sense of despair when nothing happened.

The Hudathan laughed. "If you had an ass, which you don't, you'd be shitting your pants right about now."

Kuga-Ka had more to say, *lots* more, but the doors banged open, and Knifethrow reentered the terminal. "I can see lights and hear a whole lot of voices! They're coming this way!"

"Did you hear that?" the renegade inquired, speaking into the headset that went with the pack. "No, I suppose you didn't. Well, you and I are going for a long walk in the jungle. Think about that... and we'll talk a bit later."

So saying, the ex-noncom pulled the plug on Haaby's radio, swung the pack up onto his back, and pointed to the side door. "Well, lads, I don't know about you, but I'm tired of this Hudathan's army. Let's find a new one."

5

The truth is whatever I say it is.
RAMANTHIAN HIVE MOTHER NORS IBLIBIO
Standard year 2841

Planet Algeron, the Confederacy of Sentient Beings

The road, which had been built atop an ancient trail, had been widened and improved by the Legion's pioneers many years before. But it was still subject to washouts and landslides, which made it treacherous at best. The scenery was beautiful, though, as the sun arced across a clear blue sky, and the Towers of Algeron dominated the southern horizon.

The scout car jerked as General Bill Booly shifted into a lower gear, and his wife held on to a grab bar, as the boxy vehicle negotiated a tight turn. Knobby tires spewed rocks out over the two-hundred-foot precipice even as they propelled the vehicle up through a seemingly endless series of switchbacks and deeper into what Legion briefers referred to as "a disputed zone (DZ)." Disputed, because the Earth government claimed that Algeron belonged to them, while most Naa believed otherwise. They wanted sovereignty and direct representation in the Senate like the spacefaring races had, but many wanted to maintain close ties with Earth as well.

Then, as if Maylo's husband was reading her mind, he guided the scout car around a corner and came to a stop about fifteen feet short of a pile of carefully stacked rocks. He killed the engine. "See that? Two T-2s and four bio bods died there. My great-grandfather, Wayfar Hardman, led the war party that ambushed them. It was a hard-fought battle. The last time I stopped here you could still find empty shell casings in among the rocks."

Maylo looked from her husband's face to the cairn of rocks. The brief anecdote spoke volumes about the situation on Algeron, her husband, and his family. Truly divergent species weren't supposed to be able to reproduce, yet there were thousands of so-called breeds, and just as many theories as to why. The favorite, for the moment at least, was the possibility of common ancestors. An ancient race archeologists called the Forerunners, who left enigmatic ruins on planets like Jericho, and some said Earth.

Maylo didn't care, not so long as her husband existed and was at her side. The trip was *her* idea, a way of breaking her husband away from Fort Cameron and the never-ending stream of bad news. The war with the Ramanthians was not going well, morale was at an all-time low, and there was no relief in sight. A fact that weighed heavily on Booly. She had short black hair, almond-shaped eyes, and a long oval face. "So, which side are you proud of?"

"Both," Booly answered succinctly, "because both were right in their own way."

The scout car started with a roar, and Booly guided it up through a series of blind curves and into a broad, U-shaped valley. There were signs that the land had been under cultivation in the past and would be again when spring came around.

In the meantime a large herd of shaggy dooths could be seen, standing in small groups and pawing the ground to uncover the vegetation buried beneath the snow. Vehicles were not unknown in the area, which meant that the animals remained unmoved by the sound of the scout car's engine and continued to chew slowly as it rolled past them.

* * *

Meanwhile, high above, what looked like an airborne scavenger circled the valley. But it wasn't a flyer, not the flesh-and-blood variety at any rate, nor was it searching for carrion. The RPV-L467 (Remotely Piloted Vehicle–Legion type 467) was there for one reason, and one reason only: to protect General Bill Booly and his wife. It was a task that, like so many others, fell to Chief of Staff Colonel Tom Leeger.

The officer was in his office, plowing his way through the latest reports from dozens of far-flung outposts, when a natty-looking lieutenant knocked on his already open door. Leeger looked up from his comp. "Yeah, Thinklong, what's up?"

The Naa was not only one of the brighter young officers assigned to Legion HQ. He was a graduate of the academy, something that had once been unheard of, but was now increasingly common. He had cream-colored fur with diagonal streaks of black. "It's the general, sir. He and his wife are in the valley adjacent to his ancestral village."

Leeger sighed. Much as he admired Maylo Chien-Chu and her many accomplishments, it seemed as if the woman had dropped out of space for the sole purpose of making his life more difficult. The trip into the DZ was not only a waste of time, but a dangerous waste of time, which was why he had recommended against it.

Unfortunately, Booly not only bought into the idea, but refused an armed escort, which not only put *his* life at risk but made Leeger's that much more difficult. "So?" the staff officer inquired testily. "That's where he was headed. So, what's the problem?"

"Sir, yes, sir," Thinklong replied expressionlessly, "but the video transmitted back from the RPV shows a large number of armed warriors closing in on the village from the south."

Leeger frowned. "Define 'large.'"

"About two hundred, give or take, sir."

"Shit! Notify the response team. I want them ready to lift at a moment's notice."

Thinklong already had but nodded obediently. "Sir, yes, sir."

* * *

Booly and Maylo had an escort by then. It consisted of half a dozen mounted warriors. They galloped along next to the scout car, shouted friendly insults, and waved rifles over their heads as the legionnaire guided the car between a series of defensive barriers. A voice spoke in his ear, and Booly triggered his radio. "This is Rover Six… Go. Over."

Knowing her husband's staff wouldn't call him unless it was something important, and fearful that the war had taken a sudden turn for the worse, Maylo felt something heavy hit the bottom of her stomach. She watched him listen, utter a brief reply, and break the connection. "So?"

Booly glanced at his wife and back to the road. "A group of warriors are closing on the village from the south. Leeger wants to pull us out."

"And?"

"And I said, 'no.' It's my guess that they want to talk to me rather than slit my throat."

"And if you're wrong?"

Booly felt a moment of doubt, wondered if he should have the response team come for his wife, and knew she would refuse to leave unless he left as well. He smiled. "Then we'll be in deep trouble."

Maylo had been in deep trouble before. First on Earth, where Booly had saved her life, and later off Arballa, where she had been badly wounded. That didn't matter, not much at any rate, but something else did. Something her husband didn't know about yet… but would soon become apparent. Her hand went to her abdomen. She forced a smile.

"You're supposed to be taking a couple of days off… Remember?"

"Absolutely," Booly replied. "I'll have a chat with their leaders and send the rest of them packing. A couple of hours should take care of it."

Maylo didn't believe a word of it but smiled and nodded. She had parallel jobs. The first involved running a large interstellar corporation. The second, the one she was focused on at the moment, was the more difficult of the two. The car slowed, a reception party appeared ahead, and Booly was home.

* * *

Planet Starfall, the Confederacy of Sentient Beings

If human and Ramanthian fleets were clashing in the far reaches of space, and cities were being incinerated from orbit, there was no sign of that on Starfall, where business beings cut deals and diplomats like ambassador Kay Wilmot and Foreign Service Officer Christine Vanderveen were required to attend what seemed like a never-ending round of meetings, receptions, and parties.

Vanderveen wasn't sure which she detested most, the parties that claimed two or three evenings a week, or her boss, who seemed to delight in them. Not to meet new contacts, strengthen relationships, and pick up odd bits of intelligence, but to hook up with the Clone Hegemony's military attaché, who had a taste for free breeder sex. Or so FSO-5 Mitsi Ang claimed.

It was dark, and the lights of the steadily growing city glittered as the embassy's long black limo paused to allow a similar vehicle to discharge its formally clad passengers at the foot of a covered walkway. Vanderveen looked forward to escaping both Wilmot's overwhelming perfume *and* her overbearing personality.

"That should do it," the ambassador said, as she checked her image in a small mirror and put her lipstick away. "Looks shouldn't matter… but they do."

Only to other humans, Vanderveen thought to herself, as the car in front of them pulled away and the limo crept forward.

"Don't forget to pitch Ambassador Sca Sor. He likes you for some reason… and we need the Prithians on our side. They don't have much military clout, but if they were to align themselves with the Confederacy, it would make for a very nice headline. And Lord knows the cits could do with some good news. All they see on the evening vids are transports loaded with vacuum-sealed body bags. It's depressing."

"Yes, ma'am," Vanderveen replied evenly, "I'll do my best."

Wilmot was well aware of the fact that the Prithian ambassador liked Vanderveen because both of them had been stationed on LaNor during the Claw rebellion. Although it was a connection that the older woman resented, she hoped to take advantage of it.

A uniformed robot opened the passenger-side door. Wilmot exited, and Vanderveen followed. Then, having plastered what she believed to be a winning smile on her face, the senior diplomat spotted a businessman she knew, waved to her subordinate, and was off.

Vanderveen heaved a sigh of relief, climbed the broad flight of stairs in company with the trade delegation from Earth, presented her invitation to a Thraki security guard, passed through a screening device, and was admitted to a large if somewhat sterile reception area.

Like so many Thraki structures, the Ministry of Foreign Affairs was reminiscent of the space arks on which the race had lived for so long. And even though the diminutive aliens had intentionally raised the ceilings, made the doors larger, and widened the hallways for the benefit of other species, the building's interior still had a cramped feel.

The human diplomat allowed herself to be pulled along by the crowd, exchanged greetings with the various beings she knew, and wound up in a large reception room. Tables lined the walls, each heavily laden with different types of cuisine and a wide variety of eating utensils. Robots, dozens of them, roamed the room carrying trays loaded with drinks. Thanks to his brightly colored plumage, and distinctive voice, Sca Sor would have been hard to miss. He was on the far side of the room, flanked by an exoskeleton-assisted Dweller and a black-clad Drac.

Vanderveen took a glass of wine off a tray, drifted through the crowd, and warbled a much-practiced greeting. Her efforts to learn Prithian had begun on LaNor and had continued under Sok Tok's tutelage, prior to the translator's recent death. Her command of the language was better now—but far from perfect. The Prithian diplomat replied in kind, then switched to standard. "Well done, my dear! It won't be long before we fit you with wings!"

It was an old joke, but the foreign service officer laughed anyway, and continued to sing rather than speak. That cut the other diplomats out—and gave Vanderveen the opportunity she was looking for. Her grammar was atrocious, and human vocal cords couldn't produce certain inflections, but Sca Sor was impressed nevertheless.

"Mr. Ambassador," Vanderveen began, "when the Prithian

race went to the stars, it was like a flight from the sacred mountain that soared over all below. With the passage of time Prithian shipowners prospered by serving planets that were too far off the main shipping routes for larger companies to bother with.

"Now, as the Ramanthians expand their empire, many of the paths between the stars have been closed. If profits haven't started to fall yet, they will soon, causing great hardship for your people.

"More than that great suffering has resulted from Ramanthian aggression, and will continue, unless they are stopped. According to the Book of Wings, it is the duty of each soul to advance that which is good and to fight the forces of evil. That is the course to which we and our allies are committed. I urge you to urge your government to join the Confederacy, and by doing so, to join the battle against evil."

Sca Sor had large, oval-shaped eyes. They blinked in unison. Not only was the prolonged use of his language unprecedented— but so was the reference to the Book of Wings. An ancient text comparable to the human Koran or Bible. Few off-worlders went to the trouble to read it. His crimson shoulder plumage rippled approvingly. "Your superiors chose wisely when they selected you to speak for them. Some accuse my people of benefiting from the Confederacy's work without providing support. I happen to agree with them… but lack the authority required to effect a change of policy.

"This matter has been reviewed before… but always within a commercial context. We are a minor power… and many of our leaders are loath to offend the Ramanthians. But the moral argument has weight—as does your capacity to put it forward. I will pass your message along… perhaps the council will reconsider."

It was good feedback, no, *excellent* feedback, since intelligence indicated that a group of so-called pragmatists had consistently managed to frame the question as one of trade rather than moral imperative. The Confederacy's diplomatic corps had reinforced that approach by consistently steering clear of religious matters, always framing their arguments as if everything could, and should, be driven by simple self-interest. Maybe, just maybe, Sca Sor, and beings like him, could transform the nature of the discussion into something higher. "Thank you, Mr. Ambassador,"

Vanderveen trilled. "I look forward to your response."

They parted after that, as Sca Sor headed toward one of the tables loaded with food—and Vanderveen went in search of a restroom.

A line had formed outside the first one she came to, but the diplomat had been in the building before and remembered a second-floor conference room that boasted its own restroom. There wasn't any security to cope with since the first two floors of the building were almost entirely dedicated to reception and conference rooms and considered to be semipublic areas.

The diplomat left the lift, made her way down a narrow hallway, and spotted the conference room where she had been forced to endure a three-hour meeting. The door was open, so she took a peek inside. A twelve-person table occupied the center of the space and was surrounded by adjustable chairs. Windows dominated one wall, a large holo tank claimed a second, and a pin board covered most of a third.

The door Vanderveen was looking for was off to the right. Consistent with her expectations, the restroom was vacant. The diplomat entered and closed the door.

Five minutes later, just as the foreign service officer finished checking her makeup, she heard a door slam. Next came the sound of a giggle followed by an extremely familiar voice. "Jonathan! Stop it! You're tearing my dress."

Vanderveen cracked the door open and peered through the gap. The Clone military attaché had removed Ambassador Wilmot's dress by that time, tossed it aside, and laid her on the conference room table. He had just pulled her panties off, and was in the process of removing his uniform, when the Foreign Service Officer closed the door and turned the bolt.

What followed was the longest fifteen minutes of Vanderveen's life as her boss moaned like a lost soul, yelled, "Yes, yes, *yes*!" and uttered a scream so loud that it seemed as if everyone in the building would hear it.

It wasn't long thereafter that someone tried the door. Wilmot was annoyed. "It's locked, dammit! Why would the furballs lock the can?"

"Careful," a male voice said. "Maybe someone's in there."

Wilmot said, "Shit! Let's get out of here," and Vanderveen heard the clack of high-heeled shoes followed by a solid *thud* as the outer door closed.

Not wanting to charge out into the corridor and possibly be seen, Vanderveen forced herself to wait for a full minute before entering the conference room.

But then, before the diplomat could make her escape, the outer door opened again. Concerned that Wilmot had left something behind and returned to get it, Vanderveen backed into the restroom. She pulled the door closed and relocked it.

No one tried the door. Instead, Vanderveen heard the murmur of voices, neither of which sounded like Wilmot's. Slowly, so as not to give herself away, the FSO turned the bolt and eased the door open. What she saw was very interesting indeed. There, sitting cater–corner from each other, were two of her fellow diplomats—a Ramanthian, whom she immediately recognized as Ambassador Alway Orno, and the Thraki foreign minister, Oholo Bintha. Of even more interest, however, was the nature of their conversation. Vanderveen listened intently.

"…Which means," Orno continued, "that the Sheen ships aren't compatible with the rest of our fleet. Rather than put a computer in charge, the way your ancestors did, our naval officers prefer to command such ships themselves. That means replacing the command and control systems, making modifications to each ship's weaponry, and reprogramming all of the maintenance nano."

The Thrakies were skilled roboticists, so much so that even their pets were machines, each of which was as unique as its owner. Bintha's pet robot, or "form," chose that moment to emerge from his coat pocket and climb onto the conference room table. The tiny machine morphed from something that resembled a four-legged spider into a biped that performed a series of cartwheels. The Thraki nodded approvingly. "Yes, I can understand the problem. In spite of the fact that it was our ancestors who created the Sheen and put them into motion, they chose to control their arks much as your naval officers do. Even we refuse to let machines make decisions for us."

"Yes," the Ramanthian agreed, "we are similar in that regard.

So, given the fact that your people have the skills required to retrofit the fleet, I wondered if you would be willing to assist us."

Vanderveen felt her heart beat faster. The Thrakies were neutral, that's what they claimed at any rate, so how would the foreign minister reply?

Bintha frowned. "My people are neutral—I believe you are aware of that fact."

"Yes," Orno answered smoothly, "but it isn't military assistance that I seek. My race requires certain services. The same services that you make available to others. Surely neutrality doesn't involve the cessation of all commercial activity. How would your people survive?"

"Well," the Thraki said thoughtfully, "you make a good point. A truly neutral government would support both sides equally."

"Although," Orno continued, "it might be a good idea to keep the relationship confidential, lest someone get the wrong idea."

"Absolutely," Bintha agreed, "assuming that some sort of agreement is reached."

"Which brings us to the matter of terms," the Ramanthian suggested. "We have approximately three thousand Sheen ships. How much would it cost to refit them?"

Rather than dodge the question, as Vanderveen thought that he would, the Thraki tackled it head-on. A clear indication that the question was anything but unexpected. "About two and a half million credits per ship, or 75 million all together, plus certain trade concessions at the cessation of hostilities."

There it was, an open offer to provide the Ramanthians with sub rosa support, in return for money and trade concessions. Vanderveen remembered Sok Tok's dying words: "...Don't trust the Thrakies..." and felt a tremendous surge of anger. The translator had been correct—and here was the proof.

Surprisingly, from Orno's perspective, the financial part of the package was fairly reasonable. That meant that the trade concessions, once the Thrakies put them forward, would be less so. But that was to be expected. Of more importance was the fact that the Thrakies believed that the Ramanthians would win the war and wanted to position themselves for the future. That didn't stop him from trying to get a better deal, however. "The price you put forward strikes me as a bit high, but that's what negotiations are for, and we can leave such matters to the experts.

"As for trade agreements, yes, we would be most interested in sitting down to discuss the postwar environment, and how both peoples could better themselves through mutually advantageous commercial agreements."

The human diplomat knew that behind all the diplomatic mumbo jumbo was the age-old notion of Ramanthian reciprocity, meaning, "if you scrape my chitin, I'll polish yours." There was more, but most of it consisted of self-congratulatory posturing and further assurances of sincerity.

Finally, after what felt like an eternity, the Thraki and the Ramanthian left the conference room. Vanderveen forced herself to wait, left the restroom, and crossed the conference room to the door. A quick peek was sufficient to ascertain that the hall was empty. The diplomat's heels made an angry clacking sound as she made her way down the hall. She had information, valuable information, but what to do with it? Should she turn it over to Wilmot? And reveal how the intelligence had been gathered? Or find some other way to take advantage of it, which would involve stepping outside of proper channels and acting on her own? It was a difficult choice—and one that would haunt her dreams.

Planet Algeron, the Confederacy of Sentient Beings

One of the planet's one-hour-and-twenty-one-minute-long periods of daylight had just ended as Nodoubt Truespeak and his fellow chieftains approached the outskirts of the village. Local warriors had been aware of both them and their escort for six day-cycles by then, and knew the visitors weren't hostile because of the light arms they carried, the fact that most members of the group were well past middle age, and the peace pennant that fluttered over their heads. Dooths snorted columns of warm vapor out into the air, their hooves beat the semifrozen ground into a muddy stew, and the column filled the trail from side to side.

But the process of entering a village, even a friendly one, was a complicated affair that involved ritual purification, a pro forma inspection by the local master-at-arms, and the giving of symbolic gifts. Seemingly outmoded rituals that had grown up out of a need to prevent the spread of disease, detect hidden weapons, and cement alliances.

That meant that a full night cycle was to pass before Truespeak and his companions were allowed to leave the company of their mounts, enter the village proper, and be received there. Time in which General Booly could have fled had he wished to do so—or summoned airborne troops from the fort.

But the human had done neither one, which was just as well for Truespeak, who had promised his fellow chieftains that the legionnaire would meet with them. What they didn't know was that rather than issue an invitation, which would have almost certainly been refused, Truespeak had conspired with Corporal Nowake Longsleep to take advantage of a trip that Booly had scheduled on his own. It was a security breach for which Longsleep would almost certainly pay.

Still, *if* the chiefs could get Booly's ear, *if* they could persuade him to arrange a meeting with President Nankool, the entire effort would be well worth it. A maiden offered him a cup of hot soup, and he was careful to thank her, but the Naa's true hunger was reserved for something else.

A warrior armed with a torch led Booly and Maylo into the tunnel. It was oval in shape, and vertical grooves had been cut into the rock walls to simulate the inside of a throat. The temperature fell as they moved inward, and water oozed from above and trickled into gutters. Their guide turned. He was a brindled brute, who wore nothing more than a vest, baggy trousers, and weapons harness. His voice was a growl. "Watch your step."

The warning arrived just in time. The stairs were broad, cut from solid rock, and worn toward the center of each tread. Booly remembered the passageway from childhood—and reached for Maylo's hand. "Watch out… they're slippery." Maylo thought about her condition and was grateful for her husband's help.

By then a booming sound could be heard, like the sound produced by a kettledrum, or the beating of a monstrous heart.

The air grew warmer, the stairs took a turn to the right, and the scent of incense filled Maylo's nostrils. To cover the strong odor associated with humans? Or for some other reason? There was no way to know.

Booly saw the warrior step through an oval-shaped doorway and followed him into the open space beyond. The torchlit cavern was huge. The roof arched upward to vanish in darkness. It was supported by thick, intricately carved rock. A closer inspection revealed packs of wild pooks, herds of wooly dooths, and the Towers of Algeron all woven together to support the ceiling or sky.

The floor of the cave sloped down and away from the point of entry. More than a hundred Naa were already seated toward the back, leaving room for those yet to arrive down in front. Some of the villagers had known Booly as a youth. They remembered him as the cub who could never keep up, who couldn't smell anything that wasn't right under his nose, and always wore a lot of clothes. Now he was a chief among chiefs, a powerful warrior, and a person to reckon with. Not just any person, but *their* person, by virtue of the mixed blood that flowed through his veins.

One of the villagers uttered a strange undulating cry, others joined in, and Maylo felt a chill run the length of her spine as the sound echoed back and forth between the cavern walls. The wail came to an end when the legionnaire raised a fist, shouted something in Naa, and the crowd applauded.

Pleased, but also surprised by the strength of his welcome, Booly made his way down toward the stage and the council seats that had been chipped out of solid rock. There were three to a side, with a seventh slightly raised chair in the middle.

Off to the left, standing shoulder to shoulder, were a now-antiquated Trooper I and an early-model Trooper II. Neither war form was occupied, and hadn't been for a long time, but both had been equipped with glowing red eyes. They were there for the same reason that the Legion maintained various war museums, as a testament to Naa valor and the ultimate cost of war. They had fascinated him as a boy—and still had power over him now.

Two chairs had been brought in and set up next to those that would be occupied by the council. Booly and Maylo accepted the invitation to sit down, and had just taken their seats, when Truespeak, his fellow chiefs, and their retainers entered the cavern and took their various places. The invisible drum continued to pound until Truespeak raised a hand and brought it down. The sudden silence was as effective as a demand for attention. The Chief of Chiefs gazed out over the audience. He looked impressive in full regalia, *very* impressive, and his voice carried to the farthest reaches of the cavern. "This village was once home to one of the greatest chiefs who ever lived. His name was Wayfar Hardman."

The same undulating cry that Maylo had heard before sounded once again, except that it was louder now, as the newly arrived guests joined in. Maylo knew that Wayfar Hardman was her husband's great-grandfather—and took his hand.

Booly knew it was Truespeak's way of honoring both him and the village. He managed a smile, but felt a rising sense of concern. This had all the earmarks of a serious meeting—and one for which he was completely unprepared. Somehow, based on intelligence they weren't supposed to have, the Naa had known where he would be and when. That put him at a distinct disadvantage. All he could do was listen—and see what the Naa had in mind.

"There are many stories about Wayfar Hardman," Truespeak continued, as the noise died away. "One of my favorites had to do with the manner in which he took control of a village all by himself."

Booly had heard all sorts of stories about his great-grandfather, some fanciful, and some clearly based on fact. But this sounded like a new one, and he listened with interest.

"There was a village," Truespeak intoned, "a distant village, that envied the harvest stored in your ancestral caves. They came against your forefathers during a blizzard. Many members of your village were killed, a great deal of food was stolen, and the enemy returned home. So distant were their huts, and so powerful were their warriors, that the thieves slept comfortably every night.

"Hardman knew they were strong, too strong to defeat in a

head-on conflict, so rather than take all of his warriors out to meet the enemy and leave his village vulnerable to other thieves, he traveled across the vast wasteland alone. No one knows how he neutralized their sentries, or how he killed their chief, even as he lay next to his mate in bed. Only that he did.

"But the real purpose of his mission was not to kill the chief, but to plant the seeds of fear deep within the heart of the village, where they were certain to grow. Proof of that can be found in the fact that warriors from that distant land never raided your village again."

As Booly listened to the words his mind took the story, superimposed it over the war with the Ramanthians, and produced something of an epiphany. Suddenly the officer knew *what* to do, even if he had no idea how to accomplish it, and the knowledge buoyed his spirits. Soon, very soon, the Confederacy would strike back.

Ramanthian Planet, Hive

It was slightly after noon in The Place Where The Queen Dwells, which meant that thousands of Ramanthian workers were still in the process of returning from midmeal when Suu Norr left his office at the Department of Civilian Affairs and shuffled his way toward the royal eggery. Not to hear accolades as he had so many times in the past, but to receive what could well be his death warrant, depending on how her highness reacted to the news he was about to deliver.

In fact, the official felt *so* negative regarding his chances, that he had taken the highly unusual step of notifying both the War Norr and the Egg Norr of the royal audience lest the Queen's security drones dump his body on their doorstep unannounced.

That was why Norr slip-slid along the walkway with head hung low, dreading the meeting that lay ahead. He entered the eggery via a side door, submitted himself to the usual security check, and shuffled up a series of ramps to the platform that surrounded the top portion of the royal's badly swollen body.

As the functionary arrived two dozen uniformed retainers were in the process of arranging a fresh coverlet over the

Queen's grossly distended body. After the enormous sheet was secured, the previous drape was removed from underneath, thus preserving the royal's privacy. Finally, once the process was complete, Norr was allowed to proceed. The pungent odor of recently laid eggs triggered the usual physiological reactions, which caused the official to feel protective, subservient, and even more fearful.

The Queen watched the functionary's approach via one of her monitors. His body language spoke volumes. Norr was depressed about something, but what? By the time the official arrived in front of her, the royal had prepared herself for bad news. She gave no sign of that, however, as she looked down upon one of her most distinguished subjects. "Yes, Minister Norr? What can we do for you today?"

"I came to beg your forgiveness, Majesty," Norr replied miserably.

"I see," the Queen replied icily. "Please continue."

So, having no other choice, Norr gave a report on Project Echo. The royal listened with rapt attention. It seemed that Project Echo was the latest in a long series of attempts to develop a means of faster-than-ship communication. The work, which had been carried out within a little-known bureau buried deep within the Department of Civilian Affairs, had been under way for a year and a half.

Though largely unsaid, the Queen got the impression that Norr and senior members of his staff considered the technology involved to be interesting but not especially promising, until it suddenly started to work.

It seemed that a research facility had been established on a planet called Savas, which was located thousands of light-years away. Nothing of any consequence had been heard from the research station until a series of what were purported to be hypercom messages arrived on Hive via the Project Echo equipment located there. Tests had been carried out to verify that the messages were real, and the results were clear: Thanks to Ramanthian research, faster-than-ship communication was now a reality.

More work would have to be done before hypercom sets

could be manufactured and issued to the navy, but those efforts were under way, and it was only a matter of time before the first units rolled off the assembly lines.

The royal couldn't resist the temptation to interrupt at that point. "This is excellent news! So, why beg my forgiveness?"

Norr gave the Ramanthian equivalent of a sigh, lowered his head to the furthest extent possible, and gave the rest of his report. According to communications received from a local naval officer via the Echo system, his battle group had been ambushed by a superior enemy force, which had inflicted heavy damage on his destroyer prior to landing on Savas. There was no way to know what the Confederacy forces hoped to accomplish there, but Norr feared that they had somehow managed to learn about the hypercom and dispatched a task force to grab it.

"But why not bring the device out *now*?" the Queen demanded. "You indicated that we have a destroyer off-planet."

"The ship was not only damaged," Norr reminded her, "but it's too large to enter the atmosphere."

"So, how long will it take?" the royal inquired impatiently.

"Three standard weeks for the task force to arrive, plus approximately three weeks to tear the facility down, and another three weeks to return."

"And the situation on the ground?"

Norr brightened slightly. "One of the enemy ships crash-landed in the middle of a desert. The other put down at a human settlement located more than a thousand units away from the research facility. Fortunately, it was severely damaged. Not only that, but we have a battalion of armor on Savas, which is under the command of a very competent officer. He feels confident that he can defend the facility even if the surviving Confederacy troops march overland against him."

The Queen felt a tremendous sense of relief. Think of it! A hypercom! And at exactly the right moment, too... Once in operation, the new technology would ensure military superiority until such time as billions of her offspring had matured and were old enough to conquer known space. Her words were consistent with her mood.

"While it is unfortunate that your personnel failed to take

Project Echo more seriously, this is a scientific discovery of truly monumental proportions, and the functionaries responsible for the breakthrough are to be congratulated."

It was a generous assessment, much more generous than Norr expected, or thought that he deserved. The official went to one knee. "Thank you, Majesty. I will tell them what you said."

"See that you do," the royal admonished, "and check to see what other advances lay hidden within the depths of your bureaucracy. Maybe your scientists can make me thin again!"

Planet Algeron, the Confederacy of Sentient Beings

Rather than take over the commandant's office, forcing her to find other quarters, Booly had laid claim to a conference room that was located three levels below the planet's surface. It was barely large enough to accommodate all of his guests. They included two admirals, plus Sergi Chien-Chu in his capacity as a reserve naval officer and advisor, plus members of Booly's staff, including Colonel Kitty Kirby, Colonel Tom Leeger, Major Drik Seeba-Ka, and a dozen aides who sat behind the main participants with their backs to the walls. There was a certain amount of chatter as everyone took their seats followed by the order, "Atten-hut!" as Booly entered the room.

The senior officer said, "As you were," before anyone had time to stand, and took the chair at the head of the table. "Good afternoon," Booly said, as he allowed his eyes to roam the faces around him, "and welcome to Operation Deep Strike. The objective of this meeting is to discuss an attack on the planet Hive."

All of those present were far too experienced to utter a gasp of surprise, but there were plenty of raised eyebrows, and a significant number of frowns. After all, Hive was extremely well defended, and the Confederacy had yet to successfully penetrate Ramanthian-held space. Booly nodded understandingly. "Sounds impossible, doesn't it? But that's why we should do it. Because an attack on Hive would bolster morale throughout the Confederacy, scare the hell out of the bugs, and cause them to pull additional assets back to their home planet.

"What I'm looking for is a plan that will allow us to take the war to Hive. The extent of the damage isn't especially important. The bugs will figure that if we can do it once, we can do it twice, and that will make them paranoid.

"Now, in order to pull this off we need something so far out of the box that it will take the bugs entirely by surprise. That means conventional stuff won't work. So, let's get to it."

The ensuing brainstorming session lasted all day. Dozens of possible plans were considered and ultimately rejected before the group settled on what seemed like the best idea available. A number of Ramanthian vessels had been captured during the previous few months. Volunteers would load one of them with nukes, drop into the Ramanthian home system, and use a specially designed Ramanthian-like artificial intelligence to bluff their way through the outermost ring of defenses. Once in position, the crew would launch their weapons, go hyper, and hope for the best.

The plan was far from perfect, but Booly was convinced that it was the best one put forward, and was just about to end the meeting when a hesitant voice was heard from the back of the room. "General? Are you still interested in new ideas?"

The truth was that Booly was tired and looking forward to what promised to be a romantic dinner with Maylo, but forced himself to say, "Sure, what have you got?"

One of the more senior officers said, "Stand up," so Ensign Loli Sooby stood up. She had short hair, big brown eyes, and a pinched face. She had just graduated from the academy, and other than the gold bars on her shoulders, and a standard name tag, her blue uniform bore no ribbons, badges, or other insignia. Like the other aides, Sooby was present to run errands for her betters, which was to say all of the other participants.

So, even though Booly had invited *everyone* to participate in the discussion, it had taken the junior officer more than three hours to work up the nerve to voice her idea. The ensign was so terrified that her hands started to shake, and she balled them into fists. "As established earlier, the moment a ship arrives in the Ramanthian system, the bugs rush to challenge it. In fact, based on intelligence gathered from neutrals, we know that a high percentage of incoming vessels are routinely boarded.

"However, like Earth's solar system, the Hive system includes a number of comets. Most are permanent residents, so to speak, and therefore predictable, but new ones arrive occasionally. By outfitting a warship with the equipment required to generate what looks like a plasma trail, it might be possible to enter the system unchallenged and thereby get a good deal closer to Hive before being attacked."

The proposal met with a long moment of dead silence.

Sooby tried to will herself into another dimension, and when that failed, was contemplating suicide when Chien-Chu spoke. "Damn. That sounds like one helluva good idea. How 'bout it? What do the *real* naval officers have to say?"

It was a good idea. *So* good that Admiral Hykin wished that he had thought of it himself. "I like it," he said reluctantly. "I'm not sure how the plasma trail thing would work—but the concept is worth further investigation."

Booly nodded. "I agree. Good work, Ensign. I hate to admit it, but the navy comes up with some good ideas from time to time."

There was laughter, the meeting was adjourned, and Sooby was amazed to discover that she had survived.

In spite of the overcrowding caused by all of the newly arrived government officials, the Legion takes care of its own, and Booly had a room to himself. It was spartan, but fairly large, which was good since his wife had arrived to share it with him.

The legionnaire palmed the door, peered into the dimly lit interior, and grinned. Candles flickered near the bed, soft music could be heard, and Maylo was stretched on the bed. She smiled. "Hey, soldier, looking for some fun?"

Booly closed the door and shed pieces of his uniform as he crossed the room. "That depends... How much will this cost?"

"*Everything*," Maylo answered, as he entered the circle of her arms.

"Everything? That's a lot."

"Yes," his wife agreed soberly, "it is. There are rewards, however, one of which is right here."

Booly felt her hand take control of his and guide it down over silky-smooth skin to her lower abdomen. That was when he realized that rather than being flat, the way it usually was, her stomach felt slightly rounded. He looked into her face and saw her smile. "*Really?* A baby?"

"No, not just any baby, *your* baby. *Our* baby."

Booly laughed joyfully, kissed her, and laughed again. "Can we still make love?"

Maylo looked up into his face and smiled. "Yes. For quite a while yet."

"Good. Let's celebrate." And they did.

6

I'll hide my master from the flies, as deep
As these poor pickaxes can dig.
WILLIAM SHAKESPEARE
CYMBELINE
Standard year 1609

Savas Prime, Planet Savas

It had rained during the night, but the clouds had disappeared, leaving a clear blue sky. But puddles remained, some of which were quite large, forcing the citizens of Savas Prime to navigate their way between them on their way to the only structure large enough to hold everyone. They filtered into the customs dome, milled around the mostly open duracrete floor, or huddled in small groups.

There hadn't been a whole lot of commerce in and out of the Savas system of late, not with a Ramanthian destroyer in orbit, and what little bit of traffic there was bypassed both the dome *and* the local customs officer, something he was almost powerless to stop since the locals had no love of taxes or those paid to collect them. That was why the structure was empty except for a pile of shipping containers stacked along a section of the curvilinear wall that would most likely remain there until the end of the war.

There was a stir as Colonel Kobbi arrived, and a general

movement in toward the makeshift platform, as the military officer climbed a pile of increasingly larger crates until he stood on top of a full-sized cargo module. Sunlight streamed down through the skylight at the center of the dome to bathe him in gold.

Santana and a small cluster of legionnaires stood off to one side, ready to intervene if the crowd turned ugly. The fact that he was *there*, rather than chasing Kuga-Ka and his henchmen through the jungle, made the cavalry officer angry.

However, for reasons Santana could only guess at, Captain Gaphy had assigned Lieutenant Awanda and a squad of six bio bods to find the deserters and bring them back. No small task given the fact that the renegades had weapons, an RAV loaded with stolen supplies, and a hostage.

There was nothing Santana could do, however, but stand and watch as Kobbi prepared to address the townspeople. There wasn't any PA system, but the bandy-legged legionnaire didn't need one. He had a voice that had been tested on dozens of parade grounds and never found to be wanting. "Good morning," Kobbi began. "I would like to thank the citizens of Savas Prime for their hospitality... and apologize for any hardship we brought them. There have been numerous inquiries regarding our plans, so I thought I would take this opportunity to answer those that I can.

"As most of you are aware, half of my battalion landed here... while the other half landed in the Pandu Desert. It is my intention to march north, reconstitute my force, and undertake the mission we were sent here to accomplish."

"Why?" a male voice demanded harshly. "Your duty is *here*."

Others shouted, "Yeah!" "That's right!" "You said it!"

The crowd surged forward, and Santana turned to Dietrich. "Take two bio bods. Flank them and stand by. Fire over their heads on my order."

The noncom nodded, selected two soldiers, and slipped away.

"No," Kobbi replied stolidly, "it isn't. Unfortunately, the nature of my orders prevents me from sharing them with you— nor do I have the latitude to act on my own."

"But we'll be slaughtered!" a woman wailed. "Take us with you!"

"I can't do that," the officer responded, "and you wouldn't want me to. If the battalion sees combat, which I believe ~~that~~ it will, it would be impossible for us to protect civilians. The best thing you can do is evacuate Savas Prime, hole up in one of those mine shafts, and maintain a low profile. It may be a while before the navy arrives in-system, but when it does, you'll be able to reoccupy the town."

There were angry protests, and Santana was starting to become concerned for Kobbi's safety, when a loud explosion shook the dome. Someone shouted, "It's the bugs! Run!" and the townspeople stampeded toward the exits.

Meanwhile, out in the plaza that marked the center of Savas Prime, Captain Gaphy stood and stared toward the south. One of the Ramanthian aerospace fighters had already passed overhead—and it appeared that two more were on the way.

One of the problems associated with his addiction was the fact that the joy-leeches fed whenever they chose to. That made it difficult to function at times. The officer gave an involuntary jerk as one of the creatures injected a dose of endorphins into his bloodstream and began to suck blood from his abdomen. Gaphy fought the rising sense of euphoria and struggled to concentrate. One part of his mind was focused on the oncoming fighters while the rest rode a towering wave of ecstasy.

Seemingly off in the distance, as if shouted from the top of a hill, someone told Gaphy to "Take cover!" but the officer was pretty sure that he was immortal and saw no reason to compromise his dignity.

Slowly, as if underwater, the legionnaire drew his sidearm and took aim at the oncoming aircraft. He managed to fire two rounds before his ears were filled with the roar of engines, something exploded off to his left, and a shadow flitted over his body. He wasn't wearing his body armor, and a piece of jagged steel punched its way through his chest a fraction of a second later. Gaphy fell, his head hit the pavement, and the handgun skittered away. The sky looked so blue, so very...

But then Gaphy was gone, as someone yelled, "Medic!" hands ripped at his bloodstained shirt, and the fabric was ripped away. The medic took a look at the hole in the officer's chest and knew he was dead. A private pointed to one of the leeches. "Look at that! What is it?"

Well aware of the fact that its host was dead, the leech reached out to make contact with the new food source, but failed when the medic jerked the intended victim back out of range. "I don't know, Mendez, but there's more of them. Grab his ankles... we'll drag him to cover."

The entire town shook as the *Spirit of Natu* took a direct hit from a ship-to-ship missile and exploded. An enormous mushroom cloud boiled up to blot out half the sky, even as a secondary blast sent still another column of smoke upward, and pieces of debris rattled and in one case clanged as they hit the surrounding duracrete. Then, satisfied that the objective had been destroyed, the Ramanthian pilots pulled up and away.

Santana was at Kobbi's side as the colonel stepped out of the miraculously untouched customs dome and took a look at the devastation that surrounded him. "You know," the battalion commander said to no one in particular, "those bugs are really starting to piss me off."

Even though Lieutenant Lis Awanda could look up and see glimpses of blue sky, very little light made it down through the triple canopy jungle to the ground below. That meant that while there were plenty of plants to either side of the trail, most weren't very large. Many were green, but there were pale yellow leaves as well, and some that had maroon spikes. Higher up, beyond what she could actually see, Awanda had the impression of extremely tall trees, a lot of interlocking foliage, and a tangle of parasitic vines.

The whole thing was beautiful, but frightening, too, because of the limited visibility. Anything could be hiding in the shadows including predators, Jithi tribesmen, and Gunnery Sergeant Hreemo Kuga-Ka. The first two possibilities bothered her, but the third scared the hell out of her, and the cavalry officer keyed her radio. Ito was on point. He heard the *click*, turned to look, and saw the loot hold up her hand. The legionnaire nodded, dropped to one knee, and kept his eyes on the jungle ahead. The patrol was on the right trail, Ito was certain of that, since there was no mistaking the pancake-sized RAV prints that bracketed both sides of the path.

Awanda had closely cropped black hair, brown skin, and broad cheekbones. A miniature version of the 1st REC's wreath-and-shield insignia dangled from her left ear. She was a combat veteran and knew that trails were the natural place for the enemy to lay traps, plant mines, and set up ambushes. But to travel parallel to the trail would eat time, allow the deserters to widen their lead, and lessen the chances of catching them. Still, it made sense to pause every once in a while, and listen.

Private Ricci saw the loot's gesture and relayed it back to Nugen, Eckers, and Sergeant Brio. All of them were grateful for the momentary respite. In spite of the fact that they had left Savas Prime only five hours before, they were tired. Even though the rain had stopped before they left, water continued to drip down through the foliage, leaving them soaked. Making them even more miserable was the warm humid air, constant harassment by insects, and the fact that like most cavalry they were uncomfortable in the role of foot soldiers.

Still, none of those factors bothered the legionnaires as much as the nature of their quarry. With the exception of Sergeant Brio, every single one of the troopers had been bullied by Kuga-Ka at one time or another, and they weren't all that eager to catch up with him.

The jungle teemed with life, much of which seemed determined to screech, chortle, and trill all at the same time. Awanda strained to hear something besides the ambient noise, thought she detected the distant thump of what might have been an explosion, but couldn't be sure. The cavalry officer used her right forearm to wipe the sweat off her forehead, looked up toward the sky, and directly into the thumb-sized camera-sensor unit that Knifethrow had attached to a neighboring tree trunk.

Meanwhile, a thousand yards uptrail, Sawicki shook Kuga-Ka's shoulder. "They're here, gunny, just like you said they'd be. It looks like Lieutenant Awanda and at least three troopers. There may be more, but they're out of camera range."

The Hudathan's eyes popped open; he yawned and stretched. "Are they on the move?"

"Nope. They're taking a break."

"Where's Knifethrow?"

"Right here," the Naa answered, dropping out of a tree not six feet away.

"Damn!" Sawicki complained. "Don't do that! You scared the hell out of me."

In spite of the fact that Naa physiology had evolved to cope with cold rather than warm temperatures, Knifethrow had adapted to the jungle environment by stripping down to his trousers and sweat-soaked fur. He grinned. "You'd better pay attention, Sawicki—or something will sneak up and bite your ass."

Kuga-Ka eyed the tiny vid screen, saw the patrol start to move, and reached for a headset. It was connected to Haaby's brain box. "So," the Hudathan said into the mike, "how's it going, freak? Are you all cozy in there? Just waiting to die?"

The Hudathan's voice seemed to echo through the darkness that surrounded Haaby. "Why haul the extra weight around?" she inquired. "Kill me now."

"Oh, you'd like that, wouldn't you?" Kuga-Ka said. "But that would be too quick... too painless. Besides, I have to kill someone else right now... Rather than send Santana the way I hoped he would, the leech-head sent Awanda, so she's got to die. And it's your fault. Because if you weren't such a freak, none of this would have happened. Think about it." Haaby liked Awanda, and was about to try to intervene on her behalf, when the Hudathan cut her off. Darkness closed around the legionnaire, and she tried to cry.

The ambush had been ready for hours, which meant that all the renegades had to do was take their places along the east side of the trail. Ito followed the RAV tracks up a slight rise, over a fallen tree trunk, and through a gurgling stream. But, in spite of his best efforts to take in everything around him, he failed to see the deserters as he walked past them.

Awanda was more observant, however. She saw the thin, almost invisible monofilament line just as Ito's boot broke it. She thought a warning, but never had the opportunity to deliver it, as the bounding mine jumped up out of the mud and exploded with a loud *bang*! A thousand steel spheres scythed through the air, blew Ito off his feet, and removed the officer's head.

That was when the renegades stood and opened fire with their assault weapons. Ricci, Nugen, and Floro went down in a welter of blood as Brio grabbed Eckers by the back of his combat harness and pulled him back out of the killing zone.

Then, firing from the hip, the survivors backed down the trail. The incoming fire stopped. The legionnaires turned and ran.

"I'll get them," Knifethrow said, and was just about to follow when Kuga-Ka grabbed his arm. "Let them go, Private... Once Kobbi hears what happened to the first patrol—the second will proceed more carefully. That will take time."

The Naa grinned. "Right you are, gunny. Come on, Sawicki, let's collect the loose ordnance. Something tells me that we're going to need it!"

The human nodded cheerfully as he followed the Naa out onto the gore-drenched trail. "Did you see the way the loot's head flew off? Damn! That was cool."

Meanwhile, high above, a pair of bright yellow eyes peered down through the foliage. The Jithi smiled. The off-worlders were killing each other... and that was fine with him.

Hagala Nor, Planet Savas

The wind was warm and made a gentle rumbling sound as it swept across the brown grasslands to the north, caressed the flanks of the small, cone-shaped mountain, and continued on its way. Though not the one who had decided to establish a military base inside the extinct volcano, Force Commander Ignatho Dontha was grateful to the predecessor who had since it made an excellent fortress. Especially given the new weapons emplacements linked together by a series of internal tunnels and passageways.

And that was why the officer had journeyed out into the desolate land that surrounded the fortress, to look back at it, and make sure that the work had been done correctly. And that was when Dontha noticed that a fan-shaped layer of recently excavated soil pointed up at each weapon. He turned to Subcommander Ootha Pamee, who stood at his side. "Do you see the soil below each gun? It's darker than the surrounding earth. Why stop there? You could place a red flag on each weapon to make it that much more visible."

The possibility had never occurred to Pamee—and he felt a deep sense of embarrassment. "Yes, Force Commander, I will take care of it."

"Good," Dontha replied. "Although our aerospace fighters destroyed a human ship earlier this morning, the hypercom is extremely important, so we must take every possible precaution."

"Yes," Pamee agreed. "A hypercom! Think of it! You could speak with the Egg Dontha."

"True," the more senior officer allowed, "but that would mean that she could speak with *me*."

The joke went a long way toward easing the embarrassment that Pamee felt regarding the all-too-visible dirt, and he laughed.

Dontha smiled, marveled at how malleable Pamee was, and felt grateful for it. "I have a job for you, Pamee… an *important* job."

The subcommander brightened. "Of course… Tell me how I might serve."

Dontha turned to his right, and Pamee did likewise. The arid landscape rolled away toward the desert to the south. The force commander raised a tool arm in order to point. "We have allies, Pamee… Thousands of them. And they live out there."

Like the rest of the Ramanthians on Savas, Pamee was well aware of the indigenous Paguum. At some point in the past a single race of protosentients had split into two groups. The Paguum chose to roam the steppes and deserts on coevolved quadrupeds, while the Jithi took up residence in the rain forests, and gradually adapted to that environment. The subcommander looked confused. "We have an alliance with the Paguum? I didn't know that."

"No," Dontha answered patiently, "we don't. But we *will*, just as soon as you go out there and help create it."

Pamee looked at his superior to make sure that Dontha was serious and saw that he was. "Meaning no disrespect, sir, but how would I do that?"

"Simple," Dontha replied. "There are *two* tribes of Paguum.

The northern tribe and the southern tribe. Both depend on herd animals called katha. Hundreds of thousands of them. They feed on the grass that borders the desert to the north and south. But no one area can support that many animals for long. That's why the tribes travel around the circumference of the planet in opposite directions. They pass each other once every four and a half years. As luck would have it, the 'passing' as they call it will take place a few weeks from now at a spot southeast of here."

Pamee looked uncertain. He knew the Paguum were nomads—but that was all. Like most of the Ramanthians on Savas, he considered them to be irrelevant. Or had until now. "How do you know these things?"

"Because," Dontha answered, "one of our operatives has been traveling with them for more than six months. I'll provide you with a copy of his reports. They're quite instructive."

"So, what can I do?" the subcommander inquired.

"Our operative believes that it would be in our best interest to start a war between the northern Paguum and the southern Paguum. That should be relatively easy since the two groups have fought each other on and off for thousands of years. Neither group has military supremacy at the moment, but once you present the northern tribe with five hundred Negar III assault rifles and the benefit of your leadership, hostilities should begin within a matter of days."

Pamee was malleable, but he wasn't stupid, and his head bobbed approvingly. "If the humans were to march on us from Savas Prime, they would be forced to pass between a pair of warring tribes!"

"Exactly," Dontha said smugly. "And, even if they did manage to break through, our armor will be here waiting for them."

"Truly the gods are great," Pamee said reverently. "We are blessed."

"Yes," Dontha agreed thoughtfully, "we certainly are."

Savas Prime, Planet Savas

The saloon was located at the edge of the Savas Prime city limits, where what remained of the badly devastated town made contact with the verdant jungle. It was a place where mostly men went to have a little fun, where Jithi tribesmen could slip in to buy things they weren't supposed to have, and where Hol Owens could make a comfortable living.

It was a three-story wood frame building with a saloon on the first floor, a brothel on the second, and living quarters on the third. Covered porches circled all three stories, and the windows were covered with louvered shutters that remained closed during the heat of the day. A mangy Earth hound lounged out front, a colorful jungle bird squawked from its cage, and a wind chime tinkled gently on those rare occasions when a breeze found its way down from the hills.

Owen's Place never opened until about three in the afternoon, not even on days when the town was attacked by Ramanthians, which was why it was just sitting there, dozing in the heat, when a beefy legionnaire tried the front door, discovered that it was locked, and applied a combat boot to the much-abused wood.

There was a loud *crash* as wood splintered, the door swung open, and the legionnaire stepped inside. A quick check confirmed that the room was empty. He stepped to one side and slammed to attention. "The saloon is now open for business, *sir*!"

Kobbi grinned as the sweet-sour stench of alcohol, incense, and spicy food pushed out to greet him. "That's quite a key you have there, Corporal, thank you."

The Earth hound had seen worse. He yawned, and his tail made a thumping noise as Kobbi entered. Owens had his own power plant, which meant air-conditioning, which kept the interior cool. *Too* cool for Kobbi's taste, and the officer shivered. A bar ran the length of one wall, a small stage occupied the far end of the room, and there were about a dozen tables scattered around the plank floor. Mismatched chairs were stacked on round tables. With the exception of the drunk who was passed out asleep in a corner, there was nobody present to greet them.

A flight of stairs ran up along the wall opposite the bar. Kobbi took the steps two at a time. He had just reached the top when Hol Owens appeared. The proprietor wore powder blue silk pajamas. He was armed with a lethal-looking pump gun. The legionnaires on the stairs raised their weapons and a half dozen red dots appeared on the saloon keeper's chest. He lowered the scattergun and scowled. "Who the hell are you? And what's going on here?"

"Sorry about the front door," Kobbi replied cheerfully. "Submit a form CCF-967, along with proper identification and three independent bids. The Legion will pay you in about ten standard years, assuming we win the war, and you're still alive… I'm looking for a man named Teeg Jackson… Where is he?"

Owens looked from the officer, to the legionnaires on the stairs, and back again. "Room four. Straight down the west side of the building on your left."

Kobbi smiled, brought a blunt finger to his lips, and winked. Owens had little choice but to get out of the way as the officer and his legionnaires brushed past and made their way down along the porch.

The moment they were gone Owens turned, and was just about to descend the stairs when he discovered that a Naa blocked the way. The trooper grinned and shook his head. Owens swore, turned, and went upstairs instead. There were times when it simply didn't pay to get up.

Teeg Jackson wasn't asleep—but he wasn't quite awake either. Rather he was floating in the never-never land that lay between the two. A fan blew cold air out of a vent located right over his king-sized bed. His arms were cold, but the rest of his body was deliciously warm thanks to the naked women who slept to either side of him. A rather interesting contrast.

So, if it hadn't been for the fact that his bladder was uncomfortably full, a slight headache caused by the excessive amount of alcohol consumed the night before, and the fact that his mouth tasted like the floor of a Koog bear's cave everything would have been just fine. That was when he heard boards creak and reached for the handgun stashed under his pillow, only to discover that it had migrated during the lovemaking hours before. Jackson was still groping for the weapon when the door crashed open, bodies rushed into the room, and a noncom pointed an assault weapon at his head. "Hold it right there, bucko… The colonel wants a word with you."

One of the prostitutes screamed and pulled the blanket up

under her chin, while the other sat up and allowed the sheet to fall away. She had large breasts, and the male legionnaires leered approvingly. Jackson looked from the assault weapon to the officer who had appeared at his bedside. "So what's up? Did I spit on the sidewalk or something?"

Kobbi raised his eyebrows. "Citizen Jackson I presume? Or should I say, *Lieutenant Commander* Jackson? Back before the mutiny that is."

Jackson sighed and sat up. He had thick black hair, brown eyes, and dark skin. Stubble covered his cheeks. "Give me a break, Colonel. Both the captain *and* the XO went over to the mutineers. What was I supposed to do? Arrest all 211 members of the crew? That's yesterday's news. Nobody cares."

"Oh, but they *do*," Kobbi replied. "In fact, the local customs officer was not only kind enough to show me a facsimile of a CONFED arrest warrant that has your name on it, he told me where to find you. Now, just bail out of that bed, get some clothes on, and let's go for a ride. I hear you have an MDT-764 that's equipped with a Thraki stealth generator, and I'd like to see it."

Only one of the legionnaires was female, and she watched with interest as the smuggler got out of bed, grabbed his clothes, and began to dress. He stood well over six feet tall, had a muscular build, and an unusual number of scars.

Twenty minutes later one of the mining company's trucks bounced into a jungle clearing north of town, jerked to a stop, and coughed as a legionnaire shut it down.

Kobbi jumped to the ground, rounded the front of the vehicle, and produced a long slow whistle. Camo netting had been stretched from one side of the clearing to the other in order to conceal the medium-duty transport from above. Despite the fact that her hull had been blackened by countless reentries, and the vessel was at least ten years old, she looked quite serviceable. Unfortunately, the MDT was far too small to handle half the battalion—never mind a whole bunch of Ramanthian hardware. Still, something beat the hell out of nothing. "So," the legionnaire inquired, "is your ship ready to lift?"

A soldier pushed the smuggler forward, and Jackson

nodded reluctantly. "Yeah, she's ready."

"Good. You're going to take a message to Algeron for me. A very important message. Then, within a couple of days, you're going to return here."

Jackson felt a sudden surge of hope but was careful to keep any sign of the emotion off his face. The idiot was going to turn him loose! All he had to do was play along, lift, and haul butt! He nodded soberly. "Sir, yes, sir."

Kobbi smiled thinly. "Good... I'm glad you feel so cooperative. Just to make sure that you continue to feel that way, I'm going to send a naval officer plus four ratings along to keep an eye on you. Maybe, *if* you cooperate, I'll see what I can do to get the charges against you reduced."

Jackson scowled. "Or?"

"Or I'll pull my sidearm and shoot you in the frigging head. You're good at what you do, or so the customs officer claims, but my swabbies can handle this ship as well. You decide."

"I'll take option one."

Kobbi smiled angelically. "I thought you would."

Fire Base Alpha, the Great Pandu Desert, Planet Savas

The Ramanthian troop transport passed over the wrecked ship at one thousand units, lost altitude, and circled back. Group Commander Pinther Nooba peered between the pilots at the desert landscape below. Force Commander Dontha's orders were to put down near the wreck, take a couple of prisoners if there were any to be had, and kill the rest. Once that was accomplished Nooba was to inspect the ship's cargo holds, inventory the contents, and radio for further instructions. But *how* he went about it was up to him, and the infantry officer was cautious. While there weren't any signs of life below, anything could be concealed within the ship itself. "Circle the vessel again," he instructed, "only wider this time."

The pilot obeyed. As the transport circled, Nooba scanned the desert floor for tracks, for bodies, for anything that might suggest that one or more of the humans had survived the crash. The ship continued to produce enough heat that sensors aboard the orbiting destroyer could detect it, but that didn't mean anyone was alive. In fact, based on what the experts told him, there was a good chance that the transport's power plant had survived the impact and remained on-line without human assistance.

"All right," Nooba said, as the assault ship completed a full circuit of the crash site, "put us down a quarter unit to the west. Stand by, and if I call for you, come in guns blazing. Understood?"

The pilots considered the question to be insulting but nodded anyway and put the ship down where they had been told to. Sand billowed, a ramp hit the ground, and fifteen Ramanthian soldiers shuffled out onto the surface. Each trooper wore a sculpted skullcap with a built-in com set, carried a Negar V assault rifle, and wore a saddlebag-style pack that contained extra magazines, emergency rations, and a rudimentary first-aid kit. Specialists carried additional gear, including a radio that could reach Hagala Nor, cutting torches that could cut through hull metal, and two fire-and-forget surface-to-surface missile launchers. It was a potent force and more than adequate for the task at hand.

The air was a good deal warmer than it was to the northwest, but the Ramanthians liked the additional heat and felt invigorated by it. Nooba ordered the troopers to spread out, to put more distance between themselves, and they obeyed. The ship grew larger, then towered above them, throwing a shadow to the north.

That was the moment when Calvo said, "Now!" and the carefully groomed sand parted as a pair of T-2s sat up and opened fire. Lif Hogger, better known to his teammates as "the hog," had never been in combat before. He fired his arm-mounted machine gun too early and had to walk the geysers of sand back toward the enemy.

That gave the Ramanthians three seconds' worth of warning, and they made good use of it. They fired, bullets clanged, but shattered against armor. The *real* threat lay in the shoulder-launched weapons that the bugs tried to bring to bear before the autofire consumed them. Bodies jerked and twirled as if participating in a macabre dance as Nooba and his entire team were slaughtered.

The group commander never got a message off, but he didn't need to, since the transport pilots could *see* the battle and took immediate action. They used full emergency power to lift off, activated all of the ship's weapons, and were already firing as they swept in on the human ship.

But that was when an enormous quad rounded the wreck's stern, locked on to the incoming target, and fired a single missile. The transport's onboard computer attempted to launch flares in an effort to lure the oncoming weapon away, but the range was too short. The SAM slammed into the Ramanthian hull and exploded. There was a loud *boom!* followed by a flash of orange-red light, and a cloud of black smoke. Chunks of still-flaming debris cartwheeled across the sky and dug mini craters in the sand. There was silence for a moment followed by a reedy cheer on com channel five as the widely dispersed defenders celebrated their victory.

Both Rono-Ra and Calvo had crowded into the wreck's tiny C&C compartment. The Hudathan stared at a screen as the debris fell and released a slow breath. "That was the easy one… now it will get ugly. *Very*, ugly."

Calvo nodded. "Yes," she said soberly, "I know."

Savas Prime, Planet Savas

The mine shaft yawned like a huge mouth as a constant stream of townspeople, Jithi, and legionnaires came and went through the opening. The tailings looked like a long gray tongue that spilled down a chute, passed over the gravel access road, and fanned out over the slope below. It wasn't pretty, but it made a great place to store all the material removed from the *Spirit of Natu*, which explained all the comings and goings.

Vehicles were in short supply, which meant that Santana had been forced to walk up the road to the point where a flight of heavily used wooden stairs led up toward a cluster of shacks. The officer's uniform was already soaked with sweat, and the climb did nothing to cool him down. A sentry saluted, and Santana replied in kind. "The colonel sent for me… Have you got any idea of where I could find him?"

The private nodded. "Straight back, sir. About a hundred feet or so. There's an office on the left."

Santana nodded, passed a file of heavily laden Jithi laborers who were headed the other way, and hoped Kobbi knew what he was doing. After the *Natu* had been destroyed, the community's leaders, including Cam Qwan, had announced plans to follow the battalion with or without Kobbi's permission.

Faced with that reality, the colonel decided that it was better to take control of the entire effort rather than leave the civilians to manage on their own. Or, as he had explained it to his company commanders, "I'm damned if I do... and damned if I don't. They'll blame me if I leave the cits to their own devices, and somebody gets hurt, and they'll blame me if I lead them into harm's way. I can't frigging win. But if they're coming along, let's put the bastards to work."

That seemed risky at best, but it wasn't Santana's choice to make, and that was fine. There were advantages to being a lieutenant... and not having to make certain decisions was among them.

The air was cooler back inside the hill, and Santana's wet uniform felt clammy against his skin. The office was well lit, and the colonel was visible beyond the filthy duraplast windows. The cavalry officer made his way across a pair of well-worn tracks, nodded to a platoon leader from Alpha Company, and entered the office. Sergeant Brio was there, as was Private Eckers, both of whom sat on metal chairs. The legionnaires were dirty, soaked with sweat, and covered with scratches. The noncom looked up from his muddy boots. His eyes were filled with pain. "Sorry, sir. We caught up with them... but the bastards were waiting for us."

Santana looked over at Kobbi. The officer was seated behind a beat-up desk. His face was bleak. "They killed Lieutenant Awanda, plus Ito, Ricci, Nugen, and Floro."

Anger flashed in Santana's eyes. "Let me go after them, sir. I'll find the bastards and kill them."

"Thanks," Kobbi said grimly, "but no thanks. Not right now. First I lost Gaphy... and then Awanda. That makes you the most experienced officer that Bravo Company has left. I'm putting you in command. You can choose your own XO plus a new company sergeant. Gaphy was a leech addict, and Kuga-Ka is a psychopath. That means the company was poorly served. See what you can do to whip the outfit into shape. We leave at first light. Any questions?"

Santana *wanted* to push back, *wanted* to say that Haaby deserved better, but managed to choke the words off. "Sir, no, sir."

"Good," Kobbi replied as he turned to Brio. "Don't let this eat at you, Sergeant. It wasn't your fault. Take Eckers down to Owen's Place and have a drink on me."

Brio stood. Eckers did likewise. The noncom forced a grin. "Sir, yes, sir."

"And Sergeant Brio…"

"Sir?"

"I'm counting on you to help the lieutenant bring Bravo company back to full effectiveness."

Brio nodded. "Yes, sir. The lieutenant can count on me."

Kobbi waited until both legionnaires had left, checked the time on his wrist term, and stood. "Keep an eye on Brio… He blames himself for what happened to the patrol. Maybe you can come up with something to take his mind off the ambush."

Santana raised both eyebrows. "Like the company sergeant slot, sir?"

"That's *your* decision, not mine," the senior officer replied slyly, "but I like the way you think. Come on, there's something I want you to see."

Santana followed Kobbi out of the office, back along the rails, to the opening of the shaft. Both officers squinted into the harsh sunlight. Thanks to the fact that the mine was positioned high on a hillside, they found themselves looking down on the jungle. Kobbi looked toward the north, paused for a second, and raised a short stubby finger. "*There!* Do you see it? Coming up out of the trees."

Santana watched as a spaceship rose from what had to be a clearing, hovered for a moment, and turned toward the south. "It belongs to a smuggler named Jackson," the senior officer explained. "I sent some naval personnel along to keep an eye on him. *If* he can get past the Ramanthian destroyer, and *if* he can make it to Algeron, they'll send a task force to pick us up. Our job is to have the hypercom ready for shipment when the swabbies arrive."

Santana looked from the ship back to the officer. "And if he doesn't get through?"

Kobbi grimaced. "Then it's my guess that the bugs will send a task force of their own. Assuming that we're in Hagala Nor by then, we'll destroy the hypercom and hold for as long as we can."

Santana remembered Captain Danjou, the valiant battle at Camerone, and knew what Kobbi had in mind. "Then I hope Jackson succeeds."

"Yeah," Kobbi agreed, as the ship accelerated away, "so do I."

Teeg Jackson watched the jungle slide under the *Ghost*'s belly, saw a flash of gold where the sunlight reflected off the southern ocean, and said, "Hang on!" as he brought the bow up and applied full power.

The *Spirit of Natu*'s captain was a career naval officer—and one of those who had remained loyal during the mutiny a few years earlier. His name was Posson, and he didn't like Jackson, which was why he kept a close eye on the smuggler as he pushed the MDT up through the atmosphere. "So," the naval officer demanded, "when will you activate the stealth generator?"

"When it will do the most good," the renegade answered resentfully, "now shut up and let me fly this thing."

Posson didn't like being told to "shut up," but was in no position to do anything about it and glowered as the *Ghost* entered the upper atmosphere.

Alarms had gone off aboard the Ramanthian destroyer within seconds of the MDT's departure from Savas, and fighters had been launched seconds later. By the time the human vessel emerged from the atmosphere the attack ships had already converged on the spot where their computers projected that transport would appear. Each pilot knew it was important to kill the human vessel quickly, before it could get far enough away from the planet to jump, and thereby escape.

Energy cannons fired, missiles were launched, and Captain Posson waited to die as Jackson's hands danced over the controls. That was when the smuggler slapped a red button, the hull lurched unexpectedly, and a specially designed torpedo dropped free of the hull. "Here's your stealth generator," the pilot said as he touched a series of buttons and turned the ship to port.

Even as the bottom fell out of his stomach Posson saw a huge explosion blossom on one of the screens. "What the hell was that?"

"*That* was the *Ghost* blowing up," Jackson answered succinctly. "At least that's what I hope the bugs will believe… which would leave us free to duck out the back door."

Posson imagined how the sequence would look to the Ramanthians. A ship was fired on, a ship exploded, and a ship disappeared. All very tidy. But would it actually work?

Five seconds passed, followed by ten, followed by twenty. Posson let out a long slow breath as Jackson put the bulk of Savas between the destroyer and his ship prior to accelerating away. "Well, I'll be damned," the naval officer said. "You did it."

"I'm glad you noticed," Jackson replied sarcastically. "All we have to do now is jump into Ramanthian-held space, calculate the next hop, and bingo! We'll be off Algeron."

Posson frowned. There were limits on how far a vessel could safely travel in a single jump without momentarily returning to normal space so the NAVCOMP could check its true position and calculate the next leg of the journey. But that didn't mean that one had to travel in a straight line. "Why transit Ramanthian space?" the naval officer demanded. "Why not go around it?"

"Sure," the smuggler replied with a shrug. "But doing so will tack at least three days on to the trip… Is that okay?"

"*No*," Posson answered reluctantly. "It isn't."

"Okay then," Jackson said cheerfully, "stand by."

The *Ghost* vanished thirty-six seconds later.

Dawn brought rain. Not a downpour, but a steady drizzle, that thickened the already humid air and turned the already soft trail to mud. Bravo Company had been assigned to the drag position, which meant that Santana and his troops had the opportunity to stand under a cluster of trees and watch as their fellow legionnaires and most of the town's civilians left Savas Prime for the north.

Alpha, Charlie, and Delta Companies went first, followed by a long column of civilians. In spite of twelve RAVs, which carried the bulk of their supplies and equipment, the legionnaires were still burdened with either seventy-five-pound packs or individual brain boxes, plus the life-support equipment required to maintain them.

The civilians, some of whom employed Jithi bearers, carried similar loads. Many were dressed appropriately and clearly knew what they were about, while others wore casual attire and carried superfluous items like an antique mirror, heavy pots and pans, and at least one vase. Most looked miserable, and many were crying as they glanced back over their shoulders.

Santana kept an eye out for the Qwan family, wondered if Qwis would recognize him, and was pleased when she waved. The young woman was dressed in a loose-fitting green shirt, khaki shorts, and a pair of rugged-looking hiking boots. The pack she wore looked as though it had seen use many times before, and, judging from the way she carried the scope-mounted hunting rifle, it appeared that Qwis knew how to handle a weapon. Santana waved in return, but there was no opportunity to speak, so that was the extent of their interaction.

As more civilian families streamed past, Santana was thankful for the fact that all the children under the age of twelve had been held back, and would be brought forward using the three aircraft that hadn't been destroyed during the last few months. There wasn't enough fuel to use the lifters often—not to mention the fact that more frequent flights would almost certainly bring the Ramanthian fighters down on them.

As the last of the bedraggled-looking civilians passed the checkpoint, Santana alerted his troops, and Bravo Company hit the trail. Walking drag was a miserable business thanks to the ankle-deep mud, heavy loads, and frequently obnoxious stragglers who had to be dealt with.

Not only that, but the colonists claimed that the so-called wild Jithi, which was to say 99 percent of them, weren't likely to approve of the column and might decide to attack it. A very unpleasant possibility since the indigs would have the advantage of surprise.

There was nothing the legionnaires could do, however, except stay alert and muck their way up the trail. It wasn't long before various items appeared alongside the path, including the mirror that Santana had noticed earlier and all manner of other household items. The lieutenant grinned, ordered his officers to keep a sharp eye out for military equipment, and continued up a rise. The mud made sucking sounds as it tried to pull his boots off, birds flitted between branches high above, and time seemed to slow as the rain misted the air.

The half hour lunch break had already come and gone, and the column had just passed between a couple of widely spaced hills when it arrived at the spot where Awanda's patrol had been ambushed. A team of scouts radioed their find back to Kobbi, who went forward to see for himself and quickly wished that he hadn't. The jacker had been in the Legion for a long time, and seen a lot of horrible things, but nothing like the scene laid out in front of him. His rations tried to come up, and he forced them back down.

The officer sent for Santana, along with what remained of Awanda's platoon, but specified that Sergeant Brio and Private Eckers remain behind. It took the newly appointed company commander and the other legionnaires more than fifteen minutes to make their way to the front of the column and the horror that awaited them there.

The tableau, for that's what it was, occupied the very center of the trail. The surrounding vegetation had been shredded by the mine that Ito had accidentally detonated, and white scars could be seen where hundreds of steel spheres had ripped into the surrounding trees.

The carefully staged scene consisted of heads, four in all, each on a thick, gore-drenched post. Bodies had been propped up against the uprights, but it appeared as though they had all been intentionally switched, as part of some sick joke. One corpse had fallen over, however—and all had been attacked by small scavengers.

Santana saw two columns of antlike insects. One marched up into Awanda's left nostril, while the other exited through the right, each with a tiny bit of tissue clutched in its pincers. Not satisfied with murdering his fellow legionnaires, Kuga-Ka had posed them as a way to both taunt and intimidate any pursuers who might be sent after him.

Kobbi appeared at Santana's side. "We have to keep going," the battalion commander said gently, "but I thought her platoon would prefer to take care of its own. There's no sign of Haaby by the way—so it seems safe to assume that she's alive."

"Thank you," Santana replied hoarsely. "We'll take the bodies off the trail so the column can pass. By the time Bravo Company arrives, we'll be ready to put them in the ground."

Kobbi nodded. "Here," the officer said, and handed Santana the slim waterproofed volume that he always carried in the field. "Once the company is assembled, read them a passage from this."

Santana said, "Yes, sir," accepted the book, and called his troops forward. Once the bodies had been removed from the center of the trail, the column got under way, and a single grave could be dug.

The ground was wet, and thick with humus, which meant that the digging was relatively easy. By the time the rest of Bravo Company arrived, the heads had been placed in a row, aligned with the correct bodies, and covered with a thick layer of dark earth.

One of the patrol's assault weapons had been hit by a steel sphere and rendered useless. Santana shoved it barrel-down into the dirt at the head of the grave, and a private placed a helmet on top. The jungle would close in around the site within a matter of weeks, adding the nameless mound to thousands of others that the Legion had left in its wake over hundreds of years, but never forgotten.

Then, with his company gathered around him, Santana pulled Kobbi's book out of his pocket and turned to the spot marked with a crimson ribbon. Tiny droplets of rain populated the page as the officer read the already familiar words. They had been written by Alan Seeger, a member of the Legion's Marching Regiment, who had been killed in 1916.

God knows 'twere better to be deep
Pillowed in silk and scented down,
Where Love throbs out in blissful sleep,

Pulse nigh to pulse, and breath to breath,
Where hushed awakenings are dear

But I've a rendezvous with Death
At midnight in some flaming town,
When Spring trips north again this year,
And I to my pledged word am true,
I shall not fail that rendezvous.

7

The first artificer of death; the shrewd,
Contriver who first sweated at the forge,
And forc'd the blunt and yet unbloodied steel
To a keen edge, and made it bright for war.

WILLIAM COWPER

THE TASK

Standard year 1758

Planet Savas

The river made a joyous noise as it rushed downstream, jumped off a rocky ledge, and splashed into the pool below. The water was deliciously cool, and the Jithi warriors delighted in the feel of it as they took turns climbing up onto a natural platform next to the waterfall and jumping into the spray-spattered reservoir. The foursome were supposed to be hunting, but the prospect of a swim had lured them away from the assigned task, and the noise produced by the river served to obliterate all other sounds.

Ool, who prided himself on his athletic ability, jumped into the air and turned a full somersault before hitting the surface of the water. Eyes watched the Jithi through a scope as he surfaced, swam to the bank, and took Tobo's hand. A single jerk was sufficient to pull the swimmer up onto dry land, where Camba and Uth compared his dive to that of a rock heaved off the edge of a cliff.

The entire group was laughing when Sawicki made a final

adjustment to the Legion-issue sniper's rifle. The barrel was sixty-one inches long, and the .50 caliber slugs could strike targets located more than a thousand yards away. The trigger gave, the stock thumped the human's shoulder, and a loud *crack!* bounced back and forth between the canyon walls.

Ool felt something knock his right leg out from under him, wondered what had occurred, and was still in the process of falling when the second slug hit Tobo. The other warriors went into motion at that point, both breaking to the right, hoping to recover the weapons that lay not ten feet away.

But Sawicki had anticipated such a move. He nailed Uth on the fly and Camba as he bent to retrieve a weapon. Four shots—four hits. Three left legs and one right leg. Not bad for somebody who had washed out of sniper school.

"Nice shooting," Kuga-Ka observed indulgently. "Let's get down there before the digs crawl too far into the jungle."

The initial shock had worn off by the time the deserters emerged from the jungle, and in spite of the fact that all four of the Jithi were in extreme pain, none of them made a sound. Not as proof of courage, but because they lived in a very dangerous environment, and had been taught the importance of silence from birth.

Blood trails showed where the Jithi had dragged themselves into the jungle. "Find them," the Hudathan ordered tersely. "Tie their hands, slap battle dressings on their wounds, and build a six-foot-long fire. I'll take care of the framework."

Twenty minutes later a long narrow fire was burning, the Jithi warriors dangled from a six-inch-thick tree trunk supported by two improvised A-frames, and their feet were starting to blister. Ool wanted to scream, had to scream, but refused to do so until one of his companions did. His face was contorted with pain, rivulets of sweat ran down along the flat planes of body, and he performed a series of jerky pull-ups in a vain attempt to escape the flames.

"The machine in my hand will translate for us," Kuga-Ka said, as he held the device up for the Jithi to see. "How many days will it take to reach the northern desert?"

Tobo heard a series of incomprehensible sounds followed

by stilted Jithi. Not the finely nuanced language that *his* people spoke but the harsh patois the tribes used to communicate with each other and the off-worlders in Savas Prime. The pain was all-consuming, and he could smell his roasting flesh. His voice was little more than a croak. "It makes no difference stink-thing. My people will track you down and kill you."

"Wrong answer," Kuga-Ka said coldly, as he slit the warrior open and allowed the Jithi's entrails to fall into the fire. Tobo felt the moment of release, heard his intestines start to sizzle, and passed out.

"Now, how 'bout *you*?" the Hudathan demanded pointedly, as he paused in front of Uth. "How many days till we reach the desert?"

Uth lost control of his bladder, felt warm liquid trickle down the inside surface of his right thigh, and heard the explosion of steam as the urine hit the fire. The shame of it humiliated and motivated the warrior at the same time. He called upon every bit of strength left to him to raise both of his raw, blackened feet and kicked outward.

Kuga-Ka felt the Jithi's feet thump against his chest, roared his outrage, and began to slash. Blood flew in sheets as the Hudathan vented his spleen, the other renegades backed away, and there was a fountain of sparks as Camba's dead body collapsed into the fire. That was when Kuga-Ka realized that the Jithi who had dishonored him was dead, that the others were dead as well, and that the front of his uniform was soaked in alien blood.

The other deserters watched silently as the Hudathan stripped, threw the camos on the ground, and turned toward the river. Knifethrow waited until the ex-noncom was actually in the water before shaking his head in wonderment. "Whooee. The gunny sure lost it that time."

"No kidding," Sawicki agreed soberly. "Do you think he's crazy?"

The Naa grinned. "Do colonels shit on privates?"

Both renegades laughed.

* * *

The Great Pandu Desert, Planet Savas

The dark finger of basalt rock pointed up at the feet of the Paguumi warrior who stood on top, silhouetted against the cloud-streaked sky. Farther up, high above his head, a longwing could be seen, turning lazy circles as it waited for something to die.

Srebo Riff, his subchiefs, and selected tribal elders sat in the shade provided by a large piece of Jithi trade fabric and watched as a mob of carefully groomed zurna backed and filled in the area before them. Most of the animals were tan in color, but browns, blacks, and reds weren't unknown. The quadrupeds snorted, farted, and nipped each other as both they and their riders waited for the race to start.

Riff's eldest son, a proud, some said arrogant, youth named Tithin, had drawn one of the less-desirable starting positions way out at the end of the line. It was unfortunate but not insurmountable. Especially given the fact that the youngster's steed was superior to at least 80 percent of those that milled around him.

The chieftain looked over to Kal Koussi, his most senior general, and gave a nod. The warrior was bipedal, stood about six units tall, and wore a loose-fitting robe over baggy pants and sturdy pull-on boots. Notches, one for each enemy killed, ran the full length of his bony heat-dispersing headcrest. His eyes, which were protected by semitransparent side lids, blinked as he raised a hand over his head.

The warrior on top of the rocky outcropping had been waiting for that movement and cocked his single-shot trade rifle in response.

Riff saw Tithin's mount nip the zurna on his right so viciously that the bite drew blood, smiled thinly, and gave the necessary order. *"Now!"*

Koussi brought his hand down, the warrior fired his rifle, and the mob of frantic zurna lurched into motion. One of the mounts fell and threw its unfortunate rider onto the ground, where he was trampled to death. There were cries of anguish from his relatives and long strings of oaths from those who had bets on him, but no calls to stop the race.

But Tithin had no such difficulties as he remained glued

to the saddle-shaped mass of bone and cartilage that was an integral part of the zurna's spine. The warrior saw a hole up ahead, and thanks to the spinal extension that connected their nervous systems together, the animal "saw" the same picture. He pushed his way into the momentary gap and nipped the mounts to either side.

Metal weapons were forbidden, but wooden staves were permissible, and with both hands free to use them most riders carried at least one six-unit-long pole. Tithin ducked as a stick passed over his head, used his stave as a lance, and jabbed a black zurna in the flank. The animal screamed in outrage, tried to turn toward the source of the attack, but was forced to obey as its rider sent a countervailing command.

Then came the wonderful sweet-sour stench of the animals that surrounded him, the cacophony of fierce war cries, and the moment when he and the war mount were one. The warrior screamed his joy, urged his steed forward, and gave thanks for the fact that he was alive.

But there was more riding on the race than the honor associated with finishing among the top five; there were hundreds of bets, including one that Srebo Riff had placed that very morning. If Tithin came in first, the chieftain would win a hundred prime katha. But if he failed, the warrior's father would lose a hundred prime katha, not to mention a measure of vath (face).

So even as Tithin relished the tumult of competition, Riff felt his own stomach muscles tighten as his son rounded the obelisk-shaped piece of basalt, and a pair of sturdy-looking zurna closed on him from either side. The sudden convergence of two animals, both pressing in at the same time, might have been a matter of coincidence, but Riff didn't believe it. Odds were that Sorn Dukk, the subchieftain against whom his bet had been placed, had hired a couple of low-level competitors to make sure that the advantage fell to *his* son.

Tithin felt a stick strike the padding on his shoulders, turned to deal with the attacker, and took a sharp jab from the other side. The warrior knew the simultaneous attack was no accident and felt a sudden surge of anger. He was just about to lash out when the off-worlder spoke from afar. The remote talker, plus the tiny receiver hidden in one of his ear slits, ~~were~~ _{was} among more than a dozen gifts that the insectlike alien had presented to his father. "Remove the device from your pocket," the voice advised. "Use it now."

Tithin might have refused, but the warrior on the left brought his staff down on the zurna's hindquarters, and the warrior felt the animal's pain. He stuck his right hand into his pocket, took hold of the alien construct, and pulled it free. Though designed for humans by humans, the stunner fit the Paguum's four-fingered hand a lot better than the Ramanthian equivalent would have.

Tithin aimed the device at the mount on his left, pressed the firing stud, and saw the animal go down. A quick turn to the right, and a second touch of the trigger produced a similar result.

The riders and their mounts had completed a second circuit of the rocky pylon by then, and Riff caught a glimpse of his son as the second conspirator went down and the youngster surged forward. With only one more lap to go, and having lost valuable time, Tithin found himself about halfway back in the pack. Dust boiled up around the warrior as he eyed the bodies massed ahead of him, visualized a path that would take his zurna toward the inside edge of the pack, and felt the animal change course.

A smaller animal issued a scream of outrage as it was pushed aside, a stick shattered on Tithin's crest, and hooves thundered as the mob rounded the rocky tower once again. A hole opened ahead, the zurna galloped through it, and Tithin found himself in third place. The race was nearing an end by that time, so the stick fighting ceased as the warriors put their heads down and urged their mounts to greater speed.

The number two zurna tripped, squealed as it went down, and was soon pounded into reddish mush by the tidal wave of flesh and bone that followed. That left the lead to Sorn Dukk's son, and knowing how much the race meant to his father, Tithin was tempted to use the stunner. But there was no honor in that, no zis (elegance), and he shoved the device back into his pocket. The wind ripped the words out of his throat even as he shouted them. "You can do it! Pass him on the inside! Take him *now*!"

The zurna wanted to please Tithin. What little bit of identity it had reached down, located a small reservoir of remaining energy, and tapped into it.

Riff and the rest of the northern Paguum, thousands in all, stood as the lead animals came into sight and cheered their favorites. The chieftain spotted Sorn Dukk's son in the lead, saw Tithin pull up alongside, and screamed his lungs out as the racers neared the finish line. Then it was over as the rest of the mob thundered past and a cloud of dust rose to conceal the last few seconds of the contest.

Though invited to watch, the off-worlders hadn't been given seats among the tribe's leaders, a slight intended to keep them in their place. However, thanks to their electrobinoculars, both Ramanthians had enjoyed a much better view of the race than the Paguum had. They stood just west of the VIP section, not far from Riff's dome-shaped shelter, and lowered their glasses as the contest came to an end. "So," Subcommander Pamee said as he turned to face the special operations officer, "who won?"

"Tithin did," Ruu Sacc replied. "By a nose."

"Will the judges agree?"

"Yes, I think they will."

"And that's good for us."

"Very good," Sacc agreed thoughtfully. "Tithin will tell his father about the equalizer I gave him, and he'll invite us to an absolutely disgusting dinner. That's where you will present the assault rifle. Riff will fall in love with the weapon and demand more. The rest will be easy."

Pamee considered the special operative's words! "Disgusting? *How* disgusting?"

"*Really* disgusting," Sacc replied wearily. And it was.

North of Savas Prime, Planet Savas

The legionnaires stood to just before dawn, ready should the Jithi attack through the gently undulating mist, but nothing happened. The sun broke over a hill to the east, a baby started to cry, and the day creatures took that as their signal to warble, screech, and howl in sympathy with the infant.

The Jithi clearing, which showed signs of seasonal use, had

been enlarged by felling two dozen trees but was still smaller than Santana liked. Especially given the need to cram three beat-up aircraft into the center of it. But that was the nature of the situation, and there wasn't much the officer could do about it, except give thanks that the long creepy night was over and finish his morning shave. He was still in the process of wiping the last of the gel off his face when the company's lead com tech (CT) appeared at his side. She wore a look of perpetual gloom, as if most of the messages she handled were bad, and there was no reason to believe that this one was any different. "Sorry, sir, but the old man wants to see you."

Santana raised his eyebrows. "When?"

"The message didn't say, sir."

The company commander nodded. "I imagine that means now. Tell his CT that I'll be there shortly."

It was extremely difficult to stay clean in the jungle environment, but Santana managed to brush the worst of the mud off his trousers and boots prior to grabbing his assault rifle and leaving the area assigned to Bravo Company.

The civilians had been herded into the center of the camp, which meant that once the lifters landed, the boxy aircraft had been used to anchor all manner of tarps, shelters, and tents. That, plus the crisscrossing lines, made it nearly impossible to pursue a straight course for more than a few paces before being forced to turn left or right. Santana wound his way between piles of belongings, smoky fire pits, and clusters of muddy civilians.

Some of the townspeople seemed to know exactly what they were doing, and went about their chores with the serenity of experienced campers, while others stared helplessly while their Jithi servants did all the work, or in the case of one poor woman, sat on a pack and cried.

Finally, as the cavalry officer emerged from the center of the clearing, he left the chaos and entered the civilian-free zone that the Legion had established around the perimeter. The RAVs had been dug in all around the encampment so that one mortar round wouldn't be able to destroy all of them and their nose guns could add weight to the defensive fire. Santana was careful to walk *behind* rather than in front of the robot.

Bat. HQ was deliberately modest so that a Jithi scout wouldn't be able to distinguish it by appearance alone, and rather than identify the officer to a sniper by saluting him, the sentry nodded instead. "Morning, sir."

Santana nodded in return. "Good morning. Is the colonel around?"

The legionnaire pointed. "Down there, sir. With some cits."

The officer said, "Thanks," followed a reasonably dry ramp down into the bunker. The timber ceiling was low, but cell-powered lamps provided plenty of light, and the floor was dry. Three com techs sat along one wall while other legionnaires came and went. Kobbi was present, as was Cam Qwan and his daughter Qwis. They turned as Santana entered. "Here he is," Kobbi said, "all rested and ready for a stroll in the jungle."

Both civilians laughed, and there was something about the light, almost musical, sound of the young woman's laughter that the cavalry officer liked. He smiled. "If you say so, sir."

Kobbi nodded. "I do. Come on over here and take a look at the map that Mr. Qwan was kind enough to provide us."

Santana complied and soon found himself eyeing the hand-drawn contour map that lay flat on the folding table. "We're here," Kobbi said, marking the spot with a blunt finger, "and we want to go *here*."

Santana saw the same digit fall on the words "Great Pandu Desert," and realized that the battalion had a long way to go yet.

"In order to get there, and do so in a timely fashion," the senior officer explained, "I plan to send an advance party up ahead. Their mission will be to perform reconnaissance, prepare campsites, and establish river crossings. That should cut at least five days off the overall journey. That's why I want you to take two platoons, plus Ms. Qwan and her civilian scouts, and clear the way for us. Questions?"

Santana looked at the Qwans and back again. "Sir, yes, sir. No offense to Ms. Qwan, or the other civilians, but what if the digs attack us? There could be a fight."

Kobbi started to reply, but Qwis raised a hand. She met the cavalry officer's gaze. "No offense to the lieutenant, or the members of his company, but there weren't any legionnaires on

Savas when the battalion arrived. The fact that we were there to greet you should speak to our ability to fight."

Kobbi grinned sympathetically. "Sorry, son, but you walked right into that one. I can spare one RAV. Any other questions?"

Santana knew when he was beat. He shook his head. "No, sir."

"Good. It will take this traveling circus the better part of three hours to break camp. I want you and your people out of here in one."

It took an hour and twenty-six minutes for Santana to pull his team together, unload a RAV, and reload it with the kind of gear that the mission demanded. Heavy weapons to serve as force multipliers, power saws to help clear campsites, and light monofilament cable that could be used to build bridges.

Because a normal cavalry platoon was a good deal smaller than an infantry platoon, and half his legionnaires were currently being toted around on backpacks, Santana was forced to combine the bio bods from his headquarters platoon with bio bods from two of the combat platoons to create two eight-person squads. Sergeant Dietrich would lead one, and he would lead the other. The addition of Qwis Qwan, plus two Jithi scouts, brought the total up to nineteen people. Far from overwhelming, but adequate, or that's what Santana hoped.

The last time Santana had seen the Jithi named Yamba, the well dressed majordomo had been serving dinner in the Qwan family's dining room. Now, wearing nothing other than a loincloth, cartridge belt, and bush knife, the indig cut an altogether different figure. He nodded as Qwis gave him some last-minute instructions, slung a well-maintained rifle over his shoulder, and disappeared up the trail. A similarly clad companion followed behind.

The newly constituted recon unit left ten minutes later. There were no brass bands to see them off, and such was the chaos that ruled the camp as Kobbi and his staff tried to get the civilians up and moving, that nobody other than Cam and Lin Qwan even noticed. They held hands and watched their daughter leave, before turning back to the encampment and the work that awaited.

In spite of the fact that the Jithi were theoretically on point, and that the Qwans clearly trusted them, Santana sent Suresee Fareye forward by way of an insurance policy. Qwis came next, followed by the cavalry officer, the first squad, the heavily laden RAV, and the second squad.

The jungle wrapped the group in a humid embrace and caressed the advance party with dewy leaves as it proceeded up the trail. Qwis gloried in the rich, pungent smell, the sounds that filtered down from the treetops, and the dark mysteries that lay to either side of the path. The civilian noticed small things, like the fact that the tracks that Kuga-Ka and his companions had left had been overlaid by *new* tracks, as if the off-worlders had been followed for a while. There were other signs, too, messages that took the form of notches that Yamba had cut into the trees, a pile of pebbles next to the trail, and a stick that pointed up into the canopy. A place where the Jithi scouts could not only travel faster than they could on the ground, but check to make sure that their "wild" cousins weren't waiting in ambush.

The colonist was also aware of the officer who followed a few paces behind her, a tall, silent sort, who seemed very different from the young men of Savas Prime. He was attracted to her, she knew that, and wasn't surprised. Males had *always* been attracted to her, ever since she had been twelve years old, and that was her primary source of power. That and her parents' wealth.

And she was attracted to him, at a hormonal level at least, since there was nothing more to base the feeling on. They barely knew each other—although that was likely to change. Not that it mattered much, Qwis reflected, since everything was in doubt, and there was very little point in thinking about the future. She had been planning to attend college on Earth, to see the planet her parents had been born on, but the war put a stop to that.

The colonist's eyes narrowed as the eerie, undulating cry of the koto bird cut through the other jungle sounds before gradually dying away. She turned to Santana, said, "Yamba found something!" and took off running.

Santana said, "Wait!" then swore and triggered his com set as he pounded after her. "Bravo Six to Bravo One Five... It looks like the digs have something up ahead. Bravo Three One is closing on your six. Over."

Fareye sent two clicks by way of an acknowledgment, stepped to the side of the trail, and waited for Qwis Qwan to round a bend. The Naa took note of the fact that she ran like someone who enjoyed it and wasn't surprised when she blew past him. Then, consistent with his role as point man, the legionnaire followed. No more than a couple of minutes had passed before the civilian triggered her com set. In spite of the fact that Qwis had agreed to use the Legion's com protocols, she forgot to do so when confronted with the horror of what Yamba had found off the main trail. Her voice was thick with emotion. "You need to see this, Lieutenant… You need to see what those animals did."

The rest of the column couldn't move any faster than the RAV, but Santana could, and hurried up the trail. Fareye was waiting next to what appeared to be a narrow footpath that disappeared into the jungle. "She went in there, sir."

Santana paused. "Thank you, Private. Wait for the column and tell them to take five. I don't know what this is all about… but we won't stay for very long."

The thick vegetation reached out to brush the legionnaire's face and baste his body with dew as he forced his way back through the foliage toward the sound of rushing water. And it was there, in a well-trampled clearing, that he found Qwis, Yamba, and the Jithi bodies. Three of the partially blackened corpses dangled over the remains of a fire, while the fourth lay across it. All of them were nearly obscured by a thick swarm of insects. It was horrible, and Santana was reminded of the atrocities he had witnessed on LaNor.

"Your soldiers tortured them," Qwis said, "before cutting their stomachs open."

The officer was about to ask how she knew the deserters were guilty when Yamba offered him a bloodstained camouflage shirt. It was *huge*, large enough for two humans, and the name "Kuga-Ka" was still visible over the right breast pocket.

Of course the blood could have belonged to the renegade himself, but Santana was pretty sure that it didn't and resolved to keep the garment in case the deserter was brought to trial. He looked at Yamba. "I'm very sorry about what happened here… These soldiers will be punished if we can catch them. Can you tell how long ago the murders took place?"

The Jithi knelt next to the fire pit and placed a hand over the ashes. They were cold. "A day ago… maybe more."

The cavalry officer swore. Kuga-Ka and his toadies had a lead, a *big* lead, which made it highly unlikely that he would be able to carry out his assignment and catch them as well. "I'll call for some shovels. We'll bury them before we leave."

"*No*," Yamba replied emphatically. "That would cut their souls off from the sky. Look up… Do you see the ribbons? Their tribe has already been here."

Santana looked up, saw that hundreds of multicolored ribbons had been tied to the branches over his head, and realized that the treetops were like a highway that he couldn't see, much less control.

That was when distant drums began to beat, a chill ran down the cavalry officer's spine, and Qwis Qwan took his hand. "Come on, Lieutenant. It's time to go."

Aboard the *Star Ravager*, in orbit around the Planet Savas

Torches flared and sparks flew as half a dozen space-suited Ramanthians continued to work on the destroyer's badly damaged bow. They couldn't repair the ship, that would take a couple of months in a naval yard, but they could cut away the worst of the wreckage and reinforce the bulkhead just aft of the impact zone. It was a process the ship's officers could monitor via vid cams set up for that purpose.

Naval Commander Jos Satto looked down from the vid screen and wished a pox on the Ramanthian high command. Both of the human transports had been destroyed, which meant that with the exception of the human blockade runner who had slipped through his graspers one cycle earlier, the surviving humans had been reduced to scuttling about the planet's surface like so many chit lice.

So, given the amount of damage the *Ravager* had sustained, she should have been taken off station, and sent to a Class B repair facility. However, thanks to a severe shortage of ships, and orders issued by a know-nothing civilian bureaucrat named Suu

Norr, both the destroyer and its commanding officer were stuck in-system until relieved by a mysterious task force. Something related to the research facility at Hagala Nor, Satto supposed, although Force Commander Ignatho Dontha refused to confirm that, even as he continued to make unreasonable demands.

The latest order, which had been phrased as a "request," was that Satto use the ship's guns to attack what remained of a human transport. A conspicuous waste of time and energy since any aliens still alive were stranded in the middle of a desert a long way from Dontha and his precious research facility.

But the infantry officer was insistent so Satto had agreed to attack the wreckage from orbit, a task which, though technically feasible, required moving the *Ravager* to a lower orbit, turning the ship onto its side in order to bring the starboard batteries to bear, and firing a preprogrammed series of energy bolts, which though far from precise, would probably do the job. The pilot, who had been making some last-minute adjustments to the destroyer's attitude, looked up from his controls. "The ship is ready."

Satto gestured assent. "Warn the repair crew. Delegate fire control. Run the mission."

The pilot murmured into a mike, flipped a series of switches, and touched a button. It would take 3.5 units before the destroyer was in the optimal position. In the meantime all they could do was wait.

Fire Base Alpha, the Great Pandu Desert, Planet Savas

It was early morning in that particular slice of the Great Pandu Desert, and if Captain Beverly Calvo had a favorite time of day on Savas, the period immediately after dawn was it. The sun was still low on the eastern horizon, so the air was cool, and the entire area was awash in soft pink light. That was why the maintenance officer always rose early enough to make herself a cup of tea, clump down the transport's metal ramp, and make her way up onto the top of the nearest dune.

Two T-2s, each with a bio bod riding high on its back, were patrolling the perimeter. The nearest one happened to be a couple of hundred yards away as Calvo arrived at the vantage point and looked out over the area below. The cyborg waved as the MO popped the lid off the top of her metal mug, blew steam off the surface, and took the first tentative sip of tea. It was good, and she waved back.

A good deal of progress had been made since the crash landing. Eight war forms were up and running, the cyborgs who had been assigned to crew them were becoming more competent with each passing day, and four of the transport's energy cannons had been stripped out of the ship and moved to positions at the corners of an imaginary grid. Conduit had been laid to three of them—and efforts to bring power to the fourth were under way.

The effort to free the number two lifeboat hadn't gone as well, however, because in spite of all the work carried out by a T-2 equipped with bucket arms, the cofferdam holding the sand back had collapsed, nearly killing Captain Amdo and two naval techs who had been in the bottom of the hole at the time. So, rather than invest more energy in what looked like an impossible task, the project had been abandoned.

Meanwhile, it sounded as though Kobbi was making steady, albeit relatively slow progress, as he and a menagerie of civilians worked their way up from the south.

Calvo sipped her tea, enjoyed the way the hot liquid felt as it trickled down her throat, and frowned as her eyes came to rest on the blackened remains of the Ramanthian assault boat. After the attack was repelled, the maintenance officer had expected an all-out reprisal. But nothing had happened. The question was: why? Because the bugs were short on troops? Or had decided that what amounted to a handful of legionnaires weren't worth the effort? Or their CO was an idiot? There was no way to know.

Calvo had just finished the last of her tea and turned the mug upside down to let the last few drops of liquid darken the sand when she heard a *crack!* as something passed through the planet's atmosphere. That was followed by a *bang!* as whatever it was hit the ground—and a rumble as the sound rolled out across the desert. Then, even as the startled officer was still trying to figure out what was happening, a column of sand shot twenty feet up into the air before collapsing into a blackened crater.

Amdo, who had been sitting in the *Natu*'s control room when the bolt struck, saw the impact via the main screen and switched his belt com to broadcast. "This is Delta Six! The bugs are shelling us from orbit! All personnel into the ship! Over."

"This is Alpha Six," Calvo said over the same frequency. "Both patrol forms will take cover where they are… We need to disperse our forces, not concentrate them. Can you activate the ship's shields?"

Another series of *crack! bang! boom!* sounds were heard and Amdo saw that the second column of sand was not only closer, but in line with what remained of his ship. The bastards were sitting in orbit, nibbling whatever bugs nibble, while one of their computers walked energy bolts across the coordinates where the downed transport was located. The naval officer's first inclination was to tell the legionnaire "No," that the ship's energy fields weren't designed to operate within a planetary atmosphere, which was true. But then there was another *crack! bang! boom!* only louder this time, and the naval officer wondered if the shields would offer at least some protection.

There was no time to explain, no time to discuss the idea, so Amdo took action instead. He stood, lurched across the uneven deck, and plopped down in front of the vacant engineering control station.

"Delta Six?" Calvo inquired. "Do you read me? Over."

"I read you," Amdo answered grimly, "and I'm working on it."

Individual lights changed color, power flowed to the shield projectors mounted on the top surface of the hull, and the naval officer stabbed a button a full second before the next bolt hit. The transport's force field flashed incandescent as it neutralized the incoming energy and shorted out.

Calvo was lying prone in the sand by then. She saw the fireworks as the energy bolt struck, knew something had gone wrong, and waited for the final blow to fall. It came with the usual *crack! bang! boom!* but hit twenty feet aft of the ship's stern and sent a geyser of sand up into the air. The MO came to her feet and cheered as the next shot fell a hundred yards out, and the succeeding bolts marched off to the west.

Meanwhile, in the transport's control room, Captain Amdo shook his head in wonderment. The *Spirit of Natu* might be down... but she refused to die.

North of Savas Prime, Planet Savas

Because very little sun found its way down to the jungle floor even when the sun was at its apex, evening came early down below the canopy, and even though sunset was still a couple of hours away, the legionnaires wore small, stylus-sized lights clipped to both sides of their headsets. Circles of pale white light wobbled across the thick vegetation and slipped between tree trunks, as the soldiers made their way up the trail. The RAV's headlights speared the treetops as it climbed a hill, dipped as the robot started down the other side, and threw long shadows up the trail.

The omnipresent drums had been beating for hours by then, as steady as a heartbeat. It was a psychological ploy, and an effective one, because even though Santana *knew* that the wild Jithi were trying to scare him, the device worked. "How much farther?" he demanded, and one of his headlamps played across Qwis Qwan's mud-smeared face as she looked back over her shoulder.

"We're close, *very* close."

"Good. I'd like to set up a defensive perimeter before we lose the rest of the light."

Qwis started to reply but was cut off when Dietrich came in via the platoon frequency. "This is Bravo Three Six... I have a man down. He took some sort of dart in the neck. Over."

"They're trying to slow us down!" Qwis said. "They don't want us to reach the ruins!"

"I read you, Three Six," Santana replied. "Throw him on the RAV or carry him... Come on, people... There's a clearing up ahead complete with cover. Let's pick up the pace. Over."

Santana heard the *phut!* of a dart as it whizzed past his head, felt something nudge his pack, and splashed through a stream. There was a series of disconnected *bangs* as the Jithi fired their trade rifles from high in the trees and the rattle of automatic fire as one of the legionnaires replied.

"There it is!" Qwis shouted triumphantly, as she pointed into the gloom. "Head for the structure at the center of the clearing! Their blow guns won't be able to reach it!"

Santana looked ahead, saw what looked like a flat-topped pyramid, and stepped to one side. "This is Bravo Six... Follow Ms. Qwan! We'll hole up in the ruins!"

The officer forced himself to stand there, waiting for the sting of a dart, as he motioned his troops forward. But there was no pain, no moment of ensuing dizziness, as the rest of the first squad brushed past, followed by the RAV. Servos whined as it lumbered forward, slugs whipped through the foliage as someone fired into the treetops, and Dietrich appeared. His teeth looked extremely white in the steadily growing darkness. "No offense, sir, but that's the last time I'm going for a walk in the woods with you!"

Santana grinned and waved the second squad forward.

"Come on! The last one to the ruins has to dig the latrine!"

The trade rifles continued to bang away as the cavalry officer followed the last legionnaire across open ground and into the relative safety of the ruins. A bullet spanged off ancient rock as Santana ducked through a doorway just as someone fired from within. There was a flash, followed by the *crack!* of a high-velocity rifle round, and the sound of a distant scream.

Santana turned to see who the marksman was and saw that Qwis Qwan was standing just inside the doorway with the hunting rifle still at her shoulder. That was when he caught a whiff of her perfume—and realized that there was a distinct possibility that the colonist had saved his life. Light washed across the soldier's face as she turned in his direction. Santana turned his lamps off and reached out to extinguish hers as well. They were safe behind a stone wall—but it was important to be careful.

The action brought the two of them together, and as the lights went out, the legionnaire found himself cupping her face in his hands. The kiss was soft at first, then increasingly urgent, as Qwis reached up to pull him down.

That was when a flare went off high in the air, bathed the clearing in an eerie glow, and swayed from side to side as it fell. Somebody shouted an order, and there was a steady thumping sound as the RAV opened up with one of its nose guns. Santana broke the contact, smiled, and kissed her on the nose. "That was extremely enjoyable—but duty calls." Then he was gone.

Qwis stood there for a moment, watched a second flare go off, and laughed. Life on Savas was boring, or had been until then.

Near Passing Rock, the southern edge of the Great Pandu Desert, Planet Savas

Hooves thundered as Nartha Omoni and one hundred of her best warriors swept up onto a low-lying pass, where the chieftain ordered her mount to stop and eyed the valley below. For thousands of years the northern and southern Paguum had pursued opposite paths around the planet, and since each group took roughly the same amount of time to make the journey, they met once every 4.5 years in a shallow depression under a plateau known as Passing Rock.

There had been wars, territorial disputes related to water rights mostly, but long periods of peace as well. Wonderful times when passings lasted a month or more, as hundreds of arranged marriages took place, entire herds of katha changed hands, and zurna races thundered far into the night. But that was then, and this was now.

That was before the summers grew even warmer, some of the best water holes dried up, and the southern tribe had been forced to cross into the northern savanna searching for grass and water. It was a bad thing to do, Omoni knew that, and understood why Srebo Riff was upset with her. The incursions had gone unnoticed at first, thanks to the fact that the two tribes were moving in opposite directions, but what had begun more than six years earlier was now apparent as the two tribes neared each other once again.

That was why the leader of the southern tribe was surprised to see a cluster of northern tents next to the ribbon-thin river, the peace pennant that flew above them, and a pen stocked with six katha. The number that were traditionally slaughtered at "first meet," when the advance parties from both tribes came together.

But, unexpected though the encampment was, Omoni was eager to believe in it. Perhaps Riff had matured over the last few years, had come to understand the complexities of life, and was ready to resolve problems in a peaceful manner. If so, the southern chieftain was more than ready to meet her counterpart halfway, even going so far as to pay the northerners up to twenty thousand katha for the water already consumed.

It was a good theory, a *wonderful* theory, and Omoni raised the silver-inlaid trade rifle high over her head. The undulating cry was part exultation, part announcement, as the chief and her zurna galloped down the rocky hillside.

The warriors followed, all but one of them, that is, who remained where he was. Unlike the rest of the warriors, this particular individual had no skull crest, a nose that was exceedingly small by Paguumi standards, and shoulder-length hair. His name was Nis Noia, he was human, and the only Confederacy intelligence officer on Savas. His zurna was equipped with reins, resented the fact, and lurched forward as the other animals departed.

But Noia was ready, jerked savagely on the reins, and held his mount in place. He wasn't a big man, only six feet or so, although it was hard to tell given the tan-colored robes that he wore. Most of his head was obscured by a turbanlike arrangement that featured a slit for his piercing blue eyes but couldn't conceal the fall of gray hair that hit the tops of his shoulders.

Once the agent had steadied his mount, he brought a pair of electrobinoculars up to his eyes and examined the tents below. They looked normal at first glance—but something about the scene bothered him. Noia couldn't get a fix on the problem at first—but then it came to him. People! There weren't any people! Not even tracks—because the wind had scrubbed them clean.

The human started to shout a warning, knew it was too late, and jerked the viewing device upward. It took a full ten seconds to find the northerners, hidden along the top edge of Passing Rock, but they were there with rifles angled downward. A single glance was sufficient to confirm that Omoni and her warriors were still hell-bent for leather down into the valley.

Noia said, "Goddamn it to hell," reached down, and pulled the .50 caliber rifle out of the long, narrow scabbard. It was a long shot, an absurdly long shot, but the only one he had. The agent held the zurna's reins with one hand, held the rifle with the other, and jumped to the ground. Then, with the barrel resting across the animal's sculptured back, Noia took careful aim. The telescopic sight caused the other side of the valley to leap forward. There wasn't enough time to choose targets, only to select a warrior who had the misfortune to be visible from that particular angle and squeeze the trigger.

The rifle went off with a loud *bang!* the zurna jumped, and the agent was hard-pressed to prevent the beast from running away. That's why the human didn't witness what happened when the heavy slug hit Tithin's head, or see the way the Paguum's brains splattered the Ramanthian officer crouched at his side, or watch as Omoni and her warriors skidded to a gravel-spewing stop just short of the valley's floor.

But the agent heard the ripped-cloth sound of automatic weapons fire as the northern tribe's newly acquired Negar III assault rifles came into play, yells as Omoni's bodyguards started to fall, and screams as some of the zurnas went down as well.

Then, having regained the saddle, Noia was able to watch as Omoni led the surviving warriors back out of range, then up the slope to the point where the human waited. The chieftain was furious, and judging from the animal's expression, so was her zurna. It snorted angrily and skidded to a stop. "You saw them," Omoni said accusingly.

"Yes," the human replied. "But only after you rode down into the valley."

Omoni had been a beauty once, or that's what the elders claimed, though her once-pleasing features had forever been altered by the silver patch that concealed her left eye, the scar that bisected her right cheek, and the lines that divided her skin into a thousand leathery islands. She was proud, very proud, but bowed her head. "Thank you."

"You're welcome," Noia replied gravely.

"The weapons that fire quickly," Omoni said, "where did the northern scum get them?"

"From the hard skins," the agent replied. "In return for their loyalty."

"Then the hard skins must die," the chieftain said thoughtfully.

"Yes," Noia agreed solemnly. "On that we can agree."

8

And the jungle was given to the Jithi, just as the Jithi were given to the jungle, for they are one.

JITHI BOOK OF CHANTS

Author and date unknown

North of Savas Prime, Planet Savas

Dawn came slowly, as if the sun was reluctant to raise its reddish orange head and stare down into the jungle clearing. The ruins had been there long before intelligent life had evolved on Savas, and the mist clung to them like ectoplasm rising from a grave. It shivered slightly as the morning temperature differential generated a slight breeze and nudged it from the west. Now, after a long night of monotonous drumming punctuated by sporadic sniper fire, the jungle was nearly silent.

The structure that the legionnaires had taken refuge in had four sides, each of which slanted up to a flat top, where four enigmatic statues sat back-to-back, each facing a different point of the compass. All were different in appearance, and none resembled any species that Santana had seen before. Perhaps they were mythological beings, or part of the mysterious forerunner civilization that had left its mark on Jericho, as well as other planets. It hardly mattered, not to the cavalry officer,

174

who was primarily interested in how to escape from the place.

The creature who faced south was at least fifty feet tall, had a doglike aspect, a humanoid body, and sat with folded legs. Santana stood on the ancient's mossy lap and scanned the mist-shrouded tree line. The human was within rifle range of the jungle but shielded by a pair of folded hands, both of which were stained by bird droppings.

The Jithi wouldn't be able to take the pyramid, not for a long time at any rate, but they could keep the advance party bottled up. That would force Kobbi and the rest of the battalion to pause, which would take time off the clock and make it that much less likely that the legionnaires would be able to reach Hagala Nor and the hypercom, which the bandy-legged jacker wasn't willing to countenance. The two of them had spoken just after midnight, and Santana's orders were clear: Find a way to deal with the Jithi—and accomplish it quickly.

That's why Yamba had been sent out into the jungle to see if he could convince the local chieftain that a group of renegade soldiers had been responsible for the murders and that a friendly relationship could be mutually beneficial. But that had been hours earlier, during the hours of darkness, and Santana was afraid that the dig was dead.

The legionnaire heard a boot scrape against rock and turned to find that Qwis had climbed the inner staircase to join him. No one had been able to sleep, and she was no exception. Her eyes were red, her face was drawn, and her clothes were filthy. Santana could smell her perfume, though, which meant that it had been renewed recently, in spite of her circumstances. "So," Qwis said, "what's going on?"

Santana shrugged. "Nothing so far."

"That could be a good sign," the colonist said hopefully. "The Jithi love to barter, and if the local chieftain believes he can profit, negotiations could go on for quite a while."

"Time is what we don't have," Santana replied grimly. "A safe passage would be preferable, but if that isn't possible, then we'll try to suck them into a full-scale assault."

Qwis frowned. "So you can slaughter them with automatic weapons?"

"Yes," the legionnaire answered honestly. "So we can slaughter them and save thousands, perhaps millions of other beings."

"And how will you do that?" the colonist demanded. "Why did the government send you here anyway?"

"Sorry," Santana replied. "I can't answer that."

"Can't? Or won't?"

"It doesn't make much difference, does it?" the legionnaire replied.

Qwis was about to reply, about to tell the officer where he could shove his mysterious mission, when the cry of a koto bird cut through the silence. The colonist scrambled up to the point where she could see over the ancient's beautifully sculpted hands. She pointed as a figure emerged from the tree line. "Look! It's Yamba! He's alive!"

Santana triggered his belt com. "This is Bravo Six... Hold your fire, repeat, hold your fire! Over."

The officer brought his electrobinoculars up to his eyes and found the figures below. Yamba was there, apparently none the worse for wear. He advanced with his hands in the air as two Jithi warriors followed along behind. "I don't know what Yamba agreed to," Qwis said, "but you'd better be prepared to honor it. All hell will break loose if you don't. I'll go out to meet them."

Santana followed the young woman down to ground level, issued orders for the legionnaires to keep an eye on the surrounding tree line, and watched Qwis cross open ground. The fact that nothing more than a scattering of weeds had been able to take root in the area around the building indicated that some sort of hard surface lay just below a layer of accumulated soil. The colonist looked small and vulnerable as she met the Jithi. An animated conversation followed.

Meanwhile, the sun inched higher in the sky, the mist disappeared, and the jungle sounds resumed. Finally, after a good fifteen minutes, Qwis returned alone. The cavalry officer was waiting. "They want weapons," the colonist reported. "Rifles like yours plus ammunition."

Providing indigs on a Class III world with firearms was illegal, not to mention potentially dangerous, but Santana was in a jam. "How many?"

"A thousand," Qwis replied, and held up her hand before the officer could object. "I know… that's impossible. They agreed to five."

Santana's eyebrows shot up. "Five? You got them down to five?"

"No," Qwis answered, "Yamba got them down to five, plus three hundred rounds for each weapon, and a mortar with fifty illumination rounds."

"A mortar? Plus illumination rounds?" Santana demanded. "Whatever for?"

"The locals were very impressed with your ability to turn night into day," the colonist replied smugly. "I got the impression that the next tribe to attack them during the hours of darkness will be in for quite a surprise."

"And Kuga-Ka?"

"It took some talking, but Yamba told them about the legionnaires that the deserters ambushed, and that squared with information the chieftain had received from his spies."

"He has spies in Savas Prime?"

"Of course," Qwis said matter-of-factly. "We try to vet all the Jithi workers, but it's a difficult process at best, and a few ringers always manage to get through."

"Okay," the cavalry officer agreed reluctantly. "It's a deal."

"I'm glad to hear it," Qwis replied serenely, "because that's what I told them."

South of the Great Pandu Desert, Planet Savas

It was late afternoon as the boxy transport flew north. The sun threw its slightly distorted shadow out to the east, where it skimmed the treetops like a dark bird, undulating in sympathy with the terrain. The jungle looked like a thick green carpet, impenetrable from above except for the occasional clearing or flash of water.

Wind whipped in through an open side door and Colonel Kobbi was grateful for the helmet and visor, as the slipstream tugged at his camos, and sought to push him off-balance. The aircraft hadn't been serviced in a long time, which was why one of its twin engines cut out from time to time, the air frame rattled like a bucket of loose bolts, and the cockpit alarms buzzed like a swarm of angry insects.

Even though he had already put in a long day, Cam Qwan had volunteered for the mission and stood at the legionnaire's side. He had to shout in order to make himself heard over the roar of the wind and noise generated by the engines. "There's a lot of jungle down there, Colonel... Are you sure we can find them?"

Kobbi grinned, and the slipstream pushed the expression into a grimace. "I'm sure... For obvious reasons, each RAV is equipped with a trackable transmitter. The corporal has the bastards, and he's guiding the pilot in," the officer shouted, gesturing toward the fold-down bench-style seat where a legionnaire sat with an olive drab console on his lap.

"They failed to disable the transmitter?" Qwan demanded skeptically. "That was stupid."

"Ah, but they did!" Kobbi replied triumphantly. "Or thought that they had... But none of the deserters are techs! They blew it... and now they're going to pay."

Qwan nodded and offered a thumbs-up. His daughter was somewhere below, and even though she and the advance party had successfully cut a deal with the local Jithi, the deserters posed an additional threat. They had staged one successful ambush already... Why not a second? Yes, the transport was an important asset, and the fuel supply was limited, but if Gunnery Sergeant Kuga-Ka and his cronies could be eliminated, it would be well worth the price. That was why Kobbi had risked bringing the transports forward early, offloaded the children at the ruins the advance party had secured earlier, and taken off again. Now, in a matter of minutes, the transport was covering ground it took the deserters days to put behind them. A flock of large gray birds rose from the treetops below, flapped their gigantic wings, and joined the chase.

The jungle held the deserters in its sweaty grip, wrapping them in fingers of green, gradually squeezing the life out of them. Somewhere, back at one of the many branchings, Kuga-Ka had chosen the wrong path. Now, many hard-fought miles later, the once-promising ribbon of dirt and mud had grown increasingly narrow until it disappeared. Perhaps it would have been wiser to go back, to retrace their steps, but that would involve an admission of failure. And that was something the Hudathan couldn't bring himself to do. That's why the threesome were bushwhacking their way north toward the point where the rain forest gave way to open steppe.

Because Kuga-Ka was twice as strong as the other two, he did twice the work. Not because he wanted to, but because he *had* to if he wanted to escape the jungle's clutches. A dense wall of green tubers rose in front of him, many as thick as one of his meaty thumbs, each filled with whitish fluid. The machete made steady *whack! whack! whack!* sounds as the Hudathan attacked the vegetation. The problem was that the tubers grew so thickly that it was necessary to cut them head high, then ankle low, before they would finally fall. That, plus the fact that the Hudathan had to make a hole large enough for the RAV, created extra work. Then, as if to make a miserable process worse, was the fact that the whitish sap had a sticky consistency and covered the ex-noncom's chest and arms.

But he was determined to beat his enemy and was so engrossed in the battle that Knifethrow had to tap Kuga-Ka on the shoulder in order to get his attention. "Hey, gunny, listen. I think I hear a fly-form."

The deserters had heard aircraft before, seen glimpses of them high above the trees, and even tried to signal one of them with a flare. But the bugs hadn't noticed, or had chosen to ignore the flare, which meant the deserters would have to try again. But the buzz of engines that the Naa referred to didn't sound like a Ramanthian aerospace fighter, or one of the Legion's fly-forms, not to the Hudathan's practiced ear. The renegade frowned as the pitch changed, then changed again, as one of two engines momentarily cut out.

Then the sound was suddenly transformed into a throaty roar, a boxy hull passed directly over the deserters' heads, and Kuga-Ka knew the truth. "It's the RAV!" he yelled. "We must have missed something!"

Then the transport was back. It circled the area where the transmitter said that the renegades were hiding and the seven-barreled minigun roared as it spewed six thousand rounds per minute into the jungle below. "Run!" Kuga-Ka ordered. "Get as far away from the RAV as you can!"

Knifethrow and Sawicki needed little urging as the .50 caliber rounds tore the canopy apart, cut tree trunks in two, and dug divots out of the ground around them.

But the thick vegetation made running impossible, which meant that the threesome were soon reduced to scuttling through the jungle on their hands and knees, swearing as what seemed like tons of plant material rained down on them. That was when a sustained burst from the minigun cut the RAV in two, found the ordnance it carried, and triggered a massive explosion. The jungle was flattened for a hundred feet in every direction, the whitish sap turned out to be flammable, and a fireball rose into the sky.

"Damn!" Qwan said as he leaned out into the slipstream. "Look at that!"

"You can stop firing," Kobbi shouted to the gunner, and gave her a pat on the back. "Nice work."

"Do you think you got them?" the civilian asked, as the aircraft circled the inferno below.

"Yeah," Kobbi replied thoughtfully, "I do. It's hard to imagine how anyone could have survived that. But, even if we didn't, we nailed the RAV. If any of the bastards survived, they'll be living on short rations from now on... and that suits me."

Qwan nodded, the transport turned toward the south, and the jungle continued to burn.

The Great Pandu Desert, Planet Savas

The central encampment was huge, so huge that it would have required at least half a day to gallop around it on a zurna, never mind the lesser clusters of hogas (domed tents) that circled the main camp similar to the way that planets orbit a sun.

Near the center of the encampment, a short distance from Srebo Riff's oversized hoga, a smaller but no less heavily guarded shelter had been established adjacent to the open area where the elders gathered to gossip during the evenings.

As Subcommander Ootha Pamee wound his way through the maze of domed tents, tendrils of black smoke wove their way into the pale sky as hundreds of dung cooking fires were lit, and kettles of precious water were put on to boil. Many Paguum were still in the process of getting up, so there were very few sounds other than the rumble of the wind, the flap of loose fabric, and the low murmur of the katha.

The heavily armed guards eyed Pamee as he approached the hoga but made no attempt to stop the Ramanthian from entering, since the condemned had every right to say good-bye to friends and relatives on the morning of his execution. "Ruu Sacc?" the soldier said, as he stuck his head in through the door, "It's me. Ootha Pamee."

"*Really*?" the agent inquired sarcastically from his place in the murk, "I thought it was the Queen, come to see me off." The military officer could have taken offense, but didn't, knowing the other Ramanthian's circumstances. The plan to ambush Nartha Omoni at Passing Rock, and thereby win the war with the southerners in one swift blow, had been Sacc's idea. When things had gone wrong, and Tithin was killed, the agent's fate was sealed. Paguumi justice was simple and strict. A promise had been made, a promise had been broken, and the sentence was death. "No, the Queen won't be able to make it," Pamee replied lightly. "She's too fat to get into the tent."

Sacc laughed, but it had a harsh quality, like grain in a grinder. "I should report you for that... but something tells me I won't get the chance."

The hoga was made out of neatly sewn katha hides. The lowest circling of leather had been left rough, with the insulating hair on, but the uppers had been painstakingly scraped, so that the inner layer of skin was exposed. It was translucent, which meant that as the sun continued to rise, Pamee could see the other Ramanthian with increasing clarity. He looked tired and miserable. His wings had been cut off, and bloodstained bandages covered the stubs. "Thank you for coming."

Pamee felt embarrassed. He started to say that it was his

pleasure, thought better of it, and said, "You're welcome," instead.

"Have you witnessed a Paguumi execution?" the operative inquired dully. "No, I don't suppose you have. It makes for quite a spectacle. The condemned person is led out into the arena, where everyone can watch. Four zurnas are led in… one for each extremity. Ropes are attached, a signal is given, and the animals take off in different directions. Limbs are torn off, blood flies, and the crowd cheers. Riff once told me that it's a good way to let off steam, keep grudges from simmering, and provide people with something to talk about."

Pamee looked down at the sand-scattered floor and back up again. "I'm sorry. I wish there was something I could do, but they confiscated my com set."

Sacc forced the Ramanthian equivalent of a smile. "Thank you. Ironically enough it was I who taught them the value of electronic communications. There *is* something you can do for me however."

"Anything," Pamee said sincerely. "Just name it."

"Well," the agent said, his eyes sliding away, "like it or not you'll be forced to witness my death. As I indicated earlier, it won't be pleasant, and there's the distinct possibility that I will embarrass myself. I intend to do my best, mind you, but there could be noises, or other signs of distress." The functionary's eyes came back to meet the soldier's. "I have nothing to leave my mates except their memories of me. Your discretion would be appreciated."

Pamee bowed his head to a position consistent with profound respect. "You need have no fear in that regard. Your strength is apparent to see. There is a point where our bodies seize control."

The agent bowed in return. "You are most kind, Subcommander Pamee. I will carry your name to the gods."

The conversation continued for a bit, but soon became awkward, and the soldier prepared to leave. Ruu Sacc stopped him just short of the doorway. "One last thing, my friend… I got a look at the warrior who shot Tithin, and even though his head was covered, I think he was human. That means the southern tribe has off-world advice, too… Watch for the piece of excrement and kill him if you can."

Pamee nodded, thanked the agent, and slipped outside. By that time the vast encampment was not only awake, but brimming with excitement as the Paguum looked forward to the impending dismemberment and hurried through their morning meals. Nearly all of the northerners had seen members of their own kind ripped apart, but the alien's death promised to be something special, which was why seats surrounding the arena were at a premium. What color was hard-skin blood anyway? Red? Green? Or blue? The betting was fierce.

Pamee had hoped to avoid the execution and was sitting in his hoga when the warriors came for him. Strangely, from the Ramanthian's perspective at least, it seemed that he was slated to witness Sacc's death along with Srebo Riff and the chieftain's family. Then, once the blood debt had been paid, the entire incident would be over. Not just over, but *completely* over, leaving relationships as they had been before. That meant the alliance would remain intact, the northern tribe would continue to function as an obstacle that the humans would have to overcome, and Force Commander Dontha would be pleased. And so it was that Subcommander Pamee was forced to sit side by side with Srebo Riff as the clearly terrified Ramanthian agent was dragged out into the center of the circular arena where four zurnas snorted, produced long ropes of drool, and tried to sink badly yellowed teeth into each other.

The crowd stood twelve to fifteen people deep, and everyone struggled to see as warriors attached ropes made of braided leather to Sacc's extremities, and the agent lost control of his bladder. Pamee winced as the crowd laughed, and he saw the anguished look on the other Ramanthian's face. The officer allowed himself to close his eyes momentarily as the warriors urged their mounts forward, and the slack came out of the ropes. Sacc made a pitiful clacking sound as one of his retrograde legs was broken and an arm was jerked out of its socket.

All eyes were on Riff by then, as the crowd held its collective breath, and waited for the moment when alien blood would fly. Pamee watched the chieftain come to his feet, give what amounted to a short eulogy for his son, and raise a heavily tattooed hand. There was a roar of approval as it came down, and the zurnas took off in four different directions. The soldier closed his eyes again, but there was no escaping the piteous scream, the crackle of shattered chitin, or Riff's undulating war cry. Another life had been sacrificed... and the war went on.

Just south of the Grass Path, Planet Savas

They heard the roar of the river and felt the extra humidity in the air long before they actually saw the tributary itself. The riverbed was wide at that point. So much so that the water ran fast but shallow. It foamed around the upstream side of the larger rocks, sluiced between mossy boulders, and slid over the end of a fallen tree trunk. It made for a considerable barrier. But the advance party had been traveling for many days by that time and overcome all sorts of obstacles. So many that Santana wondered if he and his legionnaires were in danger of becoming engineers rather than cavalry.

So, having already dealt with numerous crossings, the officer was able to gauge the task in front of him with a practiced eye. The river was too wide to bridge, not with the resources at his disposal, but there wasn't any need. A simple safety line would be sufficient. Once the main party arrived they would simply clip on and wade in. The last person to cross would unhitch the cable, secure it to his or her harness, and follow it over as the people on the other side pulled it in. If necessary, the monofilament line could be sent forward for Santana and his team to use again, but the legionnaire hoped it wouldn't be necessary.

The officer turned to Dietrich. "All right, Sergeant... You know the drill. Establish some security, fell enough trees so the main party can camp next to the water, and we'll secure a safety line to a tree on the other side. I'll tow it across and scout the trail."

"And I'll go along to watch his six," Qwis volunteered, coming up on the legionnaires from behind. Dietrich took note of the fact that while Santana looked surprised, he didn't object. The soldier and the civilian were attracted to each other in a wary sort of way. It didn't take a genius to figure that out—and the lady was willing to wade across the river in order to get some additional face time. So, rather than insist on a couple of legionnaires to provide security, Dietrich decided to let the matter pass. He nodded. "Sir, yes, sir."

The actual cable would have been too heavy for a single person to pull across, so a pilot line was prepared instead. Santana slung his assault rifle across his back, wrapped some cord around his left hand, and secured a grip on a freshly cut eight-foot-long walking stick with his right. Then, placing the end of the pole upstream to break the current, the officer started across.

Meanwhile, Qwis crossed the river downstream of Santana, thereby taking advantage of the eddy behind him, armed with a stick of her own should she need to use it.

The twosome allowed the current to push them slightly downstream as they crossed. That meant they hit the riverbank where most travelers did, which explained why the trail picked up there, rather than opposite the point where they entered the river.

The pilot line was across, but the cable was far too heavy to pull without some sort of leverage, so Santana shook the pack off his shoulders, removed a pulley, and secured it to a likely-looking tree trunk.

With assistance from the civilian, the officer fed the pilot line through the block and got a good grip on it. Then, by marching upstream, the twosome were able to pull the cord through the pulley, followed by the cable. Water sprang away from the monofilament as it came up out of the river and was secured at both ends.

Having checked to make sure that his knots would hold, Santana shouldered his pack and followed Qwis up the narrow path. Though not as savvy as Yamba, the colonist read trail signs better than any legionnaire save Fareye, and was good at interpreting what she saw. "Look," she said, "a lot of the lighter tracks have been erased by subsequent rain storms, but you can still see where the RAV planted its pods."

Santana looked at what he had assumed were mud puddles, realized they were far too symmetrical for that and the exact same distance apart.

"Well, this is interesting," Qwis added, as they came to the point where the path split in two. "They went left... and they should have gone right."

The legionnaire eyed the trail that led off to the left. It looked just as promising as the one that went to the right, and without the benefit of a guide, Kuga-Ka had chosen the wrong path. "Well, based on what the Colonel told me, they certainly paid for their mistake," Santana observed.

"Yes, and no one deserved it more," Qwis said fiercely. "Come on, let's find a place to get out of the rain."

Santana was about to ask, "What rain?" when he heard a breeze rustle the treetops, heard the raindrops hit the canopy, and felt the temperature drop a couple of degrees. The first drops of water found their way down through the foliage a few seconds later.

"Maybe we should head back," the legionnaire offered, but felt her hand close on his and allowed himself to be led off the trail. Vegetation brushed the officer's shoulders, something screeched from high above, and leaves bobbed as the raindrops hit. Some of the plants opened up, happy to let the life-giving liquid flow down their fibrous arms into reservoirs where it could be absorbed, while others, those that relied on root systems to obtain moisture, lowered their light-gathering extensions to create rooflike structures that enabled the sudden deluge to run off them. Qwis had taken shelter beneath such plants as a child and led Santana in under a five-foot-high skirt of overlapping leaves. The officer experienced a cold shower as he ducked through the runoff followed by a sense of wonder as he entered what amounted to a ready-made hut.

"The Jithi call it a lap-lap tree because of the way the leaves come down on top of each other," Qwis explained, "and use them for emergency shelter. Have a seat... lunch will be served in a moment."

Santana checked to make sure that his com set was on, heard a reassuring burst of static, and turned the squelch down before taking a seat on the bone-dry ground.

Qwis had her pack off by then, had spread a shelter half on the ground, and was busy placing food items on it. Some dried fruit that her mother had given her for the journey, two cans of carefully hoarded self-heating beef stroganoff that she had saved from her MREs, and a couple of candy bars for dessert. Thanks to her foresight it wasn't long before Santana was tucking into the best meal he'd had in weeks.

Neither one of them wanted to talk about the war, or the march to the north, so the legionnaire took the opportunity to learn more about the civilian. Qwis spoke of her desire to visit Earth and get an education there. Santana told stories about his years at the academy, a prank gone horribly wrong, and the month of extra duty he received by way of punishment.

Qwis laughed her wonderful melodious laugh, and it wasn't until his com set made a squawking noise that Santana looked at his watch, and realized that an hour and a half had passed. "This is Bravo Six... Go. Over."

"This is Three Six," Dietrich answered. "The old man called in. He wants to talk to you at 1800 hours this evening. Over."

"Roger that," Santana said. "We're on the way. Over and out."

The officer checked to ensure that the transmit switch was in the "off" position before reaching out to take his companion's hand. It felt very small. "Thank you, Qwis. That was fabulous. I really enjoyed it."

Qwis looked into Santana's eyes and saw that he meant it. "You're very welcome."

The kiss seemed natural, like something that had been waiting to happen, and Santana reveled in the smell of her. There was the perfume that she never failed to dab behind her perfectly shaped ears, the cook smoke that was trapped in fibers of her clothing, and the jungle that surrounded them. Things might have gone further had there been time, but Santana was forced to break it off. "Come on... before you get me into trouble."

Qwis pouted, but obeyed, and it was about an hour later when the wet twosome made use of the cable to pull themselves back across the river. Dietrich pulled Qwis up over the riverbank before extending a helping hand to the officer. The noncom wore a prominent smirk. "How did the reconnaissance go, sir? Did you find everything you were looking for?"

Santana frowned. "Screw you, Sergeant," he said grumpily. "And I mean that from the very bottom of my heart."

Dietrich smiled innocently. "Sir. Yes, sir."

Fire Base Alpha, the Great Pandu Desert, Planet Savas

The red-orange sun hung high in the sky, baked everything below in its unrelenting heat, and drove everything that could walk, crawl, or wiggle down under the surface of the sand, into the crevices between the dark basaltic rocks, or the shade provided by the rolling dunes to the south. Anything to lower the temperature if only by a few degrees and thereby enhance their chances of survival.

However, thanks to the fact that the *Spirit of Natu* could still produce her own power, the legionnaires had air-conditioning. An almost unbelievable luxury given the group's otherwise dire circumstances. All of which explained why Captain Beverly Calvo tried to minimize the number of people who were out and about during the worst heat of the day and rely on remote sensors instead. Now, having been summoned to the bridge, the MO looked over a com tech's shoulder. "There it is," the rating remarked as she tapped the screen with a much-bitten nail, "one helluva dust cloud. And it's coming this way."

Calvo checked the bottom of the screen, saw that Sensor 14 had been placed on top of a rock outcropping a couple of miles east of the crash site, and shifted her gaze to the image above. With the other war forms up and ready for action, she'd been planning to break out one of the fly-forms but hadn't found the time. Now, looking at the enormous dust cloud, the legionnaire wished that she had. "Launch an RPV," the MO ordered. "I'll notify the troops. Maybe some sort of animal migration is responsible for the cloud, but I doubt it."

The tech doubted it, too, and her worst fears were realized twenty minutes later when the remotely piloted aircraft penetrated the cloud and circled over what could only be described as an army of what the rating assumed were indigs.

Calvo was summoned and brought 2nd Lieutenant Mik Farner to the control room with her. He was a burly man, with a baby face, who always looked as though he was going to explode out of his uniform. But there was strength there, both mental and physical, and the MO felt lucky to have him. He examined the screen image from beneath a beetled brow. His voice rumbled. "They *look* primitive... but you never know. Did you scan this mob for any signs of electromechanical activity?"

The tech figured it would be a waste of time, judging from the way the riders looked, but obediently stabbed a series of buttons. The results were nearly instantaneous as a blue dot superimposed itself over the wide shot quickly followed by half a dozen red dots.

"How very interesting," Farner observed. "It looks like our supposedly primitive indigs own a com net. A relatively primitive net to be sure, but a net nonetheless. Go in on the blue target."

The tech used a joystick to position a set of crosshairs over the blue dot and touched a button. The vid cam zoomed in, and Calvo looked on in surprise as the unmistakable image of a mounted Ramanthian appeared. The RPV lost the image for a moment, turned a tight circle, and found it again.

"Well, well, look what we have here," Farner said soberly. "A bug on the hoof. And not just *any* bug, but based on the uniform he's wearing, a subcommander in the Ramanthian equivalent of our cavalry. He has the command set... so let's see who he likes to talk to."

The tech chose a red dot at random, zoomed in, and found herself looking at a heavily swathed indig. She was about to switch, and check another dot, when Farner placed a hand on her shoulder. "Hold on! Look at the weapon that bastard is holding! It's a Negar III!"

The maintenance officer turned her head. "Which means?"

Farner looked apologetic. "Sorry, ma'am. The Negar III is a Ramanthian assault rifle. They were standard issue up until five standard years ago, when the Negar IV was introduced. It's a good weapon, though... and vastly superior to the trade rifles that gun smugglers sell."

Calvo swore under her breath. First the Ramanthian, now this. "Check some more of those targets. Let's see what kind of armament they have."

A quick series of checks confirmed that all of the warriors who carried com gear had Negar IIIs as well. A random sampling of those *not* identified by a dot revealed that while some carried Ramanthian assault rifles, the vast majority were armed with trade weapons.

"Thanks, Lieutenant," Calvo said sincerely, "your analysis has been most helpful. I think it's clear that having failed to destroy Fire Base Alpha by other means, the Ramanthians are about to throw some native troops our way. We're in for a fight. The question is whether we should go out to meet them... or make our stand here. What's *your* view?"

The junior officer swallowed what felt like a rough-edged rock. Second lieutenants were rarely asked to contribute opinions on trivial matters, much less situations like this one, so he was understandably surprised. However, while the infantry officer didn't have a lot of experience, he had been to the academy and fought thousands of simulated battles, some of which were relevant to the present situation. He cleared his throat. "While the war forms could go out and engage the enemy, that would leave the ship vulnerable and open to attack.

"For example," Farner said, warming to his subject, "what if the natives are bait? Intended to suck our borgs into a fight so the bugs can drop a company of special ops troops in by air? For all we know they're already positioned ten miles out waiting for the signal to attack."

Calvo had missed the second possibility, but considered the first, and nodded. "I concur, Lieutenant," the MO said grimly. "We'll put the war forms in position, secure the ship, and bring the heavy stuff on-line. Let's get cracking."

The dust rose in a thick cloud, and while much of the particulate matter was filtered out by the scarves that the Paguumi wore wrapped around their heads, the Ramanthian had no such protection. His eyes felt raw, his throat hurt, and his chitin was covered with a layer of grit.

The custom-made saddle, which had once been the property of Special Operations Officer Ruu Sacc, did a respectable job of holding Subcommander Pamee in place, but no amount of padding could ameliorate the pounding that resulted from the way the zurna's hooves hit the sand.

And, in addition to the physical discomfort that Pamee felt, there was a growing ~~sense of~~ fear. The Paguum had returned his com set shortly after Sacc's execution, allowing the officer to make contact with the base at Hagala Nor. But, rather than pull the infantry officer out as Pamee had hoped, Force Commander Ignatho Dontha ordered him to remain in place, and engineer an attack on a small group of Confederacy soldiers in the desert.

A simple task, really, or what should have been, but what if the assault failed? It seemed as if images of Ruu Sacc's death had been burned on to the Ramanthian's retinas because he couldn't get rid of them. But events had been set into motion, Srebo Riff was leading a wave of a thousand warriors toward the west, and Pamee was like a chip of wood riding the flood. All he could do was hang on and pray that the Paguum would win.

A protective berm had been established around the energy cannon, which sat just above the level of the sand and had a broad field of fire. "Here they come!" someone shouted over the team freq, and Calvo, who was standing just behind the defensive rampart, snarled into her mike, "This is Pandu Six... Take that person's name! Radio discipline *will* be maintained. Over."

There was silence after that, on the radio at least, although war cries could be heard, followed by the *pop, pop, pop* of trade guns as the lead elements of the oncoming force fired their weapons. The digs looked like a solid mass at that point, shimmering in the heat and floating just above the surface of the desert.

The MO had never seen anything like it, or expected to, given the nature of her specialty, and was busy analyzing her reaction to the sight when Staff Sergeant Amel Haddad cleared his throat. Farner had put him in charge of the gun position, and like the officer, the noncom was standing in the open. He was a combat veteran, and his voice was calm. "Those bullets can carry quite a way, ma'am... I suggest that we take cover."

That was the moment when Calvo realized that Haddad was

risking his life to stand at her side. She grinned. "That sounds like excellent advice, Sergeant. Thank you."

A firing step had been formed around the edge of the gun emplacement, then fused into place with laser torches. Calvo vaulted over the berm, landed on the blackened glass, and raised her glasses. The oncoming horde had separated into clumps of riders by then, weapons held high, screaming their hatred. The rating who sat in the seat behind the gun was only a few feet away. He looked from the mob that filled his sight down toward Calvo. He was nineteen years old and had a hard time keeping his voice level. "They're in range, ma'am."

Calvo was about to reply, about to tell him to hold his fire a bit longer, when two aerospace fighters appeared out of the sun. The energy bolts arrived before the sound of their engines did, tossed great gouts of sand up into the air, and destroyed the gun emplacement to the north. Thunder rolled as the pilots pulled up, banked to the south, and prepared for a second run.

Captain Amdo, still ensconced on the ship's bridge, took control of the surviving cannons at that point and handed it over to the C&C computer. A firing solution was fed to the weapons, they whined as they turned, and bolts of blue light flashed into the sky. The lead fighter staggered as if it had just run into a brick wall, exploded into a thousand pieces of fiery debris, and scattered itself over the desert below.

The pilot of the second ship saw the explosion, had no time to react, and was forced to fly through it. A jagged piece of metal slammed into a stubby wing, sliced through a fuel line, and triggered a cockpit alarm. The Ramanthian knew there was no way he'd be able to make it back into orbit and turned toward Hagala Nor instead. Captain Amdo gave thanks and hit a button. The gunners saw a green light appear and knew they had control again.

Srebo Riff was in the third rank of riders, and would have been in the first had General Kal Koussi allowed it, but could still feel the wild exultation of battle. Not that the engagement was likely to last very long, since while they were purported to be well armed, the hard skin named Pamee had assured him that there were no more than fifty aliens in and around the wrecked flier. He stood straight-legged, screamed his son's name into the wind, and saw a flash of light.

There was a loud *boom!* as an energy bolt capable of punching its way through durasteel ruptured the atmosphere, tore a bloody four-zurna-wide hole through all twenty ranks of Paguumi warriors, and kept right on going. There weren't any wounded, just a long line of dead bodies, most of which were so badly charred it would have been impossible to identify them.

Srebo Riff survived the initial blast, and even though he'd never seen an energy cannon before, instinctively understood its weakness. "Spread out!" he shouted into the Ramanthian-made com set. "Spread out *now!*" And key leaders obeyed him, thereby limiting the cannon's effectiveness, as the gunner was reduced to firing on groups of two or three rather than a massed target.

But the legionnaires had *another* surprise in store for the digs—and it wasn't so easily countered. There were eight borgs, four of which were quads, and four of which were T-2s. Calvo planned to keep half of the force in reserve in case it turned out that the cavalry charge was a feint and the real attack came from somewhere else.

But that left two quads, and two T-2s, all of which had been given enough warning that they had been able to take up positions east of the wreck. None of the locals had the faintest idea what the strange apparitions were as they rose out of the sand, but it didn't take long for them to learn as machine guns opened fire, and the entire front rank of warriors disappeared in a welter of blood, shattered bone, and flying bits of flesh.

Shocked by what was taking place, Subcommander Pamee tried to turn his zurna around, discovered that the battle-maddened mount seemed determined to take the lead, and ran faster. The off-worlder soon found himself side by side with Srebo Riff. The Paguum nodded approvingly, screamed something incoherent, and charged a Confederacy cyborg. The Ramanthian felt inspired in spite of himself and followed the chieftain in.

In spite of the terrible carnage, there were still plenty of targets, and Lif Hogger's T-2 continued to mow the digs down as bullets clanged against his armor, and the native cavalry swept around him. A bio bod rode high on the borg's back. He fired his assault rifle, knocked a Paguum out of the saddle, and jerked as a bullet took him at the base of his spine just below his body armor.

"This is it!" Sergeant Haddad shouted to the legionnaires around him as the enemy swept in. "Pick your targets, make each bullet count, and remember that the nearest ammo dump is at least five lights away!"

Calvo took the noncom's advice, raised her assault weapon, and put the crosshairs on one of the lead animals. It made for a large target, and when it fell, the body might block those behind it. The rifle jerked as the MO fired bursts of three rounds each.

Pamee felt the zurna stumble, knew it had been hit, and felt himself being launched into the air. The Ramanthian hit the sand, rolled head over heels, and felt a shadow fall across him. He had pulled his sidearm, and was firing up into the quad's armored belly, when the durasteel pod came down on his head and thorax. There was a crunching sound as chitin shattered, a momentary wetness in the sand, then nothing as the cyborg unwittingly pushed the officer's remains down under the desert's surface.

The charge broke after that, as Riff and the handful of warriors who remained to him were forced to flee back the way they had come, with energy bolts sizzling past their heads.

"Cease fire!" Calvo shouted, then said it again, via the com net. "This is Pandu Six... Cease fire! Over."

There was one last burst of .50 caliber rounds as a legionnaire took her finger off the heavy machine gun's trigger, followed by nearly total silence as overheated metal pinged, servos whined, and a badly wounded zurna whimpered pitifully.

The bodies were stacked in bloody heaps where the cannon had caught them and laid out in tidy rows where the T-2s had cut them down. Haddad looked out over the battlefield in stunned amazement. "Congratulations, Captain, it looks like you won your first battle."

Calvo was afraid to speak lest her voice crack. She heard

Farner report that six legionnaires were dead, and four more had been wounded. The butcher's bill had been light, all things considered, but what about the next attack? And the one after that? How long could they hold before they were overwhelmed?

There was no answer, just the unrelenting heat and occasional gunshot as the troops put wounded animals out of their misery and directed the harried medics to warriors who needed medical attention. The maintenance officer sighed and went back to work.

The southern edge of the Grass Path, Planet Savas

The jungle and the desert had been at war for hundreds of thousands of years, which meant that the margins of the grasslands that separated them had been conquered many times before. Now, thanks to the interaction between conditions in the planet's atmosphere and major ocean currents, the desert was pushing great fingers of sand down from the north, and the jungle was in retreat. The savanna, which the Paguumi called the Grass Path, had migrated accordingly. It was dry, though, and what had once been a continuous band of rich green grass was interrupted by peninsulas of invading sand.

And it was there, at the point where the grass and scattered trees gave way to the thick jungle vegetation, that three raggedy figures stumbled out onto the savanna and collapsed. Kuga-Ka's uniform was ripped in various places, he'd lost forty pounds, and been forced to improvise a pair of sandals after his boots gave out. All he had left was the life-support pack, Corporal Mora Haaby's brain box, his assault rifle, sixteen rounds of ammunition, and a machete.

Knifethrow had acquired some sort of fungus, which though not evolved to feed on the Naa race, found the off-world organism to its liking. As a result large sections of the deserter's fur had fallen out, leaving significant islands of irritated skin. He carried an assault weapon, forty-six rounds of ammo, and two well-honed knives.

Sawicki had a bloodstained battle dressing tied around his head. It was three days old, but there weren't any more. The human had lost a significant amount of weight, had constant diarrhea, and felt cold even though it was warm.

The .50 caliber sniper's rifle, the weapon he happened to be carrying when the RAV blew up, lay at his side. The long gun had proven useless for hunting, since the huge slugs had a pronounced tendency to blow small game into even smaller pieces and frequently got caught in the jungle foliage. Kuga-Ka had insisted that he keep the weapon, however, so the human had, along with thirty-two rounds of ammunition. "Damn," Sawicki said feelingly, "it feels good to get out of that frigging jungle."

"Yeah," Knifethrow agreed as he looked out over the ocean of grass, "except what do we do now?"

Kuga-Ka lay on his back and stared up into the sky. Although it sounded rhetorical, the ex-noncom knew that the question was directed at him and fought a sudden surge of anger. How dare the mangy furball question his leadership! Sometimes he wanted to grab the Naa, twist his ugly head off, and pee into the hole. But that would be tantamount to slamming his assault weapon against a rock, throwing his machete away, or sharing the vitamins that the other two didn't know he had.

So the Hudathan waited for the resentment to subside and was careful to keep any trace of what he truly felt out of his voice. "Do you remember the flares? The ones we fired when the bugs flew over? Well, we're going to try again. We don't have any flares, not anymore, so we'll use signal fires instead. Once we get their attention, we're going to let the weird-looking bastards fly us north, pay us for our services, and drop us on a nice friendly planet."

Sawicki had wondered why the ex-noncom wanted to signal the Ramanthians, but he'd never mustered the courage to ask, and this seemed like the perfect opportunity. "No offense, gunny, but why would the bugs give us all that stuff? A bullet in the back of the head seems more likely."

"That's true," the Hudathan answered equably, "or would be, except we have something to offer them. We, which is to say I, know why the battalion was sent to Savas."

Knifethrow scratched a patch of badly reddened skin and looked hopeful. "You do? That would be great! Why *did* the brass send us here?"

"To steal something called a hypercom," Kuga-Ka answered lazily. "But once we tell the bugs what Kobbi is after, and provide them with a readout on what the 2nd can throw their way, they'll pound the battalion into bloody mush."

"That'll teach them!" Sawicki said enthusiastically.

"Yes," the Hudathan agreed dreamily. "It certainly will."

Meanwhile, deep within the hole where she lived, Haaby floated in an ocean of blackness. It was lonely there, so lonely she actually looked forward to the times when Kuga-Ka would open the com circuit and torment her. What she feared was not death itself, because she looked forward to that, but dying without getting the chance to kill the Hudathan. So the cyborg waited, her mind adrift, waiting for the only thing she cared about anymore: revenge.

9

In wartime truth is so precious that she should always be attended by a bodyguard of lies.

ATTRIBUTED TO SIR WINSTON CHURCHILL
Date uncertain

The Erini System, Thraki-held Space

Had someone been present to witness the event they would have seen the yellow-orange orb that was the sun, bright points of light that represented the system's planets, and the steely glitter of stars beyond. Then, in the blink of an eye, a hundred ships dropped out of the never-never land of hyperspace to shimmer like spacegoing minnows.

Thanks to the efforts of microscopic nano that had not only been programmed to replicate themselves, but to constantly re-create the huge ships in the same way that a flesh-and-blood body produces new cells, the now-ancient vessels were as good as new. And, even though the enormous constructs were normally served by robotic crews, rudimentary controls had been provided for emergency use. Which was why Thraki Naval Commander Dithi Holaka and a crew of three occupied hard, unpadded chairs, in a control room that was small by even *their* standards, and were happy to have most of the journey behind them.

Vid screens were mounted over gently curving control panels. With the exception of the two officers, each crew member sat with his or her hands thrust inside control tunnels where a matrix of laser beams measured each movement of their fingers and hands. A computer translated the readings into orders that controlled the vessel and its subsystems.

Holaka was fond of good food, a little overweight as a result, and notoriously irritable. A week in hyperspace with nothing to eat but prepackaged rations had done nothing to improve his temper. He slapped at the robotic form that roamed his body and sent the tiny robot diving for the safety of a deep pocket. "All right," he said crossly, "we're here. Check to make sure all of the ships made it through safely."

Myla Suro sighed. Even though she was used to Holaka's cantankerous ways, it would have been nice to hear a "please" or "thank you" every once in a while. The other ninety-nine ships were robotically operated and slaved to the computer on the command vessel. The first officer had already queried her shimmery flock and received the appropriate acknowledgements. "The entire flotilla is in place, sir."

"I'm surprised but gratified to hear it," Holaka replied grumpily. "Let the locals know we're here and set a course for Erini IV... Keep it down to half power until we receive an acknowledgment."

Having no desire to get her rear blown off by an overzealous peer, Suro had sent the codes immediately after dropping hyper, and the reply was coming in. "Yes, sir. All ahead half."

The pilot, who sat with both hands in the nav matrix, gave the necessary orders, and the additional gees pushed the crew back into their unpadded chairs as the entire flotilla turned and accelerated inward. The better part of a day passed before the Sheen ships passed between a pair of heavily armed destroyers and dropped into orbit around the fourth planet from the sun. Most of Erini IV's surface was obscured by clouds, but what could be seen on the control room's screens was brown in color and wrinkled by a continent-spanning mountain range. There were minimal polar caps, some huge lakes, but no oceans.

More than that could not be seen, but Suro knew that the only Thrakies on the planet were there to strip it of minerals, not to construct cities. The minerals that were used to feed the highly automated factories that supplied the orbital shipyards, which serviced the steadily growing segment of the Thraki navy that the Confederacy knew nothing about.

Putting one hundred ships in orbit, and doing so safely, was no small task, which meant that Holaka was downright cranky by the time that the whole process had been completed. Pictograms that showed the command ship's position relative to the orbital repair facility flashed on the screens as the pilot used tiny, almost imperceptible, movements of her fingers to guide the vessel between a pair of enormous blast doors into the zero-gee dock beyond.

Suro held her breath as the vessel glided into position, slowed as the pilot fired a series of braking jets, and came to a full stop. That was when a set of opposing tractor and repellor beams shot out from their various projectors and locked the hull in place. "Not too bad," Holaka commented grudgingly, as his form climbed up onto his shoulder. "Place all systems on standby, delegate control to the dock master, and call for a shuttle. They have a cafeteria here, and I'm hungry."

The dock master's office was high on the back wall, where he could look out through a duraplast window, and watch everything that took place below. What the diminutive civilian couldn't see from there, his robotic spy balls could, and they dashed hither and yon as if competing to see which one could add the most interesting picture to the mosaic of tilelike screens that lined the surrounding bulkheads.

Now, as his Ramanthian guest entered the office, Dock Master Wono bowed in what he understood to be a gesture of respect. "Welcome, Ambassador Orno, it's an honor to meet you."

Orno inclined his head. Although the being in front of him was small, and slightly stooped, his eyes were bright with intelligence. "Thank you. The honor is mine. Foreign Minister Oholo Bintha speaks highly of both you and your facility."

Wono, who was the oldest person on or near Erini IV, offered the Thraki equivalent of a grin. It revealed two rows of extremely sharp teeth. "The foreign minister is very kind. If I'm competent, it's because I'm old enough to have made every possible error and learned from my mistakes."

Orno produced a series of clicks that the Thraki knew to be laughter. He gestured toward the window. "Please step over here, Mr. Ambassador. As you can see, the first ship has entered the bay. All of the necessary equipment has been manufactured according to the specs provided by your navy and is waiting in orbit. The robotic systems will be removed and new ones installed."

In keeping with orders from above, Wono made no mention of the fact that specs for all of the Ramanthian systems had been shared with Thraki intelligence officials, or that each vessel would be thoroughly bugged prior to delivery. After all, just because the two races were on friendly terms today, didn't mean that they would be tomorrow.

Orno looked out into the enormous bay, saw that all manner of robotic equipment was already closing around the hull, and felt a profound sense of satisfaction. Soon, within a matter of months, the Ramanthian navy would be a hundred vessels stronger. After that they would retrofit another group of ships, and *another*, until all of them were ready to defend their new masters. The diplomat's thoughts were interrupted as Wono cleared his throat. "Not to be crass, but I was told to expect a down payment, and would like to get that out of the way."

"Of course," Orno said obligingly, "I will order my crew to remove the chests from my ship. Cash is a bit unusual... but these are unusual times."

"Yes," the Thraki said, looking at the Ramanthian's insectoid body. "They certainly are."

Planet Algeron, the Confederacy of Sentient Beings
In spite of the fact that Fort Camerone's theater had been retrofitted to serve as Senate's chambers, it still looked like what it was: a large box-shaped room with a slanting floor, five hundred folding seats, and a raised stage. The words "Legio patria nostra" had been painted over—but anyone with a sharp eye could make them out through the cream-colored paint.

President Nankool stood at the podium and waited for the politicians to walk, strut, and whir into the room. Even though the venue had changed, the Senate was the same. That meant it consisted of the same factious, squabbling, and often petty beings it had before, all except for ex-Senator Alway Orno, that is, who though no longer present, continued to be a source of trouble. In fact, the entire morning had been devoted to debating the question of whether there was enough evidence to try the treacherous bug for mass murder, destruction of government property, and grand theft in absentia, or whether it would be necessary to capture him first. All of which was understandable, but unfortunate, given all of the other high-priority agenda items awaiting the senators' attention.

But Nankool was a skilled politician which meant that even as the master-at-arms brought the gavel down and called for order, the strategy that he and key members of the Senate's leadership had devised was already in place. A respected senator made a motion to table the matter while a committee of judicial experts took a look at relevant precedents. There was a second, followed by a vote, and the measure was approved by a razor-thin margin. But a win is a win, and Nankool took the opportunity to bolster morale by introducing the Prithian representative, Senator Itnor Ikaka.

Like most of his peers, the brightly plumed politician loved the spotlight and strutted to the podium, where he ruffled his feathers and scanned the audience with saucerlike yellow eyes. He had an excellent command of standard speak, a deep, booming voice, and an undeniable stage presence. "War is a terrible thing, but so is systematic evil. To see evil, yet tolerate it, is to participate in it. Therefore, after careful consideration, the High Council has decided that Prithia will ally itself with those battling the Ramanthian empire."

There was a loud cheer, followed by all manner of applause, as the vast majority of those present came to their feet for a standing ovation. One of those present, a senior diplomat named Charles Vanderveen, had spoken with Ikaka the evening before. Because of that he knew that while his daughter would never receive credit for stimulating the High Council to reevaluate their position, it wouldn't have happened without her intervention, and the knowledge made him feel proud. He was the last person to stop clapping.

Booly, who was standing at the back of the room, clapped as well but not so enthusiastically. Though fierce fighters, the Prithians were not a populous race and had no navy other than three squadrons of ships that would be forced to remain in orbit around their home world lest the Ramanthians attack it. So, while the announcement would produce some positive headlines, the Prithians wouldn't be able to provide much help. The officer felt someone arrive at his side and turned to find Lieutenant Thinklong standing there. "Yes, Lieutenant? What's up?"

The Naa whispered into Booly's ear, the general's eyes widened, and he nodded. "Put them in my conference room. Send for Xanith, Leeger, Hykin. Oh, and put in a call for Admiral Chien-Chu as well... I'll meet them there in ten minutes."

The aide nodded, said, "Yes, sir," and slipped away. Booly took a moment to contact Nankool's administrative assistant and reserve a fifteen-minute slot on the president's schedule for later that afternoon. Whatever came out of the meeting in the conference room would have to be approved, and with so many beings vying for the president's attention, getting some face time could be tough. Everyone else had arrived and taken seats by the time Booly stepped through the door, and Leeger said, "Atten-hut!"

Booly said, "As you were," waved everyone back into their seats, and went to the head of the table. Besides Xanith, Leeger, Hykin, Chien-Chu, and Thinklong, four additional people were present in the room. The Naa hurried to introduce two of them. The others, a corporal and a private, were there in their capacity as guards. They wore sidearms and stood at parade rest behind the prisoner.

"General," Thinklong said, "I would like to introduce Captain Marvin Posson and Citizen Teeg Jackson, both of whom arrived from Savas about an hour ago."

"Welcome to Algeron," Booly said, his gaze shifting from the man in civilian clothing back to the naval officer. "I understand you had to dodge some bugs in order to get here."

"Yes, sir," Posson replied, well aware of the fact that there were two admirals in the room. "I was in command of one of the two transports that took Colonel Kobbi and his battalion to Savas. Unfortunately, both ships were damaged going in. My crew and I managed to land the *Spirit of Natu*, but the *Mothri Sun* crashed. Fortunately, all of her crew and passengers survived. Later my ship was destroyed as well.

"Citizen Jackson is a deserter, but he had a good ship, and Colonel Kobbi prevailed upon him to bring me here."

Booly raised an eyebrow. "'*Prevailed*' on him?"

Posson smiled. "Colonel Kobbi can be quite persuasive when he wants to be. It should be said that while Jackson is a smuggler, he's also one helluva pilot and deserves a great deal of credit for getting us out. The bugs pretty much own the Savas system."

It was the first time Posson had ever said anything nice about him, and Jackson was visibly surprised. Now, as Booly looked more closely, he saw that the smuggler wore wrist restraints. "I see… Is citizen Jackson dangerous?"

"No," Posson answered honestly, "I don't think so… But he's a flight risk."

"So noted," Booly replied. "Corporal, remove that man's restraints, but if he tries to run, shoot him in the leg. That goes for the rest of the people in this room."

There was laughter as the corporal removed a remote from a holster on his pistol belt and touched a button. The restraints fell away as if by magic.

"All right," Booly said, "start at the beginning."

So Posson took those present through the battle in space, the subsequent landings, and Kobbi's decision to march north, reconstitute his battalion, and continue with the mission. Booly nodded approvingly and looked at Leeger. "I knew a *Major* Kobbi once. A tough little bastard who was armed with a single swear word that he used all the time. A jacker, if I remember correctly."

"Yes, sir," Leeger acknowledged. "That's him."

"An excellent choice," Booly said thoughtfully. "If anyone can do the job, *he* can. But, assuming he does, how are we going to pull him out? Admiral Hykin? Admiral Chien-Chu? Any suggestions?"

Hykin clenched his jaw. He didn't have any reserves, so there was only one way to go. "Yes, sir. We'll pull the ships out of Task Force Zebra and retask them."

Leeger frowned. "Task Force Zebra? But that would…"

"Excuse me, Colonel," Posson interrupted, "but I would remind you that Citizen Jackson is in the room."

"Good point," Leeger agreed. "Thank you. I'll rephrase the question. Isn't there some less critical mission that we could rob?"

Hykin was about to say, "No," when Chien-Chu chose to clear his nonexistent throat. While Hykin had been talking, the industrialist had been consulting his onboard computer. "Perhaps I could help… While most of my company's ships are occupied transporting raw materials and finished products for the war effort, I believe we still have a couple of hulls that were slated for the scrap yards. They aren't very economical to run, and they aren't very pretty, but I doubt that Colonel Kobbi and his legionnaires would care. My niece would have to agree, of course… but I have reason to believe that she would honor a request from General Booly."

Everyone with the exception of Jackson and the two enlisted men laughed. "I have less influence than you might think," Booly replied, "but I'll see what I can do. We're going to need some escorts, though, so find them, and that's an order."

Hykin gave a short jerky nod, wondered which task force to steal the warships from and who would die as a result.

Planet Starfall, the Confederacy of Sentient Beings

Triad Hiween Doma-Sa hated parties, especially ones thrown in his honor, like the affair in full swing within the human embassy. A vast affair complete with the sort of decorations Hudathans never used, a band playing music that hurt his ears, and hordes of aliens. Fortunately, the being or beings responsible for organizing the torture seemed to have some knowledge of Hudathan psychology and had been careful to position the receiving line so that the huge head of state could stand with his back to a solid wall rather than out in the open. Some xenoanthropologists claimed that the racial paranoia stemmed from the extremely varied weather conditions on

Hudatha, not to mention the feudalism of the recent past, but the fact that both of Doma-Sa's peers had died violent deaths certainly had something to do with his caution as well.

Still, whatever comfort the Hudathan felt as a result of having a wall at his back was more than balanced out by the roar of conversation, the stench of alien food, and the endless procession of repulsive flesh. However, now that Doma-Sa's race had been allowed to emerge from isolation, he knew that such rituals were necessary to reassure the diplomatic community as to his people's intentions.

A Prithian squawked something unintelligible, passed on, and gave way to a human female. Ithnu Buno-Sa, the Hudathan ambassador to the Thraki people, made the necessary announcement. "It is my honor to introduce Ambassador Kay Wilmot."

The human extended her hand, and Doma-Sa engulfed it with his. There were very few humans that the head of state respected, Sergi Chien-Chu being among them, because most members of the species were weak and insipid. The female who stood before him clearly fit that category as she gushed nonsense about how much she respected Hudathan culture, how she hoped he would find time to meet with her, and the wonderful things they could accomplish together.

Doma-Sa responded with a curt bow and fervently wished that she would drop dead right there in front of him. When that failed to take place, he said, "It's a pleasure to meet you, Ambassador... My calendar is quite full, but I'll ask my staff to check and see if something is available."

Wilmot mistook the polite "No" for a "Yes," felt Doma-Sa release her hand, and allowed herself to be ushered away from the line.

Christine Vanderveen stepped into the space vacated by her superior and heard her name announced. "Foreign Service Officer Christine Vanderveen."

Vanderveen knew what she was about to do was wrong, knew it would result in dismissal if Wilmot learned of it, but was willing to take that chance. It was clear that the Thrakies had cut some sort of illicit deal with the Ramanthians, and while

Wilmot could be expected to prevent such information from being passed up the line, she couldn't interfere with Doma-Sa.

That was the idea, at least, but now, as the human looked at the alien's hard eyes, craggy features, and thin-lipped mouth, she started to have second thoughts. But it was too late by then as her hand continued the journey that it had already begun, Doma-Sa's sausagelike fingers closed around hers, and the tiny disk pressed against the surface of his palm.

If the Hudathan was surprised, there was no sign of it in his face as he gave a characteristically abbreviated bow. His voice had a deep, gravelly quality. "I am pleased to meet you, Ms. Vanderveen. I am acquainted with another diplomat having the same clan name. Your father perhaps?"

Buno-Sa took note of the fact that his superior had yet to release the human's hand and was actually taking a moment to speak with her. Although he had never spent any time with the triad before, Doma-Sa had a well-established reputation for strange behavior, and now the diplomat saw why.

"Yes, sir," Vanderveen answered simply. "Charles Vanderveen is my father."

"To the best of my knowledge he never lied to me," the Hudathan replied evenly. "A remarkable accomplishment for one of his breed."

Vanderveen couldn't tell whether the "breed" that Doma-Sa referred to consisted of diplomats, humans, or both. She nodded. "My father says that truth is the only currency that has real value."

"And he's correct," Doma-Sa agreed as he let go of Vanderveen's hand. "Please give him my best."

The diplomat said, "Thank you," and was so busy thinking about the unexpected interchange, that she was five feet away when she remembered the disk. A quick look at her hand confirmed what she already knew. The coin-sized disk was gone.

It wasn't just raining as Vanderveen walked to work the next morning, it was *pouring*, and the streets were filled with Thrakies and their pyramid-shaped umbrellas. The locals didn't like to get wet, not one little bit, and hurried to get wherever they were going. Vanderveen didn't mind the rain, but was suffering from severe guilt pangs as she passed through security and entered the embassy. Though motivated by the best of intentions, the effort to contact Doma-Sa had clearly been misguided, and might even cause problems rather than solve them. Thanks to efforts by people like President Nankool, Sergi Chien-Chu, and her father, the Confederacy's relationship with the once-hostile Hudathans had improved greatly over the last few years. What if the message on the disk did something to alter that? Perhaps she should schedule a meeting with Wilmot, confess her sins, and suffer the consequences.

Such were the FSO's thoughts as she left the elevator, made her way down the hall, and entered her office. That was when Vanderveen saw that Wilmot was not only there, but sitting at her subordinate's desk, wearing a scowl. "Well, it's about damned time."

Vanderveen glanced at her watch. "I'm half an hour early."

"You're a lying, cheating, little bitch," Wilmot replied. "Explain the meaning of *this*."

Vanderveen took a couple of steps forward, accepted the printout, and scanned the words in front of her. The message was from the Hudathan embassy—and dated four hours earlier. What the FSO expected to see was the full text of what she had given Doma-Sa—and she was happy to be wrong. The copy read: "His excellency, Triad Hiween Doma-Sa, requests the pleasure of Foreign Service Officer Christine Vanderveen's presence at 1000 hours (local) this morning, at the Hudathan embassy." And it had been signed by none other than the imperious Ambassador Buno-Sa. Wilmot's peer. Vanderveen felt her fear turn to anger. "You've been monitoring my electronic communications."

"That's right," Wilmot replied tersely, "which I have every right to do if I think it's necessary. Read the regs sometime... They spell out what an FSO-4 can do. Playing diplomatic footsie with a head of state isn't one of them," Wilmot said grimly. "I repeat... what is the meaning of this outrage?"

Vanderveen remembered what Doma-Sa had said regarding her father's honesty even as the half-truth formed itself on her lips. "Triad Doma-Sa is an old friend of my father's. This so-called outrage is nothing more than a courtesy call."

Vanderveen's response was so smooth, so mundane, that Wilmot was left with little choice but to believe it. And then, having confronted what she believed to be the truth, to realize the extent to which she had embarrassed herself. With nothing to say, and no way in which to save face, the diplomat stood and stormed out of the room.

It took a full minute for Vanderveen's pulse to slow, but when it finally did, she couldn't help but smile.

Rather than an embassy the structure the Hudathans had commissioned on Starfall looked more like a three-story duracrete bunker than what it actually was. And, as Vanderveen struggled to exit the small Thraki-sized robocab, she was struck by the extent to which the low, blocky-looking building matched what she knew of the Hudathan psyche. As she approached the huge doors, adjectives like "hard," "wary," and "defensive" came to mind.

One of the enormous durasteel doors sensed the human's presence and slid out of the way. That was when she entered a locklike chamber, where a pair of brusque Hudathan troopers ordered the human to step through a screening device, eyed their screens, and reluctantly allowed her to pass.

From there Vanderveen entered a Hudathan-sized lobby and had no choice but to confront the mountain of flesh and blood who sat behind a barricade-like reception desk. He frowned ominously as the diplomat gave her name, consulted a data screen, and uttered a single word: "Wait."

The reception area was empty of chairs, plants, and art. All there was to look at were duracrete walls, stone floors, and durasteel fittings. The human smiled. "Nice decor... Who is your decorator?"

The Hudathan frowned. "What is a 'decorator'?" Vanderveen was about to reply when a second Hudathan arrived on the scene. He was a smaller specimen, weighing only 250 pounds or so, and part of the so-called new clan of government officials that Doma-Sa was trying to create. He recruited youngsters for the most part, well-educated individuals who were willing to abandon the clans into which they had been born, to accept membership in a new group bound together by a common vision, dedication to those they served, and the rule of law. It wasn't possible for a Hudathan to smile, not really, but the official did the best he could. "Ms. Vanderveen? Good morning. My name is Rinwa Molo-Sa. I am one of the triad's aides. His excellency's schedule is extremely full… but he agreed to see you while he takes his morning exercise. I hope that's acceptable."

"Of course," Vanderveen agreed. "It was very kind of him to see me at all."

Molo-Sa didn't say anything, but clearly agreed, as he led the human around the reception desk and down a long, highly polished hallway. Finally, at the very end, the Hudathan offered her a small device and pointed to a door. "His excellency is in there. When your audience is over, please press the button, and I will escort you out."

Vanderveen could have found her own way out, but knew it was a security precaution and slipped the device into a pocket. What she *didn't* know was that it contained an explosive charge that Doma-Sa could detonate with a simple voice command.

The door slid out of the way, and the diplomat entered a well-appointed gymnasium. The air was cool but heavy with the rank odor of Hudathan sweat. Heavy feet thumped the wooden floorboards as a pair of Hudathans fought each other. Or that's what Vanderveen *thought* she saw, until she realized that the aliens were identical, and only one of them was real. The hologram swung his sword, which caused the flesh-and-blood version to duck a potentially lethal blow.

It was relatively cool inside, which meant that the Hudathan's skin was gray. Now, nearly stripped of clothing, Vanderveen could see how large the head of state truly was. Leather cross-straps bulged where they met at the center of his chest, muscles rippled along massive arms, and his legs were like twin pillars.

The diplomat's father had been present for the now-famous duel on the surface of Arballa, when Doma-Sa had battled one of Ambassador Alway Orno's mates, and what had been a matter of politics was transformed into something intensely personal. In fact it was her father's account of the fight, plus the head of state's timely visit to Starfall, that triggered Vanderveen's attempt to enlist Doma-Sa's assistance.

The sword, an ancient weapon named Head Taker, had been handed down through Doma-Sa's family the way all things were. *By force*. It had two edges, one straight and one with teeth. Metal flashed, and the real Doma-Sa was forced to jump into the air as his double attempted to take him off at the knees.

There was a realistic cry of anguish as the head of state hacked downward, sliced through his opponent's collarbone, and cut deep into the other Doma-Sa's chest. That was when the holo exploded into a thousand motes of light, which sparkled as they disappeared. Doma-Sa turned to greet his visitor. "Good morning. Thank you for coming on such short notice."

Vanderveen shook her head. "No, Excellency. It's I who should thank you."

"Maybe, and maybe not," the Hudathan answered. "Like my sword, your visit could cut two ways. You may live to regret it."

"Yes," the human acknowledged soberly. "In some ways I already do."

Doma-Sa's craggy brow rose a fraction of an inch. "Really? Then why come?"

Vanderveen thought for a moment. "All of us battle ourselves. You do it with a sword. I fight battles in my mind."

The Hudathan gave his deepest bow. "You are wise beyond your years. Come... You will talk, and I will listen."

Five minutes later the human diplomat found herself in a private dining room where Doma-Sa sat down to breakfast and she was served what turned out to be a surprisingly good cup of coffee. "All right," the Hudathan said, as he tucked into an enormous bowl of what looked like steaming oatmeal, "start at the beginning. I want to hear *everything*."

So Vanderveen told the head of state about the party, her trip to the restroom, and the liaison between her boss and a certain Clone. Doma-Sa stopped eating long enough to utter the Hudathan equivalent of a chuckle. "No wonder you were hesitant to share the information with your superior."

Vanderveen nodded, felt another pang of guilt, and managed to suppress it. With the situational material out of the way, the diplomat told Doma-Sa about the meeting between the Thraki foreign minister, Oholo Bintha, and the Ramanthian ambassador, Alway Orno. She finished with the details of the financial part of the deal, the mutually beneficial trade agreements that were supposed to follow.

A human, or a Dweller, might have reacted with surprise and anger, but Doma-Sa was Hudathan and therefore *expected* those around him to be treacherous. He wiped his mouth with a napkin the size of a dish towel. "Someone will catch up with Ambassador Orno one of these days, and I hope that person is me. In the meantime we need to expose the Thrakies for the liars they are… and force them to sever the relationship with the Ramanthians. That will slow efforts to retrofit the Sheen fleet, buy the Confederacy some much-needed time, and aid the war effort. Doing so will require two things, good intelligence and a bit of muscle. You supply the first… and I'll take care of the second. Agreed?"

Vanderveen took a sip of coffee. It suddenly tasted bitter. Intelligence? How would she get that? Especially with Wilmot looking over her shoulder. But she was committed by that time, so there was nothing to do but nod. "Yes, Excellency. We are agreed."

The Hive System, the Ramanthian Empire

There were 642 observatories in orbit around Hive's sun, which sounded like a lot, but given the vastness of space were comparable to individual atoms in an ocean of black seawater. Though normally focused on scientific research, the advent of the war had caused the platforms to be "repurposed." Now, like it or not, each tiny space station had been transformed into a two-person observation post.

So, when an alarm went off, and the onboard computer informed astronomer Hotho Ackla that the observatory's sensors had detected an intruder, the scientist dropped what he was doing to scan the heavens for an invading fleet. Within a matter of moments a powerful telescope and other sensors were focused on the object in question, and data began to arrive. It soon became apparent that rather than a ravening horde of barbaric humans, Ackla had discovered a heretofore-undocumented short-period comet.

But, even though it was clear that the incoming object was something other than a fleet of bloodthirsty Hudathans, there was something else to be concerned about. Based on data gathered so far, the comet was going to pass within a few million units of Hive. Nothing to cause much concern, especially given the object's small size, but still worthy of note. For that reason, Ackla added his observations to the report that he and his companion sent out every eight days, then went back to work on his *real* love, which was electro-magnetic radiation.

The ship that constituted Moya Frenko's body looked more like a spaceborne chemical plant than the warship it actually was. The vessel consisted of six globe-shaped tanks, positioned in two rows of three each and connected by a cylindrical cross member to form the letter H. Powerful engines, both mounted aft of the trailing tanks, provided in-system propulsion.

But, unsightly though they might be, the tanks were necessary if the *Flaming Bitch* was going to pass for a comet. The big globe-shaped containers held a highly pressurized mixture of gases, which, when released through nozzles and injected with dust particles, created a long tail similar to that of a comet. The guise wouldn't hold forever, the mission planners knew that, and so did Moya. But it didn't matter. All the *Bitch* had to do was penetrate far enough to close with Hive, plunge through the atmosphere, and hit the ground.

There were targets, plenty of them, but any sort of touchdown would do. The whole point of Operation Deep Strike was to scare the crap out of the bugs, force them to pull naval assets back into their home system, and boost the Confederacy's morale.

That's why the possibility of a full crew had been rejected in favor of a single cyborg, an officer with combat experience, who was the sole survivor of a battle with a Ramanthian cruiser. A woman who had been killed once—and wasn't afraid to die again. The truth was that Lieutenant Commander Moya Frenko was a little crazy, a little *too* focused on revenge, which was exactly what the mission called for. A guidance system that cared, was capable of hate, and could improvise if called upon to do so.

And so the goddess of death fell through the emptiness of space, her long silvery hair streaming out behind her, mind focused on a pinpoint of distant light. That's where the Ramanthians were—and that's where Frenko was determined to go. Victory may be sweet—but payback is a bitch.

The Erini System, Thraki-held Space

In spite of the fact that the Hudathans weren't supposed to have any ships as part of the peace pact that Doma-Sa had negotiated with the Confederacy, a few had been manufactured out beyond the rim and crewed by the offspring of veterans from the last war. The *Deceiver* was one such vessel, and ironically enough, the stealth technology that theoretically made her invisible to conventional sensors had been illicitly acquired from the Thrakies more than a year before.

Vanderveen felt the usual moment of nausea as the Hudathan warship dropped out of hyperspace and into the Erini system. But rather than disappear as it usually did, the hollow feeling was still there well after the transition was over, and the diplomat knew why. She was scared. And for good reason. Having secured Doma-Sa's promise to help expose the true nature of the relationship between the Ramanthians and Thrakies, she had needed intelligence about where the clandestine conversions were taking place. Unfortunately, the diplomat didn't have the foggiest notion of how to obtain it. Not until she spotted Wilmot and her Clone lover sneaking off for a three-hour lunch and had a moment of inspiration. After hostilities between the Clones and the Thrakies, the relationship had warmed once again, which meant that even if she couldn't come up with the necessary information, Jonathan Alan Seebo-11,602 probably could. Especially if the right sort of pressure was applied to him.

Having lied to the ambassador and withheld information

from her as well, the FSO-4 proceeded to compound her crimes by blackmailing Wilmot's lover into using his position in the Hegemony's armed forces to learn where the conversions might take place. For there was no greater sin within the highly regimented Clone culture than for an individual to have free breeder sex and thereby run the risk of creating a functionless life. So, rather than face the possibility that Vanderveen would rat him out, Wilmot's lover handed over three sets of coordinates, two of which had already proven to be wrong.

Now, as the *Deceiver* entered Erini system, it was the diplomat's last chance to succeed. Failure would not only bring disgrace to her, but to her father as well, given all the unethical things that she had done. So even though it made sense to be scared, the knowledge did nothing to make her feel any better, as the crew waited to see if the ship would be challenged.

But it seemed that the Thraki stealth generator that lay at the heart of the ship's defensive capabilities was working because even though the *Deceiver*'s sensors registered the presence of other ships in-system, no attempt had been made to contact the Hudathan vessel. Vanderveen was seated in an enormous chair at the rear of the control room. Doma-Sa swiveled to look at her. "Everything looks good so far. Most of the system's electromechanical activity seems to be centered around the fourth planet from the sun. We'll start with that."

The human nodded, felt some additional gees, and awaited her fate.

The Thraki picket ship hung motionless in space, its stealth generator on, its sensors reaching out to monitor electromechanical activity within a full quarter of the Erini system. Not because the Thrakies were expecting trouble but because the admiral with responsibility for the sector was so cautious that he often wore a belt and suspenders. A habit that seemed to have stood him in good stead since no one had ever seen the officer with his pants down.

More than that, Admiral Nukama was a crafty soul, who was well aware of the fact that rather than reserve Thraki-developed stealth technology for the military, thereby ensuring that the navy would have an important edge over potential enemies, his civilian counterparts had sold it to anyone who had sufficient money or political leverage. Which explained why Nukama not only placed obvious picket ships around Erini IV, but salted the area with vessels like the Ghost-class PSS-789 as well, hoping that intruders would focus their attention on what they could electronically "see" and thereby give themselves away.

All of which was fine in theory, except that it hadn't worked, not yet anyway. That's why Nubu Harl, the tech on duty, yawned when the alarm went off, flipped a series of switches, and waited for the system to clear itself. False readings were common, and there was no reason to believe that this one would be any different.

But it *was* different, something that quickly became apparent as a series of readings scrolled onto the screen in front of her, and Harl summoned her commanding officer. Flight Warrior Stee Hoso was an industrious sort who had a tendency to take everything a bit too seriously. Still, that was a good characteristic where the business of threat detection was concerned, and he frowned when he saw the screen. Not just because someone equipped with stealth technology was approaching Erini IV, but because the readings suggested a ship unlike anything cataloged in the Thraki data banks, which constituted a threat in and of itself. "Shall I summon the crew to battle stations?" Harl inquired hopefully, eager for some excitement.

"Yes," Hoso replied, "but leave all the weapons on standby. Let's follow our visitor for a while and see what he's interested in. *Then* we'll take him out."

It was a good plan, a smart plan, and Harl felt confident as she touched a button, heard the klaxon, and sent the balance of the small crew to their battle stations. The hunt was on.

Thanks to the Thraki-manufactured stealth generator, the *Deceiver* was able to slip between the picket ships guarding the approach to Erini IV and drop into high orbit. Meanwhile, Thraki vessels came and went all around them, seemingly unaware of the spy in their midst, as Vanderveen continued to hold her breath. The human had never been so frightened. But if the Hudathans felt the same way, the huge aliens gave no sign of it as they activated the ship's sensors and started to collect information on the number of ships in orbit, the way they were configured, com traffic, surface installations on the planet itself, and much more. "There they are," a tech said matter-of-factly. "The force fields must be set low, just enough to block orbital debris, but you can see the telltale shimmer."

Vanderveen felt a sense of triumph as she looked up at the main screen and saw a much-enlarged image of three alien warships floating over the heavily marbled planetscape below. They were Sheen ships all right—and the energy fields that protected them flickered as tiny bits of matter hit them. "We've got them!" the human said excitedly. "You're recording this?"

"Of course we are," Doma-Sa replied matter-of-factly, "but I can't say that I agree with your overall assessment. This proves the Thrakies have some ships they aren't supposed to have, and while that might prove embarrassing, there's no link to the Ramanthians. And that's what we came here to find."

Vanderveen's previously high spirits plummeted as she realized that the Hudathan was correct. Though suspicious, there was nothing to connect the ships to the bugs other than the fact that the Ramanthians had stolen them. Something was better than nothing, but the thought of taking her evidence to higher authorities, only to have them pick it apart, was more than the diplomat could bear. She was casting about for ideas when the docking facility loomed ahead. It was huge, and the evidence she was looking for could easily be inside. "Does the *Deceiver* have a lifeboat?"

"Two of them," Doma-Sa confirmed, as the Hudathan looked back over his shoulder. "Why?"

"Because there's lots of traffic," the human replied, pointing to a screen on which a multiplicity of vessels were being tracked. "Something small, like a lifeboat, might be able to get in closer than the *Deceiver* can. If we could capture video of a Ramanthian ship near the docking facility, or find some other connection, it would make all the difference when we present our report to the Senate."

Doma-Sa understood the need even better than Vanderveen did—and was busy considering the diplomat's idea when a tech interrupted his thoughts. "The Thrakies are on to us! I had a visual on a ship that doesn't register on our sensors! It's following about fifty units astern."

Doma-Sa hit the release on his harness and stood. "Ms. Vanderveen and I will take one of the lifeboats. Break orbit the moment we depart. Lead the Thraki ship into space. You can return for us later."

The plan had flaws, *lots* of them, not the least of which was allowing the Hudathan ruler to take off on a mission fit for a junior officer. The ship's CO was about to say as much when a warning tone sounded and a ship-to-ship missile exploded against the *Deceiver*'s shields. The warship shook like a thing possessed. "Come on!" Doma-Sa yelled as he lurched aft. "Let's go!"

Vanderveen released her harness, came to her feet, and followed as the Hudathan thundered down the main corridor toward the launch bay. "They'll need a pilot!" the stealth ship's commanding officer shouted, gesturing to his second officer. "Go!"

By the time Doma-Sa and Vanderveen entered the bay, the pilot had caught up with the unlikely pair and waved them forward. "The number two boat is best! Follow me!"

The deck tilted as the *Deceiver* took evasive action, shuddered as a quick flurry of energy bolts pounded the protective energy shields, and jerked as the vessel fired, in self-defense. Servos whined as the lifeboat's main hatch closed, the single in-system drive came on, and the pilot spoke into his mike. "We're ready to launch."

Cognizant of the fact that he would not only have to open the launch bay door, but drop the ship's shield in order to launch the lifeboat, the commanding officer winced. But there was nothing he could do except give the necessary order, cut power to the energy field, and hope for the best.

The lifeboat was gone in the twinkling of an eye, and the launch bay door had already started to close, when a Thraki torpedo shot through the opening, hit the port bulkhead, and exploded. An orange-red flower bloomed, lived its short life, and was forever snuffed from existence. The *Deceiver* and her crew were gone.

Doma-Sa swore bitterly as the tiny ship darted away from the explosion and started to close with the free-floating dock. Warning lights strobed, directional signs flashed, and nav lights blinked as the Hudathan lifeboat weaved its way through the heavy traffic to close with the facility ahead. "Look!" Vanderveen said, pointing up at the main screen. "They have a Sheen ship in the dock."

The Hudathan head of state saw that the human was correct—and saw something else as well. "Do you see the one-person sleds? The ones shaped like cylinders? Aren't those bugs riding them?"

Vanderveen looked and saw that Doma-Sa was correct. Ramanthian space armor was just as distinctive as were the aliens themselves. "Yes! Could we capture one of them? That would give us the proof we need."

The pilot swore silently as he conned the tiny ship between the enormous blast doors and into the dock's brightly lit interior. His name was Reem Boka-Ka, and he wasn't sure which passenger was worse, the little alien with the high voice or the hulking triad in the copilot's seat. "You heard the human," Doma-Sa said in Hudathan. "We need to capture one of those bugs."

The word was out by then, and not only were all of the utility craft scuttling for cover, the Ramanthians were trying to clear the area as well. "Damn!" the pilot said, as two lines of energy bolts stuttered over the top of the hull. "We have a fighter on our tail!"

"Ignore him," Doma-Sa ordered grimly. "Go after one of those sleds... I'll spear the bastard with a tractor beam. Once we have him, you can make a run for it."

Boka-Ka was going to die, he knew that now, and accepted it. He chose one of the targets, jinked to throw his pursuer off, and bored in. His quarry was crossing the pilot's field of vision from left to right and moving rather slowly.

Ipra Tychno was one of more than fifty technical experts sent to monitor the conversion process, and because he had accidentally turned his com set off, he hadn't heard the warnings broadcast by traffic control.

Therefore, it wasn't until the Hudathan lifeboat was already closing in on him, and a burst of Thraki cannon fire whipped past his head, that the Ramanthian realized that something unusual was taking place. He opened the throttle on his sled and felt it surge forward, but the effort came too late. A pair of invisible arms reached out to grab on to the engineer's sled and pull it in.

The tractor beams were normally used to moor the lifeboat to larger ships, or to manipulate small objects, but it took skill to operate two opposing joysticks and Doma-Sa made a mistake. One of the beams slipped off, Tychno fell free, and was quick to take advantage of the fact. Thrilled by his miraculous escape, and planning to take cover among the maze of installations that covered the Sheen ship's hull, the Ramanthian steered the sled in that direction. "I lost him!" Doma-Sa shouted. "Get the bastard!"

The Thraki fighter was so close that Boka-Ka felt he had no choice but to ignore the order, pull up, and roll in behind his pursuer. Human lifeboats weren't armed, but the Hudathan equivalents were, and the small craft had a pair of forward-firing energy cannons. They burped coherent light, the fighter took a bolt up its tailpipe, and blew up. The lifeboat's shields flared as it passed through the debris field and shot out the other side.

Doma-Sa could be quite unreasonable at times and slammed a massive fist onto the console. "Quit showing off! Are you deaf? I want the bug!"

Boka-Ka didn't have time to reply. He put the ship into a tight turn, reacquired the target, and applied more power. Doma-Sa spotted the still-fleeing Ramanthian, grabbed him for a second time, and wrapped the sled in an unbreakable hug. "All right! I've got him! Let's get out of here!"

The pilot didn't need to be told twice. He put the lifeboat into a sweeping turn, headed back toward the enormous blast doors, and saw that they had started to close. The Thrakies were trying to lock the invading ship inside the dock! Boka-Ka opened the throttle all the way, bit his lower lip, and tried to gauge his chances. Would the lifeboat slip through? Or slam into solid durasteel? It was too close to call.

Vanderveen watched the slit narrow to what looked like a vertical crack. The human grabbed hold of the huge armrests and closed her eyes. There was a moment of silence followed by a grunt of acknowledgment from Doma-Sa and some rare words of praise. "Not bad."

The human opened her eyes as the lifeboat sailed through a sixty-foot-wide gap, realized that they were through, and heaved a sigh of relief. They were alive!

Tychno, who had witnessed the entire sequence from outside the hull, legs still clamped around the cylindrical sled, discovered that he had soiled the inside of his space armor. The stench was incredible.

But the wild ride wasn't over. The lifeboat was equipped with a hyperdrive, but it would be necessary to escape Erini IV's gravity well before the fugitives could use it, and there were dozens of Thraki vessels in the way. Fortunately, most of them couldn't open fire without running the risk of hitting each other. Boka-Ka took advantage of that fact for as long as he could before shooting out into space with three fighters on his tail. Then, the moment the lifeboat was clear of the planet's gravitational influence, he stabbed a button. The fighter pilots saw the Hudathan vessel shimmer and vanish even as their missiles flew through the space it had occupied only moments before.

That much was good—but what about the Ramanthian clamped to the outside surface of the hull? Would he be able to survive within the protective force field that surrounded the lifeboat? Or would the strange environment of hyperspace scramble his organs like a breakfast omelet? There was no way to know. But one thing was for sure, no matter which way it went, the entire effort was riding on the alien's fate. Because if they lost their prisoner and came out of hyperspace empty-handed, there would be no way to prove an alliance between the Thrakies and Ramanthians. The weight of that knowledge rode Vanderveen's shoulders like a mantle of lead.

Planet Algeron, the Confederacy of Sentient Beings

Six inches of well-churned brown muck covered the road that led between the snow-encrusted domes of Naa Town, up through the strictly maintained free-fire zone, and through the gates of Fort Camerone. The slushy material geysered up around the dooth's plate-sized hooves as the animal plodded up the incline and grunted to communicate how it felt. Conscious of the fact that alien eyes were upon him, Nodoubt Truespeak sat tall in the saddle, eyed the ramparts above, and saw pockmarks where Naa bullets had struck them.

Thousands of Naa had lost their lives trying to conquer the fortress that rose above him, even while thousands more had become part of the very organization that built it and gone off to fight on distant worlds. Only to be treated as second-class citizens by those they fought for. *But not anymore*, the chieftain thought to himself as a sentry uttered a challenge. *Not if I can help it.*

But there was a problem, a *big* problem, because even though the humans seemed willing to accept their former "protectorate" as an equal, other races feared that were the Naa allowed to have their own seat in the Senate, they would vote in concert with their sponsors, even though the entire notion was patently absurd.

Strangely, from his perspective at least, Truespeak had other opponents to worry about as well, including the self-styled true bloods who opposed any sort of congress with the off-worlders and wanted a return to the isolation of the past.

Truespeak dismounted, allowed a human legionnaire to scan him for weapons, and wondered if full-fledged senators were subject to the same indignity. Then, once his companions were back in their saddles, the chieftain led them up to a pair of much-abused durasteel gates. They parted to allow a pair of Trooper IIs to exit, remained open long enough for the Naa to enter, and clanged as they closed.

Lieutenant Thinklong had been detailed to meet the dignitaries and was waiting when Truespeak and his advisors entered the main courtyard. He caught hold of the first dooth's bridle and waited for the chieftain to jump to the ground. "Welcome to Fort Camerone, sir."

"Thank you," Truespeak replied darkly. "I'm happy to report that we didn't have to shoot anyone in order to gain entry."

Thinklong was from another tribe, but was familiar with the other Naa's reputation for straight talk and grinned sympathetically. "I'm sure the Legion is happy about that as well, sir. Private Oki will take care of your mounts. If you and your advisors would be so kind as to follow me, I'll escort you to the Senate's chambers. They're running a bit late, but that's typical, I'm afraid, so it may be necessary to wait for a few minutes."

The Naa allowed themselves to be led into the inner part of the fortress and through a labyrinth of bustling corridors. The walls were confining, like the depths of a cave, or the stomach of some enormous beast. There were strange smells, many of which made Truespeak feel nauseous, and low ceilings that caused him to yearn for the open sky. The only pleasure the Naa felt stemmed from the fact that his leg had healed so well that he could walk without the aid of a cane and thereby avoid any appearance of weakness. Not that passersby turned to look at him because there were so many of his kind in the Legion that the presence of a small group of civilians wasn't considered to be noteworthy.

Finally, after numerous twists and turns, Thinklong led his guests into what had become the Senate's chambers and invited them to seat themselves toward the rear, while the senators continued to debate the merits of two competing tax proposals. Wars cost money, lots of it, and it had to come from somewhere.

Truespeak listened intently, trying to understand the nature of the discussion, but was soon lost in a blizzard of highly specialized terminology. He wondered how long it would take to absorb the knowledge necessary to understand what the senators were talking about and feared that the complexity of the whole thing might be beyond him. But younger, more flexible minds were available, and if given a chance, could surely master the intricacies of interstellar economics. Individuals like Lieutenant Thinklong were evidence of that—and the knowledge gave him comfort.

Meanwhile, not far away, a civilian named Rockfeel Wallstack wheeled a cart of refreshments into the back of the room and removed the sheet that covered the food. Like all true bloods, he believed that the Naa should push the aliens off-world rather than join them in oppressing others and was willing to sacrifice his life to the cause.

It was nearly impossible for a day worker to smuggle a firearm into Fort Camerone, or to steal one from a legionnaire, but there was plenty of cutlery in the huge kitchen. He had chosen a knife with a long narrow blade for the task at hand, believing that it would penetrate Truespeak's leather body armor and find a path between the bones in his back. The aliens would kill him after that, but not his name, which would live forever in the heart of his people. The thought of it caused Wallstack's chest to tighten with emotion. He checked to make sure the weapon was where it was supposed to be, took comfort from the sight of it, and set to work clearing the ravaged buffet table.

Being the president of a major corporation, Maylo was interested in the tax debate and was seated toward the back of the room. She turned to look as Lieutenant Thinklong led the Naa delegation into the room. The human recognized Truespeak from the visit to her husband's ancestral village. Though officially neutral on the subject, she knew that Booly favored direct representation for his grandmother's people and hoped Truespeak's efforts would succeed. That was why the military officer had used his influence, not to mention her uncle's, to push for a hearing. The timing was right, that's what he believed at any rate, and she agreed. *If* Truespeak did well, *if* the naysayers could be countered, the Naa would take their rightful place within a government of equals. Something Maylo wanted for her husband, and for her as-yet-unborn baby, who would share some of his father's genetic heritage.

The executive turned back toward the stage as the allotted time for debate regarding the controversial value-added tax expired, and a final vote was scheduled for later that day. "Now," President Nankool said, as he eyed that day's agenda, "we have one more item to take up prior to lunch. Specifically I'm referring to SR-5706 which proposes that the Naa be given direct representation in the Senate, that the planet Algeron revert to Naa control, and that their status as a protectorate be lifted. Senator Pama? You wanted to say a few words, I believe?"

The senator from Earth stood and made his way up onto the stage. He was tall, slender, and wore a formal, ankle-length robe. He had dark skin, serious eyes, and high cheekbones. "Thank you, Mr. President. In a moment you will have an opportunity to hear from Nodoubt Truespeak regarding the merits of this proposal. In the meantime I would like to remind you that more than 30,000 Naa have given their lives for the Confederacy—and more than 250,000 Naa presently serve in the Legion. A large number given their relatively small population—and a strong testament to their support for a government that has thus far denied them direct representation. We, the people of Earth, have been partially responsible for that injustice and hope to address it.

"Nodoubt Truespeak holds the title Chief of Chiefs, and as such, has been authorized to speak on behalf of his people. Please join me and SR-5706's four cosponsors in making him feel welcome."

There was scattered applause as Truespeak rose, stepped out into the aisle, and started toward the stage. Booly, who was seated toward the front of the room turned to look, and saw that his wife was clapping loudly enough for both of them. He grinned, saw a white-jacketed waiter start down the aisle behind the Naa chieftain, and wondered what he was up to. That was when Wallstack produced the long, glittering blade, raised it high into the air, and charged.

Maylo saw the knife, understood the Naa's intent, and came up out of her chair. She wasn't as fast as she might have been, not given the weight of her pregnancy, but all she had to do was get in the way.

Wallstack saw a human female lurch out in front of him, slashed at her with the knife, and heard a cry of pain as the blade sliced through flesh. The Naa tripped over the alien as she fell, but was able to recover and stagger down the aisle.

Truespeak was turning, preparing to defend himself, when Lieutenant Thinklong fired. It was a tricky shot, since a bullet meant for the assassin could easily strike the chieftain or one of the senators beyond, but the officer was extremely good. The slug hit Wallstack between the shoulder blades and threw him forward, where Truespeak struck the already dead body a mighty blow. The corpse was still in the process of falling when Booly yelled, "Maylo!" sprang out of his chair, and charged down the aisle.

Maylo lay on the floor, blood running down her arm to stain the carpet, her body curled up into the fetal position. Booly shouted for a medic and knelt at her side. She saw his face and attempted a smile. "I'm sorry, honey. The baby... something hurts."

Booly said something, but the words sounded distorted, and she couldn't make them out. Maylo felt darkness gather around her, tried to push it back, but felt it roll back in. A shaft seemed to open beneath her, she fell into the blackness, and heard herself scream.

10

Many people think it is impossible for guerrillas to exist for long in the enemy's rear. Such a belief reveals lack of comprehension of the relationship that should exist between the people and the troops. The former may be likened to water and the latter to the fish who inhabit it.

MAO TSE-TUNG
STRATEGIC PROBLEMS IN THE ANTI-JAPANESE GUERRILLA WAR
Standard year 1939

Near Hagala Nor, Planet Savas

The boxy Ramanthian troop transport lost altitude as it approached Hagala Nor from the south, Sawicki's ears popped, and the deserter made a face. That was about all he *could* do since restraints had been attached to the human's wrists and ankles, his body was strapped to a bulkhead, and a battle dressing had been shoved into his mouth. The gag was dry, *very* dry, but a piece of tape kept him from spitting it out.

Knifethrow had been treated in a similar fashion, as had Kuga-Ka, who was beginning to question his decision to surrender. Rather than the warm welcome he had envisioned, the officer in charge of the Ramanthian scouts had refused to listen to the Hudathan's story, placed *three* pairs of restraints on his massive wrists, and chained him to D-rings that were welded to the deck.

Now, as the transport touched down at the bottom of the volcano's crater, Kuga-Ka wondered if he and his companions would be interrogated or simply taken out and shot. He hoped for the first, but feared that the second was more likely.

Not surprisingly, the prisoners were separated shortly after they were removed from the transport and locked in separate cells, where they wouldn't be able to communicate with each other.

Now, as Force Commander Ignatho Dontha made his way down into the holding cells originally intended to house military prisoners, the Ramanthian knew that standard interrogation protocols called for him to ignore the Confederacy soldiers for at least a day. The problem was that he couldn't muster the self-discipline required to carry the strategy out. According to the report that had been submitted by the officer in charge of the scouting party, the prisoners lit a grass fire in order to draw attention to themselves. And that was what stimulated Dontha's curiosity. Why would Confederacy troops signal their presence, throw down their weapons, and allow themselves to be captured?

There were no obvious answers, so rather than let the enemy soldiers sweat for a while, the Ramanthian officer decided to interrogate them right away. So, given the fact that the humans were known to dominate the Legion, Dontha figured that the individual named Kras Sawicki was most likely in command.

Metal groaned as a Ramanthian trooper pulled the durasteel door open, and the human got to his feet. It was an extremely small space, so when Dontha entered, the two of them were nearly face-to-face. Though humans weren't especially attractive even at the best of times, Dontha couldn't help but notice that this particular specimen was especially scabrous. He had a filthy bandage wound around his head, and his clothes hung in tatters. Not only that, but he smelled, his face twitched uncontrollably, and words spewed out of his mouth like water from a hose.

Not being bilingual like some of his peers were, Dontha had chosen to wear a translator, and wondered if it was functioning properly as Sawicki launched into a nearly incoherent list of complaints and demands.

About thirty seconds into the human's rant, Dontha grew tired of the prisoner's rantings and closed his right pincer. Then, using the chitinous member like a club, the officer backhanded the deserter across the face. Sawicki's head jerked around, he stumbled, and fell. Then, sitting on the floor, the human felt his jaw. "Hey! That hurt. What's the problem?" Dontha made no answer—but turned and shuffled out of the cell instead. The door crashed shut a moment later. The guard heard a series of muffled thumps and incomprehensible shouts as the human beat his fists on steel and begged the officer to return.

Dontha didn't know much about the Naa, only that they served the humans and that some of them had enlisted in the Legion. That was why he chose to visit Knifethrow next. Once inside the legionnaire's cell, the Ramanthian discovered that rather than being voluble like the human, the fur-covered prisoner was completely silent. Almost ominously so. Questions were met with terse replies. "Who are you?"

The Naa's catlike eyes blinked once. "My name is Knifethrow."

"And your rank?"

"Ex-Private."

"*Ex*-Private?"

"We're deserters."

Dontha tried to hide his surprise, realized the Naa couldn't possibly read his nonverbal expressions, and let the reaction show. He felt both disappointed and elated at the same time. Disappointed because he'd been hoping for a higher caliber of prisoner, yet elated because deserters could be useful, especially if one knew how to employ them. "So, you're the leader?"

"No, sir. That would be the gunny."

"The 'gunny'?"

"Gunnery Sergeant Kuga-Ka."

"The Hudathan."

"Yes, sir."

"Thank you, Private, you've been most helpful," Dontha said, and backed out of the cell.

Kuga-Ka heard a series of muffled pops and clicks as the Ramanthians spoke with each other, followed by a whir as someone passed a key card through the reader on the lock, and the squeal of unoiled metal as the door swung open. A new bug appeared, and this one wore the tabs of an officer. The Hudathan came to attention, his eyes focused on a point over Dontha's head. "Sir! Gunnery Sergeant Kuga-Ka, at your service, sir!"

Though their military traditions were different, there was no mistaking the gesture of respect or the message that it was intended to convey. The Hudathan was not only willing to cooperate, but eager to cooperate, which made perfect sense given his situation. Dontha didn't know what form of punishment awaited the renegade if he were caught, but it seemed safe to assume that it would be far from pleasant. That meant the Ramanthian had the upper pincer already, and there was no need to be intimidating. "At ease, Sergeant. Follow me. Let's find a more comfortable place to talk."

The Ramanthian turned and shuffled out of the cell. The guards watched in amazement as Dontha led the seemingly passive Hudathan down the corridor and into a vacant squad room. Once inside the Ramanthian slipped over a saddle-style seat and pointed at another. "I don't know how comfortable you'll be, but you're welcome to sit down."

Kuga-Ka had already positioned himself with his back to a wall. He eyed the chair and shook his head. "I think I'll stand if it's all the same to you, sir."

"It is," Dontha, assured him. "Now, let's talk about the unit that you were formerly part of and why it was sent to Savas."

This was the opportunity that Kuga-Ka had been waiting for, and he was ready. The Hudathan began with a detailed readout on the battalion's capabilities and followed up with an almost word-for-word rendition of the orders he'd seen.

Dontha was shocked. The situation was much worse than he had imagined. Rather than protect Savas Prime, or capture Hagala Nor as he had assumed, the Legion had been sent to take the hypercom! Still, it seemed likely that their capability to do so had been destroyed when the transports crashed, and he said as much. Kuga-Ka nodded. "Sir, yes, sir. But it isn't over yet. Colonel Kobbi is a stubborn man. The reason he's marching up from the south is to link up with the legionnaires stranded out in the desert. They're guarding most of the battalion's hardware. Begging your excellency's pardon, but if Kobbi manages to marry those brain boxes with the war forms stored in that transport, then it's going to be damned hard to stop them."

Dontha remembered the so-called brain box that had been confiscated along with the Hudathan's weapons and wondered why the renegade bothered to haul it around. Was the cyborg a friend perhaps? Not that it made any difference. "I have a battalion of armor at my command," the Ramanthian countered calmly, "but your point is well taken. Why fight this Colonel Kobbi head-to-head if I don't have to?

"Unfortunately the second group, the ones with the war forms, fortified the wreck. We launched repeated attempts to neutralize it, but none of them succeeded. Now I fear that I would have to throw armor at them in order to get the job done."

"Which you don't want to do, because if you pull your armor out of Hagala Nor, the hypercom would be vulnerable," Kuga-Ka put in.

Dontha looked at the hulking Hudathan with a newfound respect. "That's correct, Sergeant. You're very perceptive."

Kuga-Ka looked at a point over the Ramanthian's head. The interplay reminded him of his previous relationship with Captain Gaphy. It seemed that officers, regardless of race, were always surprised to learn that their subordinates had the capacity to think. "Thank you, sir."

"Fortunately," the force commander continued thoughtfully, "there are other assets that we can call upon. Previous efforts to utilize them have met with mixed results. But who knows? A noncommissioned officer of your intelligence and experience may be just the thing to turn that situation around."

Kuga-Ka brought his eyes down to make contact with the Ramanthian's. They bulged slightly and were black as space. "Are you offering me a job, sir?"

"Yes," Dontha said, "I am."

"And my troops?"

"Yes."

"And pay?"

Dontha cocked his head to one side. "What do you want?"

"Five hundred credits per day for myself, three hundred credits a day for my troops, and transportation to a neutral planet after the battalion is destroyed."

Dontha gave the Ramanthian equivalent of a smile. It would

be a good deal less expensive to pay the renegades off with three rather inexpensive bullets, but who knew? Maybe they'd do a good job. And maybe he'd be in an expansive mood that day. "It's a deal," the officer said evenly. "Welcome to the Ramanthian army, Unit Commander Kuga-Ka."

The Grass Path, Planet Savas

Nis Noia moved the electrobinoculars a hair to the left, acquired the image he'd been searching for, and a took a moment to scan the column of legionnaires and civilians. They were well spaced, and well equipped, if a bit ragged. He handed the device to the person who lay at his side.

Nartha Omoni had looked through the off-world device before, but still regarded what she called the "bring it closer" with something akin to awe and handled the device with care. It took the chieftain a moment to find the image she was looking for, but then she did, and what had been little more than dots exploded into full-fledged beings. The Paguum scanned the column, then scanned it again, before handing the electrobinoculars back. "I'm sorry, my friend, but I don't see how your warriors can help. Even allowing for the power of their off-world weapons, such a small number of soldiers could never stand against the northern tribe. The night people would slaughter them."

"I appreciate your concern," Noia answered patiently, "but consider the hard skins. How many are helping Srebo Riff? One? Two? Three at the most? Yet they make a difference. Surely the dawn people could benefit from some off-world military advice as well. Why not talk to them? See what they have to say. Then, if you still feel that they have nothing to offer, you can ride away."

Omoni lay there for a moment, considering the intelligence operative's words, before turning to look at him. "You have a way with words, human... but so do those who are completely mad."

Noia grinned. "Is that a 'yes'?"

The Paguum sighed. "Yes, damn you, but beware... If I meet with your warriors, and they turn out to be fools, *you* will feel the full weight of my displeasure."

The agent brought the electrobinoculars back up. The column

leaped forward. The legionnaires were too far away to discern who was in command. But the hypercom was important, vitally so, and it seemed safe to assume that the officer in charge was someone reliable. As for why the Confed troops had decided to march north, rather than ride, that was something of a mystery. The intelligence officer had some com gear, but there hadn't been any reason to carry it around, and it was stashed with the rest of his supplies a couple of hundred miles to the west. That was why he hadn't been in contact with the legionnaires before. "Yes, ma'am," Noia replied gravely. "I understand. Well, let's find out what we have here... Friend or fool."

Having admonished the legionnaires in the drag position to keep a sharp eye out, Colonel Jon Kobbi set out to reach the front end of the column again and made it a point to chat with people along the way. Especially the civilians, some of whom were still having difficulty adjusting to military discipline and the aggressive pace. Soon, within a matter of days, the column would be forced to march at night in order to avoid the steadily increasing heat. Moving around in the darkness would add still more dangers to an already long list. Ramanthian heat detectors would be able to pick them out more easily, the possibility of an attack would increase, and people could get lost. Nothing for the officer to look forward to.

The grass, which the locals assured him should have been tall that time of year, was short and brown. It crackled under Kobbi's boots, insects made popping noises as they jumped out of the way, and the ever-present sun warmed the officer's shoulders.

Though still considerably south of Fire Base Alpha and the fortified wreck, Kobbi took pleasure in the fact that his half of the battalion was clear of the jungle and well into the savanna.

Although water was going to be a problem once they hit the desert, it felt good to be out in the open, where they could see for miles around. That, plus the RPVs that Calvo sent south to circle above the column during most of the day, added to the sense of security. Not only did the remotely piloted devices reduce the risk of ambush, they allowed the column to move much more quickly than it could have had it been necessary to send out scouts and advance behind them.

Unfortunately, in spite of the fact that the column was unlikely to be ambushed by ground forces, it was open to attack from above. Although it was damaged, the Ramanthians had a ship in orbit plus smaller vessels that could operate in the atmosphere. Kobbi's worst nightmare was that one or more such aircraft would catch the column out in the open and pound it into mush. With that in mind the cavalry officer had positioned crews armed with man-portable surface-to-air missiles along the entire length of the column and worked continuously to prevent his flock from bunching up. The officer's train of thought was broken as a com tech spoke in his ear. "Nomad Three Four to Nomad Six. Over."

Kobbi touched the unit on his belt and spoke into the wire-thin boom mike. "This is Six. Go. Over."

"Alpha Base reports six, repeat *six*, mounted nomads closing with the column from the northeast. Over."

"Okay… Tell 'em we appreciate the heads up. Nomad Six to Bravo Six. Over."

Santana had been monitoring the transmission, and given the fact that he and one of his platoons were walking point, wasn't surprised to hear his call sign. "This is Bravo Six. Over."

"Take a squad and go out to meet our visitors, Bravo Six. Let's see who they are and what they want before we invite them home for dinner. Over and out."

Santana clicked his transmit button twice, signaled Dietrich to round up his squad, and waited for the troops to dump their packs in a pile that another legionnaire would guard. Then, lightened by sixty-plus pounds each, the reaction force jogged out to meet the incoming riders. They were in good shape, and the ground was relatively flat, so the legionnaires made good time. Once a sufficient buffer had been established, the officer brought the squad to a halt just short of a low rise and nodded to Dietrich. "Deploy your men, Sergeant. The indigs are mounted—so keep that in mind."

Like any good cavalryman, the noncom knew what mounted troops could do to unwary foot soldiers and had no desire to die in a meaningless skirmish on a third-rate planet like Savas. With that in mind he placed his best marksmen to either end of the line, where they could deal with any attempt to turn the corners, and sited the squad's light machine gun right at the center to counter the possibility of a head-on charge. Then, with those preparations in place, the noncom sent Fareye to keep an eye on the back door, confident that the Naa would spot anyone trying to sneak up on them from behind.

The fact that Santana watched his preparations, but made no comment, was both a compliment and one of the reasons Dietrich respected him. Many officers always found something to comment on, not because they had identified a genuine problem, but as a way to continually reaffirm their authority. It was a practice that not only served to undermine their NCOs but limit their effectiveness. His peers felt the same way and, being rid of Gaphy, were pleased to report to the new loot.

Santana stood on top of the rise and eyed the oncoming riders through his electrobinoculars. Now, as the indigs spotted him, the zurnas started to slow. It was the human's first look at the big animals and the bipeds who rode them. Most had their hoods thrown back, and it didn't take a degree in xenobiology to see the similarities between the Jithi and the Paguum. But their skin color was different, as were the pronounced hooklike noses, and the front to back skull crests. The Paguum had larger frames, too, all except for one individual, who had undeniably human features. A rather interesting if unexpected development. The riders came to a stop at the bottom of the rise, milled around for a moment, and disgorged a single rider. It was the human who rode up the slope, which given the circumstances, made good sense.

Nis Noia eyed the tall, dark-haired legionnaire as he used his knees to guide the specially trained animal up over the burned-looking grass. The agent considered himself to be a professional, an operative so seasoned he could work by himself for years without becoming homesick, but much to his surprise the sight of a human face produced what he felt to be an unseemly degree of eagerness. Noia struggled to keep his emotions under control as he reined the zurna in and felt the animal's head drop to crop at what little bit of forage there was. The operative delivered a perfunctory nod. "Good morning, Lieutenant. Nis Noia at your service. I'm the Confederacy's trade representative on Savas. Nartha Omoni is among the people at the bottom of the slope. She leads the southern tribe, and they control this swath of land. We'd like an audience with your commanding officer. Is he or she available?"

Santana didn't believe that the man with the hard features, the deep tan, and the native robes was a trade representative. Not for a moment. But kept his opinion to himself. "My name is Santana. It's a pleasure to meet you. Colonel Kobbi is back with the column. I'll let him know that you're here."

Rather than provide Noia and the digs with a close-up look at his troops and their armament, Kobbi chose to join them on the rise. And, since it would have been unseemly to run, a good twenty minutes passed before he arrived. The meeting that followed lasted even longer. So long that the column was ordered to stop and make camp two miles to the north, where a hill and a jumble of rocks offered some cover. Eventually afternoon faded into evening. A breeze came up, found the cook fires, and sent gouts of sparks up into the sky. Qwis Qwan was sitting on a rock, her fingers wrapped around a mug of hot soup, when Santana passed between her and the nearest blaze. She watched the officer pause to speak to one of his legionnaires, wondered if he was what she truly wanted, and looked up into the sky. Stars powdered the sky, but all of them were silent.

Fire Base Alpha, the Great Pandu Desert, Planet Savas

The house-sized combine that her parents had sacrificed so much to buy had broken down again, and being the best "wrench" on the family farm, Calvo had been summoned to repair it. She could see the huge machine sitting atop a distant rise, drive wheel deep in the golden tuf-wheat, but no matter how hard she pushed the little four-wheel utility vehicle, it never seemed to get any closer. It was frustrating, *very* frustrating, and...

"Captain Calvo? Sorry, ma'am, but a man-sized biological just passed through the outermost ring of detectors." Calvo groaned, sat up in her bunk, and rubbed her eyes. Finally able to see, the officer swung her feet over the side of the rack as Private Nishi handed her a cup of tea. A servo whirred as the MO accepted the mug and took a tentative sip. The hot liquid felt wonderful as it trickled down the back of her throat. "Do we have a profile on him?"

"No, ma'am," Nishi replied matter-of-factly. "But given the fact that he's walking upright and packs the right amount of heat mass, Lomo's betting on a dig. A scout probably—come to take a look at us."

The theory made sense so Calvo nodded. "Notify Lieutenant Farner. Tell him I want this one alive. Who knows? Maybe we can squeeze some intel out of him."

The legionnaire nodded, said, "Yes, ma'am," and disappeared. Calvo took another sip of tea, wondered how her parents were doing, and hoped they had the latest crop in.

The sand gave under his boots, a pinnacle of rock obscured some of the stars, and the only thing the intruder could hear was the sound of his own breathing. It was dark, *very* dark, and Sawicki felt very much alone. A Ramanthian transport had dropped him off about five miles to the north and he'd been walking for what? Two or three hours now? Following the course Knifethrow had drummed into his head. And that was a problem because Sawicki didn't like being alone. He enjoyed being with people, *lots* of people, which was one of the reasons he joined up. Only now he wasn't part of the Legion anymore, and rather than the sense of freedom that Kuga-Ka and Knifethrow seemed to glory in, all he felt was a sense of loss. The renegade hadn't told *them* that, but that's how he felt.

Now, having been selected to talk his way into the fortified wreck, the human missed having someone to tell him what to do. Senior noncoms were a pain in the ass mostly, always coming up with work for him to do, but there was a certain comfort in the certainty of it all. A shadow fell out of the sky as Staff Sergeant Amel Haddad dropped off a ledge, threw an arm around the intruder's throat, and Corporal Baza rose like a ghost from the ground. Sawicki gave a grunt of expelled air as the second noncom buried a fist in his gut, then he doubled over and fell to his knees. He was busy trying to barf when a light came on. "What the hell?" Haddad exclaimed. "This bastard is human!"

Baza checked, confirmed that the other noncom was correct, and helped the man in the tattered civvies get back to his feet. "Sorry, bud, we thought you was one of them."

Sawicki wanted to punch the little corporal's lights out, but knew it wasn't what the fictional him would do, and answered with a croak. "No problem… I understand. Would either one of you have some water?"

Other legionnaires had arrived by then, and the deserter held his breath as he chose one canteen from many and took a long pull. Sawicki had never been one to hang out with tech heads, and nobody had recognized him as yet, but the Legion was like a large family. All it would take was one person he'd swilled some beer with, and a "Hey, man, what are *you* doing here?" to put him in chains. But no one spoke, the deserter handed the water bottle back, and wiped his mouth with the back of his hand. "Thanks! The name is Horn. Jason Horn. I live in Savas Prime. The bugs cooked my air car about two weeks back. I've been walking ever since. An old Paguum gave me some water a few days ago, but I ran out yesterday afternoon."

All of which was true, except that the real Horn had been *killed* when the bugs attacked his air car, and was buried hundreds of miles to the east.

"Well, you're safe now," Haddad said gruffly. "Can you walk okay?"

"Yeah," Sawicki replied, "I believe I can."

"Good," the noncom said. "Follow Corporal Baza. He'll lead the way."

Sawicki wasn't back in the Legion, not really, but it felt like home.

Twelve hours later, having told his story to Calvo and pretended to be devastated about the destruction of Savas Prime, Sawicki was feeling pretty good. The raggedy civilian clothes, the cover story that Kuga-Ka had drilled into him, and his natural ability to lie had all combined to put his hosts at ease. Not only that, but a quick check with the civilians in Kobbi's column confirmed that a man named Horn was missing, and added weight to the newcomer's story.

Now all the renegade had to do was accomplish the mission he'd been sent to carry out, namely to scope out the improvised security system that had been deployed around the wreck and come up with a way to neutralize it prior to the attack that would take place at 0200 the next morning. Or, as Kuga-Ka put it, "Don't dork around, and don't talk to anyone you don't have to. You aren't smart enough to fool anyone for very long."

One problem had surfaced, however, and it was a lulu. Even though Sawicki hadn't hung out with the battalion's cyborgs, he and Knifethrow had been present when Kuga-Ka intentionally ran a truck over a tech named Poltero back on Adobe, before throwing the then badly damaged borg into the back to play with later. Then, having had their sadistic fun, the threesome disposed of the badly damaged spider form by dropping the mangled remains into the canyon that served as the base's garbage dump. Poltero had lain there for two days, unable to move, before somebody heard his cries for help.

Now, on a planet hundreds of lights away, Sawicki had the bad luck to run into the same box head! The good news, such as it was, lay in the fact that Poltero had never been allowed to see his tormentor's faces, which was why no alarm bells went off when the cyborg met the civilian named Horn. Still, there was no point in pressing his luck, so the renegade resolved to give the tech a wide berth while he continued to familiarize himself with the wreck.

Given his supposed background, and unaware of his true identity, Calvo had given the man named Horn the run of the ship. The renegade made use of the freedom to visit the C&C, look in on the compartment that served as an armory, and visit the holds, where he chatted with a couple of techs.

And that's where Poltero was, running a maintenance check on a quad, when he heard Sawicki laugh. It sounded like a donkey braying and ended with a series of loud snorts.

The sound jerked him back to the moment of impact, hours of torture, and days spent laying in the dump. Though unable to see through the makeshift hood that had been thrown over his sensors, Poltero had been able to hear, and the laugh was unmistakable. Impossible though it seemed, one of his tormentors was not only present, but standing just a few feet away!

Servos whined as the tech ducked out from under the quad's belly to see who was responsible for the laugh. A group of three stood a few feet away. It consisted of a spider form named Woomer, a bio bod named Gulas, and the newly arrived civilian. A self-adhesive bandage covered the cut on the side of his head, his face was sunburned, and his eyes darted from place to place. The ragged civvies had been exchanged for baggy camos and a new pair of combat boots. None of which meant jack shit since Poltero had never seen the people who tortured him.

That was when Gulas said something, Horn brayed, and Poltero felt the same sense of terror he had back on Adobe. It didn't make sense, the tech knew that, but he couldn't shake the conviction that one of his tormentors was present on the ship. None of the threesome turned to look as the cyborg spidered away.

Calvo was in the ship's wardroom, sitting at the end of a long narrow table that she used as a desk, when she heard metal click on metal. The officer looked up from her comp, saw Poltero, and nodded. Because all the spider forms were identical in appearance, they were required to wear name tags. But there were other ways to tell them apart as well, like the tool drive that Poltero habitually wore on his left tool arm, in keeping with the fact that the cyborg had once been left-handed. The officer prided herself on knowing such things and motioned for the tech to enter. "Hey, Pol, how's it going?"

"Not too bad," the cyborg answered. "Not too bad at all. I'd say we'll be ready when the old man gets here."

Calvo grinned. "I'm glad to hear it—'cause that's what I told him! So, what can I do for you?"

"It's about Horn," the tech said hesitantly. "I think he's lying."

Calvo's eyebrows rose. "Lying? About what?"

"About who he is," Poltero replied darkly.

The MO listened as the tech reminded her of what had

occurred on Adobe and described the distinctive laugh. Calvo frowned. "No offense, Pol, but a laugh isn't very much to go on. Not only that, but this guy is a civilian, and was here on Savas when you were attacked."

"I can't explain it, but he's lying," the cyborg maintained stubbornly. "I know it sounds crazy, ma'am, but I would recognize that laugh anywhere, and Horn was on Adobe."

"Okay," the officer said sympathetically. "I can't put him in the brig for his laugh, but I'll keep an eye on him."

"That's all I ask," Poltero said gratefully. "Sure, I'd like to see those bastards punished, but there's more to it than that… Assuming I'm right, how did this guy get to Savas from Adobe, and what's he up to?"

They were good questions and continued to haunt Calvo long after the cyborg was gone.

Night had fallen once more, and with it came the slight turbulence that resulted from the change in temperatures. The Ramanthian transport shuddered as it hit some rough air, Kuga-Ka pressed his back against the durasteel bulkhead, and wondered how many hours of night flying the bug pilot had logged.

But there was nothing he could do about the pilot, so the Hudathan tried to make himself comfortable in the makeshift seat and turned his attention to the task at hand. The raid had two objectives. The first was to damage, if not destroy, the fortified wreck. The second, which was more important to him, was to impress Dontha with the value of his new employees. With that in mind Kuga-Ka had been careful to manage expectations down, even going so far as to characterize Sawicki's activities as "a diversion."

Not only that, but a success, even a limited one, would still be better than what the bugs had accomplished thus far. And with a win to his credit, the Hudathan could proceed to the *real* task, which was working with the indigs. Who knew? Maybe he would use the indigs against Kobbi, or maybe he'd use them against *both* sides, and build a nice kingdom of his own. Time would tell.

The transport hit an air pocket, dropped twenty units, and

stabilized. The Ramanthian subleader seated across the aisle from the renegade stared at him, and the Hudathan stared back. The tension between the two was almost palpable, and Knifethrow smiled knowingly.

Calvo was dreaming. It was the same dream that had troubled her before. The little four-by-four wobbled as it bumped through a gully, then roared as she twisted the throttle and sent it skittering up the opposite slope. The combine was still there, sitting on top of the hill, silhouetted against the sky.

But then the image seemed to morph as the previously inert piece of equipment suddenly came back to life and turned in her direction. Then it was charging her, rolling downhill at an increasing rate of speed, clearly intent on crushing the farm girl beneath its awesome weight. That was when Calvo screamed, fought her way up out of the dream, and lay panting on a sweat-soaked sheet. Had the scream been real? Or part of the dream? The officer listened and was glad when no one arrived to see if she was okay.

Convinced that she wouldn't be able to return to sleep, the MO rose, donned her camos, and made her way down the main corridor. Her wrist term said that it was 0147. The galley was empty, but her favorite mug was upside down on a shelf, and there was plenty of hot water.

Two minutes later, tea in hand, the legionnaire made her way to the C&C and peered through the hatch. It looked normal enough, except for the fact that Horn was present, shooting the breeze with one of the naval techs. Calvo remembered Poltero's accusation and frowned. Partly because she found the civilian's presence strange—but partly because he was a distraction. Rather than monitoring her readouts, the tech was engrossed in conversation. Had the chief in charge of the watch been present, he would have set her straight, but it appeared he was out making his rounds. Calvo opened her mouth to say something but was preempted by a com tech, who spotted her out of the corner of his eye. "Attention on deck!"

Everyone came to attention, *including* Horn. And that was

the moment when the MO realized that Poltero was correct. A civilian wouldn't come to attention unless…

But Calvo's thoughts were interrupted as Sawicki realized his mistake, whipped the stolen handgun out from under his baggy shirt, and shot the navy tech in the face.

Blood was still spraying the deck when Sawicki turned toward the hatch and took a mugful of scalding-hot tea in the face. He screamed but still managed to squeeze the weapon's trigger and send a round whizzing past Calvo's head. The officer yelled, "Battle Stations!" and saw the com tech slap a large red button, just as the renegade shot her between the shoulder blades. The raid was under way by that time, and all manner of reports had started to filter in even as the battle klaxon went off and off-duty personnel rolled out of their racks.

Sawicki was hurt, but still on his feet, and determined to clear the C&C so he could lock himself inside it. That was his only hope now, and the renegade knew it.

Calvo saw the deserter's weapon swing her way, put her head down, and charged. The renegade brought the handgun down in an attempt to pistol-whip the officer, but missed her skull by a sixteenth of an inch and hit her shoulder instead. Calvo felt the impact followed by a sharp pain, heard the imposter say "Oomph!" as her head hit his gut, and she collapsed on top of him.

Help had arrived by then, and the MO felt strong hands grab the back of her shirt, pluck her off the deserter, and heard the man swear as Captain Amdo kicked the weapon out of his hand. There was a metallic clatter as the pistol skittered away followed by a muffled explosion.

The MO's left shoulder was numb by then, and the officer put her good hand on it, as she switched her attention to defending the ship. Other techs had dropped into the vacant chairs by then and were busy relaying data. "Gun emplacement one has been destroyed, ma'am," a petty officer said. "It sounds like they got close enough to throw a satchel charge in under the mount."

Calvo remembered the tech who had been talking to the imposter instead of monitoring her sensors and swore. "Who the hell are we fighting? The digs? Or the bugs?"

The ship shook as an explosion strobed the night and gun

emplacement three ceased to exist. "They're bugs, ma'am. Special ops types from the looks of it. I had one report of a Hudathan fighting with them."

"All right," Calvo said grimly, "tell everyone to fall back on the ship, take up defensive positions, and hose them down. We have enough firepower to level a small city. Let's use it."

There was near chaos down in the hold as bio bods worked feverishly to transfer cyborg brain boxes from their spider forms to standby war forms. In the meantime, there were only two T-2s outside, but they were putting out a lot of fire, and the Ramanthians were forced to take cover.

Kuga-Ka said, "Follow me!" and elbowed his way forward as a stream of tracers whipped over his head. He had carried the neural input device or zapper all the way from Savas Prime. Protecting it from the rain, keeping it even when other items had been discarded, certain he would have a use for it one day.

Now, as he came within range, and the nearest T-2 swung his fifty toward the big heat blob, the renegade pointed the device at the cyborg and pressed the red button. The results were dramatic. The machine stopped firing, spasmed, and fell forward onto its face. "Now!" Kuga-Ka yelled. "Grab the bastard and pull him back!"

The Ramanthians rushed forward to obey. The cyborg was heavy, but the sand was smooth, and they were strong. They grabbed the trooper's arms and were well clear of the wreck when two additional T-2s exited the ship and immediately opened fire. The newcomers were beyond the range of the zapper, so Kuga-Ka restored the device to his pocket and marked one of the two remaining gun positions with a clumsy laser pointer. "Put some fire on that gun!"

The words were automatically translated into Ramanthian click speech, but that didn't mean Subleader Ruu Hogo had to agree with or follow the Hudathan's orders. His instructions were clear. Follow the renegade's lead to the extent that it made sense—but remember it was *he* who would be held responsible if anything went wrong.

So as additional cyborgs joined the fray and the counter-fire increased, Hogo ordered his troops to pull back. Kuga-Ka was outraged. "What the hell are you doing? Fire your shoulder-launched missiles! Take the scum out!" But the Ramanthian troops weren't listening, not to him at any rate, and systematically fell back.

Kuga-Ka was still fuming when the raiding party arrived at the dust-off point. Not about Sawicki, who he assumed was dead, but about Hogo's decision to break the engagement off. Still, the raiding party had been able to destroy two gun positions and capture a war form. Not bad, not bad at all, and the renegade felt sure that Dontha would be pleased.

The T-2 had been dragged up into the transport's dimly lit interior and secured to the deck with steel cables. Servos whirred and massive limbs flexed as the trooper started to come around. The Hudathan reached into his pocket, found the zapper, and pushed the button. The cyborg arched his back, screamed, and lost consciousness again.

Hogo, who didn't understand what was going on, looked on in amazement.

Kuga-Ka checked to ensure that Knifethrow was awake, saw the Naa nod by way of a response, and allowed his back to make contact with cold metal. He was asleep three units later.

The Great Pandu Desert, Planet Savas

A trail wound its way up around the spire of basaltic rock known as God's Finger. But it was only two handbreadths wide, and very steep, which meant that Nartha Omoni had to cling to such handholds as were available, her face so close to the rock face that she could see the tiny crystals that were embedded in it as she sidestepped her way toward the top.

The strain of it served to remind Omoni of the toll that the years had taken on her body, of the fact that she wouldn't be able to make the same climb by the time the dawn people completed their next circuit of the planet, and the fact that other things were changing as well. Climatic changes were pushing her people toward the north, the political environment was growing increasingly complex, and new ideas and technologies were sweeping the surface of the planet. All of which had to be evaluated, accommodated, and otherwise dealt with if her tribe was to survive.

Omoni felt a piece of heavily weathered rock break away under the weight of her body, grabbed a likely-looking knob, and was able to reestablish her footing. Then, hopeful that rockfall hadn't injured any of those below, the chieftain sidestepped her way to the top, where a calloused hand reached out to grab her wrist.

Omoni thanked the warrior who pulled her up onto the surface above and promptly forgot how tired she was as the sun announced its imminent arrival by painting the eastern horizon with streaks of pink light. Dawn held special meaning for her people, just as sunsets had symbolic value for Riff's tribe, and the chieftain took the moment necessary to kneel where her younger self had knelt, and gave thanks for the gift of another day.

Then, having been led to the three-sided tent where a chair awaited her, it was time to sip her morning tea and look out over the spectacle below. A contingent of mounted warriors could be seen out in the desert—and a larger group milled around the base of the spire. The human appeared as if conjured from the rock itself. "Good morning."

The chieftain raised her mug by way of a salute. "So, you survived the climb."

Nis Noia was used to Omoni's gruff humor by then and smiled. "Yes, and I see that you did as well. Not bad for a couple of old geezers."

The Paguum laughed. "Watch your mouth, human... or I'll have you thrown off the cliff. Is the demonstration ready?"

"Yes," Noia replied. "Both groups are in position."

"Excellent," Omoni said. "Let the attack begin."

Rather than the neat orderly ranks that Santana had originally envisioned, the officer found himself at the edge of a maelstrom of snorting, nipping, and farting zurnas. They surged back and forth as their riders jockeyed for better positions. It seemed that all of them wanted the honor of leading the charge, even though the whole point was to fight as infantry rather than cavalry, something that the officer and his troops had spent the better part of three days trying to communicate.

But the off-worlders had learned a few things during that time, including the methods that the indig leaders used to maintain discipline, like pushing their way into the center of the mob while yelling orders and wielding a whip. Something made more difficult by the fact that each legionnaire was seated behind a Paguumi warrior who had to relay his instructions to his zurna before anything could happen.

Finally, after what felt like a full-scale melee, the attacking force had been herded into color-coded groups and stood facing the dark pillar of rock. Though of no value in and of itself, the spire was intended to represent the towers that guarded the Well of Zugat, which lay to the north. Omoni needed to take control of the well since Riff was unwilling to share the water that had traditionally been his. Meanwhile, eager to reassemble his battalion and go after the hypercom before the bugs could bring in reinforcements, Kobbi and the rest of the unit were marching toward Fire Base Alpha. And, boring though that was, Santana suddenly found himself wishing that he was back with the main column.

Noia was good at any number of things, but radio procedure wasn't one of them, and he forgot to use his call sign. His voice boomed in the legionnaire's ear. "Okay, Lieutenant, let 'em rip."

Not having com sets to distribute to the Paguumi leaders, Santana had been forced to fall back on the equivalent of a bugle as a means of communications. The officer tapped the warrior seated in front of him on the shoulder. He had to yell in order to make himself heard. "All right! Sound the charge!"

The young male had been practicing for days and looked forward to his role. He raised the long Jithi-made horn, blew a series of crystal-clear notes, and sent the necessary order to his impatient steed. The zurna took off like a shot. Santana, who had no saddle other than some makeshift padding held in place by a strap, managed to grab hold of the warrior's weapons harness. By that time hundreds of other animals were thundering along behind and a fall meant certain death.

Fortunately, Santana managed to hang on. Then, by standing in a pair of improvised stirrups, the officer was able to peer ahead.

The make-believe defenders, all of whom were mounted, milled about the base of God's Finger. Unlike the warriors under his command, they had not received any special training and could be expected to react like Paguumi cavalry always had. They would charge, try to flank the attackers, and crush them with the weight of their numbers. And, given the fact that they outnumbered the invading force two to one, that looked like a foregone conclusion.

However, once the defenders came face-to-face with a *new* type of mounted warrior, one they had never encountered before, Colonel Kobbi believed that the indigs would be forced to give way in spite of their superior numbers. The whole notion of mounted infantrymen who rode into battle but fought on foot was very similar to the concept of mechanized infantry. Something the Legion made good use of.

Like all cadets, Santana had been taught about dragoons during his time at the academy but forgotten them soon thereafter. Not Kobbi, however, who though never having set foot in the academy, was a student of military history and saw mounted infantry as a way for the dawn people to gain a momentary advantage over their cousins to the north. Momentary, because the tactic could, and would, be imitated.

But the notion of putting *two* riders on each zurna, thereby doubling the number of warriors each animal delivered into battle, that was Santana's idea and one that he hoped would work. The key was to dismount and form up *before* the cavalry could hit them, which was why the legionnaire leaned forward to shout into the warrior's ear slits. "Sound the second signal!"

The Paguum raised his horn, blew a quick series of notes, and ordered his zurna to halt. The animal had been bred to run and wanted to keep on going, but reluctantly agreed. Both riders were thrown forward as the beast skidded to a halt.

The defenders were just starting to move, just starting to trot, when the attackers seemed to slow. A cloud of dust rose to obscure their movements, and unsure of what was going on, the defenders paused. Then, as the dust blew clear, they saw that the oncoming horde had not only dismounted but were advancing on foot! A seemingly suicidal tactic that made no sense whatsoever.

Firearms were forbidden to both groups, as were edged weapons, but the defenders had long Jithi-supplied lances minus their metal points. The defending general was named Kuzo. He marveled at how stupid the off-worlders were, raised his weapon into the air, and shouted "Charge!"

The order was relayed down the long, undisciplined line, and since it was expected, resulted in an almost immediate response. The earth shook as thousands of hooves hit the ground and a thunderous wall of blood, flesh, and bone hurtled forward.

It was a war game, which meant that with the exception of a few accidents there shouldn't be any casualties. Santana knew that, but couldn't help feeling an emptiness at the pit of his stomach as the Paguumi charge began, and the infantry square marched to meet it. Their mounts, true to the last orders given by their riders, formed groups and trotted toward the rear.

The officer wasn't alone. The newly created Paguumi dragoons were as scared as he was, and if it hadn't been for Sergeant Dietrich and the legionnaires under his command, the hollow square would have come apart. But the acting noncoms were everywhere, pushing confused warriors back into line, shouting words of encouragement, and leading the troops by example.

There were very few historical instances where cavalry had been able to break formed infantry, that's what Kobbi maintained at any rate, but Santana continued to have his doubts as the front rank plowed forward. It was the wrong place for a commanding officer to be, but his presence in the line was equivalent to a statement of faith, and so long as an off-worlder was there no Paguum could break formation and run. Not without losing face, family, and membership in the tribe.

The legionnaire could *feel* them to either side, their shoulders brushing his, their feet stamping the ground. He could see their taut faces, smell their sweat, and hear the clatter of their equipment. And suddenly, as if strapped into a time machine, the soldier was transported back to a time when all warfare was up close and personal.

Then the time for thinking was over as Santana shouted an order, the square crashed to a halt, and a thousand staves were jammed down into the sand. Some pointed straight up at the sky, or toward the rear, but most were slanted toward the enemy.

The oncoming cavalry saw the wall of wood and automatically started to slow. Then, forced to break left or right, the defenders flowed out around the front of the square only to discover that the sides were equally dense. Wood clattered, zurnas squalled, and warriors swore as the assault stalled.

That was the cue for the off-world advisors to order the front ranks to fall back, and move the second ranks to step forward, forcing the cavalry to deal with fresh troops. The evolution was anything but smooth, but the change was made, and the newly created dragoons started to gain confidence.

Frustrated, and unsure of what to do next, Kuzo ordered his cavalry to withdraw toward the spire. It took the better part of five minutes for his instructions to reach all of the defenders but eventually they did. Santana had been waiting for such a move and ordered an advance. The result looked sloppy, and staves waved like grass in the wind, but the square managed to lurch forward. The formation had traveled a hundred paces before Kuzo realized what was taking place and ordered his forces to attack once more. They obeyed, but the dragoons refused to stop this time and continued to march forward undeterred. The cavalry wheeled, but to no great effect, and the attackers entered the shadow cast by the spire.

Meanwhile, up on top of the rock formation, Noia turned to Omoni. "So, what do you think?"

"I'm surprised," the chieftain admitted. "While it's true that the cavalry would be more effective if armed, the reverse would be true as well. Especially if the front rank of dragoons fired in unison while sharpshooters had at them from the center of the square. We must perfect this tactic and use it against Riff."

Noia thought about the effects that off-world meddling would inevitably have on the local balance of power and felt a sense of regret. But if the bugs had the hypercom technology all to themselves, and were allowed to use it in battle, billions of sentients might die as a result. "Yes," the operative agreed soberly, "I'm afraid that we must."

Neither person saw the distant wink of light that originated from the top of a rise more than a mile away. It lasted for only a fraction of a second and could have been caused by sunlight reflecting off a piece of quartz, a gun barrel, or a telescope. The desert knew—but kept its secrets well.

11

Those who choose to walk toward the rising sun can scarcely deny its light, complain of its heat, or fail to embrace the darkness that it leaves in its wake.

PAGUUMI PROVERB
AUTHOR UNKNOWN
Standard year circa 120 B.C.

Hagala Nor, Planet Savas

In contrast to the vast well-kept underground cities of Hive, the maze of tunnels and passageways that had been bored into the ancient volcano were rough and very often narrow. *Still,* Force Commander Ignatho Dontha thought to himself as he stepped over a drainage channel, and followed the corridor's gently curving earthen wall toward the science section, *why invest more?* Especially since the entire complex might be empty within a matter of weeks.

A noncom approached from the opposite direction, closely followed by a file of elite techno warriors, all dressed in their special helmets and fire-retardant uniforms. They belonged to the famous Pincer of Steel Battalion, the unit that *he* had the honor to command and which had never lost a battle. *And never will,* the officer assured himself as the noncom clacked his right pincer respectfully and continued down the tunnel.

The first indications that Dontha was nearing the science

section were the crates, stripped-out consoles, and unidentifiable components that littered both sides of the corridor. An offense to Dontha's eye, his military sensibilities, *and* common sense. The "junk," as he thought of it, was an impediment to the normal flow of traffic, and might prove disastrous should an emergency vehicle need to pass through. Given how messy and the disorganized they were, the officer was amazed by the fact that previous generations of scientists had somehow managed to invent the wheel, plumb the mysteries of the atom, and create a workable hyperspace drive.

A side tunnel led back toward the science section. Piles of cast-off equipment nearly touched the ceiling and looked poised to collapse into the passageway. Dontha frowned as he followed a clutch of unauthorized power feeds back into the warm, dimly lit labyrinth beyond. Never one to spend much time on administrative matters, Nudu Tepho's hopelessly littered office was predictably empty. That forced the military officer to hunt for him, a task that wasn't all that difficult because while the outer part of the chamber was filled with junk, all of the passageways that cut through it led to a raised dais at the center of the cavern. That's where a group of scientists stood like worshipers gathered around an altar.

The object of their attentions was big and ugly, to Dontha's eyes at least, though it was doubtful that the hypercom's acolytes would have agreed with him. When they looked at the steel frame, the jury-rigged holo tank, and the mishmash of components stacked all around it, what *they* saw was a sleek unit no larger than a standard com set. Not the hypercom the way it was, but the hypercom the way it *would* be, once their efforts were complete. There was a high-pitched whine, followed by a flood of static, and feedback from a pair of mismatched speakers. It stopped as one of the functionaries pinched a squeeze switch. Another spotted Dontha and spoke to the older scientist who was standing at his side.

Chief Scientific Investigator Tepho had never been one to worry about appearances, and now, toward the tail end of one of the legendary sixty-hour workathons, he looked especially shabby. He was in the process of molting, but rather than remove pieces of dead chitin the way most Ramanthians did, the scientist simply ignored them. That gave him a strange, mottled appearance, which, when combined with his filthy clothing, conveyed the impression of an aging lunatic rather than one of the empire's premier scientists. "So," the chief functionary said with his usual lack of tact, "how much of our time do you intend to waste today?"

"That depends on whether that unlikely-looking pile of junk actually works," Dontha replied caustically. "Assuming it does, I hope to be out of here within fifteen units or so. By the way, tell your subordinates to clear the equipment out of the adjacent corridors, or my troops will do it for them."

"We have an insufficient amount of space in which to pursue our research," Tepho replied tartly. "Lay one pincer on our equipment, and I will lodge a complaint with your superiors."

"Who should be waiting to speak with me right about now," the officer replied impatiently. "So, let's get on with it."

The scientist issued a series of orders. His assistants turned to their makeshift control boards, ran through a series of carefully documented protocols, and threw the final switches. The results seemed rather mundane as something whirred and what looked like a blizzard of light motes appeared within the confines of the metal framework. A functionary appeared. Something tore his face apart, something else put it back together again, and when he spoke his voice was distorted. "You're breaking up… Increase the power."

A technician made an adjustment, and the scientist on Hive nodded. "That's better… Is Force Commander Dontha present?"

A rectangle had been taped onto the duracrete floor. Dontha shuffled forward. "I'm here."

"Excellent… General Partho is present at this end. Please begin."

Dontha knew the War Partho, and didn't like him, which no doubt accounted for why the fates had seen fit to place him under the older officer's command. A pleasantly distant relationship until Tepho and his team of misfits had discovered a way to hook the two officers together. The general had an unusually large head, a tendency to preen too often, and a slightly superior manner. "Nice to see you, Dontha… I have good news."

"That would be most welcome," Dontha replied carefully, "especially if it is connected with the task force."

"Which it is," Partho replied heartily. "One cruiser, two destroyers, and two transports are en route to Savas. They should drop into orbit approximately two standard weeks from now."

"I'm gratified to hear it," the force commander said. "We'll shut the hypercom down, pack the equipment, and wait for extraction."

"What?" the general demanded, obviously alarmed. "I assume you're joking. What about the Confederacy troops? What if they attack you? No, it's imperative that you keep Project Echo up and running until the incoming ships arrive. You may need my advice." Partho nodded, as if agreeing with himself, and preened the area to the right of his beak.

Dontha took a deep breath as part of a concerted attempt to control a steadily rising sense of frustration. "Your advice is always welcome, Excellency, but if we delay packing until the ships arrive, the process will consume extra time. At least a week and possibly more."

"Nonsense!" the general said emphatically. "The scientists at this end assure me that it will take half that amount of time. Besides, what are you afraid of? A few soft skins traipsing around the desert? You have a battalion of armor… Use it!"

The last comment came dangerously close to suggesting that Dontha lacked courage. An outrageous assertion given his record and one that left the officer nearly speechless. "But, Excellency, I…"

"No, no," Partho said apologetically, "I don't mean to be harsh, but it's imperative that we remain in contact for as long as possible. Besides, it will give the tech types that much more time to perfect their toy. Trust me. I'm rarely wrong."

Dontha *didn't* trust the general, not by a long shot, but knew the discussion was over. "I'll do my best."

"That's the spirit!" Partho said enthusiastically. "Now, be sure to…"

But Dontha never got to hear what the senior officer wanted him to do because the prototype chose that moment to drift out of phase with the hyperspace "tunnel" through which the signal had been routed. There was an explosion of static as the image flew apart. Tepho swore and issued a series of rapid-fire pops and clicks as his subordinates rushed to find the source of the problem and correct it.

In the meantime, Dontha, who had little to no interest in reestablishing contact with General Partho, followed the illicit power feeds back out to the main corridor. Though never defeated in an actual battle, the officer had a pretty good idea of what the experience would feel like.

The Southern Pandu Desert, Planet Savas

The transport was hidden at the bottom of a nearly dry watercourse, not far from a stagnant pool and covered with camouflage netting. The worst of the heat had passed, the first stars had appeared in the blue-violet sky, and the camp was starting to stir. There were thirty-six people altogether, twenty-eight of whom were children, all under the age of twelve. There had been more originally, but that was back before two of the three transports had been put out of commission, forcing the older youngsters to join the main column. One lifter had given up the ghost and been abandoned, and the Ramanthians had destroyed the second on the ground, which left the aircraft that everyone now referred to as *Old Faithful* to carry on alone.

Now, having just awoken from their long logy naps, the children were cranky. But the adults were used to that and had developed routines to deal with it. Three of them fired up a mismatched collection of camp stoves and went to work preparing a hot meal, while Qwis Qwan, her mother Lin, and a woman named Flo Anders led the youngsters down to the same pool that had been used to fill all of the water containers a few hours before.

The children charged into the pond, yelling and screaming, splashed water at each other, or paddled about. The women allowed the youngsters to play in the water for a good fifteen minutes before introducing bars of soap into the mix, thereby transforming the free-for-all into a bath. The key was to finish before darkness fell so there was enough light to dry the youngsters and get them into clean clothes. Qwis laughed as one of the boys splashed her, then waded in and splashed him back.

Meanwhile, just under the ship's blunt nose, Cam Qwan and a grizzled pilot stood under the cone of light thrown down by a landing light and peered at a map. The aviator smelled of alcohol, grease, and sweat. "We're here," Has Norby said, tapping the printout with a grimy fingertip, "and assuming them soldiers have it right, they're about *here.* "

Qwan looked at the gap between the two locations and figured it would take *Old Faithful* about an hour and a half to catch up. Six rotations had elapsed since the children had leapfrogged forward, and they missed their parents.

"Okay, assuming there's no sign of Paguumi warriors in the vicinity, let's land one full day's march in front of them," the colonist suggested. "Kobbi is traveling at night now... so the entire group can spend the following day together."

Norby nodded agreeably. He'd been flirting with one of the women from Savas Prime, and it would be nice to see her again. "Sure, why not? When would you like to lift?"

The businessman consulted his wrist term. "How does 21:30 sound?"

"Works for me," the pilot replied.

"Good," Qwan said. "And no drinking... not till we land. Understood?"

"I wouldn't think of it," Norby lied easily, and faded into the shadows.

Aboard the *Star Ravager*, in orbit around the Planet Savas
The lights were dim, and it was cool inside the control room, too cool for Naval Commander Jos Satto's comfort, but that's what the machines around him preferred. In spite of the damage sustained during the battle with the Confederacy ships, the *Ravager* could still function as a glorified space station, even though the vessel should have been sent home for repairs. A fact that continued to frustrate Satto, who looked forward to the day when the task force would arrive, thereby allowing his ship to depart.

The Ramanthian officer still had three aerospace fighters at his disposal, however. And, based on a request from Dontha, continued to launch them at targets of opportunity. A human transport had been destroyed on the ground, a Paguumi encampment had been incinerated, and the column of legionnaires and civilians had been attacked three times during the last five days. The problem was that the alien ground forces had a plentiful supply of shoulder-launched missiles and were quite adept at using them. In fact, one of his five aircraft had been destroyed, while another had been damaged and forced to land at Hagala Nor.

But now, after days of careful observation, it appeared that a somewhat softer target was in the offing. If he couldn't stop the Confederacy column itself, perhaps Satto could choke off its supplies by destroying the last of their civilian transports. The naval officer watched the three-dimensional map appear over the surface of the plot table and listened as his intelligence officer delivered a preflight briefing to the remaining fighter pilots.

"Rather than fly every day, the soft bodies often let four of five rotations pass before moving forward," the younger officer explained. "That makes it more difficult to track them. But since six local days have passed since the last advance, we think they're due."

"We almost nailed them last time," Flight Leader Sagdo put in defensively. "But it usually takes at least a couple of standard hours to launch the ships, penetrate the planet's atmosphere, and arrive in the strike zone. By the time we arrived the soft bodies had gone to ground."

"Yes," the intelligence officer replied patiently, "we understand that. Which is why you're going to launch at the conclusion of this briefing, land a day's march to the rear of the Confed column, and wait for our signal. The moment the transport takes to the air, we'll call you. The rest will be easy."

"What if the ship is on the other side of the planet when the soft bodies depart?" Sagdo inquired pragmatically. "What then?"

It was a good question, and the briefer responded with the Ramanthian equivalent of a smile. "Our techs built three crude but serviceable satellites and launched them six standard hours ago. They aren't very fancy, but they can supplement our surface coverage and close some of the gaps. I can't offer you any guarantees, but there's an extremely good chance that if the aliens take off, we'll know about it."

Sagdo was impressed and conveyed that sentiment by clacking his right pincer. The pilots withdrew, launched their fighters shortly thereafter, and Satto watched the arrow-shaped aircraft fall toward the planet below. The attack wasn't much, not nearly enough to make up for the damage done to his ship, but some measure of revenge was better than none.

The Southern Pandu Desert, Planet Savas

Old Faithful shook, and the hull rattled, as Has Norby took one last look at the instrument array, ran the transport's engines up, and felt the ore carrier break contact with the ground. The pilot was used to handling heavy loads, and the ship felt light. Though far from drunk, Norby had consumed half a pint of locally made rotgut an hour before liftoff and felt pretty good as he turned toward the northwest and opened the throttles. The glow from the instrument panel lit his grizzled face from below, and he began to whistle. Outside of the light produced by the stars it was pitch-black outside. A fact for which Norby was grateful, knowing that the darkness, plus the enormous amount of surface area the bugs had to monitor, were the only forms of protection that he and his passengers had.

To the rear of the tiny cockpit, in the grimy ore bin, the children had been strapped into the makeshift bench-style seats that lined both of the bulkheads. Most were quiet at the moment, but Qwis knew that if left to their own devices it wouldn't be long before some of them began to fidget, and the youngest started to cry.

One of the other adults launched a round-robin-style song; those children who were old enough chimed in, while the rest listened with interest. Soon it was Qwis's turn to sing, and she was just about to create a new verse, when a heat-seeking missile hit the port engine and exploded.

There was no time to do anything more than scream as the port engine pod shattered into hundreds of jagged pieces. Some of them ripped through the hull as *Old Faithful* did a wingover.

Inside the cargo compartment the jury-rigged lights strobed on and off as a steel shard decapitated an eleven-year-old girl and sent a gout of blood shooting up into the air. A boy slumped forward, having been struck between the shoulder blades, and a second lost his left arm.

Children screamed, and Lin Qwan hit the release on her harness just as the transport performed an unintended barrel roll. With nothing to secure her, the colonist slammed into the overhead, then fell to the deck before Norby managed to regain control.

But the ship was in a steep dive, and Qwis knew her mother was dead even as her father bellowed his wife's name, and the pilot said something unintelligible over the intercom. Then the transport hit with a spine-jarring jolt, bounced back into the air, and skidded for the better part of two hundred feet before it slammed into a rock formation and sent everything that wasn't secured flying toward the stern.

Norby was killed instantly, as ~~was~~ *were* one of the adults and the infant she was holding. A fire started, but *Old Faithful*'s onboard computer detected the blaze and managed to put it out. That was when the power went down, the lights failed, and the cargo compartment was plunged into total darkness.

Hagala Nor, Planet Savas

Like any mechanized outfit, the Pincer of Steel Battalion had an armory as well as an extensive maintenance facility. And, like everything else in Hagala Nor, it was located underground. Something Kuga-Ka didn't like because he felt trapped down there.

But, like it or not, that's where the captured Trooper II had been taken and chained to a couple of steel support columns. The Ramanthian-style lights were extremely dim, so Kuga-Ka and Knifethrow had rigged more, which when combined with the Hudathan's intimidating presence had been sufficient to drive idle onlookers away.

Although they had experimented with various aspects of cybernetics, and learned a great deal from captured cyborgs, the Ramanthian psyche had never been comfortable with the concept of machines controlled by disembodied brains. As a result Dontha was willing to let Kuga-Ka maintain dominion over the T-2 so long as it furthered his purposes.

Although Kuga-Ka wasn't qualified as a cyber tech, the process of exchanging Private Oko's brain box for Haaby's was intentionally simple and could be accomplished in less than a minute. More difficult, however, was the process of rewiring the T-2 to override selected functions. *That* required some technical expertise, most of which came from a Ramanthian electronics tech. His name was Vahgo, and while not trained in cybernetics, he was a whiz where control systems were concerned. He had to wear goggles in order to cut the glare created by the additional lights, and had a difficult time using the tools included in the T-2's onboard kit, but eventually got the job done.

So, having secured Vahgo's assistance and completed the necessary changes, Kuga-Ka made the necessary switch. Floating in eternal darkness, and not having had any contact with the outer world other than the sadistic conversations that Kuga-Ka insisted on once a day, Haaby was no longer sure of her own sanity. Having no form to reside in, and therefore unable to "see" or "hear," the cyborg had nothing else to do but roam her own psychological landscape in search of things to relate to.

Fortunately the cyborg had a friend, a companion with whom she could talk and thereby fight the loneliness. Haaby knew that Missy was dead, having accidentally killed the youngster herself, which made the relationship that much more remarkable. Though not exactly happy about her death, Missy had learned to accept it, and being very close to dead herself, the legionnaire found inspiration in the youngster's attitude.

So, by the time Haaby's tormentor removed Oko's brain box and replaced it with hers, the cyborg had grown accustomed to, if not comfortable with, her enforced isolation. The sudden and completely unexpected restoration of her electronic senses was so pleasurable, so intoxicating, that the Haaby felt as if she were drunk.

Video blossomed, Haaby saw what appeared to be a maintenance facility, and felt a sudden surge of hope. Then she realized that the equipment didn't look right and that something was seriously wrong. That impression was confirmed when ex-

Gunnery Sergeant Kuga-Ka stepped into view.

Heavy chains rattled, then snapped taut as the newly resurrected T-2 sought to bring her arms forward so she could aim the war form's weapons at the Hudathan and kill him. Kuga-Ka offered the equivalent of a smile. "Nice try, dra for brains, but I'm not that stupid. And don't attempt to break those chains unless you'd like a taste of *this*."

The Hudathan held the illegal controller up for Haaby to see, and the very sight of the device was sufficient to send a lance of imagined pain into the center of the cyborg's brain. "And that isn't all," the renegade continued smugly. "I have a *new* toy. See this remote? I can use it to turn your weapons systems on and off. Get the picture?"

Haaby looked at the unit in Kuga-Ka's enormous hand and knew exactly what it meant. By alternating between the zapper and the cutout switch, the Hudathan could make her do just about anything. "That's right," Kuga-Ka said knowingly. "And there's more. I pulled a box head named Oko out of that unit in order to make room for you. He's on life support right now, the same system you were hooked up to, and that's where he's going to stay. But one wrong move on your part, and the freak dies. Do you understand me?"

Haaby wanted to give up, to let Kuga-Ka kill her, no matter how painful the process might be. But Missy was made of sterner stuff. "Go along with him," she urged. "We'll get our chance, and when we do, the ridge head is going to die."

Haaby wasn't so sure, but heard herself say, "I understand," and saw the Hudathan nod.

"Good. I have a job to do, and you're going to help me do it."

Haaby was awake, but the nightmare continued.

The Great Pandu Desert, Planet Savas

It was just after daybreak, the air was still cool, and the dawn people were in the process of breaking camp. Enormous dust clouds rose as guy ropes were released, and dome-shaped shelters collapsed to be folded into bundles. Skittish zurna squealed, snorted, and balked as the children who were going to ride them hung heavily loaded panniers across their sturdy hindquarters. Warriors ran hither and yon. Some were on actual errands, but many were simply posturing in hopes that one or more of the busy young females would notice how dashing they were.

One of the warriors, a youngster named Guppa, brought his zurna to a skidding halt in front of one of the few hogas still standing. He instructed the animal to stay put, and the animal snorted by way of an objection as its owner walked away.

Guards stood to either side of the shelter's single entrance, but they had been told to expect Guppa and motioned for the youth to enter. The sun hadn't parted company from the eastern horizon as yet, which meant the interior was dim. What light there was emanated from a scattering of a few tallow lamps and the single off-world glow strip that dangled from the ceiling. Most everything else had been packed into leather panniers that ringed the walls.

Nartha Omoni turned as Guppa entered and took pleasure in how strong her nephew looked. His eyes flashed as he nodded respectfully to both the chieftain and her guests. Omoni saw the veil cover his eyes but knew what he was thinking. Like his father, Guppa was distrustful of off-worlders, and who could blame him? His older brother had been among those killed during the ambush at Passing Rock. An act of treachery clearly engineered by the hard skins. Now he burned for revenge. It was a passion that could get him killed. The chieftain gestured to her companions. Her words were translated by the device that hung from her neck. "Welcome, Guppa. I believe you know Nis Noia. This is Lieutenant Santana."

Guppa acknowledged the aliens with two perfunctory nods and waited to see what his aunt wanted of him.

"Please," Omoni said, "take a seat." To be seated with his elders was an honor, even if off-worlders were present, and Guppa hurried to do as he was bid.

Santana knew why the youngster had been summoned and took the opportunity to look the warrior over. Thanks to a briefing from Nis Noia, the officer knew that Guppa was like a son to Omoni and that the chieftain hoped to protect the lad by sending him on what amounted to an unpleasant errand, while the rest of the tribe rode north to fight the night people. But could Guppa successfully lead the legionnaires across the finger of desert that separated them from the point where the transport had gone down? *His* life, not to mention dozens of others, could very well depend on the answer. According to the information provided by Colonel Kobbi, Qwis had survived, but there had been a number of casualties, including her mother. The survivors were vulnerable, *very* vulnerable, and it was important to reach them quickly.

Omoni locked eyes with her nephew. "I know you have seen the machines that fly through the air," she began. "During the hours of darkness Ramanthian machines attacked a human machine, and it went down. Some of the passengers were killed, but the majority survived. One of their talk boxes still works, and they called for help. Lieutenant Santana and his warriors have been ordered to secure the crash site and protect the survivors until another air machine can pick them up."

Santana knew that Omoni's description of his orders was only accurate up to a certain point. The problem was that the colonel didn't have any more aircraft at his disposal, not unless he and the rest of the column managed to reach Fire Base Alpha and the fly-forms stored there. But that was a secondary issue. He and his troops needed to reach the crash site first.

There was resentment in Guppa's eyes. "With all due respect, Aunt Omoni, I am a warrior, and it is my job to fight! Everyone knows you are going to lead our people into battle. My place is at your side."

"Your place is wherever *I* say it is," the chieftain replied grimly. "And you *will* obey. Not just me, but Lieutenant Santana as well. Do I make myself clear?"

Guppa's eyes fell. "Yes, ma'am."

"Good. I chose two warriors to accompany you. Not the hell-raisers you like to run around with—but people I trust. If they offer advice, I recommend that you listen. Your life could depend on it. The outcasts suffer from the heat just as we do and are more aggressive of late."

Santana looked at Noia, who shrugged. The operative knew that members of both tribes were banned from time to time. Petty criminals for the most part, who were turned out to fend for themselves. Many died, but some of those who survived had banded together to form groups that followed along behind the major tribes, and stole their katha. But if the outcasts had become more troublesome of late, it was news to him.

"All right," Omoni said, her thoughts having already shifted to other priorities. "It's agreed. The rescue party will depart before the sun rises one fingerbreadth higher in the sky. May God protect you."

The desert stretched hard and flat ahead. Each rock threw a distinct shadow, and each shadow harbored dozens of insects, all of which were willing to coexist so long as the sun hung hot in the sky, but wouldn't hesitate to hunt each other during the hours of darkness. The horizon lurched with each step that Santana's zurna took, and in spite of the fact that the party had been traveling for many hours by then, the hazy horizontal line that shimmered in the distance never seemed to get any closer.

Like the three Paguumi who led the way, the cavalry officer and his eight legionnaires made use of sticks to support tentlike squares of Jithi trade fabric called tatha. Even a tiny bit of shade was welcome. The air was oven hot, perspiration evaporated quickly, and the legionnaire's throat was eternally parched. But there was a limit to how much water a zurna could carry, and given the fact that the animals would consume a great deal of it themselves, rationing was important.

Santana glanced at his wrist terminal, confirmed that the next swallow of warm liquid was still a half hour away, and gave an involuntary start as both Guppa and his mount appeared at his elbow. What else had he missed? The officer resolved to be more vigilant in the future. Thanks to the multiple layers of fabric wrapped around Guppa's head, only his hard dark eyes could be seen. "Don't turn to look, but a group of outcasts found our trail and is following behind."

Santana wanted to look but managed to restrain himself. If the bandits thought they were invisible, it made sense to let them go on believing that. "Will they attack?"

"Not now," the Paguum advised, "but later, after the sun

goes down. That's when they can close with us."

"How many?"

Guppa flashed five fingers three times. With no imminent threat to the relief force Santana had time to think. The numbers weren't all that bad, especially given the superior firepower that he and his legionnaires possessed, but what if the outlaws chose to delay their attack? And followed the rescue party all the way to the crash site? The last thing the officer wanted to do was lead the wolves to the sheep. The officer looked at the warrior. "Is there a way to kill them? *All* of them?"

It was a good question, a warrior's question, and Guppa wondered if he'd been wrong about the off-worlders. Though not especially pleasant to look upon, and less than trustworthy, it seemed they might have at least a few redeeming qualities. "Jubo knows this stretch of desert well. He tells me that we will cross a dry riverbed before long. Once in the gully, and out of sight, a group of warriors could drop off and order their mounts to proceed without them. Assuming they left their tathas in place, it would appear that they were still in the saddle."

Santana looked at Guppa with new eyes. It appeared the Paguum had a good head on him. "Once the outcasts arrived, and descended into the riverbed, the warriors would attack."

Guppa nodded. "Exactly."

"It's a good plan," Santana acknowledged. "My legionnaires and I will act on it."

"We will act on it," Guppa corrected him.

The human smiled. "All right, my friend… But don't get killed. Your aunt would murder me."

"Yes," Guppa replied cheerfully. "I imagine that she would."

Two hours later, having dismounted in the dry riverbed, Santana watched Guppa and another warrior do the same. It was only a matter of seconds before the riderless zurnas, tentlike tathas still in place, were herded up the western bank and over the top. With the exception of the zurna Santana had been riding, which was happy to rid itself of the extra weight, the other animals were reluctant to leave their owners behind and squalled loudly as they were led away.

Dietrich, who had orders to complete the journey to the crash site if anything happened to Santana, nodded as he and the other legionnaires lurched past. The officer wished he could lead them *and* take part in the ambush, but that was impossible.

No sooner had the last of the legionnaires disappeared over the far side of the riverbed than the locals retreated into the ragged run of shade that paralleled the east side of the gully and checked their weapons. Both Guppa and Jubo were armed with single-shot trade rifles, which meant that Santana's assault rifle would represent a major portion of the group's firepower.

The officer joined the Paguum in the shade, dropped into the same crouch that they favored, and felt the heat radiate up through the soles of his combat boots. The legionnaire took a sip of warm water, swirled it around his mouth, and let it trickle down the back of his throat. Then, picking a small stone off the ground in front of him, he placed it in his mouth. The pebble was warm but the saliva it produced served to cool it down. It was tempting to shed some clothing in a further attempt to cool off, but Santana knew it was the wrong thing to do. Strange though it seemed, desert travelers were supposed to wear *more* clothing rather than less, which acted to slow the rate at which sweat evaporated from their skin. The officer knew that was the reason why Guppa and Jubo were swathed in long-sleeved robes and wore pieces of cloth wound round their heads as well.

So there they sat, swatting insects and waiting for time to crawl by. Finally, after what seemed like a lifetime, Guppa stirred, scrambled up the embankment, and peered over the top. He was back thirty seconds later. The grin had a predatory quality. "It's time for everyone to take cover. You must wait until all of them have descended into the riverbed before you open fire. If even one outcast escapes, he will bring more against us."

Santana expected to *give* the orders rather than receive them, but knew that the Paguum was correct. He nodded. "Right. I'll take most of them down... You handle the strays."

The threesome took their places among a clutch of water-smoothed boulders just south of the crossing point. The other two checked their weapons one last time, while Santana took the opportunity to lay three grenades on the rock at his side. The officer felt the usual knot form in his stomach, noticed how dry his mouth had become, and knew it wasn't from the heat alone. Then there was the sound of hooves and the clatter of loose equipment, followed by a sudden cascade of dirt, as the first zurna appeared dark against the searingly blue sky. The animal extended its forelegs and skidded down the steep embankment.

The zurna's rider was a wild-looking figure attired in dusty rags and armed with a well-worn semiautomatic carbine of uncertain manufacture. A sword and scabbard were tucked under his left leg, and a pair of muzzle-loading pistols hung along either side of the animal's neck. Two rather lean saddlebags completed the outlaw's kit. Those who followed looked a lot like their leader and carried a wild variety of weaponry, including everything from firearms to spears.

River rock clattered as the lead rider proceeded to the west side of the watercourse and urged his zurna up the embankment. Santana wanted to get all of the bandits into the gully before opening fire, but Guppa was afraid that the lead rider would escape. The warrior raised his weapon and fired. The outlaw's zurna felt the same impact that he did, screamed, and stood on its hind legs. Gravel gave way, both the zurna and its rider toppled over backward, and fell in a wild tangle of thrashing legs and jumbled equipment.

That was when Santana threw the first of three grenades. They went off in quick succession, ripped half the outcasts apart, and wounded the rest. There was a loud *bang!* as one of the bandits fired his rifle and Santana felt a rock chip sting his cheek as he brought the assault weapon up into firing position. The trigger gave, the weapon started to buck, and a steady stream of steel-jacketed slugs tore at the outlaws. Riders were snatched from their saddles, animals screamed as they took hits, and Guppa uttered a long, undulating war cry.

Then the assault rifle cycled empty, which allowed the surviving Paguum to enjoy a momentary respite as the volume of fire dropped and the legionnaire slammed a fresh magazine into his weapon.

The much-bloodied outcasts took advantage of the pause to

turn on the ambushers and charge. Santana glanced up to find that a Paguum with a lance was charging at him. The legionnaire used the barrel of his weapon to parry the razor-sharp tip and fired as the zurna galloped past.

The officer saw the outlaw fall, heard someone shout a warning, and turned in time to confront three additional riders. One of them fired, and Jubo clutched his chest. The warrior toppled over backward as Guppa took aim and fired. There was a loud *crack!* and the older warrior was avenged.

Santana fired, saw one of the other riders jerk, but hang on as his zurna turned away. The remaining bandit was on him by then, swinging a long, curved sword, and clearly intent on removing the human's head. The legionnaire fired, saw the rider fly over his head, and heard a *thump* as the warrior landed. Santana was still spinning, still trying to turn, when Guppa plunged a dagger into the bandit's back.

The human heard the clatter of falling rock and turned just in time to see a zurna disappear over the top of the western embankment. "One of them got away!" Guppa shouted, and fought his way up through a cascade of loose rock. Once he arrived on top of the bank the Paguum brought the long-barreled trade rifle up to his shoulder in one smooth motion and pulled the trigger. Santana heard a sharp *crack!* and saw a puff of smoke as the warrior fired. Two seconds later the legionnaire saw Guppa's shoulders fall and knew that the outcast had escaped. The ambush had failed.

Santana triggered his com set. "This is Bravo Six to Bravo Three Six. It didn't work. Send someone back to pick us up and give everyone else a break. We're going to travel all night. Over."

There were two clicks by way of a response, and dust rose as Guppa skidded down the embankment, picked his way across the body-strewn watercourse, and knelt next to Jubo. The prayer for the dead had a sad singsong quality.

The legionnaire took a look around. The bottom of the gully looked like a charnel house. Blood, bodies, and loose equipment were scattered everywhere. The sole-surviving zurna bawled mournfully and nosed a corpse as if hoping to bring its owner back to life. Santana thought about the civilians who were waiting for him and swore. The desert swallowed his words and sent a gust of wind by way of a reply. It turned circles, ran out of energy, and disappeared.

The Great Pandu Desert, Planet Savas

Warriors shaded their eyes, and zurnas stirred uneasily as engines screamed, and the Ramanthian shuttle circled the main encampment. Not because there was a need to do so but because Kuga-Ka wanted to make an impression.

Having successfully announced its presence, the boxy aircraft swooped in over the empty area reserved for its use and hovered within a whirlwind of dust before slowly lowering itself to the ground. Although many of the Paguum had seen the shuttle before, the aircraft could still draw a crowd. That's why the renegade allowed the dust to settle before ordering the pilot to open the rear hatch and drop the ramp. The Hudathan wanted to impress the crowd, cause a lot of talk, and start what he hoped would become a legend.

The onlookers stared into the black rectangle, saw a glint of reflected light, and uttered a mutual gasp as something truly monstrous clanked down the incline and out into the harsh sun. The thing was huge, and judging from its metal skin, qualified as a machine rather than a flesh-and-blood being.

But that wasn't all. The construct carried an alien on its back, a creature so large that it looked all out of proportion to its electromechanical mount, and was even more fearsome to look upon than the hard skins. Waves of heat radiated away from the shuttle, metal pinged as it started to cool, the smell of ozone hung in the air.

Conscious of how she was being used but powerless to stop it, Haaby scanned the surrounding encampment. The cyborg saw a crowd of aliens, the concentric rings of hogas beyond, and the rising tendrils of a thousand cook fires, and wondered where she was going. She had asked repeatedly but to no avail. Information was power, and Kuga-Ka took pride in releasing the minimum amount of both.

There was a disturbance out beyond the edge of the crowd,

and the Paguum scurried to get out of the way as a black zurna forced its way through. Srebo Riff sat high on the animal's back. The chieftain was glad he had chosen to ride rather than walk. The extra height put the Paguum on the same level as the newly arrived alien, a horrible beast that looked as if had been born in the bowels of hell. The machine on which he rode added to the overall feeling of menace.

But so long as Omoni took counsel from aliens, he had little choice but to do likewise. Not for long, however. Once the southern tribe was defeated and the matter of water rights was settled, Riff planned to kill all the aliens and resume the eternal globe-spanning journey to which all of his kind were dedicated.

Thus reassured, Riff offered a greeting appropriate to a warrior of middle rank, who was a member of the tribe and respected by his peers. "My name is Srebo Riff." The words that came out of the Ramanthian-made translator sounded like gibberish, but the Paguum had learned to ignore them. "Welcome to our encampment. I hope your journey was both peaceful and prosperous."

Not only did Kuga-Ka know next to nothing about the Paguum, he had no interest in trying to learn. His reply was clumsy verging on rude. "Thank you. My name is Kuga-Ka. I'm glad to be here, wherever 'here' is. Are the troops ready?"

Riff found the lack of courtesy to be annoying and changed the form of address to that used between slightly hostile strangers having no tribal connection. "Yes, the warriors are ready and waiting."

Oblivious to the shadings that had no equivalents in standard, and therefore unaware of the manner in which his social standing had thereby been reduced, Kuga-Ka nodded agreeably. "Good. Let's get going."

Riff's bodyguards and members of his staff were arrayed behind him by then. The chieftain turned to a burly subchief, ordered him to handle the matter, and left, without wishing Kuga-Ka well. Still another insult had the Hudathan been knowledgeable enough to understand it.

"Follow me," the subchief said, and ordered his zurna to turn around.

Now we're getting somewhere, the renegade thought to himself, and opened the intercom. "You heard the hatchet face—follow him."

Haaby did as she was told. Kuga-Ka was a lot heavier than the average human, so hauling him around affected her balance and required a lot of energy. *Still*, the cyborg thought to herself, *it feels good to have a war form again*.

Then Haaby remembered Oko and immediately felt guilty knowing that the war form actually belonged to *him*, and he was where she had been, floating in an uncertain darkness, cut off from the rest of the world, wondering if he was going to die. But there was nothing the cyborg could do about it, and servos whined as she followed the subchief through the crowd. They passed between dozens of dome-shaped shelters and out into the shadow cast by one of the spires guarding the Well of Zugat. Six sphere-shaped remotes floated along behind her. Each Ramanthian-made remote was equipped with a speaker, a spotlight, and a stun gun.

The warriors waiting at the foot of the spire stood and cheered. Not for Kuga-Ka, or for Haaby, but for the subchief. He ordered his steed to stop, stood on its back, and addressed the crowd. In spite of the fact that he didn't have a PA system to help him, the Paguum had little difficulty making himself heard. "The dawn people want our water. The humans taught them new ways to fight. Obey warrior Kuga-Ka as you would me."

The final admonition was met with silence as the Paguum turned their attention to Kuga-Ka, the machine he rode, and the remotes that sped out to hover above their heads. Even veteran warriors were frightened though none of them would have been willing to admit it. "All right," Kuga-Ka said, his voice booming out through the airborne speakers, "listen up!"

Most of the warriors turned their attention to the Hudathan, but a few continued to look up at the remotes. One took a bolt from a stun gun, convulsed, and fell. The crowd stirred uneasily and hands went to weapons. "You're supposed to be looking at *me*, not the frigging remotes, or the idiot lying on the ground," Kuga-Ka said impatiently. "He'll be up and around in a few minutes—but his head will ache all afternoon.

"Now, as long as we're getting acquainted, here's something else to consider. See the boulder over there? Watch what happens to it."

The orders came in over the intercom, Haaby "saw" a ready light come on as the Hudathan released control of her weapons systems, and felt a moment of temptation. If she could buck the Hudathan off her back and turn quickly enough, perhaps she could nail him. But Missy insisted that the renegade would be ready for that, especially the first time out, which meant he'd zap her. So, convinced that she didn't have any other choice, the cyborg raised her arm. The energy cannon fired, there was a loud *bang!* as the superheated rock flew apart, followed by the rattle of falling debris. There was an audible gasp as the warriors saw what the T-2 could do.

"So," the Hudathan said meaningfully, "even though most of you are going to hate my guts by the time the sun goes down, don't take a shot at me unless you're in a hurry to die.

"Now that we have the preliminaries out of the way," Kuga-Ka said cheerfully, "it's time to talk about the purpose of this training. Based on information gathered by your scouts, we know that the southern tribe is planning to attack you with cavalry *and* foot soldiers. You already know how to fight mounted warriors—so my job is to teach you infantry tactics. Or a single tactic in this case, since the enemy is on the way and we don't have time for more. Different cultures have different names for the evolution you are about to learn. The humans call it a massed column, but my people call it the Intaka, or blow of death. The basic concept is that of overwhelming force. Now, unless some idiot has a question, we'll get to work."

What followed wasn't especially pretty, lasted for six hours, and resulted in nearly a hundred casualties as warriors were stunned for making mistakes, dropped from heat prostration, or were injured during mock-combat sessions. But when the training day finally ended, the beginnings of a new weapon had been forged, and ex-Gunnery Sergeant Hreemo Kuga-Ka was pleased.

* * *

The Southern Pandu Desert, Planet Savas

Having arrived at the crash site, Santana waited for sunset before leading the survivors out into the desert and away from the blood-splashed transport and the row of carefully marked graves next to it. The decision was based on the possibility that the Ramanthians might return to the wreckage and the fact that metal was so valuable on Savas that *Old Faithful* was bound to attract all sorts of looters.

Except for the soft ghostly light provided by the thousands of stars that glittered above and the glow sticks issued to a few of the adults, it was completely dark as the Paguum led the off-worlders across the trackless desert. A zurna snorted, equipment creaked, and one of the children coughed as Santana gave thanks for the fact that he was in *front* of the animals rather than behind them. An unpleasant place to walk given their foul-smelling bowel movements.

The goal, assuming it was where the Paguum named Saddo said it was, consisted of an ancient though parsimonious well. Though too small to support an encampment, or a herd of katha, the digs claimed the pito (water seep) would be sufficient to support the forty beings that Santana had responsibility for. But for how long? Kobbi was closing on Fire Base Alpha, but there was no chance of a pickup until he arrived, and all sorts of things could delay him.

The officer's thoughts were interrupted as Qwis appeared at his elbow. She was one of the adults authorized to carry a glow stick, and the rod lit her face from below. Though still recovering from the shock of her mother's unexpected death, the young woman now found herself responsible for all of the civilians, including her father. In the wake of his wife's death, the once-confident and energetic businessman had been reduced to little more than a shambling scarecrow whose eyes were eternally focused on the horizon. The combination of burdens weighed heavily on Qwis, and she looked tired. "Here," Santana said, handing the colonist an energy bar. "It tastes like shit, but it'll give you a boost."

Qwis accepted the bar, peeled the wrapper off, and forced a smile. "If Private Cho wasn't back there, watching for stuff like this, there would be a trail of litter all the way back to the wreck.

We told the children to put the trash in their pockets, but they have a tendency to forget things like that."

Santana glanced over his shoulder, but the far end of the column was lost in darkness. "We have to try—but it's hopeless. We're leaving tracks, not to mention enormous piles of Zurna poop, and what Guppa calls 'fita.' By which he means tiny clues that only a Paguum would see."

Qwis bit off a chunk of energy bar and nodded. "I never spent any time with the Paguum, but a skilled Jithi can track a doo bug through the jungle, so I believe it. You were right by the way... This thing is *awful*."

Both of them laughed and continued to walk side by side. The desert was cold at night, and the legionnaire shoved his hands down into his pockets. "How's your father?"

Qwis shook her head. "Not very well. Mother and he were extremely close. So much so that I always felt like an outsider."

"Maybe that's the way it's supposed to be," Santana replied, and remembered what it was like to look into Christine Vanderveen's eyes.

"Yeah," Qwis agreed soberly, "maybe it is. But look what happens when something goes wrong. It rips your entire world apart."

There had been an attraction between them, and there still was from Santana's point of view, though not on a level with what he felt for Vanderveen. Still, what seemed like an unbridgeable social chasm existed between the diplomat and himself, so why yearn for the impossible? Especially if Qwis was available. Or was she? Maybe she was trying to tell him something. That attachments were dangerous? That she wasn't ready for an ongoing relationship? The legionnaire tried to see into her eyes but couldn't find them in the darkness. "True," Santana responded gravely, "but I'll bet that your father would agree that some people are worth the risk."

"Yes," Qwis replied, "I'm sure he would." She reached out to squeeze the officer's hand, and said, "Thanks," as one of the children started to cry.

Santana was about to reply when the hand was withdrawn, and she disappeared.

* * *

Fire Base Alpha, the Great Pandu Desert, Planet Savas

The column had been marching at night to avoid the heat of the day, but when dawn came, Kobbi made the decision to complete the journey in the daylight rather than bivouac less than ten miles away. The long line of soldiers and civilians wound past a flat-topped rock formation, struggled up a long sandy slope, and emerged onto the flat area east of the wreck. "My God," Major Matala said, eyeing the expanse ahead. "What happened here?"

Kobbi found himself staring at a sea of sand-drifted bones. Some were large, and might have belonged to zurnas, while the rest were smaller and consistent with what the officer imagined Paguumi bone structure might be like. Some of the sun-whitened sticks still bore pieces of sun-dried gristle, but the rest had been picked clean and would eventually be buried by the wind. Bits of brightly colored cloth could be seen in among the bones, half-buried by the sand, but still willing to flap if a breeze came along. "A battle was fought here," Kobbi answered simply. "Our people took on what must have looked like an ocean of Paguumi warriors and fought them to a standstill. Not line troops, mind you, but support staff, many of whom normally fire a weapon once or twice a year. Captain Danjou would be proud."

"Proud? Hell, he'd be amazed," Matala said, as the column picked its way through the field of bones.

Once clear of the battlefield the column followed the deep ditch the ship had plowed into the planet's surface up to a blast-blackened berm and the formation that stood arrayed in front of it. There were six war forms, all the group could muster at the moment, and a small group of bio bods. They were at rigid attention, eyes front, as Captain Calvo took two steps forward and delivered her best salute. Her skin was a deep brown color and looked as though it had been stretched over the bones of her face. "Welcome to Fire Base Alpha, sir. It's damned good to see you."

Kobbi returned the salute, and said, "At ease. You and

your people did one helluva job, Captain. And that's the best-looking wreck I've ever seen."

There was a cheer as both groups broke ranks, and the battalion was reborn.

The Great Pandu Desert, Planet Savas

After nine hours of walking Santana had fallen into a sort of ambulatory stupor. His body continued to place one foot in front of the other, but his senses were dulled, and his mind was adrift. That was why the legionnaire didn't realize that the Paguum had stopped until he was about to walk past them and Guppa reached out to grab his arm. "Lieutenant? We're there."

Santana came to a halt and blinked repeatedly. A wash of pink light heralded the reappearance of the sun, the air was cold, and the officer could see his breath. "There? Where?"

"At the well," the warrior replied patiently.

The interaction served to clear his mind, and Santana looked around. The ground around them was featureless. Surely there had been a mistake. "No offense, my friend, but I don't see a well."

"That's because you are standing on top of it," Saddo said mischievously. "If the lieutenant would be so kind as to back away, we could remove the lid."

The legionnaire looked down and saw nothing but his boots and the sand beneath them. Surely Saddo was wrong. Only someone who had access to modern technology could pinpoint one square foot of sand in a trackless desert. But there was only one way to find out. "Sorry," Santana said, and took a full step backward.

The rest of the column had caught up by then, and there was a considerable ruckus as zurnas squalled, children demanded the right to get down, and exhausted adults worked to sort things out.

Meanwhile the Paguum were down on hands and knees, digging with their hands. Sand flew, and it wasn't long before a flat piece of rock appeared and gradually grew larger. Santana's eyebrows rose as he saw that a series of pictographs had been revealed. "What does it say?"

"It says that the well belongs to the dawn people," Saddo

replied, "and that those who use it without permission will be cursed."

The legionnaire watched in amazement as even more sand was removed, the edges of the lid were revealed, and Guppa used a Jithi-forged blade to pry one side of the rock up out of its roughly circular bed. Then, with Saddo's help, the officer managed to lift the cover up and out of the ground. It was heavy, had clearly been brought to the location from somewhere else, and threw sand into the air when they let it fall.

"I will need a rope plus one of those lamps that you wear on your head," Guppa announced from behind them. Santana turned to discover that the warrior was perched on the edge of the newly created hole with his legs dangling inside.

"How deep is it?" Santana inquired, shrugging the pack off his shoulders.

Guppa didn't know how deep the hole was. But he was determined to lead rather than follow. "I don't know how you measure things," the warrior said, as Saddo positioned a recently acquired sword hilt up across the middle of his back. "But there could be snakes down there, so don't let anyone enter until I give the all clear."

"Here's some rope," Dietrich said, dropping a coil at Guppa's side. "The other end is tied to a zurna. Give a holler, and he'll pull you out."

Santana rummaged through his pack until he came across the Legion-issue headband with lights attached to either side and gave it to Guppa. The warrior put the device on his head, fumbled with the switches, and gave a grunt of satisfaction when twin beams appeared. Then, having thrown the rope down into the hole, he went in after it.

Santana peered down into the hole, saw the lights play across ancient brick walls, and knew that he was looking at the remains of a town or a city rather than simply a well. Had the area been different back then? Before the desert took over? And the eternal migrations began? There was no way to be sure, but it certainly appeared so.

"Bravo Three Seven to Bravo Six," Fareye said over the squad freq. "Company is on the way. Over."

The civilians had gathered around the hold, and Santana pushed his way through them and out into the open. The officer saw that Fareye was standing on top of a Zurna peering toward the south. He raised his electrobinoculars, saw what looked like a dot, and touched the zoom control. The image grew larger as a rider topped a rise and went down the leading slope. That was when a *second* rider appeared, and a *third*, and so on until a total of sixty-three bandits had followed their leader down into a dip from which they would soon emerge.

"What have we got?" Dietrich inquired, having materialized at the officer's side. "Sixty-three of the bastards," Santana answered grimly. "And they're coming fast."

"Even if we may have water, there isn't any cover," the sergeant observed. "Not so much as a good-sized rock."

"Yeah," Santana agreed soberly, "and we don't stand a chance out in the open. Send someone to assist Guppa whether he likes it or not. Tell Miss Qwan to organize the civilians. Lower the children into the hole the moment she's ready. The zurnas will make a pretty good barricade."

Dietrich looked at the nearest zurna and back again. The animals were obnoxious, but he had come to respect them. He hated to kill them, but the order made sense. "Sir, yes, sir."

The next few minutes were filled with frantic activity as the zurnas were stripped of their loads, children were lowered into the ground, and some of the legionnaires prepared what Fareye described as a "surprise" for the oncoming bandits.

Finally, when all of the civilians were safely below, the zurnas were pushed, pulled, and prodded into a circle. The animals squalled, snorted, and tried to balk as Saddo covered their eyes with blindfolds, and whispered words of comfort into their ears. Then, when everything was ready, the Paguum shot the first zurna in the temple. The huge two-thousand-pound body went down hard, hit with a loud thump, and caused the other animals to stir uneasily. Then they went down as well, one after another, until the black hole was like a bull's-eye at the very center of a target.

Saddo shot his own zurna last, and there was no mistaking the look of sorrow on the warrior's face. The two of them had literally grown up together, and while far from equals, were bonded in a way that only a Paguum could understand.

Santana felt sorry for both the animals and their owners, but knew there was no other way to defend the underground sanctuary. The officer made his way over to the point where the squad's com tech was busy scooping a firing position out of the sand, knelt next to the long-range set at her side, and removed the handset. "Bravo Six to Nomad Six… Over." There was a burst of static followed by a male voice. "This is Alpha Two Four… Hold on… Nomad Six will be with you in a moment. Over."

As Santana waited he watched Dietrich and another legionnaire wire the dead zurnas end to end to prevent the outcasts from swooping in, hooking on to one of the corpses, and towing it away. A tactic which, if successful, would open a hole in the defensive barricade.

"This is Nomad Six," Kobbi said. "Go."

Santana delivered a brief, emotionless sitrep, but Kobbi could imagine the hole, the corpses arrayed around it, and the battle to come. The odds didn't sound good, but Santana already knew that, and there was no reason to state the obvious. And, making a bad situation even worse, was the knowledge that there was nothing he could do to help. Kobbi struggled to keep his voice level and matter-of-fact. "I wish I could send a fly-form, but we're sitting in the middle of a hellacious sandstorm, and there's no telling how long it will be until we can launch. Hang in there Bravo Six… we'll get to you as soon as we can."

Though heartened by the fact that Kobbi and his column had been able to reach Fire Base Alpha, the news that they couldn't provide him with any air support left what felt like a rock riding low in Santana's gut. "Roger that, Nomad Six. Let us know when the storm clears… and set some extra places for dinner. It's been a long time since we had any home cooking."

The voice sounded a lot like Top Santana's, and it was just the sort of thing that the grizzled noncom might have said. "Will do," Kobbi replied gruffly. "Over and out." There was a click as Fire Base Alpha went off the air, leaving Santana and his charges on their own.

The legionnaire replaced the handset and stood. Fareye was just inside the fleshy barricade, staring through a pair of glasses.

It was getting warm, and the Naa's fur was matted with sweat. "How close are they?"

"Twenty minutes out, sir. Twenty-five at most."

"Good," the officer replied. "That means I have time to bleed my tanks, have breakfast, and check to see if this situation is covered in the manual."

Those who were close enough to hear laughed and felt a little bit better. After all, if the loot wasn't worried, then why should they be?

The sun inched higher in the sky, the bandits drew closer, and the seconds ticked away.

12

Few men are brave by nature, but good order and experience make many so.
Good order and discipline in any army are more to be depended upon than
courage alone.

NICCOLO MACHIAVELLI
ART OF WAR
Standard year 1520

Savas Prime, Planet Savas

Having been bombed by the Ramanthians, then looted by the
Jithi, the town of Savas Prime was little more than a collection
of burned-out buildings that sat baking in the sun. There were
exceptions, however, like the beautiful arbor that Lin Qwan had
established behind her house. In spite of the damage done to
the structure itself, the garden remained relatively untouched,
which was why Force Commander Ignatho Dontha had chosen
it as the venue for a very important meeting. Against all odds
the Confederacy forces originally trapped in Savas Prime had
been able to link up with the legionnaires in the desert. And,
based on the information provided by the renegade Kuga-Ka,
there was little doubt that they would march on Hagala Nor in
an attempt to capture the hypercom.

Although the Ramanthian felt confident that his armor could
defeat the Confederacy forces, he saw no reason to tackle them
alone if others could be induced to help. Which was why Srebo

Riff had been flown in, taken on a tour of the ravaged city, and hosted to lunch. Dontha needed some cannon fodder, and the northern tribe fit the bill. "So," Dontha began at what he judged to be the right moment, "you've seen the city. Capable though they may be, you'll notice that the Legion troops were unable to protect Savas Prime."

"That's true," Riff allowed cautiously, "insofar as it goes. However, it should be pointed out that your people attacked the city from the air, and had it been otherwise, things might have gone differently. In fact, it's my understanding that the Confederacy soldiers not only escaped into the jungle, but recently joined forces with their companions in the desert."

Primitive though his people might be, Riff was no fool, a fact that Dontha had a tendency to forget. "Yes," the Ramanthian admitted smoothly, "and that's why it's so important to destroy them *now*. Or would you like to wait until they control the entire planet?"

It was a powerful argument, because unbeknownst to Dontha, Riff wanted to eliminate *all* aliens, including the Ramanthians. If he could play one group off against another, then so much the better. There were problems, however, not the least of which were the horrible death-spitting machines of the sort that he had faced near the wreck and the thing that Unit Commander Kuga-Ka rode as if it were a zurna. "No," the Paguum said as he sipped from a glass of incredibly cold tea. "Nor do I want to lose thousands of warriors battling off-world machines. Have you ever faced them? No? Well, I have. Subcommander Pamee was at my side. He's dead, and by some miracle I'm alive."

"That was unfortunate," Dontha acknowledged. "But, if you will agree to fight alongside us, we will neutralize the machines."

"Truly?" Riff inquired. "You could do that?"

"Yes, we could," Dontha answered truthfully, knowing full well he had no intention of actually doing so. "Not only that, but we know where the enemy will go next, and that means we can lay a trap for them."

It was seductive stuff, and even though Dontha was still learning to read Paguumi facial expressions, he could see the conflict in Riff's eyes. Convinced that the moment was right, the Ramanthian went in for the kill. "You would need some modern weapons, of course, which is why we would give you a thousand Negar III assault rifles, plus a quarter million rounds of ammunition. And once we defeat the Legion, you could use your new weapons to defend yourselves from the southerners."

That was the tipping point for Riff, the offer that countered all of the chieftain's doubts and brought the internal debate to a close. "When would we receive the weapons?"

Dontha popped the last grub into his mouth, felt it wiggle, and bit down. "How does tomorrow strike you?"

"That would be fine," the Paguum replied, and the deal was done.

The Great Pandu Desert, Planet Savas

The sun was high in the sky by the time the battle started, which meant that the zurnas had already started to rot when the first bullets slammed into them, and the *pop, pop, pop!* of rifle shots was heard. "Hold your fire," Santana cautioned, as the defenders peered over the corpses arrayed in front of them. "Make every bullet count."

There was a pause while the outcasts steeled themselves against what was to come followed by a bloodcurdling scream as the outcasts urged their mounts forward, and sand spewed out from under their plate-sized hooves as they advanced. Dietrich went to work with his grenade launcher, and the lead rider and his mount quickly disappeared in a welter of blood and fractured bone.

"A cavalryman without a horse is afoot." That was the old saying, and knowing the outlaws would be a lot less dangerous on foot, Santana aimed for a broad, sweat-flecked chest. The rifle slammed into his shoulder, blood spurted, but the zurna kept on coming.

Desperate now, the officer shifted his aim to the animal's head and saw it jerk as the first bullet struck. The zurna went nose down in the sand, skidded forward with its rider still in place, and hit the makeshift barricade. The warrior was catapulted into the air, flew over the legionnaire's head, and landed on all fours.

Santana tried to turn but the outcast was on his feet by then with a sword held high over his head. Sunlight winked off the blade as the Paguum started to bring the weapon down. The legionnaire was still coming around when Qwis shot the warrior in the back. The bandit pitched forward and lay facedown in the sand. The officer thanked the colonist with a quick salute before turning back to the fray.

The outcasts were circling the defensive laager by then, firing their weapons at targets of opportunity, then dashing away to reload. There were five or six empty saddles and a couple of cases where warriors were riding double.

That was when Santana heard Dietrich yell, "*Now!*" and Fareye activated a handheld remote. The explosives hidden beneath the sand didn't detonate all at once, but exploded in a continuous roll of thunder, as zurnas were heaved into the air, body parts cartwheeled across the sky, and blood fell like rain. It was a stunning blow and one that broke the attack. The surviving outcasts withdrew, galloped out of range, and circled their leader.

Meanwhile, Santana took advantage of the momentary break in hostilities to assess the situation. At least a third of the outlaws had been killed or wounded but the legionnaires had suffered casualties as well. Private Farrell had taken a bullet right between the eyes, Private Hulu was down with a chest wound, and a couple of others sported assorted bandages. Fareye interrupted the officer's thoughts by touching his shoulder and pointing to the north. "Take a look at that, sir… What do you make of it?"

What looked like a brown smudge obscured the horizon. It reminded the officer of smog, the kind he'd seen on heavily industrialized worlds, but when Santana raised his glasses he found himself looking into what he knew to be a sandstorm. The *same* sandstorm Kobbi had referred to. In fact, the legionnaire could already feel the insistent push of the wind and the sting of windblown sand, as the disturbance came his way.

Santana turned toward the enemy, saw the bandits wheel, and knew they were determined to carry out one more attack before the sandstorm hit. Once they managed to overwhelm the legionnaires, the outcasts would drop through the opening and slaughter the civilians. The officer activated his com set. "Okay people, a storm is coming. That means this is their last shot at us. Get those goggles on… and hit 'em hard."

There was no time to say more before the Paguum attacked. It was clear that the outlaws had something different in mind this time as they came straight in, ordered their mounts to jump, and flew over the low barricade. Not all of them, because the inner circle was too small for that, but five or six.

Dietrich came to his feet firing, brass arcing away from his weapon as his bullets knocked a warrior out of the saddle, and his mount jumped the opposite barrier.

Santana shot a zurna in the head, managed to dodge the falling body, and yelled, "Watch the bastards on the outside!"

A Paguum chose that moment to jump the lieutenant from behind, and the assault weapon went flying as he fell facedown in the sand. It was difficult to move with so much weight on his back but Santana managed to buck the warrior off. Then, having rolled over onto his back, the officer used one hand to intercept the assailant's knife arm and the other to reach for his sidearm. The moment the weapon came free of its holster, Santana jammed it into the body above and pulled the trigger. There were two muffled thuds, and the Paguum jerked in response and suddenly went limp.

Desperate to see what was happening, Santana threw the body off, scrambled to his feet, and found that the wind-driven haze was all around him. The sun was little more than a dimly seen glow by then, it was impossible to see what was going on more than ten or fifteen feet away, and the officer realized that he had forgotten to wear his goggles. Zurnas circled half-seen in the flying sand, autofire stabbed the murk, and a legionnaire screamed as a lance went into her thigh.

Eyes slitted against the storm, Santana shot the Paguum who held the blood-reddened lance, saw Fareye jump up to pull a rider off the saddle, then haul the outlaw down to the ground. Steel flashed, the bandit's head flopped, and blood sprayed the air as the Naa-forged steel did its work.

Then there was a strange, almost surreal moment as a Paguum bellowed orders, and the surviving outcasts withdrew, and were immediately swallowed by the storm. "Lower the wounded into the hole!" Santana shouted over the wind. "Collect all the gear you can! We're going to need it!"

It took the better part of ten minutes to get everyone down the hole, tug the stone lid back into place, and descend into the dimly lit chambers below. The moment his feet touched solid ground Santana posted guards at the bottom of the shaft and ordered Dietrich to establish a quick-reaction force.

Then, satisfied that the single entry was secure, the officer set off on a tour of the surrounding rooms. All manner of candles, glow sticks, and cell-powered lights had been used to illuminate the maze of ancient corridors, dusty galleries, and cavelike chambers.

Now that the battle was over, a dormitory was being established to house the children, and a first-aid station was open for business. Santana ducked under an archway and entered to find that "Doc" Obi and a civilian volunteer were hard at work doing what they could for the wounded. The officer made the rounds, spoke to each patient, and emerged to find that Qwis was outside waiting for him. She took his hand. "Come with me. There's something I want you to see."

Santana followed the young woman through a series of passageways, past a row of bricked-up windows, and into a circular chamber. A pool of crystal-clear water occupied the very center of the space and reflected light from the candles that occupied niches all around the room.

Saddo, the Paguum who had led the off-worlders to the ancient well, crouched beside it. A bloodstained bandage had been tied around his head, but he was otherwise untouched. "You were correct," Santana said simply. "Thank you."

The Paguum shrugged. "It was God's will, not mine. My uncle showed me the well, and I passed the knowledge to you. Such was your destiny."

Santana descended a flight of shallow steps, knelt next to the pool, and scooped water up into his face. It felt wonderful. The legionnaire drank some and used the rest to wash his face. "Take as much as you want, but don't let any fall back into the well," Saddo admonished. "It is our sacred duty to keep it clean."

Santana felt embarrassed and was quick to apologize. "Please forgive me, Saddo. That was stupid."

"Not stupid," the warrior corrected him. "Only those who live with wells understand what they need."

Santana nodded, came to his feet, and allowed Qwis to lead him away. A few steps down the corridor brought them to a doorway and an alcove beyond. The officer saw his pack, what he knew to be *her* pack, and one of the water bladders that had been salvaged from *Old Faithful*. It was wet on the outside and newly fat with water.

"Do you see that corner over there?" Qwis inquired. "There's a hole in it. And if you were to hang the water bladder up there," she said, pointing at an overhead beam, "we could take a shower."

Santana raised an eyebrow. "*We?*"

"Of course," the young woman replied innocently. "We have to conserve water."

The legionnaire nodded soberly. "Quite right… Thanks for reminding me. But before I can clean up, I have to…"

"You don't have to do anything," Qwis interrupted. "Sergeant Dietrich knows where you are—and expects you to relieve him in four hours."

It was a setup, one that granted Dietrich more information about Santana's private life than the officer wanted the noncom to have, but the temptation was too strong. He grinned. "You thought of everything."

"Yes," Qwis agreed smugly, "I did."

Because of the sudden need to kiss each other while removing all sorts of military paraphernalia, it took an unusually long period of time for both of them to get undressed. But, with some enthusiastic help from Santana, Qwis was eventually able to shed her underwear and step under the dribble of liquid that flowed from the water bag.

Her body had always been slim, but after weeks of hardship, her ribs were visible. Qwis looked up into the cool water, ran her fingers through her hair, and gave a tiny moan of pleasure as the liquid trickled down across her chest. Brown nipples hardened in reaction to the water. Santana stepped in and held up a bar of soap. "May I?"

"Yes," Qwis said huskily, "you may." Santana applied the

soap to cool skin, starting with her shoulders and gradually working his way down to pert, upturned breasts, a flat stomach, and the dark cleft between her legs.

Qwis uttered a tiny gasp as his hand lingered there before finding its way around to her buttocks, where the other hand joined it. Then she was up off the floor with her legs wrapped around his waist as Santana nudged his way inside. Their lips met, and the couple remained like that, their bodies locked together, until the steadily rising tide of passion caused both of them to move.

Qwis broke the kiss, held on to the legionnaire's shoulders, and looked up into his face. She wanted to memorize it, so it would always be there, stored against the time when they would part. It was a reality he hadn't considered as yet, but she had, and was already trying to deal with. Qwis took pride in the pleasure that she was giving, the little sounds that he made, and the way their bodies fit together.

Then, as their lovemaking intensified, and the tension started to build, Qwis pulled herself up to renew the kiss as the final moment of pleasure came. And it was good, better than what she had expected, which led to a desire for more.

Finally, reluctant to release Qwis and thereby bring the interlude to an end, Santana continued to hold her, reveling in the trickle of cool water, the contrasting warmth of her body, and the smell of soap.

Later, as the legionnaire lay asleep on their makeshift bed, Qwis said a silent farewell. *If* they survived, *if* they found a way off the planet, Santana would be sent on another mission while she went to Earth. Her father had some money there, which meant that he could heal, she could further her education and find whatever life still had in store for her. The soldier turned, an arm fell across her stomach, and Qwis felt a tear roll down her cheek.

Fire Base Alpha, the Great Pandu Desert, Planet Savas
The day after the storm had dawned bright and clear, bringing with it the opportunity to dig out from under sand drifts and

put the battalion back together. The wreck was a scene of frantic activity as Kobbi stood atop a neighboring dune and watched still another quad clank down the ramp to join its mates. Bit by bit, as more war forms were activated, the perimeter had been pushed farther out.

The officer turned as engines screamed and a skeletal-looking fly-form rose on its repellors, turned on its axis, and fought for altitude. It had orders to fly south, land in the desert, and bring the crash survivors out. Something a lot of very worried parents were looking forward to.

The fact that Santana and his party had survived repeated attacks by the outcasts was good news but did nothing to resolve the central problem. The officer felt sure that the hypercom was still on Savas because the Ramanthians hadn't left, as evidenced by the attack on *Old Faithful* and the high-altitude flyovers they conducted at least twice a day. The hands-off exercise suggested that what aircraft they still had were considered too precious to risk by attacking the wreck.

But the question, the one that kept the jacker awake at night, had to do with time. How much of it remained before some sort of Ramanthian task force dropped into orbit, loaded the hypercom in their holds, and carried it away? Days? Weeks? Certainly no more, given the amount of time that had elapsed since the battalion's arrival. Whatever the answer, Kobbi knew that he and his battalion would have to reach Hagala Nor in a very short period of time, take on a substantial force of Ramanthian regulars, and defeat them *before* their reinforcements could arrive.

The next problem was how to get the captured equipment off planet, but there was no way to know if Captain Posson and the smuggler had been able to get through, so all the officer could do was seize control of Hagala Nor and hope for the best.

"Good morning, sir," Calvo said cheerfully as she topped the dune and handed Kobbi a sealed container. "I hope you like your coffee black because that's how it is."

"I like my coffee any way that I can get it," the senior officer replied appreciatively. "We ran out a full week before we got here."

The MO nodded and took a sip of tea before gesturing to the scene below. A squad of T-2s, each with a bio bod strapped to its back, were jogging toward the east side of the perimeter. "Things are going well. We'll be able to pull out by 0600 tomorrow."

"You did a helluva job, Captain. And so did Rono-Ra and Amdo. I'll put every damned one of you in for a decoration if we make it off this pus ball alive."

Calvo was about to credit her troops when a fly-form screamed in from the southeast and circled the fire base like a bird checking its nest before settling onto pad three. "That will be Nis Noia," Kobbi predicted. "Come on, let's see what the frigging spook has to say."

Although Nis Noia had seen the wreck from the air, it wasn't until he stepped out of the fly-form onto what looked like black glass that he could appreciate the size of it. The ship, or what remained of it, had the bulk of a high-rise office tower laid on its side. A legionnaire arrived to take him inside. The operative was struck by the fact that once inside the hull, and with no ports to look out of, he could have been in space. Thanks to all the miracles performed by Amdo and his crew, the lights remained on, deliciously cool air whispered through the ducts, and only the slight tilt of the deck hinted at where the ship truly was.

Kobbi, Matala, Calvo, and Amdo arrived in the wardroom at the same time Noia did. There was a quick flurry of introductions followed by a readiness report from the XO and a tray of refreshments. Once the rating who had brought them left the compartment, Kobbi wasted little time getting down to business. His eyes locked with Noia's. "I know you understand the urgency of our situation. Hell, you were the guy who found the Ramanthian air car out in the desert and sent for help. What, if anything, can you tell us about what the bugs are doing right now?"

Noia brought his fingers together into a steeple. "My scouts tell me that the Ramanthian machines, by which they mean armor, are positioned to defend Hagala Nor."

Calvo nodded. "That's consistent with the latest images obtained by our RPVs. It looks like the bugs have a full battalion on the ground. It's hard to get an exact count, since the Ramanthians are trying to hide them, but the standard strength for that kind of an outfit is fifty-six armored vehicles. So far they don't show any signs of coming out to meet us."

"So," Kobbi said soberly, his eyes roaming the faces around him, "it looks like the bugs know what we're after and plan to make a stand. We need to get our hands on the hypercom *before* they receive reinforcements, so it looks like we'll have to tackle them head-on."

Noia cleared his throat. "That may be hard to do, Colonel. My sources inform me that the northern tribe broke camp this morning and is riding west. I believe they will stop, turn south, and engage you. They won't be able to win, not against your cyborgs, but the fight could last for two or three days. Especially if the Ramanthians provide them with arms, which I predict that they will."

Kobbi directed a look at Calvo, who knew what the colonel wanted, and left the room as the jacker turned back to Noia. "We can't afford to let the bugs stall us for one day, much less three. Captain Calvo will send an RPV to check on the northerners. Now, assuming that we can confirm your intelligence, here's what I want you to do... Use your influence with the southern tribe to bring them into contact with northerners. While the Paguum are busy butting heads, we'll go around the conflict and engage the bugs head-on. Do you follow me?"

Noia winced, and his eyes dropped to the surface of the wardroom table. Even though he wasn't supposed to get emotionally involved, he'd been on Savas so long that he had come to value Paguumi culture and love the planet as much as they did. No, the off-world part of him couldn't approve of Omoni's tendency to usurp northern wells, but the Paguumi part of him understood. Survival comes first.

Now the intelligence officer was being called upon to guide his adopted people toward a conflict that would almost certainly result in thousands of casualties. And he didn't have to follow Kobbi's orders. The organization that Madame X led fell well outside the military chain of command and had been created to gather intelligence, not act on it.

But there were other sentients to whom he was beholden. *Billions* of them, spread across hundreds of systems, all of whom would be vulnerable if the Ramanthians had sole possession of the hypercom.

The silence had grown distinctly uncomfortable, and Kobbi had just cleared his throat as a prelude to restating his request, when Noia looked up from the table. His voice cracked as he spoke. "I'll do what you ask under one condition."

Kobbi wasn't used to having conditions imposed on him, not by civilians dressed in ratty-looking native garb, but managed to control his temper. "And the condition is?"

"The Ramanthians will supply Srebo Riff and his tribe with arms," Noia answered. "I'm sure of it. You don't have weapons to give away, I know that, but you could supply the southerners with a group of advisors. They were practicing the tactics Santana taught them when the lieutenant and his troops were pulled away. Send him back, let him lead the dawn people into battle, and I'll do what you ask."

Now it was Kobbi's turn to be silent as he considered all of his alternatives. It wasn't fair to Santana to throw him into the situation that Noia had described, not after what he'd been through, and he was short of competent company commanders. But it was clear that Noia felt strongly about helping the southerners, and judging from the fervor in his eyes might say "no" if he didn't get his way.

"All right," Kobbi conceded, "I'll send Santana. But only for the first engagement. He has a scout company to lead... and I'm short of officers. Agreed?"

"Yes," the intelligence operative agreed, expelling his breath with the word. "Thank you."

"Just keep the northern tribe off our backs," Kobbi replied curtly. "*That* will be thanks enough."

The Great Pandu Desert, Planet Savas

The fly-form's slipstream whipped through the open hatch, blew Santana's hair straight back, and threatened to snatch anything that wasn't strapped down. It felt good to fly rather than walk, even if it meant that he and his troops were headed back into the desert again, where they were supposed to provide the southern tribe with "advice and leadership." A euphemism for helping one group of digs kick the crap out of another.

What little comfort there was stemmed from the fact that the rest of the battalion was headed north to engage the Ramanthians. Not that Santana and his tiny command had been issued a free pass, since they were supposed to rejoin the battalion, "as early as possible after the successful execution of the unit's orders."

In the meantime, out on his own once more, Santana wanted to take a look at the night people before joining their cousins to the south. And since the two tribes were only about eighty standard miles apart, and moving toward each other at a speed of about five miles an hour, the detour wouldn't take all that long.

An RPV had been monitoring the northern tribe's movements, so it was easy to find them. The first thing the legionnaire saw from the fly-form's starboard hatch was the five-mile-long cloud of dust created by thousands of warriors all riding in a line abreast. Or trying to, since some of the terrain was easier to cross than other parts, which meant that what might have been a straight line looked like an elongated S instead. Since there was no clear reason for using that particular formation en route from one place to another, the legionnaire guessed that he was looking at some sort of training exercise. Farther back, and raising their own cloud of dust, were the elders and children, all protected by a vanguard of well-armed females.

As the fly-form passed over the first rank Santana caught a glimpse of dust-cloaked warriors, the hulking animals on which they rode, and something completely unexpected. What looked like a Trooper II! There were isolated flashes of light as a few of the northerners fired their weapons, then the fly-form was past the first group of Paguum and headed for the second.

Santana opened the intercom and spoke to the pilot via the boom-style mike in front of his lips. "Can we make another pass over the warriors? I need to check on something."

The pilot held the same rank Santana did, so the reply was casual. "Okay," she replied, "but look fast. We took at least some of them by surprise on the first pass, but they're ready for us now." The pilot's words proved prophetic as she put her electromechanical body into a tight turn and headed back toward the cloud of mistlike dust. The entire length of the line erupted into flame as virtually every Paguum who had a gun fired it. Fortunately, most were too far away to be very effective. And because those directly below the aircraft had never fired at one before, most of them aimed at where the target had been rather than where it was about to be. An error that wasted thousands of rounds of ammunition.

There was one exception, however, a cyborg named Haaby, who though embedded in the line, and moving just as quickly as the zurnas were, stuck out like a sore thumb. She was bigger for one thing, ran on two legs, and carried a 350-pound Hudathan strapped to her back. She had a lock on the fly-form, knew exactly what it was, and what Kuga-Ka wanted her to do. It would have been hard not to since the renegade was shouting at her over the intercom. "It's coming back! Blow the fly-freak out of the sky! *Now*, damn you!"

Haaby didn't want to fire, but knew what the penalty would be if she didn't, and skidded to a stop. Then, having turned to face the target, the cyborg opened fire. She intended to come close, but not *too* close, lest she harm one of her friends. The T-2's laser cannon burped coherent light, and a hundred rounds of .50 caliber armor-piercing slugs stuttered up toward the target, before Kuga-Ka shut the machine gun down to conserve ammo. The fact that the fly-form continued on apparently undamaged sent Kuga-Ka into paroxysms of rage. He beat Haaby's shoulders with his ham-sized fists and screamed abuse at her as the aircraft moved out of range.

Meanwhile, the fly-form shook but remained undamaged as the aircraft took unexpectedly heavy ground fire. "Holy shit!" the pilot said. "What have they got down there? A frigging antiaircraft battery?"

"Nope," Santana said calmly, "but they do have a Trooper II with a Hudathan riding on its back."

"A Hudathan?"

"And not just *any* Hudathan," the officer replied grimly, "but a psychotic sonofabitch who hates cyborgs."

"Then let's grease him," the pilot said enthusiastically, "*and* the T-2 he rode in on."

"I wish we could," Santana replied, "but where did the

scumbag get the T-2? Whose brain box did the bastard load into it? And is the borg shooting at us because he or she wants to, or because they have to?"

"Beats me," the pilot replied, "so I think I'll dump you and your team in the desert before you drive me crazy."

"Sounds fair," Santana agreed. "But make sure that you include the T-2 and ex-Gunnery Sergeant Kuga-Ka in your report. Maybe the old man can make sense of it."

"That's a roger," the cyborg replied, and turned toward the southwest. Fifteen minutes later the pilot spotted another cloud of dust and made an announcement over the intercom. "Five to dirt. I'm putting you down about three miles in front of the digs."

There was a solid thump as the fly-form put down. Santana exited first, followed by Dietrich, Fareye, and the rest of the squad. The legionnaires removed their hats and hung on to them as Santana thanked the pilot via his com set and the cyborg took off. With no slipstream to cool the legionnaires, and no shade to protect them, the heat fell like a hammer. Kepis went back on, the soldiers deployed flaps to protect their necks, and everyone started to sweat.

Once the aircraft was gone, and the dust had started to settle, Santana looked to the east, where three black dots could be seen. Unlike the northerners, who had been arrayed in a long line abreast, the southerners rode in three parallel columns. A sensible formation that allowed the noncombatants to travel at the center while warriors protected both flanks.

The fly-form had been visible from miles away and it wasn't long before a group of scouts galloped forward to meet the off-worlders and provide them with the worst mounts available. After all, the Paguum reasoned, if the aliens lacked the organs necessary to establish *thu* (oneness) with a zurna, what difference did it make?

As a result, so much time was spent loading the intractable animals that the legionnaires had barely finished by the time that lead elements of the formation arrived. Each member of the squad was equipped with a translator, and Santana made use of his to ask where the newly created dragoons were. Since none of the southerners knew how to employ the new unit, and the fact that there was no one to speak on behalf of it at leadership councils, Santana's students had been relegated to the ignominious job of riding drag in the outer right-hand column.

That meant the legionnaires had to sit and eat dust while the entire tribe rode by before the dragoons finally drew abreast of them. The Paguumi warriors made a splendid sight, to Santana's eyes at any rate, and were clearly identifiable by the red pennants their leaders carried, the identical tathas that sheltered them from the sun, and the uniform manner in which their weapons were slung across their backs.

Santana was both surprised and secretly pleased by the high-pitched undulating wail that broke out when the dragoons spotted their instructors, and the lead warrior turned to deliver a Legion-style salute. His name was Pobo, and he grinned as the off-world officer jerked on his mount's reins and was forced to kick its flanks before the beast finally took its place in the formation. "Greetings, Lieutenant Santana! It's good to see you! Your riding has improved."

"It's good to see you, too," the legionnaire replied over the loud rumble of his zurna's digestive system. "But, if you think my riding has improved, then you're going blind."

Pobo laughed and gestured toward the riders in front of them. "I apologize for the position that we find ourselves in, but lacking any battle honors, the unit was automatically assigned to the rear."

"No problem," Santana assured him. "We *like* dust."

However, as the day progressed, and the formation left the whitish hardpan for the softer desert sand, there wasn't all that much dust for the officer to cope with. And, for reasons known only to it, Santana's zurna was unusually placid. All of which contributed to a sense of lurching peace. A semiconscious state in which the off-worlders were vaguely aware of their surroundings—but pleasantly detached from the physical discomfort to which their bodies were being subjected.

Finally, after what seemed like a lifetime within the strange, heat-induced stupor, the formation came to a halt. Then, rather than the flurry of orders and confusion that Santana expected from so large a group, the dawn people seemed to simply drift apart as everyone did what they had already done hundreds of times before. The left and right columns circled back to meet themselves, and once that evolution was complete, the noncombatants found themselves surrounded by not one but *two* concentric rings of warriors. At that point every other fighter was excused to help set up camp.

When Santana inquired about the tribe's katha, Pobo informed him that they were well to the south, guarded by a contingent of cavalry. And, unless the enemy drove some sort of change, it sounded as if the noncombatants would remain right where they were when the warriors rode out in the morning.

Santana, who had a better idea of how close the tribes were to each other than Pobo did, agreed with that theory and spent the evening traipsing from one fire to the next meeting with his dragoons. Cooking pots bubbled, and the hard-looking warriors listened as the off-worlder reminded each group of what he expected of them. "We will do it the same way we did it at the Finger of God," Santana assured the warriors, "only better, because we know how to work together now.

"Some of the northerners may have off-world weapons, and you might see a big fighting machine that walks like you do, but hold formation unless you hear the bugle sound the retreat. Barring the unexpected, and assuming that we'll be dealing with cavalry, the best-disciplined troops will carry the day."

Finally, nearly hoarse from talking, Santana returned to where his legionnaires were camped to discover that a messenger was waiting for him. The youth had never seen aliens before, and his voice quavered as he delivered the carefully memorized words. "Chief Omoni is meeting with her generals. You are to accompany me to her hoga."

Santana nodded and turned to Dietrich. "I'll be back as soon as I can. Make sure that everyone gets as much rest as possible—and warn the tube team that we may have a renegade Trooper II to deal with tomorrow. I want them to ride with the dragoons but operate independently. If Kuga-Ka shows up on that T-2, it's going to take a missile to stop him, and we only have two of them."

The sergeant said, "Yes, sir, I'll get on it," and watched the officer disappear into the night. While it was true that a shoulder-launched missile could theoretically destroy a T-2, the odds were against a clean kill. That meant that the cyborg could, and probably would, track the weapon back to its source and blow the launch team into bloody confetti. Santana knew that, of course, but had no other choice.

Dietrich circled the fire, located the two-person tube team, and gestured toward their launcher. "I'm going to carry that thing tomorrow… Who's going to give me a refresher course?"

After a long, winding journey past dozens of fires, and hundreds of hogas, Santana followed his diminutive guide to a larger-than-average structure surrounded by heavily armed guards. Meanwhile, way off in the distance, there was the *pop, pop, pop* of gunfire as scouts from both tribes probed each other's lines. A sure sign that a battle would be forthcoming in the morning.

The legionnaire was searched and forced to divest himself of both his knife and handgun prior to being admitted to Omoni's compound. When Santana inquired as to the reason for such precautions the warrior in charge pointed into the shadows. That was when Santana saw that two bodies had been laid out side by side. Assassins most likely—sent to end the battle before it could begin.

At least twenty Paguum had gathered inside the hoga, which meant that it was warm. *Too* warm by Santana's standards so he stood next to the open door where an occasional breeze found its way through. Opposite him, on the far side of the circle, Omoni sat with Nis Noia at her side. Firelight reflected off the chieftain's silver eye patch, and the scar that bisected her cheek made her look even more fearsome than usual.

The rest of the participants were senior officers equivalent to majors, colonels, and generals. The legionnaire's translator was on and fed audio to the plug in his left ear. "So," General Kuzo continued, "rather than fight them at the Well of Zugat as originally planned, we will meet them here, on the plains that lead to Hagala Nor."

"But why?" a sturdy-looking officer inquired.

"Because we must fight them somewhere," Omoni replied

patiently. "It hardly matters where so long as the terrain is flat and open. Our wells are drying up, while the night people wallow in water and spill it into the desert. They must learn to share."

The assertion that the northerners had intentionally wasted water was false, as everyone in the hoga knew, but a certain amount of exaggeration was not only expected but appreciated by those looking for words that they could adopt and pass on to their troops.

But some of the generals hoped to succeed Omoni one day, and even though they stood ready to take her orders, weren't above a bit of posturing. One such individual took the opportunity to speak up. He had an especially predatory nose and had lost an arm in battle. "Is this about water? Or has the alien seated at your side turned your head? Why should we die for *him*?"

It was a tough question, but Omoni was ready for it. Her voice was level and calm. "The Ramanthians are at war with a group of tribes called the Confederacy. Both sides possess weapons that could destroy Savas. The northerners formed a relationship with the hard skins—and that left us with no choice but to form an alliance with their enemies. All they asked us to do was to fight the night people here rather than at the Well of Zugat. And, to help us win the upcoming battle, they sent Lieutenant Santana to lead our dragoons. So, to answer your question, we should die for them because they are willing to die for us." That, too, was something of a misrepresentation, since even if Santana and his tiny command were completely obliterated, it wouldn't begin to compare with the slaughter likely to be visited upon the dawn people the following day.

But the symbology was there, the answer was sufficient to silence Omoni's critics, and the conversation turned to more tactical concerns. Santana listened carefully as General Kuzo outlined the overall battle plan. It wasn't very sophisticated, which wasn't too surprising because while the tribes raided each other's katha herds from time to time, their counter-rotational migratory paths rarely brought them into contact, and the two groups hadn't fought a pitched battle in many years.

Finally, after Kuzo had reviewed what amounted to a half dozen sequential cavalry charges, and no mention had been made of Santana's highly mobile infantry, Noia cleared his throat. "And how do you plan to employ the dragoons?"

Kuzo hemmed and hawed, but it soon became apparent that the nontraditional troops were destined to be part of a reserve that could be called upon if needed. Santana took the opportunity to intervene. "While the concept of a reserve makes sense, sir, I wonder if you would be willing to consider using the dragoons in a slightly different manner?"

Omoni nodded, which meant that Kuzo had little choice but to agree as well. The ensuing discussion lasted for the better part of two hours as Santana used a stick to draw diagrams in the sand around the fire, explained how the dragoons could potentially be used, and dealt with all manner of questions.

The officer was exhausted by the time the meeting came to a close and everyone spilled out into the cool night air. Having retrieved his weapons, Santana turned to find that the youngster was still there, waiting to guide him back, and shivering in the cold.

The legionnaire dropped his jacket over the youth's shoulders and followed him through the labyrinth of shelters. A Ramanthian-manufactured flare went off to the north, floated slowly to the ground, and was swallowed by the darkness.

It was still dark when the war drums started to beat, and the vast encampment began to stir. Fires were rekindled, meals were cooked, and warriors looked to their weapons. Rather than the chatter and laughter typical of most mornings the Paguum were somber, as if already mourning those who would soon be dead, but still walked among them.

The legionnaires used heat tabs to boil some of their strictly rationed water, made coffee, and ate two chewy ration bars apiece. Santana didn't feel like eating but forced himself to do so both as an example to the others and to provide his body with the fuel it would need.

Once the last mouthful of dry food had been washed down the officer set off to visit all of the ten warrior units that comprised the dragoons. Different though their physiologies were, it was apparent that the Paguumi warriors suffered from the same precombat jitters that humans did, and welcomed a word of encouragement, an attempt at a joke, or a small piece of advice.

Once the unofficial inspection was over Santana gathered what amounted to his personal staff together and ordered the bugler to play assembly. By that time messengers were dashing back and forth between the various cavalry outfits, and thousands of mounted warriors were streaming out of the defensive laager and onto the surrounding plain. Then, following the order of battle that each unit leader had memorized the night before, they formed up into the broad U-shaped configuration called the horns.

Per Santana's suggestion the dragoons took their place at the bottom of the U, which meant that as the southerners moved forward, Omoni's cavalry would screen both flanks, allowing the double-mounted infantry to proceed up the middle.

Then, assuming that the flankers held, and Kuzo managed to keep the initiative, the U-shaped formation would evolve into a W as the dragoons drove in toward the very center of the northern line. At that point any number of things could occur. Assuming that Srebo Riff led from the center, the position favored by Paguumi leaders over the years, the dragoons might be able to kill or capture the chieftain and his staff. And if things went especially well, they might even cut the northern army in two, thereby opening both halves to an attack by Omoni's reserves. Or, and this was what Santana feared most, the combination of off-world weapons and leadership by the likes of Kuga-Ka might shatter the horns before they could rip into the enemy formation. But there was nothing that he and his troops could do except wait for the huge formation to coalesce, go straight up the middle, and hope for the best.

In the meantime the officer could see a smudge that he knew to be the enemy, but they were so far away that it was impossible to make out any details, even with the electrobinoculars to help him.

An uncomfortably long period of time passed before Kuzo gave the necessary order, a horn sounded, and the drums began their deliberate beat. Santana waited for the cavalry to begin their charges. Something they did with much waving of weapons, extravagant screaming, and unreserved bravado. Then, sure that the horns had gone in, the legionnaire turned to the bugler riding behind him. "Sound the advance."

Crystal-clear notes rent the morning air, and the dragoons moved forward. Gradually the zurnas transitioned from a walk, to a trot, to a canter. Then, as the entire line swept forward, the first sounds of battle were heard. Santana gritted his teeth as he heard the cloth-ripping sound of automatic weapons, the characteristic *thump, thump, thump* of a .50 caliber machine gun, and the firecracker-fast *pop, pop, pop* of trade rifles going off. He couldn't see the T-2 yet, but knew the cyborg was up ahead somewhere, with Kuga-Ka on its back. Could the southerners continue to advance against such intense fire? Only time would tell.

The horns consisted of six columns of seasoned warriors each. The moment they penetrated the northern line four ranks turned outward, pushing the night people away, while the other two lines of cavalry turned in as they tried to hold those riders caught within the U where they were.

Meanwhile, having waited in vain for the Ramanthian war machines to arrive, and thereby ceded the initiative to the southerners, Srebo Riff had no choice but to tackle the enemy alone. He sent cavalry to counter the horns and hoped that the Hudathan could hold the center.

Haaby, Kuga-Ka, and what the renegade liked to refer to as his personal guard were out in front of the dragoons and determined to make a stand. They were all armed with Ramanthian assault rifles and, thanks to the Hudathan's training, knew how to use them. They went to the prone position, waited for the enemy to come within extreme range, and opened fire.

The warrior on the zurna to Santana's right was snatched out of the saddle, as were a dozen more. The officer forced himself to ignore the mayhem around him and ordered the bugler to sound the six-note call for "Charge!" The dragoons hadn't fired a shot as yet, so the sooner they could dismount, the sooner they'd be able to shoot back.

The legionnaire kicked his mount's flanks and felt the animal stretch into a clumsy gallop. The zurna took three long strides, stumbled as a bullet struck its chest, but recovered and kept on going. Suddenly, for the first time since he had been thrown into contact with the ornery quadrupeds, Santana felt a moment of genuine admiration for the lung-shot beast as it forged ahead in spite of its wound, air wheezing through distended nostrils, sand flying from immense hooves.

But valiant though the animal was, the zurna couldn't last forever, and when the legionnaire saw a cluster of brightly colored pennants ahead, he knew the time had come to bring the charge to a halt and begin the second phase of the attack.

A series of rising and falling notes sounded, hundreds of animals skidded to a halt, and the slaughter continued. Two ranks forward of him Dietrich saw three warriors literally come apart as the .50 caliber slugs struck them, and felt a warm mist touch his face as he hauled on the reins. The zurna slowed, finally came to a stop, and stood patiently while bullets whipped around it.

The .50 caliber slugs had to be coming from the T-2, and the noncom felt anger clog the back of his throat as he freed the launcher from the ties that held the weapon in place, turned toward the northern line, and swore as a riderless zurna came out of nowhere to block his shot.

Santana screamed to make himself heard over the constant yammering of the enemy guns and ordered his troops to form up even as the deadly autofire cut them down. As the officer strode back and forth in front of them, he noticed a sword lying on the ground and felt a bullet tug at his sleeve when he bent to pick it up. He waved the weapon over his head, shouted "Advance!" and felt a moment of pride as the Paguum swept past him.

In the meantime the zurna that had been blocking Dietrich's shot had gone down when a .50 caliber slug ripped through its neck, and was still gushing blood as the dragoons lurched forward. The noncom forced himself to ignore everything around him, peered into the sight, and thumbed the zoom control. The target leaped forward. The T-2 towered over the northern troops—and the Hudathan seemed to be staring straight at him as Dietrich pulled the trigger.

But, just as the weapon left the tube one of Kuga-Ka's warriors accidentally fired a flare. It hit the ground, spun in circles, and burned white-hot. The missile's guidance system took note of the fact that the new source of heat was hotter than the first target it had been offered, made the necessary correction, and struck home. The resulting explosion killed more than a third of Kuga-Ka's guard and threw the rest into a state of confusion.

The renegade eyed the carnage, knew that a second missile would be along soon, and ordered Haaby to withdraw. The cyborg was backing away when the next rocket struck the ground ten feet in front of her. The explosion knocked half a dozen warriors off their feet and shrapnel rattled against the Trooper II's armor as she continued to pull back.

That was when the renegade sent word for the group he liked to refer to as the "hammer" to administer the Intaka, or "blow of death." Eager to join the fray, the members of the six-warrior-wide one-thousand-warrior column came forward on the double as the sound of their huge kettledrums beat a deep, booming counterpoint to the steady *thump, thump, thump* generated by the smaller instruments the dragoons carried. The airborne remotes that Kuga-Ka had introduced for training purposes accompanied them, thereby ensuring that his orders would be heard.

Though unaware of the way in which Dietrich had attempted to kill the T-2, Santana knew the rate of incoming fire had slackened and was extremely grateful. Somehow, in spite of the horror all around them, the dragoons had maintained their formation and were marching north with the precision of a machine.

When the six-warrior-wide column appeared, and the legionnaire saw the remotes flying above them, he knew it was Kuga-Ka's doing and swore through gritted teeth. Both groups were in range by then, so Santana shouted a series of orders that were repeated by unit commanders to both the left and right. "Dragoons, halt! Front rank kneel... Fire!"

Rifles crashed and muzzle flashes rippled all along the line as the infantry fired their weapons into the flying column. The first rank of warriors in the advancing column went down; they were plowed under by those behind and left half-buried in the bloody sand. One of the remotes, a tendril of smoke trailing behind it, spiraled into the ground and exploded.

The second rank of northerners raised their Negar III assault rifles and fired back, but because the column was only six warriors across only a tiny fraction of the entire force could use their weapons, while every dragoon still able to take his place in the line could reply. They were in a rhythm by then and moved forward like a machine as Santana bellowed orders. "Second rank advance! Kneel! Fire!"

Then, as the third rank came forward, the legionnaire ordered the dragoons to halt. That allowed the unit to deliver alternating volleys as one rank fired while another reloaded, and still another prepared to fire.

Kuga-Ka held the electrobinoculars to his eyes and swore as the hammer faltered, wavered, and broke under the withering fire. The Paguum were brave, but their training had been all too brief, and this was their first engagement. The column disintegrated, the warriors came streaming back and swirled around him. The renegade shouted orders over the T-2's PA system, and even went so far as to shoot a few of the fleeing troops, but all to no avail. The Intaka had failed. Only the remotes remained, hovering over the carnage like high-tech harbingers of doom.

The northern counterattack had failed, but there was still plenty of incoming fire. Santana turned to his bugler, saw the youth's head snap back as he took a bullet between the eyes, and was forced to rely on his voice instead. "Dragoons! Advance!"

Those Paguum who still could stepped over and around their fallen comrades, held their rifles at port arms, and marched grimly forward. Even though the dragoons were still some distance away, they had Srebo Riff's attention by that time, and the chieftain found himself in something of a quandary. Not only had the strange foot soldiers defeated Kuga-Ka's hammer, but they were headed straight for *him*. Orders were issued, a messenger was dispatched, and *another* troop of cavalry was thrown into the fray.

Santana got the word over the team freq from Dietrich. "Bravo Three Six to Bravo Six. Over."

"Go Three Six."

"It looks like we have cavalry attacking from the left flank. Over."

"Form a square. Pass the word. Over."

Orders were shouted, warriors wheeled, and the dragoons

created the box-shaped formation that Santana had taught them during the days leading up to the exercise at the Finger of God. And not a minute too soon because all of the distances had closed by then, and the northern cavalry thundered straight in. They rode full out, lances extended, expecting the impertinent foot soldiers to scatter like dust in the wind. But the dragoons not only held, but fired their weapons in concert, sweeping dozens of warriors from their saddles. Paguum screamed, zurna squalled, and the killing continued as Santana shouted words of encouragement to his troops. "That's it! You've got them now lads... Reload! Aim! Fire! Steady there... Fill that gap. Good job! Somebody shoot that officer... Yes, the one with the pennant!"

But roughly 25 percent of the cavalry were armed with Negar III assault rifles, and even though most of them weren't very good at using them, some enjoyed remarkable success. One of them went down when his zurna was hit, took shelter behind the animal's bullet-riddled carcass, and hosed the dragoons with autofire. The front rank on the western side of the square fell like grass to a scythe.

But Dietrich, who considered himself to be something of an artist with a grenade launcher, lobbed a round high into the air. Such was the noncom's timing that the round exploded *over* the warrior, blowing him to bloody bits. That, plus well-coordinated return fire from Santana and the four legionnaires still standing, eliminated the riders who had proven themselves most effective with the off-world auto rifles.

Finally, having been unable to break the square, and with most of their officers dead, the surviving cavalry were forced to retreat. By the time they thundered past the pavilion that had been established to protect Srebo Riff and his general staff from the blistering sun, it had already been abandoned. What remained of his once-powerful army followed, streaming back toward the Well of Zugat, leaving thousands of dead warriors for the dawn people to bury.

Twenty minutes later Nartha Omoni and Nis Noia allowed their zurnas to choose a zigzagging path through the horrible litter of battle before finally taking shelter under one of the awnings that had been rigged for Riff's comfort. "So," Noia said, leaning forward in the saddle, "victory is yours."

Omoni looked out across the plain. The noncombatants were arriving by then, rushing out onto the battlefield to find sons, brothers, uncles, fathers, and even grandfathers. Some wailed over their horribly mangled finds, while others shouted excitedly and gestured for still others to come help when a wounded relative was located.

Closer in, only a hundred yards from the pavilion itself, the dragoons stood at ease, still trying to absorb what they had been through. Of the thousand warriors assigned to the experimental unit, fully half were wounded or dead.

Santana, his voice little more than a croak, could be seen instructing small groups of troops to go in search of their casualties. "You are dragoons," he told them, "and dragoons take care of their own."

Omoni shook her head. "If this is victory," she said sadly, "then God protect me from defeat."

13

Everything which the enemy least expects will succeed the best.
FREDERICK THE GREAT
"INSTRUCTIONS FOR HIS GENERALS"
Standard year 1747

Planet Algeron, the Confederacy of Sentient Beings
When the Hudathan lifeboat dropped out of the nowhere land of hyperspace the little vessel had something strange clutched to its side. Not one object but three. A cylindrical space sled, a suit of space armor, and the bug sealed inside of it. One of more than a dozen technical experts sent to the Erini system, where the Thrakies were hard at work modifying Sheen warships for use by the Ramanthian navy. It was a highly secret endeavor, or had been, until FSO-4 Christine Vanderveen and Triad Hiween Doma-Sa had dropped in unannounced.

Now, as the pilot hurried to identify his vessel to the Confederacy naval units in orbit around Algeron, Doma-Sa was already exiting the tiny ship to bring the Ramanthian inside. Although Vanderveen wanted to go with him, the fact that the Hudathan lifeboat wasn't equipped with human space armor made it impossible for her to help. Four standard days had elapsed while the little vessel was in hyperspace. Had the

Ramanthian survived? And if so, was he still sane after such a traumatic experience? And if he was sane, could he be convinced to talk?

The questions were extremely important because although the lifeboat's sensors had been able to pick up and store a significant amount of data where the inside of the Thraki repair facility was concerned, testimony from a Ramanthian would serve to buttress that evidence.

Meanwhile, as Vanderveen sat and worried, Doma-Sa had worked his way down along the port side of the ship. He was big, so his space armor was even bigger, and a good deal more complex than the triad would have liked. In spite of the fact that the Hudathan leader had spent a significant amount of time in space, he had never been trained as a naval officer, which meant that he hadn't logged all that many hours in a suit. Something he had neglected to mention to either the pilot or the human.

Now, as Doma-Sa fought to control the armor, he was beginning to question that decision. Especially since the controls were so sensitive that his first attempt to use the built-in propulsion system sent him jetting out into the blackness of space and it required a concerted effort to make his way back.

Once in contact with the hull, the Hudathan followed recessed handholds to the point where a tractor beam held the Ramanthian space armor firmly in place. Having prepared a line, Doma-Sa called on the lifeboat's pilot "to release the bug."

The naval officer complied, and the sled had just started to drift away when Doma-Sa clipped the line to the fitting located just behind the Ramanthian's helmet. There were no signs of life from the entity in the suit, a fact that didn't bode well. When the short length of monofilament ran out, it jerked the alien space armor off the cylindrical vehicle, which drifted away.

Now, with the alien in tow, the Hudathan made his way back to the relative safety of the lifeboat's lock and pulled himself inside. After that it was a relatively simple matter to reel the Ramanthian in, close the hatch, and repressurize the compartment. It was a pleasure to shuck the suit, and hang it on a rack.

The next step, which was to open the bug's armor, proved

more difficult. But form follows function, and the bugs were no different than other races where the issue of emergency access was concerned. There had to be a way to open the suit from the outside. Doma-Sa was still exploring the suit with big clumsy fingers when the interior hatch opened, and Vanderveen appeared. The human took one look at what the triad was attempting to do, and said, "Here, let me give you a hand."

Within a matter of seconds the diplomat located a small plate and flipped it open to reveal a typical Ramanthian squeeze switch. It took all of her strength to generate the amount of pressure that a pincer would, but she felt the device give and heard the hiss of equalizing air pressures. An almost indescribable stench escaped, along with the pent-up atmosphere. Vanderveen gagged, and even the normally stone-faced Hudathan turned away. "He's dead," Doma-Sa proclaimed. "Let's blow him out through the lock."

"You're probably right," Vanderveen agreed, "but we'd better check to make sure."

The clamshell-style space armor had opened along the Ramanthian's back by then. Vanderveen made a face as she used both hands to reach inside, grabbed the alien under his chitin-slick armpits, and dragged him out onto the deck. There was no response, but Doma-Sa thought he heard a slight exhalation, and frowned. "Hold on... Let me try something."

There were all manner of things stored in the lockers that lined both bulkheads, and the Hudathan rummaged through them until he came up with a reflective sun visor. The triad held the brightly chromed surface in front of the Ramanthian's parrotlike beak and Vanderveen saw the surface fog over as the prisoner exhaled. "My God, he's alive!"

"But just barely," Doma-Sa said, as he mashed the wall-mounted intercom button. "Boka-Ka! Tell the squats that I'm aboard and demand a high-priority landing vector. Tell them we have an injured bug on board and to have a medical team waiting for us when we land."

Vanderveen took note of all the ethnic slurs inherent in the triad's orders and hoped that Boka-Ka would have the good sense to edit them out. Not that it mattered much, because by the time the full extent of their activities became known, both of them would be in trouble. Except that only the Hudathan people could dismiss Doma-Sa from *his* job—while just about anyone could fire her. The FSO remembered Wilmot, winced, and went to work on securing the Ramanthian prisoner for landing. Her career might be over, but if the information gathered in the Erini system was sufficient to destroy the Ramanthian-Thraki alliance, then the loss would be worth it.

Near Fort Camerone, Planet Algeron, the Confederacy of Sentient Beings

The military cemetery was located six miles south of Fort Camerone. The graves were arranged in concentric rings. And there were hundreds of rings and thousands of graves. Each marker wore an icy cap, and each mound was covered by a shroud of freshly fallen snow. A stainless-steel obelisk stood at the center of the graveyard, and the same inscription had been etched into all four sides:

AND HERE THEY LIE,
THEIR BLOOD FOREVER MINGLED,
THE LEGION OF THE DAMNED.

And not far from the outermost ring, in a section reserved for civilians, a large crowd had gathered around a freshly dug grave. President Nankool was there, as was Chien-Chu, as was most of the Senate, two dozen military officers, and an equal number of civilian officials. Some Naa were present as well, more than a hundred in all, singing the death chant. Nodoubt Truespeak's voice could be heard above all the rest. The deep baritone made the perfect instrument with which to express the tremendous sorrow that he felt. Sorrow mixed with a measure of guilt, because the assassin had been sent to kill him and would have almost certainly succeeded had it not been for Maylo Chien-Chu.

Now she and her husband stood at the edge of the small rectangular hole that had been hacked out of the planet's frozen surface, only partially visible through the driving snow, as the tiny casket was lowered into the cold, stony ground. Similar burials took place in Naa villages every day, but Truespeak found this one to be especially poignant not only because of the issues that lay behind the tragedy, but the fact the little girl was part Naa.

Booly pulled Maylo close as their daughter's casket came to rest at the bottom of the grave, and the ropes were withdrawn. He felt her shoulders shake as tremendous sobs racked his wife's body and bit his lip as the first shovelful of crusty soil went into the hole. The assassination attempt, the miscarriage, and the funeral all seemed like part of a surreal nightmare.

Finally, it was over. The bereaved couple leaned on each other for support as they made their way to the convoy of vehicles waiting to carry the mourners back. So many tears had been wept, and so many words had been spoken, that the couple had nothing left to say to each other as the driver guided the staff car back toward Naa Town and the fort beyond. If it hadn't been for the spirals of smoke that rose to merge with a lead gray sky, and buttery yellow light that glowed from behind dozens of thick panes, the low, snow-covered domes would have been nearly invisible.

The car bounced over ridges of ice, waddled through some potholes, and passed a snow-dusted quad just back from patrol. Booly and Maylo were huddled together, lost in the mutual misery, when the vehicle came to an unexpected halt.

Booly looked up, saw that hundreds of leather-clad Naa had spilled out onto the road in front of them, and was reaching for his belt com when the mob started to dissipate. The townspeople didn't go far, just to both sides of the road, leaving the middle clear. Then, as the staff car started up again, Booly saw that more of the locals lined both sides of the road. So many that it appeared as if the entire population had turned out, not to attack the car as he had initially feared, but to demonstrate their sympathy for those inside it. There were no secrets on Algeron, not around Fort Camerone, and word of the assassination attempt had spread.

Maylo looked out through the half-fogged window, instinctively understood what the gesture meant, and felt the tears start to flow. She sobbed as the car wound its way through Naa Town, the snow-flecked citizens stood silently by, and another two-hour-and-forty-two-minute day came to an end.

Ramanthian Planet, Hive

It was nearly midnight when Admiral Enko Norr read the very latest intelligence report, ordered an entire assault group to attack the invading object, and surrendered to the inevitable. Like it or not, he had no choice but to inform the Queen. An already cranky monarch who didn't like to be awoken in the middle of the night, and had a well-established tendency to abuse those who delivered bad news. Something that his mate, Suu Norr, the long-suffering Minister of Civilian Affairs, had already experienced firsthand.

The journey from the admiralty to the royal eggery passed all too quickly from the naval officer's perspective, and it wasn't long before Norr found himself being escorted up the switchbacking ramps to the platform that encompassed the Queen's enormous body. Norr gave silent thanks for the fact that most of the royal's army of courtiers, toadies, and sycophants were home asleep. And, judging from the sound of the monarch's high-pitched voice, the rest were under attack. "If I am to be awoken at all hours, and tortured with all manner of problems, the least you could do is fetch me some tea... now move, or I'll have the entire lot of you sent to an ice world, where you can huddle around a fire fueled by your own excrement!"

The servants were well aware of the fact that Norr was the real cause of their misery and eyed the military officer resentfully as he completed his journey and stopped to bend a knee. "A thousand apologies for interrupting your sleep, Majesty."

"Don't be silly," the monarch replied caustically. "I love to be awoken in the middle of the night and subjected to the rantings of a uniformed imbecile. I shall be fascinated to hear what manner of menace is so important that it couldn't wait for a more civilized hour."

Norr withstood the barrage of words, nodded gamely, and swallowed. It didn't work. The hard, dry lump remained lodged at the back of his throat as he spoke. "An object that was first thought to be a comet, but was later determined to be an alien construct, is on a collision course with Hive. It is expected to touch down somewhere within the western hemisphere unless we're able to stop it."

"*What?*" the Queen demanded incredulously. "You're telling me that some sort of missile is going to hit Hive?"

"Yes, ma'am, I mean *no*, ma'am," Norr corrected himself. "It isn't a missile so much as a custom-built spaceship designed to look like a comet. That's how the Confederacy brought it into the system—and that's why we weren't aware of it sooner."

The Queen was fully awake by then and so concerned about what the naval officer had to say that she forgot to sound aggrieved. "Tell me what you know… *Everything*."

So Norr told the monarch how the object came to be classified as a comet, how the better part of two weeks passed before the Department of Astronomy took a closer look at the object and ran standard calculations on its orbit. That was when the bureaucratic alarms started to sound, a scout ship was dispatched to inspect the newcomer, and the truth became known. Rather than a comet, the incoming object was a ship designed to *look* like a comet, and had no doubt been sent for the express purpose of attacking Hive.

The Queen interrupted at that point. Her voice was filled with concern. "Are they after my eggs?"

"We aren't sure that the Confederacy even knows about your eggs," Norr replied. "But it hardly matters. An assault group has been dispatched to destroy the enemy vessel, the odds are against a hit on this location, and the eggery is extremely well protected."

"An assault group?" her royal highness demanded incredulously. "I would have thought that two or three warships would have been sufficient to handle a single intruder. Or is there something you failed to tell me?"

Norr didn't want to tell her, but had very little choice. "I sent three ships. But, while the incoming vessel doesn't mount the sort of offensive weaponry one might expect, it is equipped with some very powerful shields. So powerful that my task force was unable to penetrate them. It's my hope that a stronger force will be able to get the job done."

"What about the ship's crew?" the Queen wanted to know. "Have our forces made contact with them?"

"Yes," the admiral answered wearily. "A human who identified herself as Lieutenant Commander Moya Frenko is in command. Our intelligence people theorize that she's a cyborg—and may be the only person on board."

"So let me see if I understand," the monarch said, glaring down at the officer from the summit of her gigantic body. "A fake comet, piloted by a cyborg, is on a collision course with Hive."

Norr looked down at the floor. "Yes, Majesty, I'm afraid so."

The Queen turned to look at her Chief of Security. "Kill this fool and send his head to the Egg Norr with my condolences. She'll be better off without him."

Admiral Norr wanted to object, wanted to comment on how unfair his execution would be, when a bullet interrupted his thoughts. The officer dropped like a sack of rocks. A puddle of blood formed around his shoulders.

"Get him out of here," the monarch said coldly, "and summon the rest of my staff. My eggs are at risk."

Planet Algeron, the Confederacy of Sentient Beings

The dimly lit two-bed room held only one patient, and he lay unconscious in an improvised sling-bed. Readouts glowed, sensors beeped softly, and the sharp smell of disinfectants hung in the air. But in spite of the fact that Fort Camerone had an excellent medical facility, and efforts were under way to expand its capabilities in order to deal with all the different physiologies represented by the Senate, it wasn't equipped to handle Ramanthians. So, even though the doctors were doing their best to treat the individual that Doma-Sa and Vanderveen had captured in the Thraki-controlled Erini system, there was no guarantee they would be successful. That fact remained at the forefront of President Nankool's mind as he led a small group in to peer at the prisoner, then back out to the corridor. The news that the Thrakies were providing the Ramanthians with sub rosa support had come as a shock, and he was still trying to absorb it.

"He doesn't look very good," Booly ventured doubtfully.

"There's no certainty that he'll ever come to. And even if he does, some of the doctors believe he'll be a vegetable."

"What if General Booly is correct?" Christine Vanderveen inquired worriedly. "Will the Senate accept the rest of the proof?"

"I don't know," the president answered honestly. "The visuals you brought back are very convincing, but Senator Obduro could claim that they were faked. A witness would certainly help."

"Maybe there's another way," Sergi Chien-Chu said thoughtfully. "Rather than tackle the problem out in the open, we could meet with Obduro privately and show him video of Sheen ships being repaired in a Thraki facility. Then, if he and his superiors were led to believe that the Ramanthian would testify, there's a good chance that they would break their ties with the bugs."

"But that would be a lie," Vanderveen objected hotly.

"That's a strange objection coming from *you*," Nankool replied with a frown. "First there were your activities on LaNor, and now this. While I'm grateful for what you have accomplished, your methodologies leave a great deal to be desired. In fact, some would say that this situation is of *your* making."

Vanderveen felt blood rush to her face, knew Nankool was correct, and willed herself to disappear.

"Unusual times call for unusual strategies," Hiween Doma-Sa rumbled in defense of his coconspirator. "But I agree with my colleague. If we could trick the fur balls into severing their relationship with the bugs, it would save a whole lot of trouble."

"All right," Nankool agreed reluctantly. "Let's set it up. Who's going to take the lead?"

Slowly, all heads turned toward Chien-Chu. "You're one of the sneakiest bastards I ever met," Nankool said affectionately. "If anyone can do it, you can."

"Thanks," the cyborg replied dryly. "You say the nicest things."

The Hive System, the Ramanthian Empire

Moya Frenko was the *Flaming Bitch*—and the *Flaming Bitch* was her. She could "see" via her sensors and "feel" the feedback that the ship's systems sent her, but she couldn't touch. Not yet, until her hull body made contact with the surface of Hive and her pain was consumed by the ensuing explosion. That was the moment when she would be freed from the metal prison in which she rode, the incessant loneliness, and the painful memories.

The bugs were onto her now, had been ever since the scout ship had swung by, and there was no need to behave like a comet anymore. Now she was a missile, a missile on a mission, and the target was up ahead. Hive still looked small, no larger than the head of a pin, but it was growing bigger by the minute.

Three ships had been following her, firing steadily, until they had no more torpedoes left to launch and were reduced to harassing her with cannon fire. Now they had been replaced by a dozen warships, including two battlewagons, three cruisers, and a squadron of destroyers. All preparing to fire on her.

They had called upon her to stop, to surrender, to avoid certain death. But what they didn't understand was that she *wanted* death, *needed* death, and *hungered* for death. Because that was where hundreds of her shipmates were, still strapped into the wreckage that had been their ship, cartwheeling through space in holed fighters or orbiting an alien sun in their half-slagged space suits. They whispered into the officer's nonexistent ears, called to her in her sleep, and were out there waiting for revenge.

So the cyborg ignored the incoming calls, kept her sensors focused on the target, and hummed to herself as the distance continued to close. Frenko didn't have any offensive weaponry other than her strange, H-shaped body, but she was equipped with the most powerful defensive shields ever mounted on a single vessel, and they were operating at full capacity when the Ramanthians opened fire.

Suddenly, the *Flaming Bitch* was at the epicenter of a barrage of incoming missiles, torpedoes, and cannon fire. The weapons converged on the shimmery energy field that surrounded the ship, created what looked like a new sun, and sent waves of violent energy expanding outward.

Certain that no single vessel could possibly withstand such an attack, the Ramanthian in charge of the attack group was already starting to compose a glowing report when the

Flaming Bitch shot out of the blazing confluence of energy and continued her journey toward Hive.

The admiral stared up at the screens arrayed above him in disbelief, made a grinding noise with his beak, and ordered his ships to give chase.

Meanwhile, Frenko "felt" what equated to pain, ran a systems check, and immediately identified the problem. The shields overlapped each other like scales on a reptile. One of them had given way under the force of the barrage, an energy bolt had slipped through the resulting gap, and the port in-system drive had suffered a direct hit. The system was already in the process of repairing itself, but the damage had been done, and with her speed reduced by 50 percent, the *Bitch* would be even more vulnerable.

Frenko considered her options as she shut the power plant down, and was just about to conclude that she didn't have any when a really strange possibility entered her mind. She didn't have lips anymore, but if she had, they would have curved upward.

The onboard NAVCOMP didn't like Frenko's plan and refused to implement it. But the naval officer had the necessary override code, the computer was forced to comply, and the *Flaming Bitch* simply disappeared.

Near Fort Camerone, Planet Algeron, the Confederacy of Sentient Beings

The snow had stopped some twelve hours earlier, thereby giving birth to an uninterrupted series of bright, sunny, and all-too-brief days. Wonderful interludes during which the sky was clear, the air was crisp, and billions of ice crystals sparkled like diamonds. Perfect weather for some sort of outing, or so it seemed to Chien-Chu, who went in search of his niece. But after calling her quarters and asking around, it soon became clear that Maylo had not only left the fort but failed to notify her bodyguards.

Though not overly fearful for his niece's safety, the industrialist was concerned and decided to track her down. While not a *real* admiral, not in his mind at least, Chien-Chu was entitled to wear the uniform, which meant he could requisition all manner of things, including staff cars.

The noncom in charge of the motor pool was surprised when the cyborg appeared, requested a vehicle, and got behind the wheel himself. Would he wreck it? Probably, the sergeant decided, but that was General Booly's problem.

Chien-Chu had a pretty good idea of where Maylo was, or thought that he did, and followed the main road down through Naa Town to the point where it intersected with the main north-south thoroughfare.

Waves of slush flew up and away from the oversized tires as the industrialist turned south. The vehicle rocked from side to side as it negotiated a series of potholes before gaining the better surface that lay beyond.

The top of the obelisk appeared first, soon followed by a clear view of the entire monument, as the vehicle rounded a low hill and started down a slight incline toward the cemetery below. Chien-Chu saw no sign of another vehicle, and was about to conclude that he'd been wrong, when he spotted what looked like a dot south of the main cemetery.

The cyborg pulled into the parking lot, got out, and followed the only tracks there were. He wasn't dressed for the conditions, but didn't need to be, and barely noticed the snow that found its way into his shoes and clung to his pant legs.

Maylo heard movement, felt a tiny stab of fear, and turned to find that her uncle had approached her from behind. "I thought I'd find you here," Chien-Chu commented. "Are you all right?"

Maylo forced a smile. "Yes, of course. Bill is extremely busy, and I didn't want to bother him."

"I doubt that he would consider it to be a bother," her uncle replied. "And it's dangerous to leave the fort without your bodyguards. What if you were taken hostage? Or killed? Promise you won't do this again."

"I promise," Maylo said contritely. "I know my daughter isn't here, not really, but I miss her."

"Yes," Chien-Chu said gently as he looked down on the tiny mound. "I know exactly how you feel. As you know, my son Leonid died fighting the Hudathans on a planetoid called Spindle. Later, when the war was over, I went there to find some closure. It didn't help."

"No," Maylo said sadly, "I don't suppose it did."

"And nothing will ever fill the hole he left inside me," Chien-Chu said. "But I learned to accept it, to go on with my life, and create happiness around the emptiness. You're young, Maylo. There will be other children. As many as you and Bill want. So let go of this hole in the ground and keep your daughter where she belongs. In your heart."

Maylo put her arms around her uncle's electromechanical body and gave it a hug. "You're right as always. Thank you." The sun started to set once more, but the sky was clear, and the stars seemed unusually bright.

Their footsteps echoed down the long, sterile corridor as Lieutenant Thinklong led Nodoubt Truespeak and his party toward the Senate chambers. A pair of heavily armed legionnaires marched behind. While there weren't any indications that the Naa who referred to themselves as "true bloods" had infiltrated the Legion, humans had been chosen for the detail to ensure that the Chief of Chiefs wasn't attacked by one of his own bodyguards.

What many senators had originally regarded as a minor issue had been brought into sharp focus by Truespeak's initial appearance and the assassination attempt that followed. That was why the newly refurbished theater was already packed to overflowing when the Naa dignitaries arrived and were shown to their seats.

Knowing that many eyes were upon him, Truespeak resisted the temptation to fidget as President Nankool opened the meeting. "So," Nankool continued, "having been unable to consider SR-5706 the last time it was introduced, we are slated to vote on the measure this morning. Senator Pama? Would you care to reintroduce Chief Truespeak?"

Pama rose, made his way to the podium, and delivered an eloquent restatement of the issue before them. There was discussion, especially around the question of precedent, with Senator Obduro being the most vocal opponent. "What about worlds like Drang?" the politician demanded. "If we grant independence to Algeron, the sentients indigenous to Drang will demand sovereignty as well. There will be no end to it."

But the Thraki's arguments weren't able to gain much traction since most of those present felt that it would be a long time before the sentients on Drang developed a culture and technology that were advanced enough to qualify them for membership in the Confederacy. The discussion period came to an end, and a voice vote was called for.

Truespeak listened to the slow monotonous tally, felt his spirits soar with each "aye," then plummet whenever he heard someone say "nay."

But finally, when all the votes had been tallied, the "ayes" had it, and SR-5706 passed. Algeron was free. The reality of that was so astounding, so wonderful, that Truespeak sat speechless while all of those who supported the measure broke into spontaneous applause.

Then, as the noise died down, President Nankool stepped up onto the platform. "Please allow me to be the first to congratulate the Naa people and welcome them as full members of the Confederacy. I imagine they will want the Legion to pay rent… but that's okay so long as they pay their taxes!" There was an explosion of laughter, Nankool declared a thirty-minute recess, and Truespeak found himself besieged by admirers, not to mention those eager to enlist his newly acquired vote in any number of causes.

Meanwhile, as senators and staff poured out of chambers, Senator Obduro felt a group of bodies close in around him. Admiral Chien-Chu was present, as was Triad Doma-Sa and General Bill Booly. "Excuse me, Senator," the legionnaire said genially, "but we wondered if we could have a moment of your time."

Obduro glanced back and forth. It was a distinguished group, and while he liked to be part of important gatherings, there was something ominous about the manner in which the aliens hemmed him in. "Yes, well, that would be nice, but this is a short break and…"

"Don't worry," Doma-Sa assured him, taking a firm grip on the Thraki's right arm. "The meeting won't take very long, and I'm sure you'll find it to be most interesting." Then, with the others crowded so closely around him that passersby couldn't see what was taking place, the roly-poly politician was hustled away. Obduro tried to object, but no one was listening, and by the time it occurred to the Thraki to shout, his abductors had left the main corridor for the labyrinth of passageways beyond.

"This is an outrage!" Obduro spluttered, as Doma-Sa and Booly lifted the politician off the ground and carried him forward.

"No," Chien-Chu corrected him, "it's a medical facility. There's someone here we'd like you to meet."

"Well, not exactly meet, because the poor bastard is asleep," Booly put in. "But you can look at him."

A few moments later Obduro found himself in a two-bed room looking at a Ramanthian. All of the medical equipment previously connected to the unconscious alien had been either removed or concealed, which made it appear as if the technical expert was asleep rather than in the grip of a coma. "He's had a rough time of it," Chien-Chu whispered, "so we don't want to disturb him. He was captured in the Erini system, where a whole bunch of your people are busy converting Sheen warships for use by the Ramanthians."

"Yes," Booly added sotto voce. "That was very naughty of you."

"Especially since you broke any number of treaties in order to do it," Doma-Sa growled.

"You must be joking," Obduro said. "I don't…"

"Quiet!" Chien-Chu insisted, holding a finger to his lips. "You'll wake him up. Come on, let's continue our discussion in a conference room."

Seconds later, the befuddled politician found himself being carried down a corridor into a conference room normally reserved for use by medical staff. Everything had been set up in advance, and Obduro soon found himself sitting in a vastly oversized chair, looking up at a screen. "This is the Erini system," Doma-Sa informed the Thraki, as the video began. "And *that* is an orbital repair facility, which we can only assume is owned and operated by your government."

The senator had never heard of Erini system or seen the enormous dock before, but felt a sudden emptiness at the pit of his stomach. Knowledgeable though he was regarding governmental affairs, the politician knew there were activities that he and his staff were ignorant of. And a good thing, too. Because while Obduro's superiors thought it best to side with the Confederacy at the moment, he knew some of them feared the possible consequences of a Ramanthian victory, and were uneasy regarding the way the war was going. Had they taken steps to insure the Thraki people against such a possibility? Yes, Obduro feared that they had, and here was the consequence of their double-dealing.

"Oh my," Chien-Chu said mockingly, as the camera invaded the dock's vast interior. "What have we here? Some of the very Sheen warships that were hijacked by the Ramanthians shortly after they destroyed the *Friendship*. Oh, and look at the personnel zipping all about... They look a lot like Ramanthians, don't they? Or did your government get a special deal on surplus Ramanthian space armor?"

Obduro swallowed, tried to think of something cogent to say, and swallowed again. The aliens scared him. Especially the huge Hudathan. The politician felt his bowels start to loosen. "I didn't know anything about this... I swear."

"And we believe you," Booly said soothingly. "Every government has a few lawbreakers to contend with. Unfortunate individuals who seek to turn a profit regardless of whom they harm. Who knows? Perhaps the individuals who set up the secret base in the Erini system and proceeded to cut a deal with the Ramanthians are common criminals."

Chien-Chu watched the words sink in. Obduro was no fool and was quick to recognize a lifeline when one was thrown his way. His eyes brightened, and his ears rotated toward the front of his head. "Yes! That would account for it! I will notify my government immediately."

"Good," Doma-Sa growled ominously. "Because we'll be watching. It's our expectation that the Sheen vessels will be seized and turned over to the Confederacy, the dock will be destroyed, and every effort will be made to bring the criminals to justice."

"Yes," Chien-Chu agreed. "Otherwise, it will become necessary to raise the matter with the Senate, listen to hours of testimony from our Ramanthian witness, and request sanctions against the Thraki government. All of which would be exceedingly tedious."

"Have no fear," Obduro said determinedly. "I will take care of everything."

"That's what we hoped you'd say," Booly acknowledged, "and we're grateful. Lieutenant Thinklong will escort you back to the Senate chambers."

There was a short but heartfelt celebration once the Thraki was gone. "I feel pretty sure that it's going to work," Chien-Chu said, as the threesome prepared to leave. "We'll have to keep an eye on them, however."

Booly nodded. "What about Christine Vanderveen? What happens to her?"

"I'll speak to Nankool," the industrialist replied. "I don't know that she'll get the promotion she so richly deserves, but the Confederacy can't afford to lose talent such as hers. The president knows that, and he'll come around."

"I'll put in a word as well," Doma-Sa put in. "If the Confederacy doesn't want her, *my* government would be happy to hire her. She's rather competent for a squat."

The humans grinned, and all of them went their separate ways. Booly was concerned about Maylo—and had been for days. While he felt a deep sense of loss where his unborn daughter was concerned, the emotion was muted to some extent by the fact that he had never seen or held her. But Maylo's grief had been deeper than that. So deep that he was beginning to wonder if she would ever emerge from it.

The guards stationed outside the general's quarters came to attention and rendered a rifle salute as Booly approached. The legionnaire returned the courtesy, palmed the door, and stepped inside. The lights had been dimmed, soft music could be heard, and the mouthwatering smell of an oriental stir-fry wafted through the air.

Booly followed the wonderful odor back past a nicely set table to the small and rarely used kitchenette, where his wife was busy cooking. She turned and offered her lips for a kiss. The legionnaire complied, put his arms around her waist, and pulled her close. "How did you know I was coming?"

Maylo smiled for the first time in days. "I have spies."

"Lieutenant Thinklong?"

"You'll never get it out of me."

"Never?" Booly inquired lightly. "Perhaps I should interrogate you."

"I think that would be an excellent idea," his wife whispered softly. "Do your worst."

"It could take a while," Booly said, reaching over to turn off the stove.

"I have all the time in the world," Maylo responded.

"And so do I," Booly replied, and swept his wife off her feet.

The Hive System, the Ramanthian Empire

The Ramanthian admiral experienced a moment of unrestrained joy as the blip that represented the Confederacy ship disappeared from the screens, and his subordinates clacked their pincers by way of applause.

But the brief moment of jubilation was quickly followed by a sense of consternation when there was no explosion. That was when one of his officers gave voice to the suspicion that had already taken root in the back of the admiral's mind. "It looks as though the enemy ship entered hyperspace, Excellency."

The admiral felt his spirits soar. Entering or exiting hyperspace in the vicinity of a planet or a sun was extremely dangerous. Although they couldn't see into hyperspace, odds were that Lieutenant Commander Frenko had been killed while attempting to escape her pursuers. A perfectly acceptable outcome unless... And that was the moment when another possibility occurred to the Ramanthian, and a terrible fear gripped his mind. It was difficult to speak, but he managed to squeeze the necessary words out. "Contact the admiralty. Tell them..."

But there wasn't enough time to tell anyone anything as Frenko gathered her memories around her, the NAVCOMP brought the *Flaming Bitch* out of hyperspace three miles *under* Hive's carefully manicured surface, and the bomb she had brought so far exploded. Frenko saw a flash of white light, felt a wave of warmth hit her, and let it carry her away. The results of the attack were far more spectacular than anything that General Booly and his staff had imagined. The underground explosion triggered a quake that destroyed the city of First Birth, including the underground cavern where tradition held that the first mother had produced the first egg, and took 1.7 million lives.

Though more than a thousand miles away, the Queen felt a slight tremor and was demanding information even before it began to flow in. Soon, based on a report from the home fleet as well as officials located in the vicinity of First Birth, the truth became known. The planet that had felt so impregnable an hour before wasn't, a terrible new weapon had been introduced into the war, and victory was a lot less certain.

Such were the realities as the Minister of Civilian Affairs Suu Norr stood on the very spot where one of his mates had been executed less than one rotation before and looked up into the royal's face. The odor produced by the eggs stored in the vault below her seemed especially strong at that moment, and the functionary felt an almost overpowering need to please the monarch in spite of what she had done to the War Norr.

"So," the Queen continued sternly, "the navy will pull two fleets back to reinforce security in our home system. Meanwhile, you and your department will treat the explosion as a terrible but nonetheless natural seismic event. We must avoid panic. Do I make myself clear?"

"Yes, Majesty," Norr replied. "Very clear."

"Good. Now, what progress has been made where the hypercom is concerned? It's absolutely imperative that you recover that equipment lest it somehow fall into enemy hands."

Norr had been home when the royal guards delivered the War Norr's head to his single surviving mate. He heard the Egg Norr's anguished cries from another room, rushed to her side, and tried to console her. Could she withstand another such loss? He wasn't sure.

Conscious of the fact that his life was on the line, the functionary chose his words with extreme care. "I have good news, Highness. The task force assigned to bring the equipment to Hive arrived off Savas. Loading will commence soon."

The Queen's eyes were as black as space. "And the enemy? What of them?"

"They have a battalion of troops on the surface of Savas and are marching toward our base, but the local commander remains confident that he can stop them."

"He'd better," the monarch said darkly. "Keep me informed. In the meantime, do everything in your power to help the communities around First Birth. And remember, the destruction resulted from a quake, nothing more. You may withdraw."

"Yes, Highness," Norr responded as he bent a knee. "It shall be as you say."

The Queen watched the functionary depart, felt the now-familiar pressure in her abdomen, and allowed a clutch of five hundred eggs to join those already stored below. More than a million lives had been lost—but millions were on the way.

14

*Finally, when all the diplomatic dra is over, someone has to go
in and kill the bastards.*
TRIAD HIWEEN DOMA-SA
Standard year 2840

Hagala Nor, Planet Savas

One of the many things that made the extinct volcano an ideal
fortress was not only the deep crater located at its center, but
the landing pad that had been constructed at the bottom of
the cavity. It was circular in shape and bordered by stacks of
cargo modules that were waiting to be loaded. Each container
held part of the hypercom or a piece of auxiliary equipment
associated with it.

A space black shuttle squatted at the center of the pad as Force
Commander Ignatho Dontha slip-slid onto the blast-scarred
durasteel and surveyed the area. Rather than the carefully
orchestrated process that he had imagined, chaos was the rule
as civilians yelled orders at his troops, and they yelled back.

Dontha produced the Ramanthian equivalent of a frown and
snapped an order at the nearest noncom, who blew a shrill blast
on his whistle. The gabble stopped, heads turned, and the officer
spoke. "Who can tell me what is going on here?"

After a moment of hesitation, a junior officer raised a pincer. "I guess I can, sir. We were given a list of which modules to load first, but the civilians say we should ignore it."

"I see," Dontha replied gravely. "And which civilian were you speaking with?"

"*That* one," the officer said, pointing to the ragged figure who had just exited the shuttle's cargo compartment.

Dontha wasn't particularly surprised to see that the individual in question was none other than Chief Scientific Investigator Tepho. "I'll speak with him," the force commander said reassuringly. "Tell your troops to stand by."

The officer clacked a pincer respectfully before scurrying off to have a word with his subordinates. As Dontha stepped out of the shadow cast by the crater's east wall he felt the full warmth of the sun and took pleasure in it. The scientist turned at his approach. "There you are! We've been looking all over for you… These laggards refused to obey my orders! Please set them straight."

Dontha fought to control his temper. "The lists that they're using were written by *you* and your staff. All they're trying to do is to make sure that the most important components are loaded first."

"We changed our minds," Tepho replied imperiously. "Some of the most important items are still being packed. Besides, what difference does it make? First, second, third. It's all the same."

"No," Dontha replied patiently, "it isn't all the same. The Legion went around the native troops put in place to block them. We estimate that they will arrive here within the next twelve hours. What if the barbarians force their way into Hagala Nor? And capture whatever happens to be sitting on the pad? Important components could be lost."

"And whose fault would that be?" Tepho demanded caustically. " *You're* in charge of security. Stop them."

"I intend to," Dontha grated, "but it makes sense to take every precaution we can. That includes sticking to the original load-out. By the way, since the pad can't accommodate more than one shuttle at a time, speed is of the essence. I suggest that you and your staff clear the immediate area."

"All right, all right," the scientist responded grumpily. "Do it your way."

"Thank you," the soldier replied. "I will."

South of Hagala Nor, Planet Savas

The tip of the Confederacy force consisted of twelve twenty-five-foot-tall quads, each carrying a full load-out of munitions and traveling at a stately twenty miles per hour. Dust boiled up around them, was caught by the wind, and blown back over the column. Farther to the rear, and protected on both flanks by platoons of Trooper IIs, came the command quad, the medical quad, maintenance quads, air support quads, and half a dozen transport quads carrying civilians and supplies. The rear guard consisted of another company of quads plus B Company's T-2s.

Kobbi referred to the formation as a "two-headed snake," meaning an entity that could travel forward or backward with equal facility, although there was only one direction in which the crusty officer wanted to go, and that was forward. And so far the advance had been easy, *too* easy, or so it seemed to Santana.

The cavalry officer knew that the decision to drop B Company into the drag position was Kobbi's way of giving him and his troops a break after the fight at the water hole and the battle in the desert. Still, the legionnaire would have preferred to see where the battalion was headed instead of where it had been. But orders are orders, and his were to make sure that the bugs didn't attack the battalion from behind, or stop them if they did.

As the battalion cleared some extensive ruins, B Company entered them and followed electronic markers north. Hundreds of years of heat, cold, and occasional rain had reduced the earthen city to a labyrinth of twisting streets, slowly melting walls, and shattered domes. Everything was beige, tan, or brown, with only the occasional tinge of reddish iron oxide to provide some color.

Fresh damage could be seen where dozens of quads had marched through the ancient city, sideswiped heavily weathered buildings, crushed dwellings, and blasted anything that struck them as suspicious. Many walls remained, however, and Santana found himself tempted by the shade that they provided. The bio bods needed to take a leak every now and then even if the cyborgs didn't, and the ruins looked like a good place to take a rest.

With that in mind Santana ordered the 1st and 3rd platoons to take a five-minute break while the second stood guard. After the first two-thirds of the company drained their tanks, the rest of the legionnaires would get their turn.

Santana notified the command quad as members of the 1st and 3rd platoons hurried to dismount. Most ducked into the shadows to take care of personal business, and the rest availed themselves of the opportunity to scratch what itched or tweak their support gear.

Sergeant Dietrich was no different. The legionnaire had just wet the sand in front of him and was in the process of zipping his pants when a set of tracks caught his eye. Not T-2 tracks, or quad tracks, but parallel crawler tracks that incorporated the distinctive chevron pattern that the bugs preferred. And not little tracks, but *big* tracks, each being about four feet wide. No big deal in and of themselves, especially since the Ramanthians had occupied that particular piece of real estate only hours before, but this particular set of tracks ended right in front of a blank wall!

Dietrich took a second look to ensure that he wasn't mistaken, opened his com, and meandered toward his T-2. "Bravo Three Six to all Bravo units... I have reason to believe that the bugs left some armor hidden within the ruins. Members of the 1st and 2nd will return to their mounts. *Slowly*, so they don't know we're onto them, and prepare to engage. Over."

Santana heard the noncom's orders along with the rest of the company, felt a chill run up his spine, and turned toward Okuma. The previously innocent ruins had an ominous feel now—and the officer resisted an impulse to look back over his shoulder. Assuming Dietrich was correct, the Ramanthians had intentionally allowed the battalion to pass through the ancient city without firing on them. That suggested that the bugs intended to attack the formation from the rear. But would they make their move *before* the rear guard departed the area? Or after? There was no way to know, and the cavalry officer fought the temptation to dash across the street and leap onto the T-2's back.

Meanwhile, about two hundred feet away, and fifteen feet below street level, Knifethrow sat within the cramped confines of the Ramanthian command tank. It was hot, *extremely* hot, and his fur was matted with sweat. The deserter eyed the video supplied by tiny sensors that his crew had left above ground. He knew the legionnaires above him, and when every single one of them turned toward their borgs, he knew they were responding to an order. "The bastards are onto us! Hit 'em!"

The Ramanthians were ready, had been for hours, and seemed to explode up out of the ground. Each beetlelike tank weighed about forty tons and was powered by two tandem engines. That meant the big black beasts had power to spare, and they used it to push up through the seemingly undisturbed streets and crash through the walls that had been constructed to conceal them. Santana broke into a run as the enemy tanks burst out of concealment, and a .50 caliber machine gun started to chug in the distance.

Okuma turned his back to the bio bod and willed the officer to hurry. Santana literally ran up the steps that were built into the back of the T-2's legs and was still in the process of buckling himself in when a tank crashed through a wall across the street.

Okuma fired his energy cannon. The bolt left a scorch mark on the Ramanthian-made armor but had no other effect as Santana plugged into the T-2's com system and made his report. "Bravo Six to Nomad Six. We are under attack! Repeat, under attack by an unknown number of Ramanthian heavies! They were hidden in the ruins. Request ground support. Over."

It was Matala who replied. The XO sounded calm and didn't waste time asking how such a thing could be possible. Questions of that sort would be dealt with later. "Roger that, Bravo Six. Help is on the way. Over."

Santana took comfort from the fact that Kobbi's two-headed snake could strike toward the rear as well as the front, but wondered if the reserve quads would arrive in time to save his company, or to bury it. A pair of fly-forms had arrived by then, but couldn't engage the enemy without running the risk of inflicting casualties on B Company and had little choice but to circle impotently while the battle continued.

Having failed to dent the tank, Okuma spun away just as a cannon shell sped through the space he had occupied a moment earlier. That was when a borg named Fillo fired one of her two missiles. It scored a direct hit, and thick though the Ramanthian armor was, it couldn't withstand the force of a shaped charge delivered at point-blank range. The primary explosion was followed by two secondary explosions that combined to tear the tank apart. Masonry shattered, razor-sharp shrapnel hummed through the air, and a deep, resonant *boom!* echoed between ancient walls.

Santana felt the resulting wave of heat wash across his face and allowed Okuma to handle the tactical situation while he scanned the symbols projected on the inside surface of his helmet visor. The multicolored dots and deltas were so intermingled that the officer knew it would be impossible to maneuver his company as a unit. He could allow the free-for-all to continue or order his troops to disengage. Conventional doctrine argued in favor of option two, especially in the face of superior firepower, but the T-2s were extremely agile, and reinforcements were on the way. Santana opened his mike. "Fire at will, but keep an eye out for friendlies, and don't let them suck you into the open."

At that point the officer switched to a schematic that provided him with a graphic depiction of the enemy's communications patterns. A glance was sufficient to establish that 86 percent of all the Ramanthian communications were being initiated by a single tank. The company commander forwarded the screen to Okuma, ordered the T-2 to find that particular unit, and felt the borg respond. *After all*, Santana thought to himself, *the quickest way to slay any beast is to chop off its head.*

Okuma made his way down a side street, spotted a pile of rubble heaped against a wall, and turned the debris into a ramp. Once on top Okuma discovered that the flat surface was barely wide enough to accommodate his foot pods. The T-2 ran the length of the two-foot-wide divider even as chunks of adobe crumbled away from his feet.

Santana held on, felt his stomach lurch as the borg jumped a six-foot gap, and let his knees absorb the subsequent impact. Okuma's right foot went through the roof, but the Trooper II kept his balance, and jerked the pod free. Then, eager to reach his destination, the borg made for the far side of the debris-strewn surface. Santana winced as a tank fired, and one of his T-2s vanished from the heads-up display.

Then Okuma was there, right where he wanted to be, four feet *above* the command tank. It was parked at the end of a dead-end street pointed the other way. The huge beetle-shaped war machine belched smoke and rocked slightly as it fired a self-steering, antiarmor-seeking round at a target a thousand yards away. The noise was deafening, and Santana wished he had earplugs.

The range was too short for Okuma to use his remaining missile, so the cyborg jumped onto the vehicle's upper deck and directed his energy cannon at the top hatch. It was armored, but not against a blast of energy fired from two feet away, and it wasn't long before the metal started to liquefy. Meanwhile, down in the bowels of the machine, Knifethrow heard a double clang as something landed on the metal over his head, knew it was a T-2, and swore as the hatch started to melt and a drop of red-hot metal landed on the back of his neck. There was another way out, though, a belly hatch, if the renegade could reach it in time. The Naa pulled his sidearm, shot the tank commander in the back of the head, and dropped to the lowest level. The gunner absorbed two slugs in the back, closely followed by the loader, who took a round in the face.

Having eliminated the crew, the Naa dropped through the shaft located next to the main magazine, and tapped the foot switch. The hatch opened smoothly, allowing the ex-legionnaire to drop through the resulting hole. Dust spurted away from the renegade's boots and Knifethrow proceeded to duckwalk out from under the tank.

The deserter had just emerged when a weight dropped on him from above and threw him facedown in the dirt. The Naa felt someone pull his pistol out of its holster and gave thanks when they failed to appropriate the knife. The weight disappeared, allowing him to push the ground away. "Hey," Knifethrow objected, as he came to his feet and turned toward his attacker. "Take it easy! I was captured! Damn, it's good to see…"

"Thanks," Santana interrupted calmly. "It's good to see you, too. Where's Kuga-Ka?"

The Naa raised his hands as if to surrender. That put them very close to the knife that was hilt up at the nape of his neck. "The gunny? Hell, he's…"

The renegade was fast, *very* fast, but Santana saw his hand move and fired. As the bullet struck his body armor, Knifethrow staggered, pulled the knife, and was about to throw it, when a second slug ripped through his throat. The Naa clutched at the wound, tried to stop the bleeding, and failed. He said something in his own language, frowned, and collapsed.

"Bravo Three Six to Bravo Six," Dietrich said via the company push. "The heavies are here. Over."

And Santana realized that the quads *were* there as one of the huge machines put a foot through the structure on his left, and fired its main gun. The cavalry had arrived.

Five miles to the north Kobbi and his staff sweltered in the command quad as fans whirred, com sets burped reports, and data scrolled across screens. The cone-shaped mountain was clear to see now, as was the shuttle that lifted out of the crater within. They watched the spacecraft turn on its own axis, fire chaff in an effort to distract the missiles that lashed up at it, and speed away. The transport, plus the markings it wore, served as a sure sign that a task force had arrived off Savas and was in the process of recovering the hypercom. Kobbi shook his head regretfully as the shuttle entered a steep climb, but he knew there was nothing he could do about it.

"It looks like more bugs are coming out to play," the battalion's intel officer commented, as the staff switched their attention to a video provided by the battalion's sole surviving RPV. The drone was flying at its operational ceiling, zigzagging on a random basis, and using electronic countermeasures to avoid ground fire. It was only a matter of time before a missile brought the little aircraft down, but it was nice to have the shot for as long as it lasted. The aerial view showed Hagala Nor, the landing pad located at the bottom of the volcano's crater, and tiny spurts of dust as black specks emerged from protective tunnels to venture out onto the plain beyond. "The tanks located to the rear were the anvil," Kobbi observed, "and here comes the hammer."

Major Matala saw that the jacker was correct as the RPV zoomed in to provide its audience with some additional magnification. At least two dozen tanks had emerged from the mountain onto the plain below. There were smaller targets, too, including some speedy ground effect vehicles that could inflict quite a bit of damage if they were able to close with the quads. Assuming that the T-2s would be kept busy dealing with the lesser vehicles, it looked as if the quads would be outnumbered two to one. Not a pleasant prospect, but now that a fresh batch of Ramanthian ships had dropped into orbit, there wasn't any choice.

Orders went out, and the quads formed a staggered line abreast. A formation that would enable all of them to engage the enemy at once, minimize the chance of firing on each other, and force the enemy to deal with the entire line rather than concentrating their fire on a few cyborgs.

Dontha watched from a position high on the extinct volcano's rim as his tanks opened fire. There was a bloodcurdling shriek as the rounds arced through the air, followed by flashes of light as they exploded, and a series of dull *crumps*. Columns of earth shot up into the air, and the first quadrupeds to enter the killing zone walked through the falling debris apparently untouched. Then a fifty-ton cyborg vanished in a clap of thunder as a smart shell corrected its glide path, struck the quad's hull, and detonated the missiles loaded onto its racks.

Meanwhile, as salvos of surface-to-surface missiles flew back and forth, a seemingly impenetrable matrix of computer-directed energy beams reached up to intercept them. Many exploded prematurely and rained hot metal onto the battlefield below, but a few made it through. Ramanthian tanks erupted in flame, weapons vanished in puffs of dirt and smoke, and thunder rolled across the land.

There was a series of loud cracking sounds, and the ground shook, as a clutch of missiles hit the antenna array three hundred units to Dontha's right. The explosions were not only loud but somewhat unnerving. The Ramanthian refused to flinch, hoped that the officers grouped behind him would emulate his example, and thereby steady the troops.

Now, as both groups started to close with each other, the advantage seemed to shift slightly as packs of the smaller two-legged cyborgs joined their larger cousins and attacked the Ramanthian tanks as teams.

Dontha watched in amazement as a quad lost a limb to a missile but continued to drag itself forward while a pack of T-2s guarded its flanks. The larger cyborg fired, a tank blossomed into a red-orange flower, and jerked spasmodically as the ammo stored inside its hull cooked off.

But then, just when it looked as if the scales were tipping toward the Legion, help arrived from on high. Contrails clawed the clear blue sky as two flights of Ramanthian fighters entered the atmosphere, fell on the Confederacy fly-forms like birds of prey, and immediately sent two of them spiraling into the ground. In the meantime, those aircraft not engaged in the aerial dogfight were free to skim the surface of the battlefield and fire their missiles at the Legion's quads before circling around to make another pass.

The airwaves crackled with static as the cyborgs used electronic countermeasures to confuse the incoming weapons, and launched surface-to-air missiles, but the damage had been done. A fighter belched black smoke and vanished behind Hagala Nor, but that didn't make up for the loss of two additional quads, and Kobbi had no choice but to order a retreat. It was an orderly withdrawal, with designated quads serving as antiaircraft batteries while others worked to suppress enemy tank fire. In the meantime, rescue units dashed in to pull brain boxes, salvage damaged T-2s, and pick up stranded bio bods.

Both sides had taken heavy casualties, but Dontha was gratified to see that only half of the cyborgs that had lumbered into the battle continued to be operable as the engagement came to a close. The Ramanthian's only regret was the fact that the fighters had to hold nearly half their fuel in reserve in order to reach orbit. That meant they couldn't linger and inflict even more casualties. Still, the engagement had been successful, and Dontha could return to his command center secure in the knowledge that the Pincer of Steel remained undefeated.

Aboard the light cruiser *Worber's World*

The cruiser's bridge was large and spacious. The command crew sat in a broad semicircle facing the bow. Captain Marta Wells, their commanding officer, occupied a raised platform directly behind them. Commodore Marvin Posson and Teeg Jackson were seated in two of the six seats that curved along the rear bulkhead. The atmosphere was thick with tension, and all eyes were riveted to the screens that tiled the forward bulkhead. The Confederacy task force had been in hyperspace for more than a week by then, and as Posson's ships prepared to enter the Savas system, the ranking naval officer wished that he could forever hide the vessels rather than expose them to the dangers that probably lay ahead.

Commodore was a temporary rank, one that would probably be taken from him once the mission was over, but the responsibility was real enough. Posson's task force included a new world-class cruiser, two destroyers so old that his mother had served in one of them, and a couple of Chien-Chu Enterprise-supplied transports that had formerly been slated for the scrap yards.

But old though most of his ships were, every single one of them was crewed by living, thinking, feeling beings, any or all of whom might be killed as the result of decisions that *he* made. That's why Posson wished he could somehow delay the moment when everything was at risk, the responsibility for hundreds of lives fell on him, and there was no going back. But he'd been chosen to lead the task force because he'd been to Savas, because he had a relationship with Teeg Jackson, and because the navy was short of qualified officers. Why else would they choose someone who had been passed over for promotion twice?

Because I'm expendable, Posson thought to himself, and grinned.

Wells had black hair, which she parted up the middle. It fell in two wings, each marked by matching streaks of white, and swung freely as she turned to look over her shoulder. "All right... Mr. Jackson's decoys should have entered the system some eight hours ago... Plenty of time to pull any Ramanthian naval units in the vicinity away from Savas."

"They aren't *my* decoys," Jackson said defensively. "The idea was mine, but if something goes wrong with the electronics, that's the navy's fault."

"So noted," Wells replied darkly, "realizing that you're still going to die along with the rest of us if they don't work." There was no love lost between the two, and a smile tugged at the corners of Posson's mouth as the captain turned her back to Jackson.

Wells focused on the screens in front of her and dug her fingernails into the padding of the chair's armrests. *Worber's World* had barely returned from her shakedown cruise when she was given her first mission and designated as Pusson's flagship. There were technical bugs to work out, the crew hadn't had time to gel, and the commodore had never been responsible for a group of ships before. Throw in a surly smuggler, plus the possibility of some bloodthirsty Ramanthians, and there were plenty of things for the naval officer to worry about. She felt the familiar lurch, knew her ship had entered the contested zone, and kept her eyes glued to the screens. The entire bridge crew held their collective breaths as the ship made the transition from one reality to the next, data began to flood the screens, and their brains raced to interpret it.

"There are the decoys!" someone exclaimed.

"And there are the bugs," Wells added thankfully. "Clear on the other side of the system from where we are! Congratulations, Mr. Jackson—your plan was a success."

Posson looked for the rest of his task force on the screens, saw that all of them were present, and gave silent thanks. "Well done. Signal the task force to form on *Worber's World* and call for maximum speed. I intend to have control of Savas, plus any ships that happen to be in orbit, by the time the Ramanthians return.

"And Captain Wells…"

The officer looked back over her shoulder. "Sir?"

"Tell the com section to try to contact Colonel Kobbi. I imagine he'll be happy to hear from us."

Hagala Nor, Planet Savas

For some reason there hadn't been any further air attacks on the battalion, and Kobbi was determined to take advantage of that fact. The colonel knew that his troops were exhausted and that the volcano would be a bitch to take, but he couldn't afford to wait the bugs out. First, because the Ramanthian fighters could return at any moment. Second, because Kobbi was pretty sure that a goodly portion of the hypercom had already been removed from the crater, and third, because it went against the jacker's nature to sit around and wait for things to happen.

Kobbi's T-2 had been specially modified so he could stand a little taller and see a little better. He took advantage of the additional height to examine the formation arrayed to either side of him. By rotating the cyborgs that had previously been at the rear of the formation to the front, the pugnacious officer had put a new edge to his blade. Farther back, trailing along as best they could, veterans of the first assault could be seen. Included among them was the three-legged quad now known as "Hopalong," a one-armed T-2, and half a dozen other units that were damaged but still capable of fighting.

Behind them, armed with whatever Calvo and her techs had been able to cobble together, were all of the battalion's support quads. Some carried civilians who had volunteered to fight as infantry. It was a ragtag force, but it was all he had, and that would have to do. Kobbi stood on tiptoes in the hopes that at least some of the legionnaires could see him. "This is Nomad Six… There's only one way off this piece of shit—and that's through the frigging bugs! Battalionnnn, charge!"

Santana saw Kobbi's T-2 lurch toward Hagala Nor and shouted over the company push. "You heard the colonel! Let's get the bastards!"

Other officers did likewise, and the entire battalion seemed to leap forward. The Ramanthians were waiting for them and unleashed every bit of firepower they had. A Ramanthian tank fired on a quad, scored a direct hit, and the cyborg exploded.

But even as pieces of the quad tumbled out of the sky, Santana led a platoon of T-2s against the tank and circled it. Fareye's borg carried the Naa in close, the warrior tossed a demolition pack under the monster's belly, and barely managed to get clear before the charge went off. Santana heard a dull *whump!* followed by a horrible screeching sound as the beetle-shaped vehicle turned a full circle.

That was when the top hatch opened and a bug appeared behind the big ring-mounted machine gun. The Ramanthian pulled the arming lever back, and was just about to open fire, when Santana shot him in the head. The dead body slumped into the compartment below as Dietrich fired a pair of grenades. The noncom swore as the first bounced off the edge of the hatch, but felt considerably better when the second dropped through and detonated within. The round cradled in the loader's arms exploded, the ammo stored in the main magazine went up, and there was a tremendous *boom!* as the tank flew apart.

But there was no time to celebrate, no time to gloat, as Santana rallied the platoon around him and urged them to catch up with the rest of the battalion. Okuma was running at about 50 mph by then, and raced by a scene that the company commander would never forget. Somehow, by a means that wasn't clear, one of the quads had managed to close with a tank and placed both forelegs on the behemoth's back. One of the enormous pods functioned to hold the tank in place while the other fell like a trip-hammer. Not just once, but over and over, until metal surrendered and finally gave way.

The legionnaire wanted to see what would happen next, but the mad charge continued, and the tableau was left behind. Santana scanned the area ahead, looking for what he thought might be Haaby with Kuga-Ka mounted on her back. But the renegade and his prisoner were nowhere to be seen, and the cavalry officer had other matters to attend to.

Now, having dealt with most of the smaller tracked vehicles, more and more Trooper IIs moved to support the quads. Teams of Trooper IIs identified likely-looking targets, fired any missiles they had left, and opened up with their energy cannons. Thick though their armor was, the Ramanthian tank commanders couldn't afford to ignore concentrated fire and were forced to respond. That took some of the pressure off the badly outnumbered quads, which continued to lumber forward even as the Trooper IIs used their superior maneuverability to run circles around the beetle-shaped fighting machines.

But there were fewer and fewer tanks, and those that remained were suddenly isolated as Force Commander Dontha was forced to make a terrible decision. No longer certain of victory, and fearful lest the Legion enter Hagala Nor via one of the tunnels that provided access to the desert floor, the officer gave orders to blow them, thereby cutting off the Pincer of Steel's only line of retreat.

So, even as the battalion washed up against the foot of Hagala Nor, they were soon reminded of the fact that the battle was only half-won, since they had yet to enter the fortress itself. Kobbi's bodyguards hurried to establish a protective cordon around the officer as the jacker dismounted and eyed the fortress ahead. He could see the track that zigzagged its way up the mountain's flank, knew it was the only way in, and knew the Ramanthians would be waiting. Major Matala arrived right about then and followed the jacker's gaze. "Damn... That looks bad."

"Yes, it will be," Kobbi predicted soberly. "You'd better send for Lieutenant Santana."

Aboard the *Star Ravager* in orbit around the Planet Savas, the Contested Zone

Naval Commander Jos Satto slip-slid down the main corridor of the Ramanthian ship *Star Ravager*. He was proud of the fact that both it and the rest of the interior spaces were spotless in spite of the damage to the ship's bow. In fact, to the extent that such a thing was possible under the circumstances, Satto was happy for the first time in weeks. The newly arrived task force was under the command of Admiral Hos Hikko, which meant that Satto no longer had to bear the burden of responsibility where naval matters were concerned, and that included dealing with the enemy ships that had entered the system some nine units earlier. Hikko had taken all four of the warships under his command and gone after the intruders, leaving the *Ravager* to protect the transports until his return. Something that would be easy to do since there weren't any other ships in the system.

Or so Satto assumed until the ship's battle klaxons sounded, and the destroyer's crew were forced to rush to their battle stations. A false alarm? Satto certainly hoped so as he made his way into the ship's control room and took up a position behind Olthobo and the rest of the command crew. The executive officer pointed up at one of the screens. His voice was concerned. "It looks like the Confederacy sent a *second* battle group to support the first."

Satto eyed the symbols on the screen and saw that his executive officer was correct. While the warships under Hikko's command headed out to intercept one group of enemy ships, a second cluster of symbols had appeared, and they were very close to the planet itself. So close that they would be able to reach Savas *before* the admiral could even if he started immediately.

The officer felt something cold and clammy wrap itself around his stomach. The Ramanthian warships wouldn't stand a chance against *two* battle groups unless… "Contact the admiral," Satto snapped. "Ask him if there's any chance that the force he's about to close with consists of decoys rather than actual ships."

A full fifteen units passed before the reply came back. Rather than send word through the communications personnel, Admiral Hikko chose to deliver the message personally. The com screen shivered and locked up. The Ramanthian who appeared there was old, some said *too* old, and his chitin had started to lose its luster. Though impeccably clean, Hikko's uniform appeared to be one size too large for him and hung in generous folds. His eyes were bright, however—and looked like a pair of large-caliber gun barrels. "You are correct, Satto. They *are* decoys. It's up to the *Ravager* now. Do what you can to delay them. It would be a disaster if the Confederacy was allowed to capture the transports."

Satto knew that the admiral was correct. More than 70 percent of the super-secret communications equipment that Hikko had been sent to remove from Savas had already been uploaded. His throat felt dry, and it required a conscious effort to swallow. "Yes, sir."

"I'm glad you understand," Hikko said flatly. "We will return as quickly as possible, but if it looks like the transports are going to be captured, then destroy them."

The entire command crew were shocked by the admiral's orders, including Satto himself. The entire notion of firing on their own transports was repugnant, but Hikko had already considered that, and made the necessary decision. The hypercom was important, vitally so, and could not be allowed to fall into enemy hands. Satto bowed his head. "Yes, Excellency, I understand." The video snapped to black, Satto was left on his own, and the distance between the enemy and his ship continued to diminish.

The track that zigzagged its way up Hagala Nor's steep southern flank ended on the broad ledge that had been carved out of the mountainside. It had been a hard climb, especially for Haaby, since she had done all of the work. But Kuga-Ka insisted on inspecting the entire length of the path before taking up a position behind the barricade at the top. Force Commander Dontha's plan was quite simple. Nearly all of the Legion's fly-forms had been destroyed during the first assault. That meant that Ramanthian shuttles could still come and go with relative impunity. Yes, there were missiles to dodge, but chaff and ECM would probably be sufficient to deal with them.

That meant the bugs could continue to upload the hypercom even as the Legion tried to find a way into Hagala Nor. So, with the ground-level tunnels blown and no capability to attack by air, Kobbi was bound to send troops up the track in hopes of accessing the passageway that led to the mountain's core. Not that they would get very far. The Hudathan would see to that.

Here, after all the disappointments of the past few weeks, was the opportunity to get even with Kobbi, Matala, and Santana. A chance to stop them, piss on their dead bodies, and secure a place with the bugs. The renegade's dream of going into business for himself, of building a private empire on Savas, had been a casualty of the disastrous battle in the desert. Srebo Riff was sworn to kill him now, which meant that it would not only be a good idea to leave the planet, but to do so quickly.

That's why the ex-legionnaire had volunteered to fight a delaying action, and by doing so to win a seat on the last shuttle out. It was a good plan, and the renegade was in an ebullient mood when he opened the intercom to Haaby. "Hey, freak, are you awake?"

The answer was obvious, but the cyborg knew better than to say so. "Yes, gunny, I'm awake."

"That's good, real good," the Hudathan said conversationally, "because the Legion is going to attack, and it's our job to stop them. Now, I know you haven't been very happy, but if you take good care of me, I'll take good care of you. Hell, I'll even turn you loose! How does that strike you?"

"Don't trust him," Missy cautioned from her hideout deep within the cyborg's tortured mind. "It's a trick."

"I'd like that," Haaby replied, knowing full well that Missy was probably right but hoping to humor him. "What about Oko?" she asked, referring to the borg that had originally been assigned to that particular war form. "What happens to him?"

"I'll leave him here with you," Kuga-Ka lied. "The two of you can fight over who gets the war form. But remember, if you try anything funny, I'll zap you. Understood?"

"Understood," Haaby confirmed.

"Good," the Hudathan said, as a missile hit a weapons emplacement two thousand yards away. "This should be fun."

Night had finally fallen, throwing a black cloak over the corpse-strewn battlefield, thereby creating the illusion of peace. There was an audible *pop* as a Ramanthian flare went off high over Hagala Nor. It bathed the mountain's flanks in a gruesome green light, swung back and forth, and drifted down toward the ground below.

As Santana waited for the light to fade he looked straight up the sheer mountainside and wondered if the plan would work.

But it was too late to have doubts, too late to throw up, and too late to run. "Okay," Santana whispered to the support crew clustered around him, "send the RAVs."

Oblivious to the dangers that would face them, the first of twelve Robotic All-terrain Vehicles began to plod up the trail some one thousand yards to the north. Each unit consisted of two eight-foot-long sections linked together by a single pleated, accordion-style joint located at the center of their long, ovoid-shaped bodies. Four articulated legs enabled the robots to negotiate even the most difficult terrain. Though not intended for offensive purposes, each RAV was equipped with two forward-facing machine guns and a grenade launcher.

Everything looked phosphorescent green through Santana's night-vision goggles. The officer waited for the robots to get fifty feet up the trail before opening the com. "All right, Poltero, are you ready?"

The technician *wasn't* ready, not for something like climbing the side of an extinct volcano in near-total darkness, but couldn't say that. "Yes, sir."

"Good," Santana replied. "And remember to give us a holler when it's time to set those bolts. We'll make some noise."

Poltero nodded wordlessly, checked to make sure that the pack was securely strapped to his skeletal torso, and started up the wall. A T-2 could never have accomplished it, not given the awkward hands or graspers that they had, but the spider form was equipped with tool hands. Not only that, but the volcanic rock was coarse and lumpy, which made it easy to find hand- and toeholds. As a result, the cyborg discovered that he could climb at twice the rate of speed that Santana had estimated in spite of the pack and the steadily increasing weight of the steel cable that dangled below him.

Meanwhile, as the technician-cum-commando scaled the mountain, Santana and his support team waited for the inevitable explosion. It came when the lead RAV stepped on a mine. The resulting *boom!* rolled across the land and let everyone know that an attack was under way.

* * *

"Here they come!" Kuga-Ka announced via the translator strapped to his chest. "Look sharp now, it will take them a while to reach the top, but they'll be here soon enough."

The Ramanthians were ready by that time and had been for quite a while. Most of the troops resented the fact that Dontha had placed the barbaric alien over them, but there were a few who respected the Hudathan's prowess as a warrior, and they nodded agreeably as the first of the renegade's predictions came true. There was only one way up, and they had it blocked, so it seemed logical to assume that the rest would be easy.

Poltero had been told to expect a series of such explosions and knew that they were intended as a diversion. So long as the bugs believed that the Legion was coming up the trail, they wouldn't be looking for *him*, and the technician was grateful.

Then, just when it seemed that the cyborg would be able to complete the climb without running into any obstacles, Poltero was forced to stop just below a substantial overhang. If the legionnaire was to proceed, he'd have to do so upside down, and the legionnaire doubted his ability to hang on. Swearing silently, the borg spidered sideways, causing the cable that hung below him to do likewise. Santana followed the line toward the south and opened the com. "Pol? What are you doing?"

"I ran into an overhang," the tech replied. "I'm trying to get out from under it."

Santana answered with two clicks and saw a flash of green light followed by a loud explosion. *Another* RAV was history. The bugs had bought the charade so far, but for how long? All the officer could do was pray.

There was a break in the overhang, a sort of chimney through which the spider form could pass, and he literally ran upward. Light flooded the cyborg's sensors as he took a peek over the ledge. What he saw was so strange that he switched to daylight vision just to ensure that his vid pickups were working properly. "I'm at the ledge," Poltero whispered, "looking over the edge. You won't believe who's standing there in front of me. Over."

Santana felt a sense of relief combined with annoyance.

"This is no time for guessing games, Poltero... What have you got? Over."

"It's Gunnery Sergeant Kuga-Ka, sir," the cyborg replied, "riding a T-2!"

So that's where you are, Santana thought to himself as he visualized the renegade. *Just hang around. I have a present for you.* "Thanks for the warning," the officer replied. "Now get your head down, plant the winch, and let me know when you're ready to set the bolts."

The missiles hit Hagala Nor one after another, four in all, and light strobed across the mountain. Kuga-Ka heard the weapons detonate and wondered what Kobbi was up to. A diversion perhaps? Designed to distract him while some sort of assault team made its final dash upslope? Fortunately, there was a way to check. Although the Hudathan hadn't been able to lay his hands on enough sensors to monitor the entire length of the track, he had managed to scrounge half a dozen spy eyes and place them along the last two hundred feet of trail. He told Haaby what he wanted, and servos whirred as the T-2 clumped its way back to the mouth of the tunnel. That's where the tech sat facing a row of small screens. There was nothing at first, but something lurched into view a few seconds later, and the renegade produced the Hudathan equivalent of a grin. A RAV! That made sense. Rather than send bio bods up the path, Kobbi had sent a column of robots instead. The real assault would follow. The wait continued.

Having placed the winch against the face of the cliff and fired four bolts in to secure it, Poltero flipped a switch. Cable hummed onto the reel as the cell-powered device jerked Okuma off the ground and lifted the T-2 straight up the side of the mountain. Santana, who was strapped to the cyborg's back, stared upward as the rock face flashed by.

A *real* assault team had started up the trail by then, one led by Kobbi himself, which should be able to make good time along the path the RAVs had cleared. Until the group arrived on the ledge, that is, which was where they would run into whatever type of meat grinder Kuga-Ka had installed up there, and the attack could stall. Unless Okuma and Santana could tackle the defenders from behind and even the odds a bit.

Okuma swore, and metal clanged as the cyborg bounced off the face of the cliff. Santana felt his heart sink, waited for the Ramanthians to fire down at him, and was pleasantly surprised when they didn't.

Then the winch stopped, the vertical ride ended with a jerk, and Okuma found himself dangling next to Poltero. The T-2 reached up to get a grip and performed a pull-up. Santana saw some slack come into the cable, freed the hook from a hard point located between Okuma's shoulders, and was dumped sideways as the cyborg threw an enormous leg up over the edge of the ledge and slapped the flat surface, looking for another handhold.

Kuga-Ka was back out on the ledge by that time, standing behind the barrier, when a Ramanthian shouted a warning. The Hudathan swiveled in his harness, saw a T-2 groping for a handhold, and opened the intercom. "Over there!" the renegade told Haaby. "A T-2! Kill the bastard!"

Haaby turned and brought her energy cannon to bear, but stopped short of actually firing. "I said *kill* the bastard!" Kuga-Ka shouted, "or I'll pull your brain box and toss it off the cliff!"

"Do what he says," Missy agreed, "or he'll kill us!"

"You're already dead," Haaby replied grimly. "I know because I killed you myself! And there's no way in hell that I'm going to kill a T-2."

Kuga-Ka didn't know who Haaby was talking to, but knew she wasn't going to fire and freed himself from the harness.

Haaby felt the Hudathan jump free, started to turn, and felt an explosion of pain at the very center of her brain. She tried to resist it, but felt her knees buckle, and wound up with her forehead resting on the ground. Darkness swallowed her mind.

Satisfied that the cyborg was down, Kuga-Ka aimed the zapper at Okuma and shouted to his troops. "Fire, damn you! Shoot the bastard before he shoots you!"

The words served to reanimate the Ramanthians, all of whom had been frozen in place, watching the unexpected drama. They aimed their weapons at Okuma and hosed the cyborg with bullets even as the Hudathan pressed the button. The T-2 felt the projectiles shatter his right hand, felt pain lance the center of his brain, and managed to shout, "I can't hang on, sir!" before he fell straight down onto the rocks below.

Having barely made the transfer in time, Santana hung from the spider form's neck as the cyborg spidered up and over the ledge.

Kuga-Ka stared in disbelief as another cyborg appeared and a bio bod leaped free. Though unarmed, Poltero charged the renegade and staggered as the Ramanthians opened fire. Legs crumpled, bits of metal flew off his body, and the cyborg collapsed.

Kuga-Ka raised his arms. "Cease fire! Stop, dammit!" and the Ramanthians obeyed. That left Santana standing all alone, weapon out of position, with the abyss at his back. "Well, well, well," Kuga-Ka said. "Look what we have here... Mr. High-and-Mighty Santana. Planned to play the hero did you? Well, not today, asshole."

There was a roar of machine-gun fire as the forgotten RAV opened up on the barricade, followed by the *crack!* of an exploding grenade. Kuga-Ka glanced toward the sound, realized his mistake, and turned back just in time to see Santana fire a three-round burst. The bullets struck with the force of a sledgehammer, rocked the Hudathan back onto his heels, but left him standing.

The volume of fire increased as Kobbi and his assault team arrived at the barricade, the energy cannon began to pump bolts of lethal energy down into the tightly packed legionnaires, and Santana charged in hopes of knocking the renegade off his feet. It felt like hitting a brick wall. The Hudathan dropped the zapper, uttered a roar of primordial joy, and snatched the human off his feet. Then, holding the officer over his head, Kuga-Ka waddled toward the edge of the cliff.

Then, just as the ex-legionnaire prepared to hurl Santana over the edge, something took hold of the renegade's combat harness and jerked him back from the abyss. Santana fell free, Kuga-Ka managed to turn, and Haaby was there to greet him. The cyborg couldn't smile, not anymore, but tried. "*You* are about to die."

Kuga-Ka looked up at the cyborg and felt utterly defenseless for the first time in many years. He raised his hands defensively. "Wait! Think about..."

Haaby brought her gigantic fist down on the top of the Hudathan's skull, felt bone give way, and heard Santana shout. "The gun! Kill the gun!"

Kuga-Ka's dead body thumped to the ground as Haaby turned, raised her weapons, and fired. Machine-gun bullets tore the Ramanthian soldiers to bloody shreds even as an energy bolt hit the gun and it exploded.

There was a pause, followed by a hundred voices shouting "Camerone!" as Kobbi and his assault team stormed up onto the ledge. The legionnaires barely paused before turning into the tunnel and the fortress beyond. The walls had been breached.

15

War is always a matter of doing evil in the hope that good may come of it.
B. H. LIDDELL HART
DEFENSE OF THE WEST
Standard year 1950

Aboard the light cruiser *Worber's World*, off the Planet Savas
The atmosphere in the control room was understandably tense as the warship slowed, and Wells launched a third of her fighters. The rest would remain on standby but could follow within a matter of minutes if required. Savas hung huge in the viewscreens. It was tan, marbled by white clouds, and frosted at the poles. Of more interest was the Ramanthian warship that had broken orbit and was coming out to meet them. "They can't be serious!" the nav officer exclaimed. "Look at that thing... The bow's missing!"

"You can thank Lieutenant Commander Amy Exton for that," Commodore Posson said grimly. "She rammed them and was killed in the process."

"Their commanding officer certainly has balls," Jackson commented admiringly. "You've got to give him that."

"I don't believe that Ramanthian males *have* balls," Captain Wells said primly, "but I agree with the sentiment. Put in a call to him... let's see if he'll listen to reason."

* * *

Aboard the destroyer *Star Ravager*, off the Planet Savas
Naval Commander Jos Satto was watching the Confederacy task force grow larger and trying to spot some sort of weakness, when a com tech spoke over the intercom. "I have a message from the enemy battle group, sir. They are calling upon us to cut power, take our weapons systems off-line, and await further orders."

Satto took one last look at the screens. Surrender was out of the question, but the *Ravager* wouldn't last long against a cruiser and two destroyers, which meant that the transports were likely to be captured. Perhaps Admiral Hikko would be able to take them back once he returned, but there was no guarantee of that, which left the naval officer with no choice but to destroy both the ships *and* their highly valuable cargos. "Tell the barbarians that we agree to their terms. Request some additional time. Send a message to the transports. Tell the crews that they have five units in which to abandon their ships. All weapons systems will remain on-line and ready to fire."

Aboard the light cruiser *Worber's World*, off the Planet Savas
"The Ramanthians have agreed," the tech said evenly, "and they want more time."

"Look at that!" Jackson interrupted excitedly, as he pointed up at one of the screens. "It's a trick!"

"Look at *what*?" Wells demanded, unable to make out what the smuggler was so excited about.

"The transports are launching lifeboats!" Jackson said urgently.

Then Wells understood. The hypercom had already been loaded aboard the freighters, and now that it looked as if they were about to be captured, the Ramanthian warship was going to destroy them! She snapped a series of orders. "Put every weapon that will bear on the destroyer! Lock the transports out of the targeting system! Fire!"

The cruiser lurched as dozens of missiles, torpedoes, and bolts of energy converged on the already damaged destroyer. Its shields rippled with incandescent light as they managed to shrug some of the weapons off, but the area where the bow had been blown away was completely unprotected, and therefore vulnerable. There was just enough time for Commander Satto to feel a moment of regret before the flash of light consumed him. For one brief moment the *Ravager* challenged the sun's brightness, as it threw off a constellation of fiery debris and snapped to black.

"Good work," Posson said from his position behind Wells. "I want prize crews on those transports yesterday. Order one destroyer to guard them and tell the other to form on us. We have what we came for... now let's see if we can keep it."

Hagala Nor, Planet Savas

Kobbi was working his way down through the maze of passageways and ramps that honeycombed the volcano's interior when Major Matala delivered the news via the plug in the colonel's right ear. He paused in front of a window that looked out into the crater. A shuttle sat at the center of the pad, and Ramanthians were hurrying to load it. "They're here! The relief force is here! There are two Ramanthian transports in orbit, and the navy captured both of them! Over."

The battalion commander felt a tremendous sense of relief. "That's good news, Topper Five. Very good news. Did the bugs put up a fight? Over."

"They tried to," the XO responded excitedly, "but most of their warships were decoyed to the far side of the system. Over."

Kobbi felt his formerly high spirits start to plummet. "Don't tell me, let me guess... They're on the way back. Over."

"I'm afraid so," Matala admitted soberly. "But Commodore Posson is going out to meet them."

Posson! A commodore. Things had changed. "And what are the odds?"

"The bugs have three warships, and Posson has two, not counting the tin can that he left to guard the freighters. One of them is a new world-class cruiser, though. Over."

Kobbi sighed. If the Ramanthians won the coming battle, then everything would be right back where it had been. "Okay, nothing changes. The bugs are still in the process of loading a shuttle, so it's my guess that at least some of what we're after is still on the ground. That means we've got to stop them. Over and out."

Aboard the light cruiser *Worber's World*, off the Planet Savas
As the cruiser and its lone escort turned away from Savas and went out to meet the enemy, Commodore Posson found himself in the very situation that he had feared most. He knew *what* to do, which was prevent the enemy from recapturing the transports, but didn't have a clue as to how to accomplish it. Not against a cruiser and *two* destroyers. The situation was hopeless. Or so it seemed until Teeg Jackson nudged his arm. "Would the commodore mind a suggestion?"

Posson shrugged. "No, if you've got an idea, please share it."

Jackson nodded. "You've got *four* ships, right?"

"Right," Posson replied, "but two of them are transports. They have a few energy cannon, but I don't see how…"

"Slave one ship to the other and order the crew to bail out," Jackson interrupted as he got up out of his seat. "The tin can pick them up. I'll take the lead unit straight down their throats. That will divide their fire, plus who knows? Maybe I can bag one of the bastards for you. It isn't perfect, but it could even the odds a bit."

"That would be certain death," Posson objected. "I can't let you do it."

"Those ships have escape pods in addition to their lifeboats. I plan to bail out at the last minute," the smuggler replied. "Don't forget to pick me up."

Wells couldn't help but overhear and felt a surge of anger. She turned toward Posson. "Don't listen to him, sir! He's a coward and a deserter… If you put Jackson aboard one of those transports, he'll be in hyperspace ten minutes later."

Posson hit his harness release and came to his feet. He looked Jackson in the eye. "Is that true, Teeg? Would you run?"

"No, sir," the onetime mutineer said stolidly. "I'm tired of running."

Posson nodded. "Okay, take your best shot. And Teeg…"

"Sir?"

"Thanks."

Wells watched the smuggler leave the bridge and shook her head doubtfully. "People like him never change. I think you're wrong about him, sir."

"You may be right," Posson said wearily. "Time will tell. Set a course to intercept the Ramanthians. We have a battle to fight."

Hagala Nor, Planet Savas

There was a seemingly endless labyrinth of passageways, galleries, and rooms inside the volcano's walls, and the Ramanthians put up stiff resistance as the legionnaires forced their way down toward the bottom of the crater. What remained of B Company had been incorporated in Kobbi's assault force and rallied around Santana once they arrived on the ledge. They had just checked a series of empty storerooms, and the cavalry officer was busy reloading his weapon, when Dietrich pushed a strange-looking apparition out of the drifting smoke. The Ramanthian was dressed in what Santana assumed to be filthy civilian attire since it didn't look like a uniform. The bug stumbled, but the noncom held him up. "I brought you a present," the noncom said conversationally. "His name is Eeno, or that's what it sounds like."

"So?" the officer inquired skeptically. "Put him in one of the storerooms and lock his ass up. The last thing we need is a prisoner to keep track of."

"Sir, yes, sir," Dietrich said patiently, "but I thought you might like to hear what our friend here has to say. He claims that the scientist who invented the hypercom is still dirtside—and that a bug named Dontha is out to kill him. Eeno works for the scientist, or did, and wants us to save him."

Santana's eyebrows shot up. The opportunity to capture the Ramanthian responsible for developing the hypercom was a big deal indeed. "No kidding? Good work, Sergeant. Forget all the idiotic things I just said. Where *is* this propeller head?"

The civilian had studied on Earth back before the war and

spoke standard with a negligible accent. "Chief Scientific Investigator Tepho is in hiding. Follow me."

The civilian could be leading them into a trap, Santana knew that, but doubted that such was the case. It was hard to believe that the bugs still had sufficient command and control infrastructure to implement such a complicated scheme, plus the story made perfect sense. After all, anyone ruthless enough to blow all the exits and leave their tanks sitting out on the battlefield to be destroyed wouldn't hesitate to grease a scientist.

Eeno took off, followed by Dietrich, Santana, and the remnants of B Company. The strange column jogged along a passageway, paused to kill a trio of hard-core Ramanthian troops, and proceeded down a corpse-strewn ramp. It looked like a grenade had gone off right in the middle of a squad of legionnaires. Body parts and empty shell casings littered the floor, and the walls were drenched in blood. The sound of automatic fire could be heard up ahead, and Santana motioned for a T-2 to take the point. It wasn't carrying a bio bod, and had to walk half-bent over, but still represented the most potent offense they had. "That's it," Eeno said, pointing up the hall. "Go around that corner. The third door to the left is the entrance to our lab. Chief Investigator Tepho is hiding in there."

Those who knew Force Commander Dontha best would never have recognized the ragged, crazed-looking officer who stood outside the lab and fired in through the open door. "Come out of there, you coward! I have a shuttle waiting for you… We can still get clear."

"The only thing waiting for me is a bullet," Tepho shouted back. And fired a quick burst from an assault rifle that he had appropriated from a dead trooper.

"All right," Dontha said to soldiers arrayed behind him, "go in and get him. Bring me his head. You can leave the rest."

But, that was when a strange-looking machine appeared at the far end of the hall and opened fire. Bolts of bright blue energy stuttered past Dontha's head, and the Ramanthian swore as both he and his soldiers were forced to confront a new threat. Fire lashed the other way, the T-2 went down as a shoulder-launched missile exploded against its chest, and the Ramanthians started to advance.

Santana waved his troops forward, stepped over the now-lifeless cyborg, and fired from the hip. There was nothing subtle about the ensuing firelight, just a brutal exchange of bullets as the groups closed with each other. Then they merged as Dontha sought out the human officer in hopes of ending the battle by killing him quickly. He fired his rifle, but it clicked empty, and there was no time to reload. The Ramanthian swung the weapon like a club, Santana ducked, and fired his weapon. A bullet nicked Dontha's shoulder and spun him around.

Meanwhile, one of the combatants hit the legionnaire from behind. He fell, rolled over, and looked up. The Ramanthian's rifle butt was already on the way down and Santana had just started to react when the bug's head flew apart. The legionnaire felt a warm mist fall on his face, sat up, and lurched to his feet. All of the bugs had been taken down by that time, and bodies lay everywhere. The officer heard a noise and whirled to find that Fareye had his six. "Sorry about that, sir. I meant to shoot the bastard earlier, but some clown nailed me in the leg."

That was when Santana saw that one of the Naa's legs was drenched in blood. He threw an arm around the warrior's shoulders to help support him and called for a medic. "Thanks, Private. It looks like I owe you another one."

Fareye grinned. "It takes a lot of time and effort to train a lieutenant, sir. The company would hate to have to start all over again."

There was a stir as Eeno emerged from the smoke, closely followed by a second Ramanthian. Sergeant Dietrich brought up the rear. "Here he is, sir," the noncom announced cheerfully. "The bug brain himself."

"Excellent," Santana replied. "Put both of them under heavy guard and get word to Colonel Kobbi. Assuming that this guy is who he claims to be, we've got something better than the hypercom. We've got the bug who built it!"

* * *

Aboard the cruiser *Hive Sun*, in the Savas System
Admiral Hikko was seated behind the cruiser's captain and his multifaceted eyes were locked on the fractal screen that occupied most of the opposite bulkhead. Part of the Confederacy battle group was coming out to meet him, just as he had predicted it would, but the attacking formation was so unorthodox that the aging Ramanthian didn't know what to make of it. A cloud of fighters led the way, that was standard practice, but why send two transports in after them? In fact, why bring the transports along at all, unless they were actually warships disguised to *look* like transports? But why bother with that? The configuration didn't make any sense, which was why Hikko continued to dither as the range closed. His second-in-command, a relative youngster named Thunu, was growing concerned. "Should I launch our fighters, Excellency?"

"Yes," Hikko said reluctantly, "you should. I don't know what the barbarians hope to accomplish by placing those freighters in front of their warships, but let's destroy them immediately. They're a tricky lot, the attack on Hive serves as proof of that, so there's no telling what they may be up to."

Thunu knew that the admiral was right, the aliens *were* tricky, but wondered if they were simply trying to make up for the fact that they were badly outnumbered. After all, decoys had worked once, why not twice? He couldn't say that, however, not without being asked for his opinion, so the thought went unspoken. "Yes, Excellency, I will give the necessary orders."

Aboard the freighter *Dominion Star*, in the Savas System
The ship's crew had been forced to depart so quickly that it looked as if the six men and women had simply stepped down the corridor and might return at any moment. A jacket hung draped over the back of the badly worn navigator's chair, pictures of loved ones remained taped to grimy consoles, and half a cup of cold coffee rested near Teeg Jackson's elbow. It rattled in sympathy with one of the transport's mismatched in-system engines.

The smuggler glanced up at the main screen, saw that the Ramanthians had launched their fighters, and knew they would close within a matter of minutes. The NAVCOMP had not been programmed to accept his voice, so the ex-navy officer had no choice but to deliver his instructions via a grimy keyboard instead. The computer advised him against what the human proposed to do but agreed that the maneuver was theoretically feasible, and went to standby.

Jackson checked to make sure that the other transport was still following along behind, opened the ship-to-ship com, and asked for Captain Wells. She appeared on the screen a fraction of a second later. The seemingly perpetual frown looked even more pronounced than usual. "Yes?"

The smuggler grinned. "You look cute when you're pissed— which is nearly all the time. Now listen up… Something weird is about to happen. Assuming that it works, the bugs will hesitate for a moment. Get ready to take advantage of that… It's the only chance you're likely to get."

Wells demanded to know what the smuggler was going to do, but the screen had blanked by that time, leaving her to wonder what the smuggler was up to. The *Dominion Star* disappeared three seconds later. "Did you see that?" Wells demanded, turning to look at Posson. "The bastard went hyper! Just like I told you he would."

Posson stared at the screen. Something wiggled at the pit of the naval officer's stomach. Did Wells have it right? Had he been wrong about Jackson? But the bet had already been placed. His face remained expressionless. "Your concerns have been noted, Captain… In the meantime, I suggest that you prepare to take advantage of the confusion that Jackson mentioned."

"Look!" the nav officer exclaimed. "He's back!"

Wells whirled around to discover that Jackson had exited hyperspace *behind* the enemy cruiser, a maneuver so risky, so desperate, that people rarely attempted it. The margin of error for a hyperspace jump was often thousands if not hundreds of thousands of standard miles, which meant most of those foolish enough to try it had been reduced to their constituent atoms. But there the transport was, only a few hundred miles off the

Ramanthian cruiser's stem, and picking up speed. "Both engines ahead full," Wells ordered. "Delegate all weapons to central fire control… Let's hammer the bastards!"

Aboard the cruiser _Hive Sun_, in the Savas System
"The transport exited hyperspace behind us!" the pilot exclaimed. "And it's accelerating. What should I do?"

Three long seconds passed while Admiral Hikko struggled to absorb what had happened and decided to take the easy way out. "Turn toward the transport and destroy it."

_No!_ Thunu thought to himself, _that's what they want you to do!_ But the _Sun_ had already started to turn by then, and there was nothing the XO could do. There were no fighters to the rear of the Ramanthian formation, and therefore nothing to protect the cruiser, except its own weaponry. _But that should be more than sufficient_, Thunu thought, _unless the aliens get close enough to ram_. It was an alarming idea, and the naval officer's beak opened and closed as he stared up at the main screen.

Aboard the light cruiser _Worber's World_, in the Savas System
Both groups of fighters had made contact with each other by then and were busy battling it out, as the larger vessels closed and opened fire. Wells had to focus on that part of the battle, but Posson was free to watch the _Dominion Star_, as the bugs let loose on her. The transport had screens, and they flared as the first torpedoes struck, but there was no way that they could withstand a cruiser's broadside. Light flared, the elderly freighter came apart, and the daring attack was over within a matter of seconds.

But damage had been done. Not physical damage, but psychological damage, as the Ramanthian battle group came apart. One of Admiral Hikko's destroyers fell victim to the _World_'s rampaging fighters, a second was destroyed by a well-timed flight of torpedoes, and the third was busy attacking the empty transport when the Confederacy cruiser turned in on the _Hive Sun_. Missiles accelerated away, screens flared, and both vessels suffered as a series of hull-shaking blows were exchanged.

But finally, after a huge gash was opened in the *Sun*'s hull, and her last escort had been reduced to scrap, Admiral Hikko was forced to concede defeat. The old warrior ordered Thunu to take command, retired to his cabin, and put a pistol to his head. Nobody heard the shot over the wail of klaxons, the steady stream of orders being delivered over the ship's PA system, or groans of the ship's badly stressed hull as the old warrior administered his own punishment.

A few hours later, after a boarding party had been put aboard the *Sun*, and the ship had been secured, search-and-rescue craft were dispatched to check disabled fighters in hopes that at least some of the pilots might still be alive.

The S&R crews had special orders to look for escape pods, too, especially those belonging to the *Dominion Star*, but none were ever found. Commodore Posson assumed that Jackson had been killed, that the ex-mutineer had given his life in order to restore his honor, which was why the smuggler's former rank was posthumously restored.

Captain Wells was of a different opinion, however. She took note of the fact that the transport had been equipped with *two* lifeboats, one of which had still been in its bay when Jackson was put aboard, and could have been launched during the moments before the freighter was destroyed. What with a full-scale battle under way, and a multitude of targets on the screens, it would have been easy for something so small to evade detection.

So, was Jackson out there somewhere? And would she run into him someday? The naval officer certainly hoped so— because she owed the bastard a drink.

Hagala Nor, Planet Savas

Two days had passed since the battle inside the fortress, all of the remaining hypercom components had been uploaded to the Ramanthian transports, and what remained of the 2nd Battalion, First REC was ready to pull out. And, with no homes to return to and the very real possibility of retribution by either the bugs or the Paguum at some later date, the refugees were leaving as well.

Santana had not only gone in search of Qwis Qwan, he had even gone so far as to send Fareye out to look for her, but with no results. Not because the colonist wasn't there, but because she didn't want to be found, and was careful to avoid the officer and his legionnaires. Qwis was going to miss him, though, and watched from a distance as the lanky officer made his way up the shuttle's ramp, and paused to take one final look around. Then the legionnaire was gone, the ramp went up, and the shuttle lifted off.

"So, Lieutenant," Dietrich said, as Savas fell away below, "we made it."

"Yes," Santana replied, "we did."

Neither said it out loud, but both were thinking about the long trail of graves that led from Savas Prime all the way to Hagala Nor. In fact two-thirds of the battalion would remain on the planet after the Legion's transports broke orbit. Was the hypercom worth it? Santana hoped so. The cavalry officer settled into the web-style seat, felt a tremendous weariness settle over him, and soon fell asleep.

ABOUT THE AUTHOR

William C. Dietz is an American writer best known for military science fiction. He spent time in the US Navy and the US Marine Corps, and has worked as a surgical technician, news writer, television producer, and director of public relations. He has written more than 40 novels, as well as tie-in novels for *Halo*, *Mass Effect*, *Resistance*, *Starcraft*, *Star Wars*, and *Hitman*.

williamcdietz.com

THE MUTANT FILES

William C. Dietz

In the year 2038, an act of bioengineered terrorism decimated humanity. Those who survived were either completely unaffected or developed horrible mutations. Across the globe, nations are now divided between areas populated by "norms" and lands run by "mutants".

Detective Cassandra Lee of Los Angeles's Special Investigative Section has built a fierce reputation taking down some of the city's most notorious criminals. But the serial cop killer known as Bonebreaker—who murdered Lee's father—is still at large. Officially, she's too personally involved to work on the Bonebreaker case. Unofficially, she's going to hunt him to the ends of the earth.

DEADEYE
REDZONE
GRAVEYARD (March 2016)

"This is the first volume in a great new series. The world-building is impeccable… The mystery plot is solid, there's enough action to satisfy readers coming from the author's military scifi novels, and the characters are realistic."
—CA Reviews

TITANBOOKS.COM